Christ among the Messiahs

Christ among the Messiahs

Christ Language in Paul and Messiah Language in Ancient Judaism

MATTHEW V. NOVENSON

OXFORD
UNIVERSITY PRESS

OXFORD
UNIVERSITY PRESS

Oxford University Press, Inc., publishes works that further
Oxford University's objective of excellence
in research, scholarship, and education.

Oxford   New York
Auckland   Cape Town   Dar es Salaam   Hong Kong   Karachi
Kuala Lumpur   Madrid   Melbourne   Mexico City   Nairobi
New Delhi   Shanghai   Taipei   Toronto

With offices in
Argentina   Austria   Brazil   Chile   Czech Republic   France   Greece
Guatemala   Hungary   Italy   Japan Poland   Portugal   Singapore
South Korea   Switzerland   Thailand   Turkey   Ukraine   Vietnam

Published by Oxford University Press, Inc.
198 Madison Avenue, New York, New York 10016
www.oup.com

Library of Congress Cataloging-in-Publication Data
Novenson, Matthew V.
Christ among the messiahs: Christ language in Paul and messiah language
in ancient Judaism / Matthew V. Novenson.
p. cm.
Includes bibliographical references (p.   ) and indexes.
ISBN 978-0-19-984457-9
1. Bible. N.T. Epistles of Paul—Language, style.   2. Messiah—Judaism—
History of doctrines.   3. Jesus Christ—Messiahship.   I. Title.
BS2655.L3N69 2012
232'.1–dc23
2011037947

1 3 5 7 9 8 6 4 2

Printed in the United States of America
on acid-free paper

"He was some kind of miracle kid. At chess, at Torah, at languages. I heard a story about him healing a woman's cancer, not that I really believe that, but. I guess there were a lot of stories going around about him inside the black-hat world. That He might be the Tzaddik Ha-Dor—you know what that is?"

"Sort of. Yes. Anyway, I know what the words mean," Bina says.

— Michael Chabon, *The Yiddish Policemen's Union*

Contents

Acknowledgments

I AM DEEPLY grateful to a number of people who were part of the making of this book. Because the book is a revision of my Princeton Theological Seminary dissertation, pride of place belongs to my exceptional doctoral supervisor, Beverly Roberts Gaventa. Her expertise in the subject matter and her industry as a reader of my work provided an ideal environment for undertaking the research represented here. The same is true of my other dissertation committee members, Martha Himmelfarb and Ross Wagner, whose learned feedback I enjoyed at every step along the way. These three, as well as N. T. Wright at a later stage, read and commented in detail on the entire manuscript, and whatever success my argument finds is due in large part to their generous criticism.

I also benefited a great deal from the input of other conversation partners. Within my home department at Princeton Theological Seminary, Shane Berg, Clifton Black, James Charlesworth, Kara Lyons-Pardue, Amy Peeler, Loren Stuckenbruck, Laura Sweat, and Brittany Wilson went above and beyond their own duties to read and comment on parts of earlier drafts. Outside my home department, Aryeh Amihay, John Barclay, Gabriele Boccaccini, John Gager, Jeremy Hultin, and Azzan Yadin read and commented on parts of the manuscript, and David Decosimo, Richard Hays, Dale Martin, and N. T. Wright met with me to discuss aspects of the argument. James Waddell generously shared with me a prepublication draft of his monograph *The Messiah: A Comparative Study of the Enochic Son of Man and the Pauline Kyrios* (London: T. & T. Clark, 2011). My two anonymous reviewers from Oxford University Press rendered valuable feedback on points large and small. The influence of all of these scholars on my thinking is evident in what follows, not least at those points at which I record my disagreement with one or more of them. The book is far better than it would have been if not for their input, and whatever deficiencies remain are entirely my own responsibility.

I had occasion to present parts of the argument in several professional settings, in particular the Princeton Theological Seminary New Testament Colloquium, the International Enoch Graduate Seminar, the Annual Meeting of the Society of Biblical Literature, and the Mid-Atlantic Regional Meetings of the Society of Biblical Literature and the American Academy of Religion. I am grateful to Cambridge University Press and the Society of Biblical Literature, respectively, for their permission to reprint revised versions of some material that I published in earlier journal articles. Part of chapter 4 appeared in a different form in "Can the Messiahship of Jesus Be Read off Paul's Grammar? Nils Dahl's Criteria 50 Years Later," *New Testament Studies* 56 (2010): 396–412. Part of chapter 5 appeared in a different form in "The Jewish Messiahs, the Pauline Christ, and the Gentile Question," *Journal of Biblical Literature* 128 (2009): 357–373. The epigraph to this book comes from p. 168 of *The Yiddish Policemen's Union*, copyright © 2007 by Michael Chabon, and is reprinted here by permission of HarperCollins Publishers.

Over the course of the making of this book, I moved from Princeton to Raleigh to Edinburgh, in turn. The research for the book was made possible by a generous department fellowship from Princeton Theological Seminary and teaching fellowships from Princeton Theological Seminary and Princeton University. During the course of revision and editing, I enjoyed the support of the Department of Philosophy and Religious Studies at North Carolina State University, in particular William Adler, Jason Bivins, Michael Pendlebury, Ken Peters, and Ann Rives. In the final stages of production, I was similarly accommodated by the School of Divinity at the University of Edinburgh, where I am indebted to Helen Bond, Stewart J. Brown, Nicola Davidson, Paul Foster, and Larry Hurtado. The fine staff at Oxford University Press—first of all Cynthia Read, and also Sasha Grossman, Carol Hoke, Molly Morrison, Jessica Prudhomme, and Amy Whitmer—guided me expertly through every stage of the publication process.

Most important, my wife, Michelle, was an invaluable conversation partner throughout the writing process. She not only refreshed her Greek in order to evaluate my interpretations of the pertinent texts but also selflessly took time off from her own professional responsibilities to allow me to work full-time on the completion of this project. Also essential to our well-being were the love and encouragement of our extended family, both Novensons and Sedas, and a number of close friends, especially the Altmann, Barnett, Becker, Beeson, Decosimo, Edwards, and Marshall families. Finally, each of our children had a very important part in the making of this book, and I dedicate the finished product, with love, to our number three.

Abbreviations

For ancient Jewish and Christian primary sources, I follow the system of abbreviations prescribed by *The SBL Handbook of Style* (ed. Patrick H. Alexander et al.; Peabody, Mass.: Hendrickson, 1999). For classical Greek and Roman sources, I follow the system of abbreviations prescribed by *The Oxford Classical Dictionary* (ed. Simon Hornblower and Antony Spawforth; 3d rev. ed.; Oxford: Oxford University Press, 2003).

AB	Anchor Bible
ANRW	*Aufstieg und Niedergang der römischen Welt: Geschichte und Kultur Roms im Spiegel der neueren Forschung.* Edited by H. Temporini and W. Haase. Berlin, 1972–
BDAG	Bauer, W., F. W. Danker, W. F. Arndt, and F. W. Gingrich. *Greek-English Lexicon of the New Testament and Other Early Christian Literature.* 3d ed. Chicago, 1999
BDB	Brown, F., S. R. Driver, and C. A. Briggs. *A Hebrew and English Lexicon of the Old Testament.* Oxford, 1907
BDF	Blass, F., A. Debrunner, and R. W. Funk. *A Greek Grammar of the New Testament and Other Early Christian Literature.* Chicago, 1961
BETL	Bibliotheca ephemeridum theologicarum lovaniensium
BHS	*Biblia Hebraica Stuttgartensia.* Edited by K. Elliger and W. Rudolph. Stuttgart, 1983
CAH	*Cambridge Ancient History.* 14 vols. 2d ed. Cambridge, 1970–2005
CBQ	*Catholic Biblical Quarterly*
CHJ	*Cambridge History of Judaism.* Edited by W. D. Davies and Louis Finkelstein. Cambridge, 1984–
CIG	*Corpus inscriptionum graecarum.* Edited by A. Boeckh. 4 vols. Berlin, 1828–1877
CIJ	*Corpus inscriptionum judaicarum.* Edited by J. B. Frey. 2 vols. Rome, 1936–1952

CJ	*Classical Journal*
CP	*Classical Philology*
CPJ	*Corpus papyrorum judaicorum.* Edited by V. Tcherikover. 3 vols. Cambridge, 1957–1964
DJD	Discoveries in the Judaean Desert
EvT	*Evangelische Theologie*
ExpTim	*Expository Times*
FRLANT	Forschungen zur Religion und Literatur des Alten und Neuen Testaments
HB	Hebrew Bible
HTR	*Harvard Theological Review*
Jastrow	Jastrow, M. *A Dictionary of the Targumim, the Talmud Babli and Yerushalmi, and the Midrashic Literature.* 2d ed. New York, 1903
JBL	*Journal of Biblical Literature*
JJS	*Journal of Jewish Studies*
JPS	Jewish Publication Society
JR	*Journal of Religion*
JSJ	*Journal for the Study of Judaism in the Persian, Hellenistic, and Roman Periods*
JSJSup	Supplements to the Journal for the Study of Judaism
JSNT	*Journal for the Study of the New Testament*
JSNTSup	Journal for the Study of the New Testament Supplement Series
JSOT	*Journal for the Study of the Old Testament*
JSOTSup	Journal for the Study of the Old Testament Supplement Series
JSS	*Journal of Semitic Studies*
JTS	*Journal of Theological Studies*
LCL	Loeb Classical Library
LSJ	Liddell, H. G., R. Scott, and H. S. Jones. *A Greek-English Lexicon.* 9th ed. with revised supplement. Oxford, 1996
LXX	Septuagint
MS(S)	manuscript(s)
MT	Masoretic Text
NA27	*Novum Testamentum Graece,* Nestle-Aland, 27th ed.
NovT	*Novum Testamentum*
NovTSup	Supplements to Novum Testamentum
NRSV	New Revised Standard Version
NT	New Testament
NTS	*New Testament Studies*

OCD	*Oxford Classical Dictionary.* Edited by S. Hornblower and A. Spawforth. 3d ed. Oxford, 1996
OG	Old Greek
OT	Old Testament
OTP	*Old Testament Pseudepigrapha.* Edited by J. H. Charlesworth. 2 vols. New York, 1983
PBA	Proceedings of the British Academy
PG	Patrologia graeca [=Patrologiae cursus completus: Series graeca]. Edited by J.-P. Migne. 162 vols. Paris, 1857–1886
PL	Patrologia latina [=Patrologiae cursus completus: Series latina]. Edited by J.-P. Migne. 217 vols. Paris, 1844–1864
Reider-Turner	Reider, J. *An Index to Aquila.* Completed and revised by N. Turner. Leiden, 1966
RSV	Revised Standard Version
SBL	Society of Biblical Literature
SBLE	Society of Biblical Literature and Exegesis
SBLSS	Society of Biblical Literature Symposium Series
SBT	Studies in Biblical Theology
SC	Sources chrétiennes. Paris: Cerf, 1943–
Schürer-Vermes	Schürer, E. *The History of the Jewish People in the Age of Jesus Christ.* 3 vols. Revised and edited by Geza Vermes and Fergus Millar. Edinburgh, 1973–1987
Smyth	Smyth, H. W. *Greek Grammar.* Cambridge, Mass., 1920
SNTS	Studiorum Novi Testamenti Societas
SNTSMS	Society for New Testament Studies Monograph Series
Sokoloff	Sokoloff, M. *A Dictionary of Jewish Babylonian Aramaic of the Talmudic and Geonic Periods.* Baltimore, 2002
TDNT	*Theological Dictionary of the New Testament.* Edited by G. Kittel and G. Friedrich. Translated by G. W. Bromiley. 10 vols. Grand Rapids, 1964–1976
Teubner	Bibliotheca scriptorum graecorum et romanorum teubneriana
TLG	*Thesaurus linguae graecae*
TLL	*Thesaurus linguae latinae*
TSAJ	Texte und Studien zum antiken Judentum
VT	*Vetus Testamentum*
VTSup	Supplements to Vetus Testamentum
WUNT	Wissenschaftliche Untersuchungen zum Neuen Testament
ZNW	*Zeitschrift für die neutestamentliche Wissenschaft und die Kunde der älteren Kirche*

Introduction

IN THE OPENING epigraph, Meyer Landsman, a homicide detective in Michael Chabon's fictional Yiddish-speaking Jewish Alaska, asks his partner, Bina Gelbfish, whether she knows about the Tzaddik Ha-Dor, "the righteous one of the generation," who their murder victim was reputed to have been. Gelbfish's reply is significant: She "sort of" knows about the Tzaddik Ha-Dor, in the sense that she "knows what the words mean." This fictional exchange about messiah language in modern Judaism is a fitting epigraph to this study of messiah language in ancient Judaism. I approach the question by means of a case study, namely the letters of the apostle Paul, who has been regarded as anomalous in his use of messiah language but is for this very reason an especially instructive test case. The question posed by this book is, How does the "Christ" of the Pauline letters fit among the "messiahs" of other Jewish texts from the same period? Although our modern habit of speech obscures the fact, "Christ" and "messiah" actually translate the same ancient Greek word, not two different ones. If, as Bina Gelbfish suggests, knowing about the messiah consists partly in "knowing what the words mean," then how should we understand Paul's use of this particular word, which, when it is used by other writers from the same period, we generally take to mean "messiah"?

The Problem Stated

The problem can be stated simply: Scholars of ancient Judaism, finding only a few diverse references to "messiahs" in Hellenistic- and Roman-period Jewish literature, have concluded that the word did not mean anything determinate in that period.[1] Meanwhile, Pauline interpreters, faced with Paul's several hundred uses of the Greek word for "messiah," have concluded that Paul said it but did not mean it, that χριστός in Paul does not bear any of its conventional senses.[2] To summarize the majority view: "Messiah" did not mean

---

1 See chapter 2.
2 See chs. 3–5.

anything determinate in the period in question, and Paul, at any rate, cannot have meant whatever it is that "messiah" did not mean. Andrew Chester's recent statement of the situation is lucid and representative:

> We are confronted with a curious phenomenon: this title (or term) Messiah/χριστός, for which we have struggled to find more than a handful of instances in the plethora of Jewish texts over the course of three centuries (many of them directly concerned with the final age and events, and hence where one could naturally expect them to include some reference to a messianic scenario), now occurs more than 200 times in the (not very extensive) writings of a Jew of the mid-first century C.E., but it turns out to be mainly bland and apparently insignificant in the way it is used.[3]

It is this curious phenomenon that is the subject of this study. As Chester points out, the phenomenon is actually doubly curious: It has to do, on the one hand, with the relatively sparse use of messiah language in early Jewish literature generally and, on the other hand, with the extensive but idiosyncratic use of such language by the apostle Paul. Both sides of this problem need explaining.

The problem is very sharply posed in a statement by John Collins, a scholar of ancient messianism, in response to the arguments of Lloyd Gaston and John Gager, both Pauline interpreters. Collins writes:

> On the Christian side, we have had the astonishing claim that Paul, the earliest Christian writer, did not regard Jesus as the messiah. The ecumenical intentions of such a claim are transparent and honorable, but also misguided since the claim is so plainly false. Jesus is called *Christos*, anointed, the Greek equivalent of messiah, 270 times in the Pauline corpus. If this is not ample testimony that Paul regarded Jesus as messiah, then words have no meaning.[4]

It is just this, the meaning of words—specifically, the meaning of the word "messiah" as Paul uses it—that constitutes the problem. A survey of secondary literature on Paul shows that Collins's criticism actually applies even

---

3 Andrew Chester, "Messianism, Mediators, and Pauline Christology," *Messiah and Exaltation* (Wissenschaftliche Untersuchungen zum Neuen Testament 207; Tübingen: Mohr Siebeck, 2007), 329–396, here 382–383.

4 John J. Collins, *The Scepter and the Star: The Messiahs of the Dead Sea Scrolls and Other Ancient Literature* (Anchor Bible Reference Library; New York: Doubleday, 1995), 2.

more widely than he intended it.[5] If, per majority opinion, Paul does not mean "messiah" when he writes χριστός, then why should we not conclude, as Gaston and Gager do, that for Paul Jesus is not the messiah? In fact, I will argue, the problem is not with this conclusion but rather with the premise that χριστός has lost its conventional range of meaning in Pauline usage.

To put it with maximal brevity, my thesis is that χριστός in Paul means "messiah." There are two basic ways in which one might go about making this case. One is to argue, against recent detractors, that χριστός really did mean something like what pre–World War II exegetes and theologians said that it meant and that Paul really does invoke all this when he uses the word.[6] The other way is to argue, with many recent interpreters, that messiah language was quite flexible, indeed, flexible enough to allow Paul's allegedly anomalous usage. If so, then any ancient text that uses such language must be taken into account as evidence of its possible range of meaning. This is the approach that I take here. To rephrase my thesis from this perspective: Christ language in Paul is actually an invaluable example of messiah language in ancient Judaism.

Methodology

My approach is relatively conventional; I do not propose to solve an old problem by introducing a novel method into the discussion. My tools are the historical, philological, and literary ones that are common to the disciplines of biblical studies, Jewish studies, and classics. Of course, this general approach has a long and distinguished pedigree in the study of early Judaism and Christianity. I have been particularly influenced by some of Geza Vermes's comments clarifying the approach.[7] In addition, I follow Gerbern Oegema in applying it self-consciously to the study of ancient messiah texts.[8]

Although my overall method is historical-critical, I am particularly concerned with linguistic questions (so "messiah language") in response to what

---

5 See chapter 1.

6 In my analysis, this is roughly the approach taken by N. T. Wright in his important work on the question (especially with reference to Schweitzer), on which see in particular chapters 1, 4, and 5. On "the messianic idea" in pre–World War II scholarship, see chapter 1.

7 Especially Geza Vermes, "Methodology in the Study of Jewish Literature in the Greco-Roman Period," *Journal of Jewish Studies* 36 (1985): 143–158; Geza Vermes, "Jewish Studies and New Testament Interpretation," in *Jesus and the World of Judaism* (London: SCM, 1983), 58–73; Geza Vermes, "Jewish Literature and New Testament Exegesis: Reflections on Method," in *Jesus and the World of Judaism*, 74–88.

8 Gerbern S. Oegema, *The Anointed and His People: Messianic Expectations from the Maccabees to Bar Kokhba* (Journal for the Study of the Pseudepigrapha Supplement Series 27; Sheffield: Sheffield Academic, 1998; German original 1994), especially 16–20.

I perceive as a conceptual misstep in previous research on the question. In speaking of "messiah language," I am following the lead of Nils A. Dahl, who in his 1977 presidential address to the Studiorum Novi Testamenti Societas proposed the rubric "christological language" for discussion of early Christian discourse about Jesus.[9] Dahl worries that exegetes often work unconsciously with a conceptual model that is inappropriate to the evidence. He writes:

> Several works on the origins of christology speak about sources and influences in a manner that evokes the image of a complicated watershed—say the Mississippi water basin, in which water from innumerable sources runs through creeks and streams and finally comes together in a mighty river. It might be wise to exchange this image for the notion of a "language game," to use the term of Wittgenstein.[10]

That is, whatever else they may be, ancient texts that make claims about Jesus are linguistic phenomena. Banal as this observation may seem, it is in fact widely missed by interpreters, who have inherited certain habits of thought—especially ones indebted to nineteenth-century German idealism—from their forebears in the discipline.[11] As a result, careful description of ancient messiah language remains an unfulfilled research program.

More specifically, again following Dahl, I am especially interested in the syntax of messiah language, that is, the particular things that the sources do with messiah words in the sentences in which they occur.[12] Studies of messianic and christological titles (e.g., branch, righteous one, chosen one, son of man,

---

9 Nils A. Dahl, "Sources of Christological Language," in Nils A. Dahl, *Jesus the Christ: The Historical Origins of Christological Doctrine* (ed. Donald H. Juel; Minneapolis: Fortress, 1991), 113–136, here 115: " 'Christological language' is shorthand for what those who believed in Jesus after his death said about him, as well as for the ways in which they spoke about him."

10 Dahl, "Sources of Christological Language," 132. On language games, see Ludwig Wittgenstein, *Philosophical Investigations* (trans. G. E. M. Anscombe; Oxford: Blackwell, 1953). Of course, interpretation of Wittgenstein himself, which is beyond the scope of this study, proceeds apace (see, e.g., the essays collected in *Ludwig Wittgenstein: Critical Assessments,* vol. 2 [2 vols; ed. Stuart Shanker; London: Routledge, 1996]).

11 See further chapter 1. On the influence of German idealism in biblical studies, see Hans W. Frei, *The Eclipse of Biblical Narrative: A Study in Eighteenth and Nineteenth Century Hermeneutics* (New Haven: Yale University Press, 1980), especially chapter 11, "The Lack of Realism in German Letters."

12 See Laurel J. Brinton, *The Structure of Modern English* (Philadelphia: Benjamins, 2000), 11:

> Syntax is the study of the order and arrangement of words into larger units, as well as the relationships holding between elements in these hierarchical units. . . . Semantics is the study of how meaning is conveyed, focusing either on meanings related to the outside world (lexical meaning) or meanings related to the grammar of the sentence (grammatical meaning).

messiah, lord, son of God) are in ample supply, but such studies are of limited value. Dahl's bibliographical assessment is as true today as it was in 1977:

> Scholars have thoroughly investigated the vocabulary of christological language, especially the titles of Jesus. By comparison, only sporadic attention has been paid to a systematic description of the syntax of christological language, beginning with questions concerning what roles various designations of Jesus play in Greek sentences and concerning possible semantic transformations of these sentences.[13]

With Jewish messiah texts generally, as with Christian christological texts, syntactical analysis promises to shed some light that traditional word studies cannot. This approach is particularly apt to a study of Paul since his use of the word χριστός has often been judged to be non-messianic precisely for syntactical reasons.[14] I speak of "messiah language" rather than "christological language" because, unlike Dahl, I am interested not just in early Christian ways of speaking about Jesus but rather in early Jewish ways of speaking about messiahs. I want to know what conventions existed whereby ancient Jewish authors spoke of messiahs and how Paul's use of the word fits among these conventions.

Key Terms Defined

Since a large part of this study has to do with Paul, it is necessary to say what I allow to count as evidence for "Paul." In what follows I treat only the seven letters that are virtually unanimously acknowledged to be authentically Pauline: Romans, 1 Corinthians, 2 Corinthians, Galatians, Philippians, 1 Thessalonians, and Philemon.[15] That is to say, I do not use the six disputed letters or the accounts of Paul in the Acts of the Apostles as first-order evidence for the apostle himself.[16] I sometimes refer to these other texts by way of comparison, but for the purposes of this study "Paul" effectively refers to the evidence of the seven undisputed letters.[17]

---

13 Dahl, "Sources," 115–116.

14 See chapter 4.

15 Of course, there are text-critical and literary-integrity questions about even these seven letters. I address such questions on a case-by-case basis as necessary.

16 By the same token, neither do I use still later Christian traditions about Paul (e.g., those preserved in the *Acts of Paul*, the *Epistles of Paul and Seneca*, and the *Pseudo-Clementines*).

17 For the Pauline letters and other New Testament texts, I follow the Greek text of Kurt Aland et al., *Novum Testamentum Graece* (27th ed.; Stuttgart: Deutsche Bibelgesellschaft, 1999), hereafter "NA27."

Likewise, it is necessary to explain what falls under the rubric "messiah language." I speak throughout of "messiah language" and "messiah texts," where the latter are particular literary uses of the former.[18] These terms are to be distinguished from the more commonly used noun "messianism," which is best reserved for referring to a social movement in which messiah language is commonly used.[19] My point in making this distinction is not to suggest that such social movements did not exist in our period or that language has meaning apart from the social systems in which it is used. On the contrary, I think that a reasonably strong case can be made for the currency of messianic social movements in Judaism around the turn of the era;[20] and I argue in what follows that language means in the way it does precisely because of its currency in language-using social groups. One of the main points of this study, however, is that the meaningfulness of messiah language and the popular currency of messianism are separable questions.[21]

On a related note, I frequently use "messiah" adjectivally (so "messiah language") rather than use the familiar adjective "messianic" since the latter has often been used—like, and in confusion with, its counterparts "eschatological" and "apocalyptic"—to refer to a bewildering array of things having to do with future hope in ancient Judaism.[22] Such scholarly usage may not be entirely inappropriate, although it has certainly caused a great deal of conceptual confusion. In any case, for the sake of this study, which has to do not with the history of ideas but rather with conventions of use of particular words, such usage is inappropriate. In an effort to avoid any such confusion, I use "messiah language" to refer to figures of speech that include the words משיח, χριστός, "anointed," and their translation equivalencies and "messiah texts" to refer to literary works that use such language.[23]

---

18 Of course, there could be, and there certainly were, not only written but also spoken uses of messiah language, but those are beyond the ken of the historian.

19 Cf. the working definition of "apocalypticism" (in contrast to "apocalypse," "apocalyptic," and "apocalyptic eschatology") proposed by the SBL Genres Project in *Apocalypse: The Morphology of a Genre* (ed. John J. Collins; Semeia 14; Missoula, Mont.: Scholars Press, 1979).

20 With Richard A. Horsley and John S. Hanson, *Bandits, Prophets, and Messiahs: Popular Movements at the Time of Jesus* (Minneapolis: Winston, 1985); and William Horbury, *Jewish Messianism and the Cult of Christ* (London: SCM, 1998).

21 See chapter 2 below.

22 See the apt criticism of Magne Sæbø, "On the Relationship between 'Messianism' and 'Eschatology' in the Old Testament: An Attempt at a Terminological and Factual Clarification," in *On the Way to Canon: Creative Tradition History in the Old Testament* (Journal for the Study of the Old Testament Supplement Series 191; Sheffield: Sheffield Academic, 1998), 197–231.

23 On this working definition, messiah texts from ca. 200 B.C.E. to ca. 100 C.E. include the relevant parts of the following: Daniel; *Psalms of Solomon*; *1 Enoch*; *4 Ezra*; *2 Baruch*; CD; 1QS; 1QSa; 1QM; 1Q30; 4Q252; 4Q270; 4Q287; 4Q375; 4Q376; 4Q377; 4Q381; 4Q382;

On the long-standing question whether studies of messiah texts ought to include only texts that use the word itself or ought to cast their conceptual nets more broadly, I take a mediating position. In general, I take the view that a text must use the words, not just contain what seem to us like related ideas, in order to be classified as "messianic."[24] On the other hand, as John Collins has pointed out, "It is of fundamental importance that the figures who are called 'messiahs' or 'anointed ones' in the Scrolls can also be referred to in other terms."[25] This is true not only of the Dead Sea Scrolls but of other messiah texts as well: Messiahs sometimes go by other additional names. Consequently, I include in this study some terms that are used of figures who are also called "messiahs" by the same authors.[26] I exclude, however, figures who are never called "messiahs" at all.[27]

From these definitions, it follows that the scope of this study is circumscribed in several important ways. It is not my objective to examine the diverse array of mediatorial figures in early Jewish literature, only messiahs proper.[28] Nor is it my concern to cover all that falls under the traditional heading of Pauline Christology, that is, all of Paul's complex and interrelated ideas about Jesus, including the titles κύριος, υἱὸς θεοῦ, σωτήρ, and others.[29] Least of all is it my concern to investigate the vast panoply of Jewish texts and motifs that are

---

4Q458; 4Q521; 11QMelch; and the twenty-seven books in the New Testament. These are the texts on which I principally draw in this study.

24 With Marinus de Jonge, "The Use of the Word 'Anointed' in the Time of Jesus," *Novum Testamentum* 8 (1966): 132–148, here 133: "I shall use the word 'anointed' ('Messiah') only where the sources use the corresponding word in their own language. Similarly the use of the term 'messianic' should be restricted to the expectation of a redeemer who is actually called Messiah."

25 John J. Collins, "Messiahs in Context: Method in the Study of Messianism in the Dead Sea Scrolls," in *Methods of Investigation of the Dead Sea Scrolls and the Khirbet Qumran Site: Present Realities and Future Prospects* (ed. Michael O. Wise et al.; Annals of the New York Academy of Sciences 722; New York: New York Academy of Sciences, 1994), 213–230, here 214.

26 E.g., *Psalms of Solomon* 17 refers to the same figure as "messiah," "king," "son of David," and perhaps "lord." The *Parables of Enoch* refer to the same figure as "messiah," "son of man," "righteous one," and "chosen one." Likewise, Paul refers to the same figure as "messiah," "Jesus," "lord," "son of God," and more.

27 E.g., the "white bull" in the Animal Apocalypse (*1 En.* 90:37); the "king from the sun" in *Sib. Or.* 3:652.

28 Cf. the studies of Chester, "Messianism, Mediators and Pauline Christology"; Alan F. Segal, *Two Powers in Heaven: Early Rabbinic Reports about Christianity and Gnosticism* (Studies in Judaism in Late Antiquity 25; Leiden: Brill, 1977); Loren T. Stuckenbruck, *Angel Veneration and Christology: A Study in Early Judaism and in the Christology of the Apocalypse of John* (WUNT 2/70; Tübingen: Mohr Siebeck, 1995); John J. Collins and Adela Yarbro Collins, *King and Messiah as Son of God* (Grand Rapids, Mich.: Eerdmans, 2008).

29 See most recently Gordon D. Fee, *Pauline Christology: An Exegetical-Theological Study* (Peabody, Mass.: Hendrickson, 2007).

sometimes loosely and indiscriminately called "messianic" or "eschatological" or "apocalyptic."[30] Of course, it will sometimes be necessary to comment *en passant* on aspects of these broader areas of inquiry, but my goal is simply to understand how a particular term functions for Paul in relation to the language system of which he was a part.

Conceptual Models

The subject of this book, as its subtitle suggests, is "Christ language in Paul and messiah language in ancient Judaism," not just "Christ language in Paul." That is to say, my overarching goal is not simply to interpret Paul but rather to illustrate how ancient Jewish messiah language worked, using Paul as a case study. Most obviously, this means that this study involves a significant amount of work with non-Pauline Jewish texts.[31] It is necessary to be precise, though, about how these non-Pauline texts relate to their Pauline counterparts.[32] This is perhaps best achieved by distinguishing my approach from some common alternatives. First of all, this is not a study of the Jewish "background" of Paul's Christology. The ideological problems with background research, especially the tendency of some exegetes to render negative value judgments on the "background" in such a way as to advocate subtly for the "foreground," have been well documented.[33] In such research, to borrow Vermes's turn of phrase, "the background must speak only when spoken to."[34] To the extent that decisions about what counts as "background" and "foreground" have often been either ideologically motivated or simply arbitrary, the model as a whole has been unproductive for the purposes of historical understanding.

Nor, again, is this a study of Jewish "parallels" to Pauline motifs. As Samuel Sandmel showed, appeals to parallels in the study of ancient Judaism and Christianity are often recklessly employed and so are generally not helpful

---

30 On the category problems, see de Jonge, "Use of the Word 'Anointed' "; Sæbø, "Relationship between 'Messianism' and 'Eschatology.' "

31 See especially chapter 2.

32 On this point, see the taxonomy of Martha Himmelfarb, *Tours of Hell: An Apocalyptic Form in Jewish and Christian Literature* (Philadelphia: University of Pennsylvania Press, 1983), 2.

33 See Jonathan Z. Smith, *Drudgery Divine: On the Comparison of Early Christianities and the Religions of Late Antiquity* (Chicago: University of Chicago Press, 1990). On this phenomenon in Pauline research in particular, see E. P. Sanders, *Paul and Palestinian Judaism: A Comparison of Patterns of Religion* (Philadelphia: Fortress, 1977), 1–24.

34 Vermes, "Jewish Studies and New Testament Interpretation," 69.

analytical tools.[35] In the most general sense, as Plato recognized, everything is like everything else since they are all things. Then again, in the most specific sense, nothing is like anything else since everything is identical only to itself.[36] In comparative work, then, the important thing is the precise sense in which two or more things are alike or different.[37] The problem with parallel research is that the category of "parallel" underdetermines the evidence. Some putative parallels turn out to be quite illuminating, others not at all, and there is no criterion inherent in the category "parallel" to distinguish the one set from the other.[38]

The other Jewish texts of the period are best conceived neither as backgrounds to Paul nor as parallels to Paul but rather as other instances of the ancient Judaism of which Paul, too, was an instance.[39] More specifically, χριστός in Paul's letters is itself an instance of messiah language in ancient Judaism. It is best interpreted as a member of this species, and the whole species stands to be better understood as a result of its being so interpreted. One corollary of this methodological decision is that I include a considerable chronological range of ancient messiah texts. Most important, I do not restrict the scope of the study to pre-Pauline Jewish texts since I am not asking what ideas might have been current in time to have influenced Paul but rather what the linguistic system was in which ancient Jewish messiah texts, including Paul's letters, made sense.[40] My broad field of vision covers the Hellenistic and Roman

---

35 Samuel Sandmel, "Parallelomania," *Journal of Biblical Literature* 81 (1962): 1–13, the author's 1961 presidential address to the Society of Biblical Literature and Exegesis. Sandmel defines parallelomania as "that extravagance among scholars which first overdoes the supposed similarity in passages and then proceeds to describe source and derivation as if implying literary connection flowing in an inevitable or predetermined direction" (1).

36 On both counts, see Plato, *Parmenides*.

37 On this point see David Decosimo, "Comparison and the Ubiquity of Resemblance," *Journal of the American Academy of Religion* 78 (2010): 226–258.

38 See Sanders's criticism of some of the parallels adduced by W. D. Davies in the latter's *Paul and Rabbinic Judaism: Some Rabbinic Elements in Pauline Theology* (Philadelphia: Fortress, 1980). Sanders warns, "Parallels are often illuminating, as long as one does not jump from 'parallel' to 'influence' to 'identity of thought'" (*Paul and Palestinian Judaism*, 11).

39 Following Vermes, "Jewish Studies and New Testament Interpretation," 64: "For a historical understanding, the age-old distinction between the New Testament and its Jewish background should be abolished and the former looked at deliberately as part of a larger whole." This study is a small contribution, then, to Vermes's call for "a Schürer-type religious history of the Jews from the Maccabees to AD 500 that fully incorporates the New Testament data . . . a reliable guide to the diverse streams of post-biblical Judaism in all their manifestations and reciprocal influences" (Vermes, "Jewish Literature and New Testament Exegesis," 88).

40 Here I differ from the recent work of James A. Waddell, *The Messiah: A Comparative Study of the Enochic Son of Man and the Pauline Kyrios* (London: T. & T. Clark, 2011), who argues that Paul's Christology is demonstrably dependent on Enochic Son of Man traditions, albeit not on the text of *1 Enoch* as we have it.

periods, with Paul falling nearly in the middle.[41] This is a considerable length of time, but the messiah texts from the period are relatively few, and they tend to cluster around a few major historical episodes beginning with the Maccabean revolt (160s B.C.E.) and ending with the Bar Kokhba revolt (130s C.E.), so it is actually an appropriate timeframe for the subject matter.[42]

Within this timeframe, I take both Jewish and Christian messiah texts as evidence of conventions of ancient messiah language. Following many recent interpreters, I avoid as anachronistic the distinction between Judaism and Christianity in the mid-first century C.E.[43] What is more, I take it that messiah texts are not exempted from this methodological rule. As John Gager has rightly commented, "The figures of Jesus and his early followers fall completely within the bounds of first-century Jewish messianism.... The presence of the term *christos* in a first-century text, even attached to one put to death by his enemies, does not place that figure outside or even at the periphery of messianic Judaism."[44]

Outline

Chapter 1 comprises a history of the question, which shows especially how the scholarly discussion of χριστός in Paul has taken place within a series of other debates on more pressing interpretive questions. Chapter 2 addresses the problem of the meaningfulness of messiah language in ancient Judaism, tracing the rise and fall of "the messianic idea" in Jewish studies and giving an alternative social-linguistic account of how messiah language worked in antiquity. Because the discussion of χριστός in Paul has often come down to the question whether it is a name or a title, chapter 3 asks what onomastic

---

41 In a few exceptional cases, I include sources later than this period that attest to events within the period, especially the talmudic references to the Bar Kokhba revolt, because more proximate sources are mostly lacking.

42 Similarly Oegema, *The Anointed and His People,* aptly subtitled "messianic expectations from the Maccabees to Bar Kokhba."

43 Just when this distinction became a real one is a vexing question (see the essays collected in *The Ways That Never Parted: Jews and Christians in Late Antiquity and the Early Middle Ages* [ed. Adam H. Becker and Annette Yoshiko Reed; Texte und Studien zum antiken Judentum 95; Tübingen: Mohr Siebeck, 2003]), but in any case the distinction does not apply to Paul. I do, however, sometimes use the convenient and standard rubric of "Jewish," "Christian," and "pagan" as a shorthand way of referring to late antique literary corpora and religious institutions. These terms are by no means useless since the *Wirkungsgeschichte* of the ancient texts must be taken into account, too.

44 John G. Gager, "Messiahs and Their Followers," in *Toward the Millennium: Messianic Expectations from the Bible to Waco* (ed. Peter Schäfer and Mark R. Cohen; Studies in the History of Religions 77; Leiden: Brill, 1998), 37–46, here 38.

possibilities would have been available to ancient users of messiah language, that is, what categories of name-like words they might have had. Turning to the Pauline evidence, chapter 4 examines a number of set phrases that have been taken as evidence either for or against a messianic sense of χριστός in Pauline usage (e.g., "Jesus Christ," "Christ Jesus," "in Christ," "the Christ of God," "Jesus is the Christ"). Chapter 5, then, is devoted to the interpretation of nine Pauline passages that are immediately relevant to the question of messiah Christology. In the conclusion, finally, I summarize the argument and show its relevance to Pauline interpretation on the one hand and messiah research on the other.

I

The Modern Problem of
Christ and the Messiahs

IF, AS I suggest in the introduction, the messiahship of Jesus in Paul has not been properly understood in modern scholarship, it is not for lack of attention. In fact, the question of the meaning of χριστός in Paul has often been close to the center of modern Pauline interpretation, with the major interpreters of each generation commenting on it in connection with the questions that preoccupied that generation—especially the status of the law, the hellenization of early Christianity, and the relation between Jews and Gentiles. While there are some interesting episodes in the premodern history of this question, there are no extended treatments of the question prior to the European Enlightenment and the rise of historical criticism.[1] It is therefore fitting to begin this survey in the middle of the nineteenth century with that father of modern Pauline criticism, Ferdinand Christian Baur.

---

1 Ancient, medieval, and early modern interpreters give some attention to Davidic messiah passages in Paul, often under the christological rubric of divine and human natures, where Jesus's descent from David proves his true humanity. See, e.g., Cyril of Alexandria, *Rom.* ad loc. (PG 74:774–776): ἀλλ'εἰ καὶ γέγονεν ἐκ σπέρματος τοῦ Δαβὶδ κατὰ σάρκα, καὶ ὡς εἷς ἐξ ἡμῶν εἰς υἱὸν λογίζεται Θεοῦ διὰ τὸ ἀνθρώπινον, "But if he also came from the seed of David according to the flesh, the son of God is reckoned as one of us with respect to humanity"; Augustine, *ep. Rm. inch.* 1.4 (PL 35:2090): *Occurrendum autem erat etiam illorum impietati, qui Dominum nostrum Jesum Christum secundum hominem tantummodo, quem suscepit, accipiunt; divinitatem autem in eo non intelligunt ab universae creaturae communione discretam,* "[In Rom 1:3–4 Paul] was indeed attacking the impiety of those who accept our Lord Jesus Christ only according to the man whom he took up but do not understand the divinity by which he is distinguished from the fellowship of all creatures"; John Calvin, *Commentaries on the Epistle of Paul the Apostle to the Romans* (Grand Rapids, Mich.: Eerdmans, 1948), 44: "[In Rom 1:3–4 Paul] also clearly distinguishes his human from his divine nature; and thus he refutes the impious raving of Servetus, who assigned flesh to Christ, composed of three uncreated elements."

From Baur to the religionsgeschichtliche Schule

Post-Enlightenment New Testament criticism set to work first of all not on Paul but on Jesus.[2] As early as the eighteenth century Jesus had his Reimarus, but there was no comparably radical critic of Paul until half a century later when F. C. Baur published his first work on the apostle. Baur's large-scale thesis—that the history of Christianity in the first two centuries C.E. is the story of initial conflict between and eventual synthesis of Petrine Jewish Christianity and Pauline Gentile Christianity—is justly famous.[3] With the exception of a few early works, almost all of Baur's formidable corpus is dedicated to working out this ambitious research program.[4]

In his major two-volume book on Paul, *Paulus, der Apostel Jesu Christi* (1845), Baur is acutely concerned with Paul's conception of the messiahship of Jesus.[5] If for many twentieth-century interpreters χριστός in Paul is blandly empty of messianic connotations, for Baur it has emphatically messianic connotations because Baur's Paul is furiously waging a war for the purification of the messianic idea from its Jewish pedigree. Baur writes, "The apostle...saw in the death of Christ the purification of the Messianic idea from all the sensuous elements which cleaved to it in Judaism, and its elevation to the truly spiritual consciousness where Christ comes to be recognised as (that which he was to the apostle) the absolute principle of the spiritual life."[6] For Baur this redefinition of χριστός is nothing less than a change of religions, not just from one religious affiliation to another but from a lower plane of religion to

---

2 This phase of Jesus research included figures such as Hermann Samuel Reimarus, Johann Gottfried Herder, H. E. G. Paulus, Friedrich Schleiermacher, and David Friedrich Strauss, on whom see Albert Schweitzer, *The Quest of the Historical Jesus* (trans. W. Montgomery; New York: Macmillan, 1968), 1–67.

3 The programmatic statement of this thesis is F. C. Baur, "Die Christuspartei in der korinthischen Gemeinde, der Gegensatz des paulinischen und petrinischen Christentums in der ältesten Kirche, den Apostel Petrus in Rom," *Tübinger Zeitschrift für Theologie* 4 (1831): 61–206; and shortly thereafter, F. C. Baur, *Die sogenannten Pastoralbriefe des Apostels Paulus* (Stuttgart: Cotta, 1835).

4 Stephen Neill estimates, "The works published during his life-time amount to ten thousand pages; those published after his death from his notes or those of his students to another six thousand" (Stephen Neill, *The Interpretation of the New Testament: 1861–1961* [Oxford: Oxford University Press, 1964], 19).

5 F. C. Baur, *Paulus, der Apostel Jesu Christi, sein Leben und Wirken, seine Briefe und seine Lehre* (Stuttgart: Becher und Müller, 1845); Eng. trans. *Paul the Apostle of Jesus Christ: His Life and Works, His Epistles and Teachings* (2 vols.; London: Williams & Norgate, 1845–1846; repr. Peabody, Mass.: Hendrickson, 2003). Baur intended a thoroughly revised second edition of *Paulus* but died before he could complete it. The direction of the intended revisions is indicated in Baur's posthumous *Vorlesungen über neutestamentliche Theologie* (ed. F. F. Baur; Leipzig: Fues, 1864), especially 128–207.

6 Baur, *Paul the Apostle*, 2:125–126.

its zenith. "The apostle feels that in his conception of the person of Christ he stands on a platform where he is infinitely above Judaism, where he has passed far beyond all that is merely relative, limited, and finite in Jewish religion, and has risen to the absolute religion."[7]

If this account seems difficult to square with all the Pauline evidence, it is in part because Baur admits significantly less as Pauline evidence than subsequent interpreters have done. Modern Pauline studies has settled on an undisputedly Pauline corpus of seven letters, whereas Baur admitted only the four *Hauptbriefe*—Galatians, 1 Corinthians, 2 Corinthians, and Romans—as certainly authentic.[8] Even within these four letters, moreover, Baur hypothesizes textual interpolations at certain passages that reflect the sort of messiah Christology that is at odds with Paulinism as he sees it.[9] For Baur, the point is not just that Paul represents law-free Gentile Christianity over against its Petrine, law-observant, Jewish counterpart. It is that Paul liberates Christianity from Judaism by liberating Jesus from the Jewish notion of messiah. It is the apostle's novel Christology, the fact that he understands Jesus no longer as "messiah" at all but rather as "Christ," that paves the way for the elevation of Christianity to a higher plane of religion.[10]

Baur's account of Pauline Christology cast a long shadow over subsequent generations of Pauline interpreters.[11] Perhaps most important, it was a major influence upon the German *religionsgeschichtliche Schule*, a group of critics who set the terms for early twentieth-century New Testament research

---

7 Baur, *Paul the Apostle*, 2:126.

8 Baur, *Paul the Apostle*, 1:256:

> In the Homologoumena there can only be reckoned the four Epistles which must on all accounts be considered the chief Epistles [*Hauptbriefe*] of the Apostle, namely the Epistle to the Galatians, the two Epistles to the Corinthians, and the Epistle to the Romans. There has never been the slightest suspicion of unauthenticity cast on these four Epistles, on the contrary, they bear in themselves so incontestably the character of Pauline originality, that it is not possible for critical doubt to be exercised upon them with any show of reason. All the rest of the Epistles, which are commonly ascribed to the Apostle, belong to the class of Antilegomena.

9 Most important, Baur follows the text of Marcion's *Apostolicon* in emending out all of Romans 15–16. On this problem, see my treatment in chapter 5.

10 On this aspect of Baur's work, see further the discussions of Susannah Heschel, *Abraham Geiger and the Jewish Jesus* (Chicago Studies in the History of Judaism; Chicago: University of Chicago Press, 1998), 106–126; Anders Gerdmar, *Roots of Theological Anti-Semitism: German Biblical Interpretation and the Jews, from Herder and Semler to Kittel and Bultmann* (Studies in Jewish History and Culture 20; Leiden: Brill, 2009), 97–120.

11 Baur's name is indelibly connected with the so-called *Tübinger Schule*, which included Adolf Hilgenfeld, Karl Reinhard Köstlin, Gustav Volkmar, and especially Albert Schwegler. None of these students and successors of Baur, however, is a major commentator on χριστός in Paul.

on the continent and exercised considerable influence in England and the United States as well.[12] With few exceptions, German interpretation of Paul in this period overwhelmingly tended to highlight Hellenistic aspects of Paul's thought and to downplay Jewish aspects proportionately.[13] One of the chief ways in which this was done was to argue that Paul abandoned the messiah Christology of the earliest Jewish-Christian community and advocated instead a κύριος Christology that was agreeable to Gentile sensibilities.

In 1904 William Wrede of Breslau, best known for his bombshell in Markan studies, *Das Messiasgeheimnis in den Evangelien* (1901), published a short volume titled *Paulus*.[14] In that book, Wrede argues, against Julius Wellhausen and Adolf von Harnack, that Paul was not a legitimate heir to the movement that Jesus began but an interloper, albeit a brilliant one.[15] Paul's interloping, for Wrede, has especially to do with his peculiar Christology. Wrede draws a sharp distinction between the Pauline Christ and "the ordinary conception of a Messiah": "The ordinary conception of a Messiah does not suffice to characterize the Christ of Paul. For the significance of the Pauline Christ is valid, not for Judaism, but for mankind.... He is metaphysically conceived: the Son of God is as such a superhuman, a divine figure."[16] For Wrede, this different kind of Christ entails an altogether different kind of religion. "Christ is no more the Jewish Messiah, but the saviour of the world; faith in him is therefore no more a form of the Jewish faith, but a new faith."[17] The upshot of this line of reasoning is a classic *religionsgeschichtliche* statement of the liberation of Christianity out of Judaism in the work of the apostle to the Gentiles. "[Paul] not only lifted the Christian religion out of the narrowness of Judaism, but

---

12 Their influence in Anglophone circles was mediated especially by Kirsopp Lake, an Englishman who taught first at Leiden and then for many years at Harvard (see Neill, *Interpretation of the New Testament*, 165–167). On the *religionsgeschichtliche Schule*, see Albert Schweitzer, *Paul and His Interpreters* (trans. W. Montgomery; London: Black, 1912), 151–236; Werner Georg Kümmel, *The New Testament: A History of the Investigation of Its Problems* (trans. S. McLean Gilmour and Howard Clark Kee; Nashville: Abingdon, 1972), 206–324; William Baird, *History of New Testament Research* (2 vols; Minneapolis: Fortress, 1992–2003), 2:238–253.

13 On the reasons for this trend, see Dale B. Martin, "Paul and the Judaism/Hellenism Dichotomy: Toward a Social History of the Question," in *Paul beyond the Judaism/Hellenism Divide* (ed. Troels Engberg-Pedersen; Louisville, Ky.: Westminster John Knox, 2001), 29–61.

14 William Wrede, *Paulus* (Halle: Gebauer-Schwetschke, 1904); Eng. trans. *Paul* (trans. Edward Lummis; London: Green, 1907).

15 "Of that which is to Paul all and everything, how much does Jesus know? Nothing whatever" (Wrede, *Paul,* 163). See Wrede, *Paul,* 157, for his criticism of Wellhausen and Harnack.

16 Wrede, *Paul,* 86–87.

17 Wrede, *Paul,* 168. Note the reasoning that, in order to be the savior of the world, Jesus must no longer be the Jewish messiah.

tore it loose from Judaism itself, and gave the Christian community for the first time the consciousness of being a new religion."[18]

Similar is the view of Adolf Deissmann, who draws a distinction between the "dogmatic messiah" of Judaism and the "spiritual Christ" of Paul, where, again, it is Paul's non-messianic Christology that frees Christianity from its rudimentary association with Judaism: "There can be no doubt that Paul became influential in the world's history precisely through his Christ-mysticism. The spiritual Christ was able to do what a dogmatic Messiah could not have done. The dogmatic Messiah of the Jews is fettered to the country of his origin. The spiritual Christ could move from place to place."[19] Christianity before Paul was still encumbered by the dogmatic messiah of Judaism, but Paul's spiritual Christ secured Paul's—and Christianity's—enduring place in world history.

It is generally agreed that the high-water mark of the *religionsgeschichtliche Schule* is represented by Wilhelm Bousset's *Kyrios Christos*, published in 1913.[20] Approaching the history of early Christianity with an eye to its liturgy and its Christology, Bousset argues especially for the decisive importance of the κύριος cult of the Hellenistic churches for the development of the whole Christian movement in the first two centuries C.E. On Paul in particular, Bousset argues that his conception of Christ is characterized by a "personal Christ piety" [*persönliche Christusfrömmigkeit*] that is far removed from the primitive Jewish Christian confession of Jesus as messiah. "The personal Christ piety of the apostle Paul arose on this foundation of the Kyrios faith and the Kyrios cultus in the Hellenistic primitive Christian communities."[21] This is

---

18 Wrede, *Paul*, 175. Interestingly, however, much as Wrede understands Paul to represent a departure from Judaism, he does not take the notion of a divine Christ to be a Pauline innovation:

> There remains only one explanation: Paul believed in such a celestial being, in a divine Christ, before he believed in Jesus.... The Pauline Christ cannot be understood unless we assume that Paul, while still a Pharisee, possessed a number of definite conceptions concerning a divine being, which were afterwards transferred to the historical Jesus. (Wrede, *Paul*, 151–152)

19 Adolf Deissmann, *Paul: A Study in Social and Religious History* (trans. William E. Wilson; 2d ed.; New York: Harper, 1957; German original 1911), 156.

20 Wilhelm Bousset, *Kyrios Christos: Geschichte des Christusglaubens von den Anfängen des Christentums bis Irenaeus* (Göttingen: Vandenhoeck & Ruprecht, 1913); Eng. trans. *Kyrios Christos: A History of the Belief in Christ from the Beginnings of Christianity to Irenaeus* (trans. John E. Steely; Nashville: Abingdon, 1970). See, e.g., the evaluations of Albert Schweitzer, *The Mysticism of Paul the Apostle* (trans. W. Montgomery; New York: Holt, 1931), 29; Kümmel, *History of the Investigation*, 270; Baird, *History of New Testament Research*, 2:243–251.

21 Bousset, *Kyrios Christos*, 153. Like Wrede, Bousset entertains the possibility of Paul's indebtedness to Jewish precedents, but for Bousset it is only a possibility and plays no significant part in Paul's thought. "Whether with the designation of Jesus as the υἱὸς τοῦ θεοῦ Paul reached back to an older messianic title or not, in any case with him it receives a new imprint which has nothing more to do with Jewish messianology. In Paul, the Son of God appears as a supra-terrestrial being who stands in the closest metaphysical relation with God" (Bousset, *Kyrios Christos*, 207).

not to say that Paul is simply a witness to a generic Hellenistic Christianity; the apostle introduces something genuinely new to the tradition. "In the Christ piety of Paul there now sounds one entirely new note, and it becomes the dominant: the intense feeling of personal belonging and of spiritual relationship with the exalted Lord."[22]

On Bousset's account, Paul's use of the word χριστός marks its transition from an honorific title to a proper name. "We see that the old titles which have dominated the community's faith in Christ almost completely disappear. In the Pauline era the title 'Christ' is about to change from a title into a proper name.... Basically the title 'Christ' in Paul no longer has an independent life [*im Grunde hat doch der Titel Christus bei Paulus kein selbständiges Leben mehr*]."[23] This idea that χριστός undergoes an evolution from title to proper name and that Paul represents a late stage in that process has become a commonplace in scholarship even to the present day. In sum, for Bousset, although Paul is an innovator within Hellenistic Christianity, both he and it are evidence of the tectonic shift in the history of religions from the messiah Christology of the earliest Jesus movement to the κύριος cult of the Gentile church. Bousset summarizes the transition in this way:

> It is a remarkable drama of an extremely rapid development. Robes and garments which had just been woven around Jesus' figure were taken off again, and new robes and garments were woven. But if we ask the question, which was "the" new title for the person of Jesus in the Pauline epistles, there can be no doubt as to the answer. It is the designation κύριος which holds the dominant position there.[24]

Bousset's account of Pauline Christology did have some contemporary critics, the most important of whom was Albert Schweitzer, who undertook to reclaim Paul for apocalyptic Judaism.[25] Against the broad consensus that Paul either hellenized Christianity himself or else was representative of pre-Pauline Hellenistic Christianity, Schweitzer insists, "Paul was not the Hellenizer of Christianity. But in his eschatological mysticism of the Being-in-

---

22 Bousset, *Kyrios Christos*, 153.

23 Bousset, *Kyrios Christos*, 121.

24 Bousset, *Kyrios Christos*, 122.

25 See Schweitzer, *Paul and His Interpreters;* Schweitzer, *Mysticism*, here viii: "Instead of the untenable notion that Paul had combined [Jewish] eschatological and Hellenistic ways of thinking we must now consider either a purely eschatological or a purely Hellenistic explanation of his teaching. I take the former alternative throughout."

Christ he gave it a form in which it could be Hellenized."[26] It is well known that Schweitzer locates the center of Paul's thought in the motif of "being in Christ" and that he confidently traces this motif back to the Judaism of late Second Temple apocalypses.[27] More specifically, though, Schweitzer makes the latter connection on the grounds of an ostensible correspondence between the Christ of Paul and the christs of the Jewish apocalypses. About the Pauline "in Christ" motif, he writes, "Eschatology offers such a conception. It is that of the preordained union of those who are elect to the messianic kingdom with one another and with the messiah."[28] So far from being the residue of a more primitive religious plane, for Schweitzer the messiahship of Jesus is the explanatory key to Pauline theology.[29]

Schweitzer's objections notwithstanding, the Boussetian account of χριστός in Paul effectively held sway from the First World War to the Second. Rudolf Bultmann, writing a generation after *Kyrios Christos,* stands very much in the tradition of Bousset:[30] "The historical position of Paul may be stated as follows: Standing within the frame of Hellenistic Christianity he raised the theological motifs that were at work in the proclamation of the Hellenistic

---

26 Schweitzer, *Mysticism,* ix. Schweitzer attributes the hellenization of Christianity instead to the Johannine and Ignatian literature:

> The hellenization of Christianity…consists in taking over the Pauline mysticism of being-in-Christ as the proper formulation of the Christian doctrine of redemption, but giving it for content, not the eschatological conception of the dying and rising again with Christ, but the Hellenistic conception of the union of flesh and spirit. (Schweitzer, *Mysticism,* 343)

27 So famously, "The doctrine of righteousness by faith is therefore a subsidiary crater [*Nebenkrater*], which has formed within the rim of the main crater—the mystical doctrine of redemption through the being-in-Christ" (Schweitzer, *Mysticism,* 225).

28 Schweitzer, *Mysticism,* 101.

29 Even Schweitzer, however, shares his contemporaries' view that the messiah of Judaism could have been of only narrow significance: "Paul takes the belief in Jesus as the coming messiah…and thinks it out so thoroughly that it becomes freed from its temporal limitations and becomes valid for all times" (Schweitzer, *Mysticism,* 380).

30 Bultmann himself wrote the foreword to the fifth edition of Bousset, *Kyrios Christos* (1964), where he comments as follows:

> Among the works of New Testament the study of which I used to recommend in my lectures to students as indispensable, above all belonged Wilhelm Bousset's *Kyrios Christos.* … The correctness of Bousset's posing of the questions and the weight of all these themes and motifs becomes impressively clear to the student when he sees how they have developed in the works of the history-of-religions school. (Rudolf Bultmann, "Introductory Word to the Fifth Edition," in Bousset, *Kyrios Christos,* 7–8)

On Bultmann's indebtedness to the *religionsgeschichtliche Schule,* see Werner Georg Kümmel, "Rudolf Bultmann als Paulusforscher," in *Rudolf Bultmanns Werk und Wirkung* (ed. B. Jaspert; Darmstadt: Wissenschaftlichebuchgesellschaft, 1984), 174–193.

Church to the clarity of theological thinking."[31] When Bultmann turns to Paul's Christology, then, his conclusions are unsurprising. About Paul's reference to Jesus as the "seed of David" (Rom 1:3), Bultmann comments, "The title is of no importance to him." Paul's use of it "is evidently due to a handed-down formula" that does not reflect the apostle's own view.[32]

Paul's own view is reflected "in the statements in which Paul describes Christ's death in analogy with the death of a divinity of the mystery religions."[33] Bultmann, as an heir of the *religionsgeschichtliche Schule*, concludes against messiah Christology in Paul on the grounds that Paul conceives his theology in Hellenistic—specifically, mystery cult—categories, not in Jewish ones. Despite the passage of a century, this notion—that the messiah of Judaism is narrow and limited, the Christ of Paul universal and inclusive—continues to influence many. The anti-Semitic excesses of the school of thought have been roundly rejected, but the basic shape of the argument persists in mainstream Pauline scholarship.[34] If the legacy of the *religionsgeschichtliche Schule* is still with us, however, it at least has had to reckon with a serious rival.

The Postwar Turn

Coinciding very closely with the close of the Second World War, Welsh New Testament scholar W. D. Davies, then at Yorkshire United College in Bradford, UK, published his important study *Paul and Rabbinic Judaism: Some Rabbinic Elements in Pauline Theology* (1948). In that book Davies undertakes to show, against the heirs of the *religionsgeschichtliche Schule*, that all of the principal elements of Pauline theology are explicable in terms of early rabbinic parallels without any recourse to non-Jewish sources.[35] Davies was not the first to make

---

31 Rudolf Bultmann, *Theology of the New Testament* (trans. Kendrick Grobel; 2 vols; New York: Scribner's, 1951), 1:187; German original, *Theologie des Neuen Testaments* (3 vols.; Tübingen: Mohr, 1948–1953).

32 Bultmann, *Theology of the New Testament,* 1:49. For Bultmann, in dramatic contrast to Schweitzer, Jesus's own ministry was not at all messianic ("The synoptic tradition leaves no doubt about it that Jesus' life and work measured by traditional messianic ideas was not messianic" [Bultmann, *Theology of the New Testament,* 1:27]), and Paul did not understand it to be so. For both Schweitzer and Bultmann, however, Paul gets Jesus right.

33 Bultmann, *Theology of the New Testament,* 1:298.

34 Further examples are given later.

35 See Davies, *Paul and Rabbinic Judaism,* 1: "In the present work we shall not seek to deny all Hellenistic influence on him; we shall merely attempt to prove that Paul belonged to the main stream of first-century Judaism, and that elements in his thought, which are often labelled as Hellenistic, might well be derived from Judaism." Note that Davies's position is not that Paul was uninfluenced by Hellenism but rather that the influence of Hellenism on Paul was already mediated by Judaism. In this respect Davies presaged Martin Hengel, *Judaism and Hellenism:*

this case, but he was the first to make it in a way that garnered serious attention.[36] While his particular account did not win the day, the book did signal
the beginning of a trend in Pauline research at large, away from the paradigm
of Paul the hellenizer and toward the paradigm of Paul the Jewish thinker.[37]

On the question of the messiahship of Jesus in Paul, Davies is
unambiguous:

> For [Paul] the acceptance of the Gospel was not so much the rejec-
> tion of the old Judaism and the discovery of a new religion...but the
> recognition of the true and final form of Judaism, in other words, the
> advent of the Messianic age of Jewish expectation....*It was at this one
> point that Paul parted company with Judaism, at the valuation of Jesus of
> Nazareth as Messiah with all that this implied.*[38]

On Davies's account, then, Paul was simply a Jew who believed that the messiah had come and was thinking through "all that this implied." It is no simple thing, of course, to decide precisely what was implied by the messiahship
of Jesus. There is also the difficult question whether the talmudic sources do
in fact yield up the parallels that Davies finds in them, about which subsequent interpreters have not been as confident as Davies was.[39] Even so, Davies
helped move Pauline research down a decidedly Judaism-oriented path that it
has continued on to this day.

Davies's Norwegian contemporary Nils Dahl did not give any comparable
systematic account of Paul's thought, but in a number of exegetical studies he
explored the possible connections between Jewish messianism and Pauline

---

Studies in Their Encounter in Palestine during the Early Hellenistic Period (trans. John Bowden;
Philadelphia: Fortress, 1974).

36 In his 1870 translation of Romans into classical Hebrew, the Leipzig Hebraist Franz
Delitzsch gives a very similar account (see Franz Delitzsch, *Paulus des Apostels Brief an die
Römer: Aus dem griechischen Urtext auf Grund des Sinai-Codex in das Hebräischer übersetzt,
und aus Talmud und Midrasch erläutert* [Leipzig: Dörffling und Franke, 1870]; but cf. the criticism of Schweitzer, *Paul and His Interpreters,* 47). Schweitzer, unlike Delitzsch and Davies,
situates Paul in the Judaism of the apocalypses, not the Judaism of the rabbis.

37 Other representatives of this trend at this time include Leo Baeck, "The Faith of Paul," *JJS* 3
(1952): 93–110; Samuel Sandmel, *The Genius of Paul: A Study in History* (New York: Schocken,
1958); Hans-Joachim Schoeps, *Paul: The Thought of the Apostle in the Light of Jewish Religious
History* (trans. Harold Knight; London: Lutterworth, 1961; German original 1959); Krister
Stendahl, *Paul among Jews and Gentiles* (Philadelphia: Fortress, 1976).

38 Davies, *Paul and Rabbinic Judaism,* 324; emphasis mine.

39 See, e.g., Sandmel, *Genius of Paul,* 223: "Davies' case seemed to me to be this at a maximum,
that affinities between Paul and the Rabbis were limited to some minor and elusive strands";
and a bit more positively Sanders, *Paul and Palestinian Judaism,* 7–12.

Christology.⁴⁰ In 1953 Dahl wrote a short essay, "Die Messianität Jesu bei Paulus," which is arguably still the single most important thing written on the question of messiah Christology in Paul.⁴¹ In that essay Dahl articulates the central question, "Is the name [χριστός] still employed by Paul as a title, or is it only a proper name?"⁴² an issue that had for the most part gone unquestioned at least since Bousset. By way of response, Dahl makes four negative philological observations about the word χριστός in Pauline usage, namely, that it is never a general term, that it is never a predicate of the verb "to be," that it never takes a genitive modifier, and that it characteristically lacks the definite article.⁴³ Dahl is noticeably cautious in the conclusions he draws from these four philological observations: "If one understands 'Christ' only to be a surname of Jesus, all the statements of the epistles make good sense. This does not exclude the possibility that the name 'Christ' bears a fullness of meaning. However, the messiahship of Jesus is not stressed."⁴⁴

In the wake of Dahl's pioneering essay, which distilled the problem into the philological question whether χριστός in Paul is a name or a title, the 1950s and 1960s witnessed a trend in German research toward identifying grammatical criteria whereby the interpreter might tell, in a particular instance, whether Paul intends the word as one or the other.⁴⁵ Hans Conzelmann, for example, suggests that inclusion of the definite article and use as the subject of

---

40 See especially Nils A. Dahl, "The Crucified Messiah," in *Jesus the Christ,* 27–47; "The Crucified Messiah and the Endangered Promises," in *Jesus the Christ,* 65–79; "The Sources of Christological Language," in *Jesus the Christ,* 113–136; "The Atonement: An Adequate Reward for the Akedah?" in *Jesus the Christ,* 137–151.

41 Nils A. Dahl, "Die Messianität Jesu bei Paulus," *Studia Paulina in honorem Johannis de Zwaan septuagenarii* (Haarlem: Bohn: 1953), 83–95; Eng. trans. "The Messiahship of Jesus in Paul," in *The Crucified Messiah* (Minneapolis: Augsburg, 1974), 37–47; repr. in Dahl, *Jesus the Christ,* 15–25, here 15–16. My citations follow the translation and the pagination of the most recent volume.

42 Dahl, "Messiahship of Jesus in Paul," 15, echoing Bousset's name-versus-title taxonomy.

43 Dahl, "Messiahship of Jesus in Paul," 15–16.

44 Dahl, "Messiahship of Jesus in Paul," 16. Dahl's bibliographical successors have tended to be rather less subtle. If for Dahl these four observations could be called soft criteria for assessing the messiahship of Jesus, for many subsequent interpreters they have become hard criteria. See further chapter 4.

45 Roughly contemporary with this development is the major study of Lucien Cerfaux, *Christ dans la théologie de saint Paul* (Lectio divina 6; Paris: Cerf, 1951); Eng. trans. *Christ in the Theology of St. Paul* (trans. Geoffrey Webb and Adrian Walker; New York: Herder and Herder, 1959), especially 367–528. Cerfaux generally holds to the prevailing view, but less polemically than some of his predecessors. He writes, "'Christ' is the key-word of the epistles. It occurs more than four hundred times, while 'Jesus' is used less than two hundred times" (Cerfaux, *Christ,* 480). As for the meaning of the word, "Χριστός, which comes near to having the meaning of a proper name and keeps only a shadow of its appellative sense, always means the person of Christ" (Cerfaux, *Christ,* 488).

a sentence are both signs of titular usage: "Jesus trägt weiter den Messiastitel. 'Christus' hat da titularen Sinn, wo der bestimmte Artikel steht, aber auch da, wo 'Christus' (ohne den Namen 'Jesus') Subjekt eines Satzes ist."[46] In the same way, Oscar Cullmann appeals to word order as a criterion: "The letters of Paul...have a tendency to fix the word Christ as a proper name, although the passages in which Paul writes 'Christ' before 'Jesus' (i.e., 'Christ Jesus') serve as a reminder that he is still aware of its real meaning."[47]

The most important development in this trajectory was Werner Kramer's 1962 Zurich dissertation, in which the author responds point by point to all such philological arguments proposed to date.[48] Kramer contends that in no case can it ever be shown that Paul means χριστός as anything other than a proper name since the cultural transition from primitive Jewish Christianity to pre-Pauline and Pauline Gentile Christianity has emptied this Septuagintal word of all of its conventional meaning:

> When the formula ["Christ died for our sins" (1 Cor 15:3)] was taken over by Gentile Christianity, its wording remained unchanged, but Christ came more and more to be regarded merely as the name of the person to whom the events stated in the formula had happened. It was at this stage that the formula reached Paul. Although formerly a Jew, nevertheless even he uses Christ as though it were a proper name just like Jesus. For this reason the two names ["Jesus" and "Christ"] could be combined or used indiscriminately.[49]

Some fifteen years after the initial postwar turn to the Jewish Paul, the persistent influence of the *religionsgeschichtliche Schule* is evident in Kramer: Paul was only formerly a Jew; the word χριστός, once taken over by Gentile Christianity, loses its Jewish associations. This account would remain very

---

46 Hans Conzelmann, "Was glaubte die frühe Christenheit?" *Schweizerische theologische Umschau* 25 (1955): 61–74, here 65.

47 Oscar Cullmann, *The Christology of the New Testament* (trans. Shirley C. Guthrie and Charles A. M. Hall; Philadelphia: Westminster, 1963), 112; German original, *Christologie des Neuen Testaments* (Tübingen: Mohr, 1957).

48 Werner Kramer, *Christos Kyrios Gottessohn: Untersuchungen zu Gebrauch und Bedeutung der christologischen Bezeichnungen bei Paulus und den vorpaulinischen Gemeinden* (Abhandlungen zur Theologie des Alten und Neuen Testaments 44; Zurich: Zwingli, 1963); Eng. trans. *Christ, Lord, Son of God* (trans. Brian Hardy; Studies in Biblical Theology 50; London: SCM, 1966).

49 Kramer, *Christ, Lord, Son of God*, 42–43.

influential;[50] the late 1970s, however, witnessed yet another landmark in the move toward the Jewish Paul.

As history would have it, an even more influential voice in the Paul-and-Judaism movement than W. D. Davies was Davies's own student E. P. Sanders, who in 1977 published the very important study *Paul and Palestinian Judaism: A Comparison of Patterns of Religion.* The principal goal of the book, as its title suggests, is "to carry out a comparison of Paul and Palestinian Judaism." On his way to this goal, however, Sanders undertakes "to destroy the view of Rabbinic Judaism which is still prevalent in much, perhaps most, New Testament scholarship," and it is this subsidiary project that has been the book's most enduring contribution to the discipline.[51]

While *Paul and Palestinian Judaism* is in part a response to major twentieth-century developments in the study of Judaism, not least the evidence of the Dead Sea Scrolls, it is also in part a response to the author's own teacher. In particular, Sanders finds Davies methodologically guilty of "motif research," of comparing this or that concept in Paul with a putative counterpart in the rabbinic literature. Sanders proposes instead a wholesale comparison of patterns of religions, the essence of Paulinism with the essence of Palestinian Judaism.[52] Methodology aside, however, Sanders's most important material difference with Davies has precisely to do with the messiahship of Jesus, which Davies had put at the center of Paulinism, marking it as the point of disagreement between Paul and the Judaism of the rabbis. Summarizing Davies's thesis, Sanders replies, "I agree with this analysis entirely, *except for the emphasis on the fact of Jesus' messiahship*,"[53] which is, of course, the very heart of the matter. Sanders contrasts his own position with that of Davies, therefore, in christological terms: "Paul's principal conviction was not that Jesus *as the Messiah* had come, but that God had appointed

---

50 Nonetheless, it is contested, at least cursorily, by Günther Bornkamm, "Baptism and New Life in Paul," in *Early Christian Experience* (trans. Paul L. Hammer; New York: Harper and Row, 1969; German original 1958), 76: "The fact that Paul can occasionally use the name of Christ as a 'proper name' has caused the widespread view that the title 'Christ' has become almost meaningless for him and been replaced by the title 'Kyrios' (Lord). However, this is quite incorrect. Both names usually serve as titles for him, and each has a thoroughly different function"; note also Ferdinand Hahn, *The Titles of Jesus in Christology* (trans. Harold Knight and George Ogg; London: Lutterworth, 1969; German original 1963), 186: "Χριστός plays a decisive role in Paul. The usual opinion that in his letters it occurs only as a proper name, is certainly incorrect."

51 Sanders, *Paul and Palestinian Judaism*, xii.

52 For the criticism and the alternative proposal, see Sanders, *Paul and Palestinian Judaism*, 1–24.

53 Sanders, *Paul and Palestinian Judaism*, 496; italics in the original.

Jesus Christ *as Lord* and that he would resurrect or transform those who were members of him by virtue of believing in him."[54] That is, for reasons having to do with his disagreement with Davies, Sanders sees Paul emphasizing a κύριος Christology at the expense of a χριστός Christology, a move remarkably reminiscent of Bousset.

As compelling as Sanders's proposal has been to many, there is one recalcitrant difficulty, often pointed out by his critics, that is relevant here. Sanders famously writes, "In short, this is what Paul finds wrong in Judaism: *it is not Christianity*,"[55] a summary statement that, to be sure, has a certain explanatory elegance to it. As James Dunn has rightly noted, however, on Sanders's account, "The Lutheran Paul has been replaced by an idiosyncratic Paul who in an arbitrary and irrational manner turns his face against the glory and greatness of Judaism's covenant theology and abandons Judaism simply because it is not Christianity."[56] In other words, whereas Davies proposes an inner-Jewish logic whereby Paul might have come by his peculiar views, Sanders simply posits that Paul represents an altogether different religion. By doing so, he avoids the logical snares involved in drawing parallels, but he also leaves Paul strangely untethered to his native religious context and fails to explain why Paul should refer to Jesus as χριστός at all.

After Sanders

Since *Paul and Palestinian Judaism,* the secondary literature on Paul has been more concerned than it ever was with parsing the details of Paul's situation vis-à-vis ancient Judaism, including messiah Christology, but this concern has led in a remarkable multiplicity of directions. One such direction is represented by the work of Lloyd Gaston, especially his famous 1979 essay "Paul and the Torah."[57] Gaston begins by granting Rosemary Radford Ruether's controversial claim that, already in the New Testament, the confession of

54 Sanders, *Paul and Palestinian Judaism,* 514; italics in the original.

55 Sanders, *Paul and Palestinian Judaism,* 552; italics in the original.

56 James D. G. Dunn, *Jesus, Paul, and the Law: Studies in Mark and Galatians* (Louisville, Ky.: Westminster John Knox, 1990), 187. Similarly, Daniel Boyarin, *A Radical Jew: Paul and the Politics of Identity* (Berkeley: University of California Press, 1994), 44: "[Sanders's] account, however, entirely begs the question of what brought Paul to his recognition that salvation is through Christ."

57 Lloyd Gaston, "Paul and the Torah," in *Antisemitism and the Foundations of Christianity* (ed. Alan T. Davies; New York: Paulist, 1979), 48–71; repr. in Lloyd Gaston, *Paul and the Torah* (Vancouver: University of British Columbia Press, 1987), 15–34. My citations follow the pagination in the latter.

Jesus as messiah amounts to a Christian declaration of war on the Jews and that "anti-Judaism is the left hand of Christology."[58]

While Ruether, in Gaston's view, is right on this point, he suggests, "It may be that Paul, and Paul alone among the New Testament writers, has no left hand."[59] Gaston argues that Paul, because he was the apostle to the Gentiles, saw a way to have a Christology that made no claim on God's people, Israel, and so proved the possibility of a Christianity that is not anti-Jewish.[60] The theological payoff of this interpretation is considerable:[61] "A Christian church with an antisemitic New Testament is abominable, but a Christian church without a New Testament is inconceivable."[62] From this premise Gaston reasons, "It is possible to interpret Paul in this manner [i.e., as not preaching Jesus as messiah]. That it is necessary to do so is the implication of the agonized concern of many in the post-Auschwitz situation."[63]

On his way to this antisupersessionist interpretation, however, Gaston finally denies any messianic claim on Paul's part. Citing Dahl and Kramer as having proved that χριστός is merely a name, not a title, Gaston concludes: "For Paul, Jesus is neither a new Moses nor the Messiah, he is not the climax of the history of God's dealing with Israel, but he is the fulfillment of God's promises concerning the Gentiles."[64] The mainstream of Pauline interpreters have been unwilling to follow Gaston to this conclusion, but his approach has a kind of ruthless logic: If, per the majority view, χριστός in Paul does not mean "messiah," then why should we not conclude that Paul did not think

---

58 See Rosemary Radford Ruether, *Faith and Fratricide: The Theological Roots of Anti-Semitism* (New York: Seabury, 1974); Rosemary Radford Ruether, *To Change the World: Christology and Cultural Criticism* (New York: Crossroad, 1981). Among the many responses to Ruether, see especially the essays collected in Davies, ed., *Antisemitism and the Foundations of Christianity*.

59 Gaston, "Paul and the Torah," 34.

60 At this point Gaston is influenced by the earlier work of Stendahl, *Paul among Jews and Gentiles,* here 4: "Paul's reference to God's mysterious plan [in Romans 11] is an affirmation of a God-willed coexistence between Judaism and Christianity in which the missionary urge to convert Israel is held in check." Equally important here is the work of John G. Gager (*The Origins of Anti-Semitism: Attitudes toward Judaism in Pagan and Christian Antiquity* [Oxford: Oxford University Press, 1979]; John G. Gager, *Reinventing Paul* [Oxford: Oxford University Press, 2000]), whose interpretation of Paul is very close to Stendahl's and Gaston's but who demurs from claiming that Paul actually did not think Jesus was the messiah.

61 See Collins, *Scepter and the Star,* 2: "The ecumenical intentions of such a claim are transparent and honorable, but also misguided since the claim is so plainly false."

62 Gaston, "Paul and the Torah," 15.

63 Gaston, "Paul and the Torah," 34.

64 Gaston, "Paul and the Torah," 33. This may be, but if so, then Paul is not really an exception to Ruether's rule after all.

Jesus was the messiah at all?[65] There is another remarkable irony here, too. Recall that, for F. C. Baur, if Paul had had a messiah Christology, he would have been a philo-Semite, which Baur could not abide. More than a century later, Gaston reasons that, if Paul had had a messiah Christology, he would have been an anti-Semite, which Gaston cannot abide. Baur and Gaston agree, then, on the historical point that Paul did not believe that Jesus was the messiah, but for exactly opposite theological reasons.

Roughly contemporaneous with Gaston, Martin Hengel made an important contribution to the discussion of χριστός in Paul in an essay in the 1982 *Festschrift* for C. K. Barrett.[66] Hengel's essay is close in both form and content to Dahl's essay of thirty years earlier, which Hengel cites approvingly at a number of points. Hengel updates Dahl by responding to the German research of the 1950s and 1960s that proposed grammatical criteria for judging whether χριστός in Paul is a name or a title.[67] He provocatively undertakes to move the discussion away from the rubric of name-versus-title but is not entirely consistent in doing so. In places, Hengel demolishes the older categories: "In fact 'Christos' seems to be a word with a character all its own. It was neither one name among many, like Jesus, nor was it a customary Greek title."[68] Elsewhere, however, he reinforces them: "Jesus was the real proper name, 'Christos' the cognomen, and 'Kyrios' the title."[69] And again, "It is precisely as a 'proper name' that 'Christos' expresses the uniqueness of Jesus."[70] Along the way Hengel makes a number of valuable philological observations;[71] but the main contribution of his study is to update and reinforce Dahl's approach to the problem.

Only one recent interpreter has taken the discussion in a direction significantly different from Dahl's, namely N. T. Wright, who has written extensively on the question, beginning with his unpublished 1980 Oxford dissertation and continuing through his several monographs on Paul to

---

65 As I argue in chapter 3, the problem actually lies in the majority view itself, that χριστός in Paul is a meaningless proper name.

66 Martin Hengel, "Erwägungen zum Sprachgebrauch von Χριστός bei Paulus und in der vorpaulinischen Überlieferung," in *Paul and Paulinism: Essays in Honour of C. K. Barrett* (ed. Morna D. Hooker and S. G. Wilson; London: SPCK, 1982), 135–158; Eng. trans. "'Christos' in Paul," *Between Jesus and Paul: Studies in the Earliest History of Christianity* (trans. John Bowden; Philadelphia: Fortress, 1983), 65–77.

67 E.g., Hengel contends with Kramer, *Christ, Lord, Son of God,* against Conzelmann, "Christenheit," that "there is no demonstrable connection in principle between the use of the article and a rudimentary significance as a title" ("'Christos' in Paul," 69).

68 Hengel, "'Christos' in Paul," 74.

69 Hengel, "'Christos' in Paul," 68.

70 Hengel, "'Christos' in Paul," 72.

71 I respond to these observations in chapter 4.

date.[72] In his dissertation Wright argues that the messiahship of Jesus is the theological solution to the notoriously difficult problem of the interrelationship of the several sections of the Epistle to the Romans. In doing so, he introduces a very particular definition of the word "messiah":

> The Messiah, the anointed one of Israel, represents his people and sums them up in himself, so that what is true of him is true of them. When this aspect is linked to the information Paul received in his conversion, namely, that God in the resurrection had declared the crucified Jesus to be the Messiah, the main themes of his theology, and with them the main sections of Romans, are at once brought together in a new way.[73]

Wright's subsequent publications on the subject carry on this approach in all its main lines. He has consistently articulated the view that χριστός in Paul means "messiah" and that "messiah" means "the one in whom the people of God are summed up," even as he has moved outward from Romans to the rest of the Pauline corpus.[74] So in a 1991 essay on Philemon he writes, "Χριστός in Paul should regularly be read as 'Messiah,' and ... one of the chief significances which this word then carries is *incorporative*, that is, ... it refers to the Messiah as the one in whom the people of God are summed up."[75] Similarly, in his Hulsean Lectures for 2005, "In particular, the often-studied *incorporative* use of *Christos* in Paul tells heavily in favour of a messianic reference."[76] Wright marshals a

---

72 See N. T. Wright, "The Messiah and the People of God: A Study in Pauline Theology with Particular Reference to the Argument of the Epistle to the Romans" (Ph.D. diss., University of Oxford, 1980); N. T. Wright, *The Climax of the Covenant: Christ and the Law in the Pauline Theology* (Edinburgh: T. & T. Clark, 1991); N. T. Wright, *What Saint Paul Really Said: Was Paul of Tarsus the Real Founder of Christianity?* (Grand Rapids, Mich.: Eerdmans, 1997); N. T. Wright, *The Resurrection of the Son of God* (Minneapolis: Fortress, 2003), 553–584; N. T. Wright, *Paul: In Fresh Perspective* (Minneapolis: Fortress, 2005).

73 Wright, "Messiah and the People of God," 4.

74 Wright has also argued that Paul's emphasis on the messiahship of Jesus implies a polemic against the Roman empire insofar as "if Jesus is Israel's Messiah then he is the world's true Lord," and therefore "for Paul, Jesus is Lord and Caesar is not" (Wright, *Paul: In Fresh Perspective*, 69). On this particular point Wright is in agreement with Neil Elliott, *Liberating Paul: The Justice of God and the Politics of the Apostle* (Maryknoll, N.Y.: Orbis, 1994); Richard A. Horsley, ed., *Paul and Empire: Religion and Power in Roman Imperial Society* (Harrisburg, Pa.: Trinity, 1997); Richard A. Horsley, ed., *Paul and Politics: Ekklesia, Israel, Imperium, Interpretation: Essays in Honor of Krister Stendahl* (Harrisburg, Pa.: Trinity, 2000); Richard A. Horsley, ed., *Paul and the Roman Imperial Order* (Harrisburg, Pa.: Trinity, 2004); John Dominic Crossan and Jonathan L. Reed, *In Search of Paul: How Jesus's Apostle Opposed Caesar's Empire with God's Kingdom* (New York: Harper, 2004).

75 Wright, *Climax,* 41; italics in the original.

76 Wright, *Paul: In Fresh Perspective*, 46; italics in the original.

number of forceful exegetical arguments;[77] but James Dunn is bibliographically accurate when he says that "Wright...has been a lone voice" in arguing that χριστός in Paul should be understood throughout as "the Messiah."[78]

If Wright is a lone voice, then the prevailing chorus take the now standard view that χριστός in Paul is, if not meaningless, at least de-emphasized.[79] On this assumption, several recent treatments of the question propose to explain why Paul should undertake such a program of de-emphasis. One able representative of this approach is Andrew Chester, who argues as follows:

> Paul has deliberately "defused" or "neutralized" the messianic hope (thus, in some respects, it is a process analogous to that which we find in Philo). That is, the terminology is kept, especially the term Messiah/χριστός, but the sense is changed. Probably Paul undertakes this "neutralizing" of the tradition both because the messianic kingdom has not manifested itself, contrary to what had been expected, and also because the radical implications of the messianic hope would present problems for him, especially as he and the Christian movement moved more and more into the main centres of the Roman Empire. Thus to retain or develop an emphasis of this kind would mean, for Paul and his churches (as relatively small and scattered groups set within large urban centres), focusing on something that was in practice incapable of being realized within society, and also potentially politically embarrassing.[80]

---

77 I respond to all these in chapters 4–5.

78 James D. G. Dunn, *The Theology of Paul the Apostle* (Grand Rapids, Mich.: Eerdmans, 1998), 199n88. "Lone voice" is a bit of an overstatement, however. See, e.g., Stephen A. Cummins, "Divine Life and Corporate Christology: God, Messiah Jesus, and the Covenant Community in Paul," in *The Messiah in the Old and New Testaments* (ed. Stanley E. Porter; Grand Rapids, Mich.: Eerdmans, 2007), 190–209.

79 Rather different, however, is the approach of Merrill P. Miller ("The Problem of the Origins of a Messianic Conception of Jesus," in *Redescribing Christian Origins* [ed. Ron Cameron and Merrill P. Miller; Society of Biblical Literature Symposium Series 28; Atlanta: Society of Biblical Literature, 2004], 301–336; Merrill P. Miller, "The Anointed Jesus," in *Redescribing Christian Origins*, 375–416), who has argued that χριστός in Paul seems unmessianic not because Paul is downplaying it but because the word itself had no messianic associations in the first century. Miller argues, on the methodological premises laid out by Jonathan Z. Smith and Burton Mack, that the category of "messiah" in Pauline interpretation is deeply suspect: Not only does it claim a Jewish pedigree (and an epic, biblical one at that), but it also invokes a sense of radical uniqueness—*the* messiah—which breaks the first rule of comparative study of religions. I respond at length to Miller in chapter 3.

80 Chester, "Messianism, Mediators, and Pauline Christology," 385; cf. his more recent and more succinct treatment "The Christ of Paul," in *Redemption and Resistance: The Messianic Hopes of Jews and Christians in Antiquity* (ed. Markus Bockmuehl and James Carleton Paget; London: T. & T. Clark, 2007), 109–121.

Chester begins by agreeing with the standard observation that Paul writes "messiah" but does not mean "messiah" ("the terminology is kept... but the sense is changed"), but he takes this to reflect intentional defusing or neutralizing on Paul's part. Paul is driven to defuse his messianic language first because of the delay of the parousia, which might seem to falsify the messianic claim, and second because of the politically sensitive situation of his mission, in light of which Paul would not have wanted to raise any suspicions of subversive behavior.[81]

More recently still, Magnus Zetterholm has taken the same kind of approach to the problem but with an entirely different explanation for why Paul should want to downplay the familiar meaning of χριστός. Like Chester, Zetterholm cites Dahl and Kramer as having shown that Paul emphasizes the title κύριος and proportionately downplays χριστός. Unlike Chester, however, Zetterholm explains this phenomenon in terms of Jew-Gentile dynamics in the Pauline congregations:

> Paul's de-emphasizing of Jesus' messiahship, while stressing his lordship, was a result of the fact that non-Jewish adherents to the Jesus movement were already familiar with Judaism, and partly identified themselves with the salvation history of the Jewish people in which the messiah of Israel had a key role. I believe that this is the fundamental misunderstanding of the non-Jews that Paul is generally trying to correct.[82]

Extrapolating from Paul's response to his Galatian Gentiles who were flirting with circumcision, Zetterholm reasons that Paul was concerned to prevent his Gentile believers from Judaizing in any sense whatsoever. Just as Paul disapproves of their being circumcised, so also would he disapprove of their adopting a messianic view of Jesus. For them, Jesus is properly Gentile lord, not Jewish messiah. Again, "Paul's theological convictions regarding non-Jewish

---

81 Cf. the criticisms of Stefan Schreiber, *Gesalbter und König: Titel und Konzeptionen der königlichen Gesalbtenerwartung in frühjüdischen und urchristlichen Schriften* (Berlin: de Gruyter, 2000), 419–420, especially that Paul's Christology is shaped by the death and resurrection of Jesus, not by Jewish messianic traditions; and Dieter Zeller, "Zur Transformation des Χριστός bei Paulus," in *Der Messias* (ed. Ingo Baldermann et al.; Jahrbuch für Biblische Theologie 8; Neukirchen-Vluyn: Neukirchener Verlag, 1993), 163–167, especially that Paul does not transform the word χριστός but finds it already transformed. Chester, "Christ of Paul," responds to these criticisms *en route* to a restatement and defense of his position: "His [Paul's] main focus is not on Jesus as messiah; nor do messianic categories play a prominent role in his theology" (Chester, "Christ of Paul," 109); "The number of specifically messianic references in Paul is very limited, and so also is their significance" (Chester, "Christ of Paul," 112).

82 Magnus Zetterholm, "Paul and the Missing Messiah," in *The Messiah in Early Judaism and Christianity* (ed. Magnus Zetterholm; Minneapolis: Fortress, 2007), 33–55, here 40.

Torah observance and his emphasis on preserving the ethnic identities of Jews and non-Jews within the Jesus movement forced him to present Jesus in a way that would form an ideological resource for non-Jewish believers in Jesus— the gospel of Jesus Christ as lord."[83] Here, ironically, is a sort of post–New Perspective recapitulation of the late nineteenth- and early twentieth-century account of χριστός in Paul. Like Baur and Bousset, but for very different reasons, Zetterholm considers it inappropriate for Paul to present his Gentile believers with a Jewish messiah.

The dominant approach represented by Chester and Zetterholm has not been without its detractors. Dieter Zeller has responded to Chester, arguing that Paul neither ignores nor undermines the conventional messianic over- tones of the word χριστός.[84] Paula Fredriksen has suggested that the messi- ahship of Jesus helps explain certain other Pauline themes like the persecution of believers in the Diaspora synagogues and the rationale for the Gentile mis- sion.[85] Most recently, Adela Yarbro Collins has advanced an argument for the messiahship of Jesus in Paul.[86] She makes several of the customary philologi- cal observations, but she interprets them in a direction that is different from that taken by the majority: "His [Paul's] use of it [χριστός] without expla- nation or debate indicates that the proclamation of Jesus as the messiah of Israel was a fundamental part of his announcement of the good news to those who formed the core membership of the communities that he founded."[87] In other words, Paul's unornamented use of the word suggests not that he was defusing or de-emphasizing the idea but rather that he assumed it.[88] The contributions of Zeller, Fredriksen, and Collins show that, appearances

---

83 Zetterholm, "Paul and the Missing Messiah," 54.

84 Zeller, "Transformation," 167:

> Trotz unterschiedlicher Konzepte im Judentum hat der Begriff "Messias" bzw. χριστός seine jeweilige Bestimmtheit, die sich aus der endzeitlichen Auslegung der Schrift ergibt. Für das Neue Testament bildet die davidische Messianologie den Ausgangspunkt. Dieser traditionsgeschichtliche Hintergrund ist bei Paulus nur noch in Spuren wahr- zunehmen, die für die Israelproblematik wieder aufgefrischt werden.

85 See Paula Fredriksen, "Judaism, the Circumcision of Gentiles, and Apocalyptic Hope: Another Look at Galatians 1 and 2," *Journal of Theological Studies*, n.s. 42 (1991): 532–564; also Paula Fredriksen, *Jesus of Nazareth: King of the Jews* (New York: Vintage, 1999); and Paula Fredriksen, *From Jesus to Christ: The Origins of the New Testament Images of Christ* (New Haven: Yale University Press, 2000).

86 Adela Yarbro Collins, "Jesus as Messiah and Son of God in the Letters of Paul," in John J. Collins and Adela Yarbro Collins, *King and Messiah as Son of God*, 101–122.

87 Collins, "Jesus as Messiah and Son of God in the Letters of Paul," 122.

88 A point already suggested by Dahl, "Messiahship of Jesus in Paul," 18: "The messiahship of Jesus had for Paul himself a greater significance than emerges directly from the usage of the name 'Christ' in his epistles"; Dahl, "Messiahship of Jesus in Paul," 21: "For him the messi- ahship of Jesus is essential for the inner coherence of his Christology."

notwithstanding, the majority interpretation does not follow necessarily from the Pauline evidence; other interpretations are possible and perhaps even preferable.[89]

This possibility is taken even further by Stanley Stowers, who, in his 1994 monograph on Romans, proposes a constructive interpretation of Paul's idiosyncratic use of χριστός:

> My hypothesis is as follows: Paul believed that God commissioned the man Jesus, chosen descendant of Davidic lineage, to be his messiah....Jesus, however, out of faithfulness to his mandate, chose not to exercise the awesome divine powers available to him. Jesus did not exercise the powers given to him because if he had, much of Israel and most of the gentiles would have been lost. Jesus died and postponed the world's judgment out of love for the ungodly.... In forgoing his messianic prerogatives, Jesus was allowing Jews and gentiles an opportunity to repent and trusting that God would delay his mission until God's righteousness could be effected.[90]

That is, for Paul, Jesus was indeed the messiah, but one who chose to delay the judgment of the world by forgoing his own messianic prerogatives. The messiah has delayed, and for Paul now the emphasis is on the delay, not the messiah. This, Stowers claims, explains both the authenticity of patently messianic traditions in the epistles and also their relative unimportance to Paul's thought. "Jesus' act of forgoing messianic powers and privileges meant, for Paul, that although Jesus was the messiah, his all-important act was his dying for the ungodly and his assumption of the status and role given to him when God approved his faithful act by vindicating him in the resurrection."[91] It is problematic that Stowers explains the evidence in the form of a concession, that although Jesus was messiah, his all-important act was something else.[92]

---

89 Also relevant here is Jacob Taubes, *The Political Theology of Paul* (ed. Aleida Assmann and Jan Assmann; trans. Dana Hollander; Cultural Memory in the Present; Stanford: Stanford University Press, 2004; German original 1993), who is concerned with a very different set of issues but makes much of the messiahship of Jesus as a factor in Paul's thought. Significantly, Taubes is followed at just this point by Giorgio Agamben, *The Time That Remains: A Commentary on the Letter to the Romans* (trans. Patricia Dailey; Meridian: Crossing Aesthetics; Stanford: Stanford University Press, 2005).

90 Stanley K. Stowers, *A Rereading of Romans: Justice, Jews, and Gentiles* (New Haven: Yale University Press, 1994), 214.

91 Stowers, *Rereading of Romans*, 215.

92 As I argue in chapter 5, for Paul, Jesus's messiahship somehow consists in his dying for the ungodly; the latter is not something other than the former.

Nevertheless, Stowers, like Wright, represents a move toward the integration of the category of messiahship into Paul's thought.[93]

Conclusion

By way of summary, it is fair to say that the question of the meaning of χριστός in Paul has had a storied history in modern interpretation, even if the question itself has not always lain at the surface of the discussion. The reason for this storied history is that the question touches directly on so many subjects that do lie at the surface of the discussion, long-contested rubrics like Judaism and Hellenism, Paul and Judaism, and Paul and Jesus. At the present time, scholarly opinion on χριστός in Paul stands in an ironic position. While most of the major monographs, commentaries, and theologies of Paul now follow Davies and Sanders in reading Paul in primarily "Jewish" rather than "Hellenistic" terms, on the question of the meaning of χριστός they nevertheless perpetuate the old *religionsgeschichtliche* thesis that Paul is revising, transcending, or otherwise moving beyond the messianic faith of the earliest Jesus movement.[94]

Their particular accounts of Paul's Christology are quite diverse, but common to almost all is the assumption that, whatever Paul's Christology is, it is not messianic. This bibliographical state of affairs, however, actually presupposes a broadly shared notion of messiah Christology among the parties to the discussion. In other words, Pauline interpreters think they know what messiah Christology would look like, and they are certain that Paul's Christology does not look like that. This is actually very curious, however, since the last sixty years in Jewish studies have witnessed a dramatic breakdown in consensus about what messiah Christology would look like and indeed whether it existed at all in the first century C.E. As a result, the two subfields of research are like ships passing in the night. When scholars of early Judaism, who

---

93 Such integration has been suggested, e.g., by Wright, *Climax,* 42: "The time is ripe for a re-assessment of Messiahship as a major category within Pauline theology"; and by Richard B. Hays, "Christ Prays the Psalms: Israel's Psalter as Matrix of Early Christology," in *The Conversion of the Imagination: Paul as Interpreter of Israel's Scripture* (Grand Rapids, Mich.: Eerdmans, 2005), 117: "Critical studies of Pauline Christology have seriously underestimated the importance of this [messianic] element of Paul's thought about Jesus"; but it has rarely been attempted, only cursorily here by Stowers and thoroughly but very differently by Wright.

94 Wright, *Paul: In Fresh Perspective,* 48–49, gives a plausible explanation of the prewar objection to messiah Christology in Paul: "As long as the dominant history-of-religions paradigm was trying to understand Paul in terms of his mission to the Gentile world and hence in terms of a 'translation' of Jewish ideas into Gentile ones, it was bound to marginalize such a centrally Jewish theme." The persistence of this trend in the work of late twentieth- and early twenty-first-century scholars like E. P. Sanders, James Dunn, George MacRae, Andrew Chester, and Magnus Zetterholm is much harder to explain.

have cast about for any instances of the word "messiah" in Hellenistic- and Roman-period literature, find an unparalleled cache of such instances in the letters of Paul, New Testament scholars reply that Paul says it but does not mean it, that for him χριστός means "Christ," not "messiah." It is an open question, however, what "messiah" itself means. This is a problem in need of a solution, and since both the Jewish studies scholars and the Pauline interpreters are primarily concerned with the philological question of the meaning of the word "messiah," that is the subject of the following chapter.

2

Messiah Language in Ancient Judaism

AS CHAPTER 1 shows, while Pauline interpreters have confidently concluded that χριστός in Paul does not mean "messiah," twentieth-century research on messianism has shown that it is actually an open question what "messiah" means. At once the most basic and the most vexing question about messiah language in antiquity is what—and indeed whether—it meant, that is, under what circumstances, if at all, ancient authors could use messiah language with a plausible expectation of communicating with their audiences.[1] This question has always been implicit in scholarship on ancient messianism and has been raised very pointedly in the last generation or so. The present *communis opinio* has been well expressed by William Scott Green in a programmatic essay: "In early Jewish literature, 'messiah' is all signifier with no signified; the term is notable primarily for its indeterminacy."[2] In other words, Jewish messiah language in the Hellenistic and Roman periods meant so many things that it effectively did not mean anything at all. This view of the matter, however, represents a dramatic departure from pre–World War II scholarship, whose account of "the messianic idea" therefore deserves some explication.

---

1 By "messiah language," I mean forms of speech that use the Hebrew word מָשִׁיחַ ("anointed one") or its translation equivalencies (viz. Aramaic מְשִׁיחָא, Greek χριστός and μεσσίας, and Latin *unctus* and *christus*). By "messiah texts," I mean texts that include these words (on both points, see the introduction). On this working definition, messiah texts from ca. 200 B.C.E. to ca. 100 C.E. include the relevant parts of Daniel; *Psalms of Solomon*; *1 Enoch*; *4 Ezra*; *2 Baruch*; CD; 1QS; 1QSa; 1QM; 1Q30; 4Q252; 4Q270; 4Q287; 4Q375; 4Q376; 4Q377; 4Q381; 4Q382; 4Q458; 4Q521; 11QMelch; and the twenty-seven books in the New Testament. These are the texts on which I principally draw in this chapter.

2 William Scott Green, "Introduction: Messiah in Judaism: Rethinking the Question," in *Judaisms and Their Messiahs at the Turn of the Christian Era* (ed. Jacob Neusner et al.; Cambridge: Cambridge University Press, 1987), 4.

"The Messianic Idea" in Jewish Studies

The question of the meaningfulness of ancient messiah language would have struck previous generations of interpreters as unnecessary, even nonsensical. For nineteenth- and early twentieth-century historians, Jewish and Christian alike, the existence of something called "the messianic idea" had near axiomatic status in the study of ancient Judaism. Moshe Idel has drawn attention to this feature of the secondary literature: "In many modern scholarly discussions of events that span more than two millennia, the phrase *messianic idea* is quite a recurrent locution. Though the great variety of literatures under inspection would invite an assumption that many sorts of messianic ideas would compete, the phrase *messianic idea* looms too prominently in the titles of many books and articles."[3]

For its nineteenth- and twentieth-century proponents, the messianic idea was an "idea" in the sense of nineteenth-century metaphysical idealism, a concept that exists independently of historical events and literary texts but comes to expression in them.[4] A commonplace in these older treatments is an enumeration of the composite parts of the messianic idea. Emil Schürer, for example, proposes to present "a systematic statement of Messianic doctrinal theology on the foundation of the Shema, as resulting from the Apocalypse of Baruch and the fourth Book of Esdras. For the eschatological expectation

---

3 Moshe Idel, *Messianic Mystics* (New Haven: Yale University Press, 1998), 17; italics in the original. Some representative instances of the phrase include Heinrich Julius Holtzmann, "Die Messiasidee zur Zeit Jesu," *Jahrbuch für deutsche Theologie* (1867): 389–411; James Drummond, *The Jewish Messiah: A Critical History of the Messianic Idea among the Jews from the Rise of the Maccabees to the Closing of the Talmud* (London: Longmans, Green, 1877); James Scott, "Historical Development of the Messianic Idea," *Old Testament Student* 7 (1888): 176–180; Julius H. Greenstone, *The Messiah Idea in Jewish History* (Philadelphia: JPS, 1906); W. O. E. Oesterley, *The Evolution of the Messianic Idea: A Study in Comparative Religion* (New York: Dutton, 1908); Ernest F. Scott, "What Did the Idea of Messiah Mean to the Early Christians?" *Journal of Religion* 1 (1921): 418–420; Joseph Klausner, *The Messianic Idea in Israel: From Its Beginning to the Completion of the Mishnah* (trans. W. F. Stinespring; New York: Macmillan, 1955); Gershom Scholem, *The Messianic Idea in Judaism and Other Essays on Jewish Spirituality* (New York: Schocken, 1971); Isaiah Tishby, "The Messianic Idea and Messianic Trends at the Beginning of Hasidism," *Zion* 32 (1967): 1–45 (in Hebrew); Dov Schwartz, "The Neutralization of the Messianic Idea in Medieval Jewish Rationalism," *Hebrew Union College Annual* 64 (1993): 37–58 (in Hebrew).

4 For basic background, see Karl Ameriks, "Introduction: Interpreting German Idealism," in *The Cambridge Companion to German Idealism* (ed. Karl Ameriks; Cambridge: Cambridge University Press, 2000), 1–17; Karl Ameriks, "The Legacy of Idealism in the Philosophy of Feuerbach, Marx, and Kierkegaard," in *Cambridge Companion to German Idealism*, 258–281.

is most fully developed in these two Apocalypses."[5] In Schürer's systematic statement, the parts of the messianic idea run as follows:[6]

1. The final ordeal and confusion
2. Elijah as precursor
3. The coming of the messiah
4. The last assault of the hostile powers
5. Destruction of hostile powers
6. The renewal of Jerusalem
7. The gathering of the dispersed
8. The kingdom of glory in the holy land
9. The renewal of the world
10. A general resurrection
11. The last judgment, eternal bliss and damnation

If Schürer represents Christian scholarship from this period, on the Jewish side Joseph Klausner enumerates his own very similar list of the several "links" that make up the "chain" of the messianic idea:

> Thus was forged the complete Messianic chain whose separate links are: the signs of the Messiah, the birth pangs of the Messiah, the coming of Elijah, the trumpet of Messiah, the ingathering of the exiles, the reception of proselytes, the war with Gog and Magog, the Days of the Messiah, the renovation of the world, the Day of Judgment, the resurrection of the dead, the World to Come. Not all the links of this chain are found in every book of the Apocrypha and Pseudepigrapha, or in this order; but in general you find it with these links and in the order mentioned.[7]

Schürer and Klausner agree not only about the component parts of the messianic idea but also, more importantly, about what sort of thing the messianic idea is. Schürer models his list on the narratives of *4 Ezra* and *2 Baruch* because, he says, the expectation itself comes to fullest expression in these sources. Klausner

---

5 Emil Schürer, *A History of the Jewish People in the Time of Jesus Christ* (trans. John Macpherson et al.; 5 vols; 2d ed.; Edinburgh: T. &. T. Clark, 1901), 2.2:154. The "new Schürer" (Emil Schürer, *The History of the Jewish People in the Age of Jesus Christ* [rev. and ed. Geza Vermes and Fergus Millar; 3 vols; Edinburgh: T. &. T. Clark, 1973–1987]), includes the new evidence of the Dead Sea Scrolls but preserves Schürer's original outline almost exactly.

6 Schürer, *History*, 2.2:154–183.

7 Klausner, *Messianic Idea*, 385.

concedes that his "messianic chain" does not map neatly onto the several messiah texts, but he nevertheless insists that it is an apt account of the idea. In other words, if a literary text lacks some of the pieces, that is the fault of the text, not of the messianic idea. The idea exists prior to and independently of the texts.

What is more, in most modern accounts the messianic idea is described in specifically psychological terms: It is the force that animates the pious Jewish hope for redemption, either throughout Jewish history (in Jewish treatments) or at the time of Christ (in Christian treatments).[8] So Abba Hillel Silver writes that the messianic idea arises out of the Jewish experience of "helplessness in the face of overwhelming odds, a masterful love of life, and an unyielding hold upon the basic morality underlying all national experiences."[9] Similarly, Schürer writes, "As the work of the Israelite was virtually the observance of the law, so was his faith virtually belief in a better future. Round these two poles... did the religious life of the Jewish people revolve during our period."[10]

Cast in these psychological terms, the messianic idea has often done considerable ideological work for its modern proponents. There is a common motif in which the messianic idea is conceived of as Judaism's gift to the world. Klausner comments, "To the three good gifts which the people Israel have left as an inheritance to the entire world: monotheism, refined morality, and the prophets of truth and righteousness—a fourth gift must be added: *belief in the Messiah*."[11] In the same vein, Gershom Scholem writes, "What I have in mind is the price demanded by Messianism, the price which the Jewish people has had to pay out of its own substance for this idea which it handed over to the world."[12] For early twentieth-century scholars, the historical study of messianism was also implicated in contemporary debates over Zionism.[13] The historians' reasons are sometimes more, sometimes less ideologically implicated,

---

8 Here and throughout, by saying "psychological," I do not mean that such accounts are not also religious or theological; indeed, most are. I am simply pointing out that in such accounts, a particular emphasis is laid on the human disposition.

9 Abba Hillel Silver, *A History of Messianic Speculation in Israel* (New York: Macmillan, 1927), ix.

10 Schürer, *History*, 2.2:128–129.

11 Klausner, *Messianic Idea*, 13; italics in the original. And again, "We can say, without being suspected of undue bias toward Judaism, that the Jewish Messianic faith is the seed of progress, which has been planted by Judaism throughout the whole world" (Klausner, *Messianic Idea*, 531).

12 Gershom Scholem, "Toward an Understanding of the Messianic Idea in Judaism," in *Messianic Idea*, 1–36, here 35.

13 See, e.g., the preface to the second English edition of Klausner, *Messianic Idea*, x; and now the major study of Arie Morgenstern, *Hastening Redemption: Messianism and the Resettlement of the Land of Israel* (trans. Joel A. Linsider; Oxford: Oxford University Press, 2006).

but in virtually every case, as Green notes, "The real object of research is not a figure entitled 'messiah' but the religious ideology that purportedly made one possible. Thus, the standard works on the topic typically devote less attention to the concrete textual references than to discussion of a religious attitude allegedly at the core of Israelite and Jewish experience: the so-called 'future hope.'"[14]

Despite the near hegemony of the messianic idea, it did have some early detractors.[15] When D. F. Strauss published his landmark *Das Leben Jesu, kritisch bearbeitet* in 1835, arguing that the Gospel writers took over the Jewish messianic myth and wrote it into Jesus's life, Bruno Bauer criticized Strauss's account as insufficiently radical.[16] On Bauer's account, even the notion of a pre-Christian messianic myth is an uncritical concession to theological orthodoxy. The reality, Bauer argues, is that there was never a Jewish messianic myth to be taken over; the Gospel writers spun the whole thing out of whole cloth.[17] As Albert Schweitzer points out, Bauer's views, especially his later ones, were so radical that they were generally rejected by his successors.[18] The notion that there was no messianic myth in Judaism, however, was picked up and championed in a more mainstream fashion for a time by Heinrich Julius Holtzmann.[19] These few eloquent detractors notwithstanding, though, by and large the messianic idea held sway in Jewish studies for most of the nineteenth and twentieth centuries.

Its last great proponent was Gershom Scholem.[20] A student of and a critical heir to the prewar *Wissenschaft des Judentums* movement, Scholem published

---

14 Green, "Introduction," 7.

15 See Horbury, *Jewish Messianism and the Cult of Christ*, 36–37; also William Horbury, *Messianism among Jews and Christians: Twelve Biblical and Historical Studies* (London: T. & T. Clark, 2003), 2.

16 David Friedrich Strauss, *Das Leben Jesu, kritisch bearbeitet* (2 vols; Tübingen: Osiander, 1835); Eng. trans. *The Life of Jesus Critically Examined* (trans. George Eliot; Philadelphia: Fortress, 1972; 1st Eng. ed. 1846); Bruno Bauer, *Kritik der evangelischen Geschichte der Synoptiker* (3 vols; Leipzig: Wigand, 1841–1842), 1:391–416. The charge of insufficient radicalism is ironic since *Das Leben Jesu* was radical enough to result in Strauss's losing his post at Tübingen.

17 Later still, Bauer would conclude that there had not even been a historical Jesus (Bruno Bauer, *Kritik der Evangelien und Geschichte ihres Ursprungs* [4 vols; Berlin: Hempel, 1850–1851]).

18 See Schweitzer, *Quest of the Historical Jesus,* 137–160, here 159: "The only critic with whom Bauer can be compared is Reimarus. Each influenced a terrifying and disabling influence upon his time."

19 Holtzmann, "Die Messiasidee zur Zeit Jesu." By 1897, however, Holtzmann had conceded the currency of some royal messianic hope in the Roman period (see Heinrich Julius Holtzmann, *Lehrbuch der neutestamentlichen Theologie* [2 vols; Freiburg: Mohr, 1897], 1:68–85).

20 For the most part, anyway. It is arguable that the recent work of Giorgio Agamben on "messianic time" (especially Agamben, *Time That Remains*) has certain points of contact with the

a number of important studies on the messianic idea up to his death in 1982.[21] Scholem's account is thoroughly steeped in the language of metaphysical idealism. He writes of how "the Messianic idea appears as a living force in the world of Judaism."[22] He speaks in terms of its "realization," "crystalization," "appearing," and "becoming an effective force."[23] For Scholem, the history of Judaism itself consists in the history of the messianic idea. He writes, "The magnitude of the Messianic idea corresponds to the endless powerlessness in Jewish history during all the centuries of exile, when it was unprepared to come forward onto the plane of world history."[24] The messianic idea, in other words, epitomizes the ambiguous experience of being Jewish in the world.[25] For Scholem, as for his predecessors, the meaningfulness of ancient messiah language is dependent upon the existence of the messianic idea. The ancient messiah texts were the literary expressions of the messianic idea at that point in its history. The words had meaning because the messianic idea manifested itself in them. What they meant was precisely the content of the messianic idea.

Despite the prewar skepticism of Bauer and Holtzmann and the post-war confidence of Scholem, the end of the Second World War—coinciding roughly with the discovery of the Dead Sea Scrolls—effectively marked the beginning of the disintegration of the messianic idea in Jewish studies. As early as 1946, Gerhard Sevenster wrote that the words משיח and χριστός in the

---

older idealist paradigm in Jewish studies, perhaps by way of Agamben's debt to Jacob Taubes, who had himself been a student of Scholem.

21 On the *Wissenschaft des Judentums*, see Ismar Schorsch, *From Text to Context: The Turn to History in Modern Judaism* (Waltham, Mass.: Brandeis University Press, 1994). Scholem's works on messianism include Gershom Scholem, *Major Trends in Jewish Mysticism* (Jerusalem: Schocken, 1941); Gershom Scholem, *Sabbatai Sevi: The Mystical Messiah, 1626–1676* (trans. R. J. Zwi Werblowsky; Princeton, N.J.: Princeton University Press, 1973); Gershom Scholem, *The Messianic Idea in Judaism*. On Scholem, see further David Biale, *Gershom Scholem: Kabbalah and Counter-History* (2d ed.; Cambridge, Mass.: Harvard University Press, 1982). Like his more senior colleague Joseph Klausner, but with notably different politics, Scholem found in his historical research on messianism resources for articulating his own vision for the contemporary Zionist movement (here see Biale, *Gershom Scholem,* 94–111).

22 Scholem, "Messianic Idea," 4.

23 Scholem, "Messianic Idea," 1–4.

24 Scholem, "Messianic Idea," 35.

25 This is the point of Scholem's famous dictum:

In Judaism the Messianic idea has compelled *a life lived in deferment,* in which nothing can be done definitively, nothing can be irrevocably accomplished. One may say, perhaps, the Messianic idea is the real anti-existentialist idea. Precisely understood, there is nothing concrete which can be accomplished by the unredeemed. This makes for the greatness of Messianism, but also for its constitutional weakness. (Scholem, "Messianic Idea," 35; italics in the original)

Second Temple period had no fixed content.[26] In a 1966 study anticipating his entry on χρίω in Kittel's *Wörterbuch*, Marinus de Jonge wrote that Sevenster's assessment was "on the right lines" and that in fact "[the evidence] requires us, I think, to go even farther than he did."[27]

A. S. van der Woude's important 1957 monograph on the messiah texts from Qumran showed how thoroughgoing was the motif of the two messiahs in that corpus, further undermining the notion of a uniform messianic idea common to ancient Judaism generally.[28] Morton Smith argued for the indeterminacy of messiah language in a 1959 article, in which he observes that no inner connection exists between eschatology and messianism: "Just as there are messiahs without Ends, so there are Ends without messiahs."[29] Smith draws the sociological conclusion that halakha, not eschatological hope, must have been the basic principle of social cohesion in Roman-era Judaism. A feature of many of these postwar studies is what Horbury has called the "no hope list," that is, a list of ancient Jewish texts that make no mention at all of a messiah figure.[30] In this connection some historians have used the phrase "messianological vacuum" to refer to some or all of the Persian and Hellenistic periods, during which most of the texts in the standard "no hope lists" were composed.[31]

If de Jonge pointed out the theological diversity of ancient messiah texts, and Smith inquired after the sociological consequences of that diversity, by the 1980s James Charlesworth, Jacob Neusner, and others were asking the linguistic question whether ancient messiah language signified anything at all. Charlesworth, summarizing the conclusions of the 1987 Princeton

---

26 Gerhard Sevenster, *De Christologie van het Nieuwe Testament* (Amsterdam: Uitgeversmaatschappij, 1946), 75–78; cited by de Jonge, "Use of the Word 'Anointed,'" 132.

27 De Jonge, "Use of the Word 'Anointed,'" 132; see also de Jonge et al., "χρίω, κτλ.," *TDNT* 9:493–580.

28 A. S. van der Woude, *Die messianischen Vorstellungen der Gemeinde von Qumrân* (Studia semitica neerlandica 3; Assen: Van Gorcum, 1957).

29 Morton Smith, "What Is Implied by the Variety of Messianic Figures?" *JBL* 78 (1959): 66–72, here 68.

30 Horbury, *Messianism among Jews and Christians*, 38: "The Apocrypha of the English Bible have for long been a centrepiece in a regular manifestation of the study of messianism, which may be called the 'no hope list'—the list of books wherein no messianic hope is to be found"; Horbury, *Messianism among Jews and Christians*, 38–39n11, catalogues many such lists. An example is James H. Charlesworth, "The Concept of the Messiah in the Pseudepigrapha," *ANRW* 2.19.1:188–218, here 218: "Forty pseudepigrapha, therefore, either do not contain messianic ideas, or employ titles other than 'the Messiah' and its derivatives."

31 However, the aptness of the phrase is contested by Horbury, *Jewish Messianism and the Cult of Christ;* Horbury, *Messianism among Jews and Christians;* and now Keith Rosenthal, "Rethinking the Messianological Vacuum: The Prevalence of Jewish Messianism during the Second Temple Period" (Ph.D. diss., Graduate Theological Union, 2006).

Symposium, writes, "It is impossible to define, and difficult to describe the messianology of the early Jews.... There is no script the Messiah is to act out. There is no clear, widely accepted Jewish description of the Messiah. The references to him are often frustratingly vague and imprecise."[32] In his programmatic statement, Neusner lays out the methodological rule that there is no messiah at all, nor is there even Judaism; there are only so many Judaisms and so many messiahs.[33] William Scott Green gives expression to this late twentieth-century skepticism: "In Jewish writings before or during the emergence of Christianity, 'messiah' appears neither as an evocative religious symbol nor as a centralizing native cultural category." In other words, there is no "messianic idea" behind the texts. "Rather, it ['messiah'] is a term of disparity, used in few texts and in diverse ways."[34] For Green, the relative scarcity and diversity of ancient messiah texts implies things about the meaning of the word "messiah" itself. The word, as a word, is "notable primarily for its indeterminacy."[35] Absent a "messianic idea" to invest the words with meaning, the words themselves cease to mean anything at all.

Messiah Language as a Social-Linguistic Phenomenon

This newer minimalism has been a salutary development in the field. Relative to the older treatments, whose overdrawn conclusions had filtered down into the standard introductions and commentaries, it represents an important step forward. The problem with the minimalist school is that it is thought to have proved one thing, when in fact it has proven another. What Van der Woude, Smith, de Jonge, Neusner, Charlesworth, and others are thought to have shown is that ancient messiah language was entirely indeterminate; it did not mean anything. What they have in fact shown is that the extant messiah texts from the period do not warrant any form of the older idealist paradigm of the messianic idea in Judaism. It is not that messiah language does not have meaning, just that its meaning does not consist in the manifestation of a reified messianic idea.

---

32 James H. Charlesworth, "From Messianology to Christology: Problems and Prospects," in *The Messiah: Developments in Earliest Judaism and Christianity* (ed. James H. Charlesworth; Minneapolis: Fortress, 1992), 31, 31n93.

33 Jacob Neusner, "Preface," in *Judaisms and Their Messiahs*, ix–xiv.

34 Green, "Introduction," 6.

35 Green, "Introduction," 6, 4, respectively. One wonders if there are other words that are notable primarily for their indeterminacy or if "messiah" is special in this regard. Green seems to suggest the latter, which presents an interesting irony since in this case "messiah" is once again a unique word, not for its meaningfulness but for its meaninglessness.

In response to claims of the meaninglessness of messiah language, a mediating position has been proposed by William Horbury.[36] Against the postwar minimalists, Horbury makes a sophisticated case that "messianic hope was more continuously vigorous and more widespread than has been allowed in the influential body of modern opinion" and that, the diversity of messiah texts notwithstanding, the content of this hope was "sufficiently coherent to exert strong influence."[37] In other words, Horbury directly contradicts recent majority opinion and undertakes to resuscitate the idea of a prevalent, coherent messianic hope in early Judaism.[38] He does so, however, not by reviving the messianic idea of the prewar period but rather by reasoning from the extant literary evidence to the putative social and psychological contexts that will have given rise to these texts.[39] That is, Horbury distinguishes messianic hope from the messianic idea, arguing for the former but not the latter. For Horbury, the meaningfulness of ancient messiah language was ensured by the popular prevalence and the conceptual coherence of the messianic hope that prevailed at the time. There may not have been a reified messianic idea behind it all, but the words could be used meaningfully because the Jewish populace in the Second Temple period harbored the hope expressed in the texts.

Most interpreters, however, have not been persuaded by Horbury's case for the general currency of popular messianic hope through the Second

---

36 Especially Horbury, *Jewish Messianism and the Cult of Christ;* Horbury, *Messianism among Jews and Christians.* Other representatives of this school of thought include former Horbury students Joachim Schaper (*Eschatology in the Greek Psalter* [WUNT 2/76; Tübingen: Mohr Siebeck, 1995]) and Andrew Chester (*Messiah and Exaltation*). Also contrary to the majority but independent of the Horbury school is the work of Antii Laato, especially *A Star Is Rising: The Historical Development of the Old Testament Royal Ideology and the Rise of the Jewish Messianic Expectations* (Atlanta: Scholars Press, 1997). Laato's thesis, that messianism took root even before the Judahite exile and never waned, is considerably more ambitious even than Horbury's (see the review by Gary N. Knoppers in *JBL* 117 [1998]: 732–735).

37 Horbury, *Jewish Messianism and the Cult of Christ,* 37, 64. Horbury argues first that messianism was prevalent in the Second Temple period and, second, that this was the context for the emergence of the early Christ cult. Horbury's critics have generally given him credit for proving the second thesis but not the first (see, e.g., the reviews by John J. Collins in *JR* 79 [1999]: 657–659; and Kenneth E. Pomykala in *JBL* 119 [2000]: 351–353). A significant minority, however, have followed Horbury on both points (e.g., many of the contributors to Bockmuehl and Carleton Paget, *Redemption and Resistance*).

38 See Pomykala in *JBL* 119 (2000): 353: "Horbury is clearly swimming upstream against the majority of recent studies, and for now at least, the downward current is the more persuasive."

39 So Horbury speaks throughout of "messianism" and "messianic hope," never of "the messianic idea."

Temple period, even after he has disposed of the messianic idea.[40] The majority continue to take the minimalist view that no persuasive account of the meaningfulness of messiah language can be given. There is yet another possibility, however. In fact, Horbury is probably right to distinguish messianic hope from the messianic idea; the former is indeed conceivable apart from the latter. It is also possible, however, to further distinguish messiah language from messianic hope, that is, the linguistic phenomenon from the psychological one.

A few writers on the subject have pointed in this direction. For example, John Collins writes about the apparent "messianological vacuum" of the Maccabean period: "The traditions on which Davidic messianism were based were preserved, but these in themselves did not ensure any lively expectation."[41] This is an important distinction, a distinction of kind, not of degree. It is not that there was just a little bit of messianism; rather, it is that the literary resources were preserved and transmitted even when the social phenomenon ebbed low.[42] Collins makes a similar point elsewhere in reference to the Dead Sea Scrolls: "Whether we may therefore speak of a 'general messianic *expectation*' is another matter. We do not know how important these traditions were to the populace at large; interest probably fluctuated with historical circumstances. When interest in messianic expectation arose, however, there was at hand a body of tradition which could be used to articulate it."[43]

I suggest that this distinction between the linguistic phenomenon (messiah language) on the one hand and the psychological (messianic hope) and social (messianism) phenomena on the other is of the utmost importance and, indeed, that it is the proper basis for an adequate account of the meaningfulness of ancient messiah language. The critical point is that the meaningfulness

---

40 Horbury's case depends first on the premise of a demonstrable messianizing *Tendenz* among the Septuagint translators, which remains controversial (see the later discussion), and, second, on extrapolation from the evidence of literary texts to an ostensible popular psychological disposition, which is methodologically problematic. See Loren T. Stuckenbruck, "Messianic Ideas in the Apocalyptic and Related Literature of Early Judaism," in *Messiah in the Old and New Testaments*, 90–113, here 113n44: "The ways of achieving the views that were shared among the texts reviewed here can hardly be said to be coherent among themselves, not to mention how these were reapplied and readapted by Christians. I am therefore less inclined to speak as confidently as William Horbury about 'the coherence of messianism.'"

41 John J. Collins, "Messianism in the Maccabean Period," in *Judaisms and Their Messiahs*, 97–109, here 106.

42 Likewise Horsley and Hanson, *Bandits*, 99: "The fact that 'the law and the prophets' were collected and edited into a sacred scripture means that the stories of popular anointed kings were remembered. Although it may not have been manifest in any actual movements, the tradition of popular kingship was not extinct, but dormant."

43 Collins, "Messiahs in Context," 222; italics in the original.

of the words does not depend on the psychological disposition of the hearers
or readers. So when Charlesworth asks, "If most Jews were not looking for
the coming of 'the Messiah'... then why, and how, and when did Jesus' early
followers contend that he was so clearly the promised Messiah?"[44] the answer
is that it does not matter how many Jews were looking for the coming of the
messiah; what matters is that members of the linguistic community were able
to understand what was meant when someone talked about a messiah.[45]

In this respect, messiah language is no different from language generally. It is scholars of ancient Judaism and Christianity who have created the
confusion by granting special status to messiah language, supposing it to be
either uniquely meaningful, as Schürer and Klausner do, or uniquely meaningless, as Neusner and Green do. In the context of a social-linguistic model
of language, this confusion dissolves.[46] When Green says that the word "messiah" is "all signifier and no signified," he is using the terms of Ferdinand de
Saussure.[47] Against what he perceived as commonsense "nomenclaturism,"
Saussure famously described languages as socially agreed-upon systems of signifiers.[48] "A language as a structured system... is the social part of language,
external to the individual, who by himself is powerless either to create it or
to modify it. It exists only in virtue of a kind of contract agreed between
the members of a community."[49] Languages, then, do not exist apart from
communities of language users. "In order to have a language, there must be

---

44 Charlesworth, "From Messianology to Christology," 10.

45 Cf. the epigraph to this book, in which Michael Chabon's fictional detective Meyer
Landsman asks his partner Bina Gelbfish whether she knows the Tzaddik Ha-Dor, and she
replies that she "knows what the words mean."

46 On linguistics and the study of ancient history see the recent study of Elizabeth Ann
Clark, *History, Theory, Text: Historians and the Linguistic Turn* (Cambridge, Mass.: Harvard
University Press, 2004), especially 42–62, 156–186.

47 For the classic statement see Ferdinand de Saussure, *Course in General Linguistics*
(ed. Charles Bally et al.; trans. Roy Harris; 3d ed.; Chicago: Open Court, 1986); and now
also Ferdinand de Saussure, *Writings in General Linguistics* (ed. Simon Bouquet and Rudolf
Engler; trans. Carol Sanders et al.; Oxford: Oxford University Press, 2006). On Saussure, see
further Jonathan D. Culler, *Ferdinand de Saussure* (rev. ed.; Ithaca, N.Y.: Cornell University
Press, 1986).

48 "Nomenclaturism" refers to the notion of a straightforward correspondence between
names and things in the world, "the superficial view, taken by the general public, which sees a
language merely as nomenclature" (Saussure, *Course*, 16).

49 Saussure, *Course*, 14. This basic model constitutes the basis of the modern discipline
of semiotics: "A language is a system of signs expressing ideas.... It is therefore possible to conceive of a science which studies the role of signs as part of social life.... We shall call it semi-
ology" (Saussure, *Course*, 15). See further Paul Bouissac, "Saussure's Legacy in Semiotics," in
The Cambridge Companion to Saussure (ed. Carol Sanders; Cambridge: Cambridge University
Press, 2004), 240–260.

a community of speakers. Contrary to what might appear to be the case, a language never exists even for a moment except as a social fact, for it is a semiological phenomenon."[50] Within such a community, though, language works, in the sense that competent users of the system have a reasonable expectation of communicating successfully with one another.[51] This means that, as a rule, in natural languages there are no signifiers without signifieds.[52]

An important corollary of this model is that all language is conventional in the strict sense; it consists of so many social conventions, nothing else. "The language we use is a convention, and it makes no difference what exactly the nature of the agreed sign is."[53] In other words, "the linguistic sign is arbitrary" in the sense that no necessary connection exists between a concept and the sound pattern used to point to that concept in a language.[54] This is why, for example, the very different sound patterns "tree," "arbre," and "Baum"—or for that matter, משיח, χριστός, and *unctus*—can all point equally well to the same concept, each in its own language system.[55]

This arbitrariness, though, pertains to the theoretical relation between words and concepts, not to any language user's actual situation. Saussure writes, "It must not be taken to imply that a signal depends on the free choice of the speaker.... The speaker has no power to alter a sign in any respect once it has become established in a linguistic community."[56] Deep down, the relation between sound patterns and concepts is arbitrary, but speakers are not free to invent new sound-to-concept relationships whenever they like, at least, not if they hope to be understood by anyone.[57] "Once the language has selected

---

50 Saussure, *Course,* 77.

51 See Saussure, *Course,* 4: "All the individuals linguistically linked in this manner will establish among themselves a kind of mean; all of them will reproduce—doubtless not exactly, but approximately—the same signs linked to the same concepts."

52 In linguistics, a natural language is one that arises in a human community according to the normal pattern, in contrast to artificial languages like Klingon or formal languages like HTML (see further Alice ter Meulen, "Logic and Natural Language," in *The Blackwell Guide to Philosophical Logic* [ed. Lou Goble; Oxford: Blackwell, 2001], 461–483).

53 Saussure, *Course,* 10.

54 Saussure, *Course,* 67. He clarifies that, in contrast to nomenclaturism, "a linguistic sign is not a link between a thing and a name, but between a concept and a sound pattern" (Saussure, *Course,* 66).

55 Transliteration between languages further complicates the matter (cf. משיח, μεσσίας, messiah; likewise, χριστός, *christus,* Christ). On this phenomenon see further chapter 3.

56 Saussure, *Course,* 68.

57 This is the point of disagreement in the famous exchange between Alice and Humpty Dumpty in Lewis Carroll, *Through the Looking Glass and What Alice Found There* (Philadelphia: Altemus, 1897), 123:

a signal, it cannot be freely replaced by any other.... What can be chosen is already determined in advance. No individual is able, even if he wished, to modify in any way a choice already established in the language."[58]

None of this is cutting-edge linguistics by any means; the discipline has made enormous strides in the century since Saussure. Most of these strides, however, have been in directions to which Saussure pointed. His fundamental move from "nomenclaturism" to social linguistics has set the terms for subsequent research and, in its main lines, still commands broad assent.[59] Writers on ancient messianism, however, have continued to work under a theory not unlike Saussure's "nomenclaturism," presupposing the deep correspondence of a word ("messiah") to a thing (either an idea or a hope) and disagreeing only on the question whether that thing existed as early as the Second Temple period.[60] If we set aside this problematic linguistic theory, however, and

---

"There's glory for you!" "I don't know what you mean by 'glory,'" Alice said. Humpty Dumpty smiled contemptuously. "Of course you don't—till I tell you. I meant 'there's a nice knock-down argument for you!'" "But 'glory' doesn't mean 'a nice knock-down argument,'" Alice objected. "When I use a word," Humpty Dumpty said, in rather a scornful tone, "it means just what I choose it to mean—neither more nor less." "The question is," said Alice, "whether you can make words mean so many different things." "The question is," said Humpty Dumpty, "which is to be master—that's all."

In this exchange, Alice effectively represents the Saussurian point of view.

58 Saussure, *Course,* 71. Not only are individual speakers constrained by their linguistic communities, but linguistic communities are also constrained by the histories of their languages: "At any given period, however far back in time we go, a language is always an inheritance from the past." As a result, "Collective inertia resists all linguistic innovations.... At any time a language belongs to all its users. It is a facility unrestrictedly available throughout a whole community.... This key fact is by itself sufficient to explain why a linguistic revolution is impossible" (Saussure, *Course,* 71–72). This linguistic rule poses a serious objection to the notion that Paul fills the word "messiah" with entirely new content. It is more accurate to say that he stretches the semantic boundaries of the word, sometimes strenuously, in particular directions (see further chapter 5).

59 On Saussure's reception in subsequent linguistics, see Culler, *Saussure,* 15–20, 105–150; Carol Sanders, "Introduction: Saussure Today," in *Cambridge Companion to Saussure,* 1–8.

60 To be sure, there have been valuable contributions in the application of linguistics to biblical studies (e.g., the recently established *Journal of the Linguistics Institute of Ancient and Biblical Greek*), but these have tended to focus on lexical semantics, especially Bible translation theory (e.g., the several joint projects of Johannes P. Louw and Eugene A. Nida, especially their *Greek-English Lexicon of the New Testament Based on Semantic Domains* [New York: United Bible Societies, 1988]) and the proper use of word studies (e.g., James Barr, *The Semantics of Biblical Language* [Oxford: Oxford University Press, 1961]; Moisés Silva, *Biblical Words and Their Meaning: An Introduction to Lexical Semantics* [2d ed.; Grand Rapids, Mich.: Zondervan, 1994]), rather than on social-linguistic dynamics more generally, and in any case the methodological advances have not trickled down to the mainstream of biblical studies and Jewish studies (so rightly Max Turner, "Modern Linguistics and the New Testament," in *Hearing the New Testament: Strategies for Interpretation* [ed. Joel B. Green; 2d ed.; Grand Rapids, Mich.: Eerdmans, 2010], 146–174, especially 155).

instead think of messiah texts as uses of language by competent members of a linguistic community, then solutions to long-standing historical problems may begin to emerge.

To summarize the argument to this point: the meaningfulness of ancient messiah language derives neither from the self-expression of a reified messianic idea nor from the mass psychological phenomenon of a shared hope for redemption. Popular hope may have been more or less current at different times and places in early Judaism, but the meaningfulness of the language is independent of the fervency of the popular hope. People could know what the words meant whether or not they shared the sentiment expressed. In short, messiah language could be used meaningfully in antiquity because it was deployed in the context of a linguistic community whose members shared a stock of common linguistic resources. But whence came these linguistic resources?

The Jewish Scriptures as Linguistic Resources

Their cultural particularities notwithstanding, ancient Jews were members of vast, multicultural linguistic communities that came about as a consequence of the conquests of the great ancient imperial powers. Aramaic-speaking Jews spoke a democratized version of the official language of the Achaemenid Persians, under whom their ancestors had returned from Babylonian exile.[61] Greek-speaking Jews spoke the Koine dialect that was a product of Alexander's fourth-century conquest of the Near East.[62] Within these vast, multicultural language groups, however, ancient Jews—like all ethnic subgroups—had certain patterns of speech that derived from within their own tradition. In their particular case, many of these ethnic patterns of speech had roots in the Jewish scriptures.[63] Although the canonical Tanakh is a product of the early centuries

---

61 See Matthew Black, "The Biblical Languages," in *The Cambridge History of the Bible: From the Beginnings to Jerome* (ed. P. R. Ackroyd and C. F. Evans; Cambridge: Cambridge University Press, 1970), 1–10.

62 See Anna Missiou, "The Hellenistic Period," in *A History of Ancient Greek: From the Beginnings to Late Antiquity* (ed. A.-F. Christidis; Cambridge: Cambridge University Press, 2007), 325–341.

63 As a rule, I use the term "Jewish scriptures" since "Old Testament" presumes the canonical Christian Bible, "Tanakh" the canonical Jewish Bible, and even "Hebrew Bible" presumes a notion of "Bible" and, furthermore, refers only to Hebrew-language texts. Prior to the formation of the Jewish and Christian canons, just which texts count as "scripture" is of course a vexed question. For present purposes my main criterion is a functional one: All antecedent texts frequently cited by early Jewish messiah texts are among the scriptures. This is largely noncontroversial since most of these (e.g., Genesis, Numbers, Psalms, Isaiah) fall within the core group of texts that were widely recognized very early. An anomaly, however, is posed by the book of Daniel, which is quite late (second c. B.C.E.) but nevertheless comes to be widely cited

C.E., the prominent place of scripture in ancient Jewish life was already presaged by the seventh-century Josianic reforms (2 Kings 22–23), formalized in the fifth-century governorship of Nehemiah in Persian Yehud (Nehemiah 8), and reinforced for the Diaspora community by the third- and second-century B.C.E. work of the LXX translators (*Let. Aris.* 1–82; 301–322).[64] As Michael Fishbane has shown for the Hebrew Bible and Tessa Rajak for the Septuagint, the Jewish scriptures functioned for their readers not only as a corpus of holy books but also as a pool of linguistic resources, a source of ways of speaking about things both sacred and mundane.[65]

Talk about "messiahs" in early Jewish literature is just such a scripturally derived pattern of speech.[66] The word משיח itself occurs some thirty-eight times in the Hebrew Bible, always with reference to a person, usually in the singular, and usually as a substantive.[67] For their part, the Greek translators

in a very short time (on this problem see Klaus Koch, "Stages in the Canonization of the Book of Daniel," in *The Book of Daniel: Composition and Reception* [ed. John J. Collins and Peter W. Flint; Supplements to Vetus Testamentum 83; Leiden: Brill, 2001], 421–446).

64 On this point see Hindy Najman, "Torah of Moses: Pseudonymous Attribution in Second Temple Writings," in *The Interpretation of Scripture in Early Judaism and Christianity: Studies in Language and Tradition* (ed. Craig A. Evans; Sheffield: Sheffield Academic, 2000), 202–216, especially 202–207.

65 See Michael Fishbane, *Biblical Interpretation in Ancient Israel* (Oxford: Oxford University Press, 1985); Tessa Rajak, *Translation and Survival: The Greek Bible of the Ancient Jewish Diaspora* (Oxford: Oxford University Press, 2009), here 225–226: "A language for self-expression was forged by the Greek Bible.... Citations, whether verbatim or approximate, are an important vehicle for the diffusion of this special vocabulary and more broadly for asserting connection with the source text." For their part, the authors and translators of the scriptural texts will have drawn on the linguistic resources of their own communities (on this point, see Anneli Aejmelaus, "Faith, Hope and Interpretation: A Lexical and Syntactical Study of the Semantic Field of Hope in the Greek Psalter," in *Studies in the Hebrew Bible, Qumran, and the Septuagint Presented to Eugene Ulrich* [ed. Peter W. Flint et al.; VTSup 101; Leiden: Brill, 2006], 360–376).

66 This basic point is now widely acknowledged (see, e.g., Martin Hengel, "Jesus, the Messiah of Israel," in *Studies in Early Christology* [Edinburgh: T. & T. Clark, 1995], 1–71; Collins, *Scepter and the Star;* Peter Schäfer, "Diversity and Interaction: Messiahs in Early Judaism," in *Toward the Millennium,* 15–35; Stuckenbruck, "Messianic Ideas"), but precisely how this phenomenon worked at the linguistic level has not yet been explained as I undertake to do here.

67 The references, with verse numbers according the Hebrew text, are as follows: Lev 4:3, 5, 16; 6:15; 1 Sam 2:10, 35; 12:3, 5; 16:6; 24:7, 11; 26:9, 11, 16, 23; 2 Sam 1:14, 16; 19:22; 22:51; 23:1; Isa 45:1; Hab 3:13; Ps 2:2; 18:51; 20:7; 28:8; 84:10; 89:39, 52; 105:15; 132:10, 17; Lam 4:20; Dan 9:25, 26; 1 Chron 16:22; 2 Chron 6:42. For an overview of these texts see J. J. M. Roberts, "The Old Testament's Contribution to Messianic Expectations," in Charlesworth, *Messiah,* 39–51. Here and throughout, for the text of the MT I follow K. Elliger and W. Rudolph, *Biblia Hebraica Stuttgartensia* (Stuttgart: Deutsche Bibelgesellschaft, 1983); and for the text of the LXX I follow Alfred Rahlfs, *Septuaginta: Id est Vetus Testamentum graece iuxta LXX interpretes* (2 vols; Stuttgart: Deutsche Bibelgesellschaft, 1979), or particular Göttingen Septuagint volumes where available.

characteristically render Hebrew משיח with χριστός, and they reserve χριστός as an equivalency for משיח rather than any other Hebrew word.[68] At the lexical level, in other words, the messianism of the LXX is quite close to the messianism of its putative Hebrew *Vorlage*.[69] The notion of anointing with oil and the words to signify such a practice were more or less common among other Greco-Roman groups;[70] but early Jewish writers who used the word משיח and

---

68 Cf. Aquila, who sometimes glosses משיח with ἠλειμμένος (from ἀλείφω), viz. at 1 Kgdms 2:35; 2 Kgdms 1:21; Ps 27:8 (MT 28:8); 83:10 (MT 84:10); 88:39, 52 (MT 89:39, 52); Isa 45:1; Dan 9:26 (Reider-Turner, s.v. ἀλείφω). As for the LXX, there are three instances in which it does not read χριστός where MT reads משיח: Lev 4:3 LXX translates הכהן המשיח with ὁ ἀρχιερεὺς ὁ κεχρισμένος, using the participle cognate to χριστός; Old Greek Dan 9:25 lacks a clause corresponding to its Hebrew counterpart, but Theodotion-Daniel reads ἕως χριστοῦ ἡγουμένου for MT עד משיח נגיד; and Old Greek Dan 9:26 renders משיח with the cognate noun χρίσμα, so not "an anointed one will be cut off" but "an anointing will be taken away" (on the latter two instances, see Joseph Ziegler, ed., *Susanna, Daniel, Bel et Draco* [Septuagina 16.2; Göttingen: Vandenhoeck & Ruprecht, 1954], ad loc.). There are five instances in which the LXX reads χριστός where the MT does not read משיח. Two of these are not really exceptions: Lev 21:10, 12 LXX use the neuter χριστόν for the cognate noun משחה, "anointing"; and 2 Chron 22:7 LXX renders the relative clause אשר משחו יהוה, "whom YHWH anointed," with the substantive χριστὸν κυρίου, "the Lord's anointed." There are two genuine exceptions: 2 Kgdms 2:5 reads τὸν κύριον ὑμῶν ἐπὶ Σαουλ τὸν χριστὸν κυρίου, "your lord Saul, the Lord's anointed" where MT has only אדניכם עם שאול, "your lord Saul." 4QSamᵃ (=4Q51) is fragmentary at this point, but, based on the line length, Cross et al. reconstruct a Hebrew text very much like the LXX: [יהוה משיח שאול עם אדניכ]ם (see 4QSamᵃ frg. 52a [DJD XVII, p. 104]). Finally, Amos 4:13 LXX reads τὸν χριστὸν αὐτοῦ, "his anointed one," presumably for Hebrew משיחו, but MT has מה שחו, "what is his thought," so apparently an inner-Hebrew corruption has occurred in one direction or the other, but, unfortunately, the verse is not preserved in 4QXII.

69 There is an ongoing debate on the question of messianism in the Septuagint, with one school of thought arguing for a demonstrable messianizing tendency on the part of a number of LXX translators (e.g., Georg Bertram, "Praeparatio Evangelica in der Septuaginta," *Vetus Testamentum* 7 [1957]: 225–249; William Horbury, *Jewish Messianism and the Cult of Christ*, especially 46–52; William Horbury, "Messianism in the Old Testament Apocrypha and Pseudepigrapha," in *Messianism among Jews and Christians*, 35–64; Schaper, *Eschatology in the Greek Psalter*), and another school arguing that no such tendency can be discerned (e.g., Johan Lust, *Messianism and the Septuagint: Collected Essays* [ed. K. Hauspie; Bibliotheca ephemeridum theologicarum lovaniensium 178; Leuven: Peeters, 2004]; Albert Pietersma, "Messianism and the Greek Psalter: In Search of the Messiah," in *The Septuagint and Messianism* [ed. Michael A. Knibb; BETL 195; Leuven: Peeters, 2006], 49–75). This question, while historically important in its own right, is actually largely irrelevant to the question of the meaningfulness of early Jewish messiah language. Even if it is the case that the LXX was a link in the development from ancient Israelite royal ideology to early Jewish and early Christian messianisms, it was at any rate not a necessary link. As Brevard Childs rightly notes, messianic exegesis is an interpretive possibility that arises for readers of the Jewish scriptures, whether in Hebrew or in Greek, in the postmonarchy situation (Brevard S. Childs, *Introduction to the Old Testament as Scripture* [Philadelphia: Fortress, 1979], 515–517). We know, after all, that messianic interpretation of the Jewish scriptures happened independently of the Greek textual tradition, in the inner-Hebrew interpretations of the Dead Sea Scrolls and the rabbinic midrashim and the Aramaic translations of the Targumim.

70 See Walter Grundmann, "χρίω," *TDNT* 9:493–496; Martin Karrer, *Der Gesalbte: Die Grundlagen des Christustitels* (Forschungen zur Religion und Literatur des Alten und Neuen Testaments 151; Göttingen: Vandenhoeck & Ruprecht, 1991), 377–384.

its translation equivalencies almost invariably followed the particular idiom of the Jewish scriptures. In Saussurian terms, the Jewish scriptures provided the linguistic resources whereby ancient Jewish and Christian writers were able to use messiah language with a plausible expectation of communicating successfully with other members of their linguistic communities.[71]

This is a crucial point because it shows how talk about "anointed figures" can have had resonance for Jewish writers and their audiences even centuries after the ritual anointing of persons had fallen out of actual practice. This distance between the early Jewish word χριστός and its ancient Israelite etymology has been rightly highlighted by Martin Karrer, who documents how, by the time the Christians appealed to the word in the first century C.E., the Israelite tradition of anointing persons was long since defunct.[72] The practice of anointing Israelite kings was archaic, certainly no later than Zerubbabel in the sixth century B.C.E. Granted, in the Persian and Hellenistic periods high priests were anointed, but even this practice seems to have ended with Onias III in the second century B.C.E.[73] By the turn of the era, the actual practice of Jewish ritual

---

71 Even the Roman historians note that Jewish messianism was a matter of scriptural inter-pretation: Josephus, *J.W.* 6.312: "What set them to war most of all was an ambiguous oracle [χρησμὸς ἀμφίβολος], also found in their sacred scriptures [ἱεροῖς γράμμασιν], that at that time someone from their country would rule the world" (Greek text ed. Benedictus Niese, *Flavii Josephi Opera* [7 vols; Berlin: Weidmann, 1885–1895]); Tacitus, *Hist.* 5.13: "The majority firmly believed that their ancient priestly writings [*antiquis sacerdotum litteris*] contained the prophecy that this was the very time when the East should grow strong and that men starting from Judea should possess the world [*profectique Iudaea rerum poterentur*]" (trans. Clifford H. Moore and John Jackson [Loeb Classical Library; Cambridge, Mass.: Harvard University Press, 1931]); Suetonius, *Vesp.* 4.5:

> There had spread all over the Orient an old and established belief [*vetus et constans opinio*], that it was fated at that time for men coming from Judea to rule the world [*Iudaea profecti rerum potirentur*]. This prediction, referring to the emperor of Rome, as afterwards appeared from the event, the people of Judea took to themselves; accord-ingly they revolted. (trans. J. C. Rolfe [LCL; Cambridge, Mass.: Harvard University Press, 1914, 1979])

On these reports see Eduard Norden, "Josephus und Tacitus über Jesus Christus und eine messianische Prophetie," *Neue Jahrbücher für klassische Altertum* 31 (1913): 636–666.

72 Karrer, *Der Gesalbte;* see also Martin Karrer, *Jesus Christus im Neuen Testament* (Grundrisse zum Neuen Testament 11; Göttingen: Vandenhoeck & Ruprecht, 1998). Karrer's thesis has been influential in German-speaking scholarship and, more slowly, in Anglo-American circles as well. For responses, see the essays collected in Baldermann et al., *Der Messias,* especially Peter Stuhlmacher, "Der messianische Gottesknecht," 131–154; Dieter Zeller, "Transformation," 155–167; Karl-Wilhelm Niebuhr, "Jesus Christus und die vielfältigen messianischen Erwartungen Israels: Ein Forschungsbericht," 337–345. Among English-language responses, see Oegema, *Anointed and His People,* 147–150; Chester, "The Nature and Scope of Messianism," in *Messiah and Exaltation,* 208–209, 220; Miller, "Anointed Jesus," 392–394.

73 On royal and priestly anointing see Karrer, *Der Gesalbte,* 95–147, 147–172, respectively.

anointing pertained not to persons but to places, in particular to the sanctuary in Jerusalem, in a manner analogous to Greek and Roman rites of unction.[74] On the premise that the meaning of χριστός would have changed over time to correspond to contemporary anointing practices, Karrer concludes that by the turn of the era χριστός no longer signified "the Lord's anointed" in the sense of the scriptural tradition at all but rather simply designated any thing or person that, like the temple furniture, was consecrated to God.[75]

The history of Jewish ritual anointing does not entail this linguistic conclusion, however. It is a complicated matter of diachrony in lexical semantics, of relative degrees of persistence and change in the meanings of idioms over time.[76] While there are many words whose meanings change straightforwardly over time in keeping with the practices they signify, there are also many idioms that remain current long after the customs that gave rise to their coining have fallen out of use. Such idioms are especially common when there is a substantial literary deposit to ensure their continued currency. Significantly, this is exactly the situation in the case of χριστός in the late Hellenistic and early Roman periods. The word is only very sparsely attested prior to the Greek translations of the Jewish scriptures in the third and second centuries B.C.E., whence it gains currency as a translation term for Hebrew משׁיח.[77] It is a word whose meaning is dependent on its place in an archaic literary deposit. It is entirely plausible, therefore, that Jewish readers around the turn of the era will have understood χριστός to signify an anointed person, even if no one had anointed a king or a priest for centuries, because they were familiar with the scriptures in Greek.

This is a historical-linguistic claim, not a theological or metaphysical one. To say that early Jewish messiah language traded on certain scriptural idioms

---

74 See Karrer, *Der Gesalbte,* 172–209.

75 See Karrer, *Der Gesalbte,* 406:

Denn bei Prägung der Formel ist seit über einem halben Jahrtausend kein König, seit 200 Jahren kein Priester Israels mehr gesalbt worden. Der Kult und das Allerheiligste des Tempels in Jerusalem, wo Gott nah und wirksam ist wie sonst nirgends, sind zum Zentrum der Salbungsvollzüge und zum Massstab für die Salbungsaussagen Israels geworden; das Allerheiligste gilt aller Wahrscheinlichkeit nach als "das Gesalbte."

76 On this problem in general see the essays collected in *Words in Time: Diachronic Semantics from Different Points of View* (ed. Regine Eckardt et al.; Berlin: de Gruyter, 2003), especially David Kronenfeld and Gabriella Rundblad, "The Semantic Structure of Lexical Fields: Variation and Change," 67–114.

77 See LSJ, s.v. χριστός. The only earlier instances are of the neuter χριστόν ("ointment"), in Aeschylus, *PV* 480: οὐκ ἦν ἀλέξημ' οὐδέν, οὔτε βρώσιμον οὐ χριστὸν οὐδὲ πιστόν, "There was no defense, neither [healing] food nor ointment nor drink"; Euripides, *Hipp.* 516: πότερα δὲ χριστὸν ἢ ποτὸν τὸ φάρμακον; "Is the drug an ointment or a potion?"

is not to say that there was a "messianic idea" already in ancient Israelite religion that came to fuller, grander expression in Second Temple Judaism. As
I have noted, some great eighteenth- and early nineteenth-century scholars
understood it so, but in fact the latter claim does not follow from the former.[78] Perceiving this misstep, post–World War II scholarship—epitomized by
Sigmund Mowickel's 1951 monograph *Han som kommer*—has tended to insist
how great a distance there is between the משיח of, say, the Psalms and the משיח
of, say, the Qumran Community Rule.[79] Along these lines, postwar critics
often distinguish sharply between the "anointed ones" of the Hebrew Bible
and the "messiahs" of early Judaism and Christianity.[80] For example, J.J.M.
Roberts writes, "In the original context not one of the thirty-nine occurrences
of משיח in the Hebrew canon refers to an expected figure of the future whose
coming will coincide with the inauguration of an age of salvation." And again,
"Nowhere in the Old Testament has the term משיח acquired its later technical
sense as an eschatological title."[81] In other words, on one popular definition of
"messiah," there is no messiah in the Hebrew Bible.

There is indeed considerable distance between the royal ideology of parts
of the Hebrew Bible and the messianic reflection of some Hellenistic- and
Roman-period Jewish literature. In this respect, Gressmann was wrong and
Mowinckel right. Scholarly insistence on this point, however, has obscured
the fact that the later messiah texts nevertheless consist mostly of interpretations of scriptural texts. In other words, there may not be any messiahs in the
Hebrew Bible, but some Jewish authors of the Hellenistic and Roman periods

---

78 For this misconception see, e.g., Klausner, *Messianic Idea;* and Hugo Gressmann, *Der
Messias* (Göttingen: Vandenhoeck & Ruprecht, 1929).

79 Sigmund Mowinckel, *He That Cometh: The Messiah Concept in the Old Testament and
Later Judaism* (trans. G. W. Anderson; Grand Rapids, Mich.: Eerdmans, 2005), here 3: "The
word 'Messiah' itself, as a title and a name, originated in later Judaism as the designation of
an eschatological figure; and it is therefore only to such a figure that it may be applied." On
the influence of this book, see Nils A. Dahl, "Sigmund Mowinckel: Historian of Religion
and Theologian," *Scandinavian Journal of the Old Testament* 2 (1988): 8–22; John J. Collins,
"Mowinckel's *He That Cometh* in Retrospect," in Mowinckel, *He That Cometh,* xv–xxiii.

80 Recent treatments in this Mowinckelian vein include Roberts, "Old Testament's
Contribution"; Oegema, *Anointed and His People,* 40–43; Kenneth E. Pomykala, *The Davidic
Dynasty Tradition in Early Judaism: Its History and Significance for Messianism* (Early Judaism
and Its Literature 7; Atlanta: Scholars Press, 1995); Collins, *Scepter and the Star,* 20–48; Collins,
King and Messiah as Son of God, 1–74; many of the essays collected in John Day, ed., *King and
Messiah in Israel and the Ancient Near East* (JSOTSup 270; Sheffield: Sheffield Academic,
1998); and most recently Joseph A. Fitzmyer, *The One Who Is to Come* (Grand Rapids, Mich.:
Eerdmans, 2007).

81 Roberts, "Old Testament's Contribution," 39, 51, respectively.

evidently thought there were.[82] This is true not only of those formal examples of scriptural interpretation, such as some of the pesharim from Qumran or the Targumim, that interpret certain scriptures in explicitly messianic terms.[83] It is also true of almost all of the free compositions (that is, texts whose genre is not scriptural interpretation) that mention messiah figures; such texts do so in patterns of speech that derive from the Jewish scriptures.

"Creatively Biblical" Linguistic Acts

It is possible to distinguish two levels at which this dynamic is observable: the close syntactical level and the wider literary level.[84] First, at the close syntactical level, when early Jewish and Christian texts use the word "messiah," they usually follow the precedent of the Jewish scriptures not only in the choice of lexeme but also in the choice of syntagm in which the lexeme occurs.[85] In other words, when one finds the word "messiah" in an early Jewish or Christian text, one very often finds it in a phrase whose structure itself has precedent in one of the "messiah" passages in the Jewish scriptures. Such uses do not necessarily amount to what we generally recognize as citations or even allusions since there are usually not multiple key words in common.[86] In contrast to citations and allusions, these borrowed syntagms may have been mostly unconscious on the part of their authors. They are not literary evocations of particular scriptural source texts; they are simply part of the linguistic inheritance that comes packaged with the lexeme. That is to say, not only the word itself

---

82 On this point, see especially Donald Juel, *Messianic Exegesis: Christological Interpretation of the Old Testament in Early Christianity* (Philadelphia: Fortress, 1988).

83 This phenomenon has been well documented. On the pesharim see L. H. Schiffman, "Messianic Figures and Ideas in the Qumran Scrolls," in Charlesworth, *Messiah*, 116–129, especially 123–125; James H. Charlesworth et al., eds, *Qumran-Messianism: Studies on the Messianic Expectations in the Dead Sea Scrolls* (Tübingen: Mohr Siebeck, 1998). On the Targumim see Samson H. Levey, *The Messiah: An Aramaic Interpretation: The Messianic Exegesis of the Targum* (Monographs of the Hebrew Union College 2; Cincinnati: Hebrew Union College Press, 1974).

84 Here, following Dahl, "Sources of Christological Language," 115–116, I have in mind not primarily the vocabulary of messiah language, which has been thoroughly treated (see Schäfer, "Diversity and Interaction"; Collins, *Scepter and the Star*, 49–153), but rather the syntactical constructions in which the relevant words occur and their larger rhetorical contexts.

85 On the lexeme-syntagm relation in semantics, see John Lyons, *Language and Linguistics: An Introduction* (Cambridge: Cambridge University Press, 1981), 136–178.

86 On allusion see Robert Alter, *The Pleasures of Reading in an Ideological Age* (New York: Norton, 1996), 112: "Literary allusion…involves the evocation—through a wide spectrum of formal means—in one text of an antecedent literary text." The same is true, *a fortiori*, of citation.

but also its relation to other words in the sentence are linguistic resources provided by the Jewish scriptures.

Examples of this phenomenon are numerous. One is the use of "messiah" as a predicate noun following a copulative verb, that is, sentences of the form "[name or pronoun] is the messiah," such as "The herald is the messiah of the spirit [הואה משיח הרוח] of whom Daniel spoke" (11QMelch 2.18);[87] "Peter answered him [Jesus], 'You are the Christ [σὺ εἶ ὁ χριστός]' " (Mark 8:29); "This Jesus whom I proclaim to you is the Christ [οὗτός ἐστιν ὁ χριστὸς [ὁ] Ἰησοῦς]" (Acts 17:3); "As for the lion that you saw... this is the messiah [hic est unctus]" (4 Ezra 12:31–32);[88] "When R. Akiba saw Bar Koziba, he said, 'This is the king messiah [דין הוא מלכא משיחא]' " (y. Ta'an. 4:8/27).[89] Such sentences borrow from a pattern of speech attested in 1–2 Samuel, in which David expresses his unwillingness to lay a hand on Saul because משיח יהוה הוא, "He [Saul] is YHWH's anointed one" (1 Sam 24:7, 11). According to this pattern of speech, one of the ways to use the word "messiah" is to predicate it of someone or something.[90]

Another example is the use of "messiah" in temporal clauses, often with a verb of "coming" or "appearing," such as "until the appearing [עד עמוד] of the messiah of Aaron and of Israel" (CD 12.23–13.1; 14.19);[91] "at the coming [בבוא] of the messiah of Aaron and of Israel" (CD 19.10–11); "until the coming [עד בוא] of the messiah of righteousness" (4Q252 5.3–4);[92] "the time of the appearance [Syriac m'tyt'] of the messiah" (2 Bar. 30:1);[93] "when the time of my messiah comes" (2 Bar. 72:2); "from the deportation to Babylon to the Christ [ἕως τοῦ Χριστοῦ] is fourteen generations" (Matt 1:17); "when he [messiah] comes [ὅταν ἔλθῃ] he will show us all things" (John 4:25). Apropos of these passages,

---

87 For 11QMelch I follow the text of F. García Martínez et al., eds., *Manuscripts from Qumran Cave 11 (11Q2–18, 11Q20–30)* (DJD 23; Oxford: Clarendon, 1997).

88 For *4 Ezra* I follow the Latin text of R. L. Bensly, ed., *The Fourth Book of Ezra: The Latin Version Edited from the MSS* (Texts and Studies 3.2; Cambridge: Cambridge University Press, 1895); and the translation of Bruce M. Metzger in James H. Charlesworth, ed., *The Old Testament Pseudepigrapha* (2 vols; Garden City, N.Y.: Doubleday, 1983).

89 For the Talmud Yerushalmi I follow the text of Peter Schäfer and Hans-Jürgen Becker, eds., *Synopse zum Talmud Yerushalmi* (4 vols; TSAJ 31, 33, 35, 47, 82–83; Tübingen: Mohr Siebeck, 1991–2001).

90 On the importance of these predication sentences in 1–2 Samuel, see Mowinckel, *He That Cometh,* 65–69.

91 For CD I cite the text of 4Q265 per J. M. Baumgarten et al., eds., *Qumran Cave 4.XXV: Halakhic Texts* (DJD 35; Oxford: Clarendon, 1999).

92 For 4Q252 I follow the text of G. J. Brooke et al., eds., *Qumran Cave 4.XVII: Parabiblical Texts, Part 3* (DJD 22; Oxford: Clarendon, 1996).

93 For *2 Baruch* I follow the Syriac text of A. M. Ceriani, ed., *Opuscula et fragmenta miscella magnam partem apocrypha* (Monumenta sacra et profana 5; Milan: Pogliani, 1868); and the translation of A. F. J. Klijn in Charlesworth, *OTP.*

there is precedent in Daniel for using "messiah" in a temporal clause: "From the going out of the word to return and build Jerusalem until [the coming of] an anointed one [עַד מָשִׁיחַ], a ruler, shall be seven weeks" (Dan 9:25).[94]

A related example is the saying in *m. Soṭah* 9:15: "At the footsteps of the messiah [בְּעִקְבוֹת מְשִׁיחָא] arrogance shall grow and scarcity shall increase."[95] "At the footsteps of the messiah" here is a temporal clause, one in a series of such phrases in this mishnah: "when R. Akiba died," "when R. Yohanan b. Zakkai died," "when the temple was destroyed," and "at the footsteps of the messiah." Less the prefixed preposition, however, the phrase עִקְבוֹת מָשִׁיחַ comes directly from Ps 89:52: "Your enemies, O YHWH, scoff on the heels of your anointed one [עִקְבוֹת מְשִׁיחֶךָ]." The context of the psalm is very different, and עִקְבוֹת in the psalm means not "footsteps" in the sense of "coming" but rather "heels" (BDB, s.v. עָקֵב; cf. Jastrow, s.v. עֲקֵב). It is a vivid image of persecution: The wicked scoff on the heels of the messiah. Mishnah *Soṭah* borrows this construction from Ps 89 and, exploiting the range of meaning of עָקֵב, reuses the construction in a sense analogous to the temporal clause of Dan 9:25.[96] As these several examples show, early Jewish and Christian messiah texts inherited from the Jewish scriptures not only the lexeme "messiah" but also a cluster of conventional syntagms within which to use it. There are exceptions to this rule—which is natural enough, given the way words accumulate uses over time—but the rule holds in a remarkable number of instances. Early Jewish and Christian messiah texts speak in syntactical patterns inherited from scriptural messiah texts.

Second, at the wider literary level, most early Jewish and Christian messiah texts also make explicit citation of or allusion to one or more scriptural source texts. This point, in contrast to the previous one, does not pertain to the constructions within which the word "messiah" falls; many citations and allusions appear in nearby sentences and so are syntactically independent of the

---

94 On the significance of the syntax of Dan 9:25–26, see Fitzmyer, *One Who Is to Come*, 56–64, here 62: "All-important in this passage is the occurrence of the word מָשִׁיחַ in v. 25 with a temporal preposition having a future connotation."

95 For the Mishnah I follow the text of J. Rabbinowitz, ed., *Mishnah Megillah* (Oxford: Oxford University Press, 1931). On this passage see Jacob Neusner, "Mishnah and Messiah," in *Judaisms and Their Messiahs*, 265–282, especially 267–275; but cf. Craig A. Evans, "Mishna and Messiah 'in Context': Some Comments on Jacob Neusner's Proposals," *JBL* 112 (1993): 267–289.

96 This reuse of the psalmist's phrase is further attested elsewhere, as in *Tg.* Ps 89:52: "Thy enemies have scoffed…at the delay of the footsteps of thy messiah, O Lord" (trans. Levey, *Messiah: An Aramaic Interpretation,* 121); *Song Rab.* 2:13 §4: "R. Jannai said: If you see one generation after another cursing and blaspheming, look out for the coming of the messiah, as it says, [*With which your enemies taunt, O YHWH, with which they scoff on the heels of your anointed one*]" (trans. Maurice Simon, *Midrash Rabbah* [London: Soncino, 1939]).

word itself. They are marked instead by imagery borrowed, often consciously, from particular scriptural source texts. The function of these citations and allusions is to clarify what the author intends by "messiah," given the word's considerable range of meaning.[97]

The *Parables of Enoch*, for example, characterizes its messiah by means of echoes of Ps 2:2 (*1 En.* 48:10: "They have denied the Lord of Spirits and his messiah"), Isa 42:6 and 49:6 (*1 En.* 48:4: "He will be the light of the nations"), and Dan 7:9–14 (*1 En.* 46:1: "I saw one who had a head of days...and with him was another, whose face was like the appearance of a man").[98] More directly, the messiah of *4 Ezra* is identified by an interpreting angel as a character from "the vision to your brother Daniel [viz. Dan 7:1–14]. But it was not explained to him as I now explain it to you" (*4 Ezra* 12:11–12), and his representation as a lion from the house of David (*4 Ezra* 12:31–32) is an allusion to Gen 49:9–10.[99] In a similar way, the Acts of the Apostles characterizes its messiah by citing Ps 2:1–2 (Acts 4:26: "The rulers have gathered together against the Lord and against his messiah") and Amos 9:11 (Acts 15:16: "I will rebuild the dwelling of David, which has fallen"), among other scriptures.[100] Also relevant here are the patronymic formulae that occur in some ancient messiah texts (e.g., "messiah son of David," "messiah son of Joseph," "messiah

---

97 Language users commonly negotiate homonyms and polysemes by adding clarifying information, for instance: "There's a movement; there must be an animal in those bushes"; or "There's a movement; they've got hundreds of people rallying in the streets" (see Yael Ravin and Claudia Leacock, "Polysemy: An Overview," in *Polysemy: Theoretical and Computational Approaches* [ed. Yael Ravin and Claudia Leacock; Oxford: Oxford University Press, 2000], 1–29).

98 For the text of *1 Enoch* see the critical editions of R. H. Charles, *The Ethiopic Version of the Book of Enoch* (2 vols.; Anecdota Oxoniensia, Semitic Series 11; Oxford: Clarendon, 1906); and Michael A. Knibb, *The Ethiopic Book of Enoch: A New Edition in Light of the Aramaic Dead Sea Fragments* (Oxford: Clarendon, 1978). Here I follow the recent translation of George W. E. Nickelsburg and James C. VanderKam, *1 Enoch: A New Translation* (Minneapolis: Fortress, 2004). On the messiah of the *Parables of Enoch*, see further Nickelsburg, "Salvation without and with a Messiah: Developing Beliefs in Writings Ascribed to Enoch," in *Judaisms and Their Messiahs*, 49–68; Matthew Black, "The Messianism of the Parables of Enoch," in Charlesworth, *Messiah*, 145–68; and now the essays collected in Gabriele Boccaccini, ed., *Enoch and the Messiah Son of Man: Revisiting the Book of Parables* (Grand Rapids, Mich.: Eerdmans, 2007).

99 On the messiah in *4 Ezra* see Michael E. Stone, "The Concept of the Messiah in IV Ezra," in *Religions in Antiquity: Essays in Memory of Erwin Ramsdell Goodenough* (ed. Jacob Neusner; Leiden: Brill, 1968), 295–312; Michael E. Stone, "The Question of the Messiah in 4 Ezra," in *Judaisms and Their Messiahs*, 209–224. Contra Klaus Koch ("Messias und Menschensohn," in *Vor der Wende der Zeiten: Beiträge zur apokalyptischen Literatur* [Neukirchen Vluyn: Neukirchener Verlag, 1996], 235–266), the "man" of *4 Ezra* 13 is not a different character in a two-stage eschatological drama but is rather a reinterpretation of the "messiah" of *4 Ezra* 12 (so rightly Stone, "Question of the Messiah").

100 On the messiah in Acts see Mark L. Strauss, *The Davidic Messiah in Luke-Acts: The Promise and Its Fulfillment in Lukan Christology* (Journal for the Study of the New Testament Supplement Series 110; Sheffield: Sheffield Academic, 1995), 130–195.

son of God"), which are best understood as shorthand allusions to particular scriptural traditions.[101]

Gerbern Oegema has made a collation of citations of and allusions to scripture in Jewish and Christian messiah texts from 300 B.C.E. to 200 C.E.[102] He finds, first, that almost all ancient messiah texts cite or allude to one or more earlier source texts; second, that almost all of these earlier source texts are among the Jewish scriptures;[103] and finally, that just a few of these scriptural source texts account for almost all of the later citations and allusions. This last point is important: Citations of and allusions to scripture in ancient messiah texts cluster around a relatively few scriptural source texts. In other words, not only did the authors of ancient messiah texts find their messiahs in the Jewish scriptures; they found them in the same particular scriptures. The most frequently cited and alluded-to scriptural texts are the following:[104]

> Gen 49:10: The scepter will not depart from Judah, nor the commander's staff from between his feet, until that which is his comes, and the obedience of the peoples is his.
>
> Num 24:17: A star will go forth from Jacob, and a scepter will rise from Israel; it will shatter the borders of Moab and tear down all the sons of Sheth.

---

101 So rightly Joel Marcus, "Mark 14:61: 'Are You the Messiah-Son-of-God?' " *NovT* 31 (1989): 125–141, here 135: "In a situation of such fluidity, it would sometimes be advantageous, when using the term 'Messiah,' to make more precise which Messiah one had in view. One way of doing this would be by means of the restrictive appositive 'Son of x.' "

102 His list of scriptures referenced is as follows: Gen 2:2, 7; 3:22–24; 14:18–20; 15; 49:10–12; Ex 12:42; 40:9–11; Num 24:8–9, 17–24; Deut 5:28–29; 18:18; 30:4–9; 33:8–11; Judg 21:16–25; 1 Sam 1:1–2; 16–17; 2 Sam 7:13; 1 Kings 17:1; 2 Kings 2:11; Pss 2:7, 9; 23:1–2; 24; 37; 69:3; 72; 90:4; 97:7; 110:1; 117:22; Isa 2:2–4; 7:14; 11:1–12; 24:17–23; 28:16; 31:8; 43:21; 48:4–6; 49:6, 54; 56:1–5; 63:1–6; Jer 23:5; 33:15; 53:7; Ezek 1:6–11; 9:4; 34:23; Daniel 2; 7; 8; 10; Joel 4:13; Amos 5:26; 9:11; Mic 4:1–7; 5:1–3, 7; Habakkuk 2; Hag 2:23; Zech 13:7 (Oegema, *Anointed and His People*, 294–299). There is a measure of subjectivity in the identification of allusions, at least in borderline cases, but most of these identifications are uncontroversial.

103 The exceptions to this rule are several inner-Christian citations, viz. *Did.* 16.1–18 referencing Matt 24:29–31; 1 Thess 4:14–17; Pol. *Phil.* referencing 1 Pet 1:21; 4:5; *Apoc. Pet.* referencing Matt 16:27; 1 Pet 4:5; *Apoc. Paul* referencing 2 Cor 12:2–4; *Apoc. El.* 42.10–15 referencing Revelation 11; and *Odes Sol.* 39.9–13 referencing Matt 14:26 (Oegema, *Anointed and His People*, 294–299).

104 My translations from the MT. Recent writers on scriptural references in messiah texts, for all their disagreements, are virtually unanimous in identifying these particular scriptural source texts (see Joseph A. Fitzmyer, "The Use of Explicit Old Testament Quotations in Qumran Literature and in the New Testament," in *Essays on the Semitic Background of the New Testament* [Missoula, Mont.: Scholars Press, 1974], 3–58; Horbury, *Jewish Messianism and the Cult of Christ*; Oegema, *Anointed and His People*; Collins, "Messiahs in Context"; Collins, *Scepter and the Star*).

2 Sam 7:12–13: I will raise up your seed after you, who will come forth
   from your body, and I will establish his kingdom. He will build a house
   for my name, and I will establish the throne of his kingdom forever.

Isa 11:1–2: A shoot will come forth from the stump of Jesse, and a branch
   will grow from his roots. The spirit of YHWH will rest upon him.

Amos 9:11: On that day I will raise up the fallen booth of David, and
   repair its breached walls, and raise up its ruins, and build it as in the
   days of old.

Dan 7:13–14: I saw in the night visions, and behold, one like a son of
   man was coming with the clouds of heaven. And he came to the
   Ancient of Days and was presented before him. To him was given
   dominion and honor and kingship.

Perhaps the most striking feature of this list of scriptures frequently cited in
later messiah texts is that none of them actually contains the word "messiah."
As we have seen, the thirty-eight scriptural passages that do contain that word
influence the later messiah texts at the level of lexeme and syntagm, but not,
for the most part, at the wider literary level. At that level, the messiah texts
typically draw on these other scriptures instead, scriptures that do not contain
the word "messiah" but whose rich imagery funds their interpretations of the
word.[105] This irony is an important feature of early Jewish and Christian messiah texts: They take the word itself from one set of scriptures and the imagery
with which they interpret the word from a different set of scriptures.

What this latter set of scriptures have in common is not the word "messiah" but rather the promise, either in oracular or in visionary form, of an
indigenous ruler for the Jewish people. The ruler's genealogy is sometimes
more, sometimes less specific: In Numbers 24 he is simply Israelite; in Genesis
49 he is from the tribe of Judah; in 2 Samuel 7, Isaiah 11, and Amos 9 he is a
Davidide. Daniel 7 might seem to be anomalous in this respect since in the
context of the vision the "one like a son of man" would appear to be a heavenly being, but even he is representative of "the people of the holy ones of the
Most High" (Dan 7:27).[106] Later messiah texts select from among these scrip-

---

105 This suggests that messiah language was a component of other, broader strategies for
interpreting the Jewish scriptures. I focus on it here for heuristic purposes since messiah texts
share enough common features to warrant collective study, but talk about a messiah was
always part of one or more larger scripturally funded discourses about God, the world, the
people Israel, and more.

106 The identities of the "son of man" and of the "holy ones" in Daniel 7 are, of course, much disputed (see John J. Collins, *Daniel: A Commentary on the Book of Daniel* [Minneapolis: Fortress,
1993], 304–318), but my point here stands regardless of one's positions on those questions.

tural source texts according as they serve the messiah texts' own respective interests.[107] However, different interests notwithstanding, the later messiah texts are remarkably consistent in their drawing from this particular set of scriptural source texts rather than from others.

An example will serve to illustrate the point. Leaving aside the formal translations of and commentaries on Isaiah (pesharim, Targumim, etc.), there are a number of free compositions that take Isa 11:1–10—the oracle about "the shoot from the stump of Jesse"—to refer to a messiah. These chronologically and geographically diverse messiah texts include the *Psalms of Solomon*, the *Parables of Enoch*, the Epistle of Paul to the Romans, and tractate *Sanhedrin* of the Bavli. For convenience, instances of the word "messiah" are underlined, and references to Isaiah 11 are italicized:

> See, O Lord, and raise up for them their king, the son of David... *in the wisdom of righteousness* to drive out the sinners from the inheritance... *with a rod of iron to break all their substance, to destroy the lawless nations by the word of his mouth* [Isa 11:2, 4]... For they shall all be holy, and their king shall be the lord messiah. (*Pss. Sol.* 17:21–32)[108]

> [The kings of the earth] have denied the Lord of Spirits and his Anointed One. Blessed be the name of the Lord of Spirits.... For the Chosen One has taken his stand in the presence of the Lord of Spirits; and his glory is forever and ever, and his might, to all generations. *And in him dwell the spirit of wisdom and the spirit of insight, and the spirit of instruction and might*, and the spirit of those who have fallen asleep in righteousness. *And he will judge the things that are secret* [Isa 11:2, 3]. (*1 En.* 48:10–49:4 [trans. George W. E. Nickelsburg])

---

107 It is significant, for example, that Bar Kokhba, for whom there is no evidence of Davidic ancestry, is spoken of as messiah in connection with Num 24:17 (*y. Taʿan.* 4:8/27; *Lam. Rab.* 2:2 §4; *Lam. Rab.* ed. Buber, p. 101), the only one of these texts that is not a Davidic royal ideology text. At *b. Sanh.* 93b, however, the rabbis deny Bar Kokhba's messianic claim on the grounds that he cannot "smell and judge" per Isa 11:3, which is a Davidic royal ideology text. Cf. also Judah Maccabee, about whom the literature bypasses the whole problem of Davidic pedigree, capitalizing instead on his priestly credentials, for instance, by giving his father Mattathias the mantle of Phinehas (Num 25:6–13; 1 Macc 2:24–26).

108 I follow the Greek text of Rahlfs, *Septuaginta*, except in the last phrase, where the MSS preserve χριστὸς κύριος but Rahlfs proposes the emendation χριστὸς κυρίου on the grounds that the MS reading is a Christian corruption. Granted, χριστὸς κύριος is not the LXX idiom (although cf. Lam 4:20 LXX), but neither is it a blatantly christianizing phrase (see similarly R. B. Wright in Charlesworth, *OTP*, ad loc.).

<u>Christ</u> became a servant of the circumcision for the sake of God's truthfulness, in order to confirm the promises to the patriarchs, and for the sake of his mercy, in order that the Gentiles might glorify God. As it is written.... *The root of Jesse shall come, he who rises to rule the Gentiles; in him shall the Gentiles hope* [Isa 11:10]. (Rom 15:8–12)

Bar Koziba reigned two and a half years. He said to the rabbis, "I am the <u>messiah</u>." They said to him, "Of the <u>messiah</u> it is written, *He smells and judges* [Isa 11:3]. Let us see whether he smells and judges." When they saw that he was unable to smell and judge, they killed him. (*b. Sanh.* 93b)[109]

Each of these four very different texts is concerned to say something about a "messiah," and each does so by citing or alluding to one or more parts of Isa 11:1–10. None of these texts is literarily dependent on any of the other three; rather, they are independent witnesses to a convention whereby ones talks about a messiah in terms of the Isaianic "shoot from the stump of Jesse."

This is not to say that all messiah texts interpreted these few scriptures in the same way. In point of fact, they did not do so. This point has been well made by Joseph Fitzmyer: "There is no evidence at Qumran of a systematic, uniform exegesis of the Old Testament. The same text was not always given the same interpretation";[110] and by Oegema: "Those verses that have been interpreted more than once do not present a uniform messianic idea.... None of the biblical verses lead to specific and definite messianic interpretations. None of the so-called messianic passages of the Hebrew Bible has an intrinsic messianic value."[111] However, even if the interpretation was not uniform, the pool of scriptural source texts commonly cited was nevertheless quite small, and the former point must not be allowed to obscure the latter. The claim that the scriptural source texts are not all interpreted in the same way by the later messiah texts is true but also inconsequential since, in fact, no such uniform system of scriptural exegesis is attested in any ancient literary corpus. The interesting point is not that the scriptural texts in question received diverse interpretations but rather that such a pool of scriptural texts existed.[112]

---

109 For the Talmud Bavli I follow the text of I. Epstein, ed., *Hebrew-English Edition of the Babylonian Talmud* (30 vols; London: Soncino, 1960–1990).

110 Fitzmyer, "Use of Explicit Old Testament Quotations," 55.

111 Oegema, *Anointed and His People*, 302–303.

112 Here see Francis Watson, *Paul and the Hermeneutics of Faith* (London: T. & T. Clark, 2004), especially 1–29, who makes the point that Paul and a number of his contemporaries were interpreting the same relatively few scriptures in strikingly different directions.

So ancient messiah texts draw on a small cluster of scriptural source texts for vocabulary with which to talk about their messiahs, but they interpret these scriptural source texts in a number of different ways. Upon reflection, this is actually unsurprising given the very diverse social and historical contexts of the respective messiah texts: Some were written in Judea, others in the Diaspora; some date as early as the second century B.C.E., others as late as the second century C.E. (and much later, of course); some are amenable to the temple cult, others opposed, still others were written only after the temple was destroyed; some are ideologically Qumranite, others Christian, Enochic, mainstream, or otherwise.[113] In some cases, in fact, it is possible to discern in the details of the messianic exegesis something of the social and historical context of the text and its authors. It has rightly been pointed out, for example, that the Qumranic commonplace of the dual "messiahs of Aaron and of Israel" is almost certainly related to the Qumranites' opposition to the conflation of priestly and royal offices by the Hasmonean dynasty.[114]

Oegema has shown how a number of messiah texts reflect aspects of their respective political situations. Indeed, on his account, this principle of analogy goes all the way down: "Messianic expectations were conceptualized... always in analogy with the balances of power. Only thus can we explain, why certain messiah concepts are found only in certain periods."[115] Every messiah text, in other words, is a product of the process of *Konzeptualisierung*, in which scriptural tradition is reinterpreted by analogy to contemporary political reality, so that each messiah figure bears the image of the dominant power structure with which his author was familiar.[116] Doubtless some such process was in play in the writing of the early messiah texts, but it is better to think of it as

---

113 Indeed, the fact that early messiah texts are diffuse across literary corpora rather than highly concentrated is evidence that the words signified a recognizable collection of concepts (e.g., Davidide monarchy, Aaronide priesthood, Jewish self-rule, the subjection of Gentile nations) and were not simply the private language of a sectarian group. One did not have to be a disciple of Enoch traditions or a Qumran covenanter or a follower of Jesus to know what was meant when messiah language was used. All one needed was a familiarity with the Jewish scriptures.

114 This point has been recognized since Van der Woude, *Die messianischen Vorstellungen*. For a compelling recent statement see Collins, *Scepter and the Star*, 74–101.

115 Oegema, *Anointed and His People*, 305.

116 So for Oegema the book of Daniel, reflecting on the Seleucid-Maccabean conflict, patterns its Son of Man after the φίλοι, "friends," of the Hellenistic kings (Oegema, *Anointed and His People*, 55–67). The Qumran covenanters, who opposed the Hasmonean priest-kings, imagined the properly ordered messiahs of Aaron and Israel (Oegema, *Anointed and His People*, 86–97). The Tannaim, who had experienced the profound disappointment of the Bar Kokhba revolt, deferred messianic hope to an indefinite future and made it contingent on Torah observance (Oegema, *Anointed and His People*, 259–262, 274–286).

one of a number of influences.[117] Some analogies between messiah texts and their respective political situations are closer than others;[118] and some messiah texts whose political situations were similar or even shared nevertheless differ in their renderings of their messiah figures.[119] There is no necessity in the literary production of messiah texts, as if each text consisted of equal parts scripture and politics, so that the only messiah figure that could have emerged in a given time and place is the one that did in fact emerge. In the case of any given text, there are multiple contributing factors, including a degree of irreducible creativity on the part of the author.[120]

This aspect of the ancient messiah texts has been well expressed by Loren Stuckenbruck: "Such a dynamic hope drove their descriptions of eschatological events to be 'creatively biblical' at every turn."[121] This is an apt description, and both of its terms are significant: "Creatively" because it is not the case that the biblical texts already contain, somewhere in their own recesses, the "real" messianic meaning; something is always added by the interpreter. "Biblical" because, even if this is the case, nevertheless ancient messiah texts consist, in almost every instance, of interpretation of the Jewish scriptures; they are not completely free literary creations.[122] Of course, there is enormous variety in the interpretations employed, but the Jewish scriptures provided the pool of shared linguistic resources for them all.

If this is the case, if every messiah text is a "creatively biblical" linguistic act, it follows, first, that all such texts should be taken into consideration as evidence of this interpretive practice and, second, that no one messiah text has a claim to represent "the messianic idea" in its pristine form over against other

---

117 So rightly Horbury, *Jewish Messianism and the Cult of Christ,* 34: "This proposal rings true in general, but external politics should probably be reckoned as just one important factor in the formation of messianic conceptions; they interacted with an existing myth, and, flexible as it was, it had its own coherence and impetus."

118 Cf. the analogy of the Qumranic messiahs of Aaron and Israel to the Hasmonean priest-kings with Oegema's putative analogy of the Danielic son of man to the φίλοι of the Hellenistic kings.

119 E.g., *4 Ezra* and *2 Baruch.*

120 Interestingly, Oegema makes a concession to this effect in the case of Paul, whose letters he takes as evidence of messianism: "It is therefore possible [on the evidence of Paul] that not only do messiah concepts develop in an analogy with the political balance of power, but also that social and religious factors play a role" (Oegema, *Anointed and His People,* 192).

121 Stuckenbruck, "Messianic Ideas," 113.

122 In this connection Philip Alexander has observed that "though full of new colourful detail, the post-70 messianic tradition was, on the whole, not innovative" (Philip S. Alexander, "The King Messiah in Rabbinic Judaism," in *King and Messiah in Israel and the Ancient Near East,* 473). This is quite right, and the same may be said of messiah texts from the pre-70 period, as well.

messiah texts that do so less adequately.[123] Rather, all messiah texts are on a par in this respect since every particular messiah text is just one instance of the use of certain scriptural linguistic resources. It is at just this point, however, that research into messianism bumps up against Pauline scholarship since Paul's nearly three hundred uses of the word "messiah" have been thought not to pass muster as properly messianic. The reason most often given for this problematic conclusion is that Paul, unlike his contemporaries, uses the word χριστός not as the title of office that it is but rather as an empty proper name. This claim warrants considerable scrutiny, which is the task of the next chapter.

---

123 So rightly James H. Charlesworth, "From Jewish Messianology to Christian Christology: Some Caveats and Perspectives," in *Judaisms and Their Messiahs*, 225–264, here 248: "These are the major discrepancies; they must not be ignored in an attempt to construct a content for Jewish messianism. Definitions of messianism must be rewritten to absorb the aforementioned complexities."

3

Names, Titles, and Other Possibilities

IN THE PREVIOUS chapter I showed that there were certain linguistic conventions in Jewish antiquity whereby a speaker or writer could refer meaningfully to the concept of a messiah by alluding to a small but significant group of scriptural texts. It is a further methodological question, however, how a modern interpreter might tell what particular role messiahship plays in the thought of a given author. One might start by inquiring into the frequency of the word משיח and its translation equivalencies in that author's corpus. This approach turns out to be of real, but limited, worth and is most helpful when it yields negative results. It is surely significant, for example, that 1 and 2 Maccabees never use messiah language to characterize Judah Maccabee or his brothers or that the Epistle of James uses χριστός only twice (1:1; 2:1) and the Gospel of Thomas apparently not at all.[1] Paul, however, uses χριστός some 270 times, counting only the seven undisputed letters, more than he uses any other word for Jesus and more than any other ancient Jewish author uses that word. Strictly by volume, then, Paul could be called the most messianically interested of any ancient Jewish or Christian author. But of course, things are not so simple. It is not frequency alone but the particular uses of words that matter most for questions of interpretation.[2]

---

1 On this aspect of the Maccabean literature, see Collins, "Messianism in the Maccabean Period"; Jonathan A. Goldstein, "How the Authors of 1 and 2 Maccabees Treated the 'Messianic' Promises," in *Judaisms and Their Messiahs*, 69–96. On James, see J. Ramsey Michaels, "Catholic Christologies in the Catholic Epistles," in *Contours of Christology in the New Testament* (ed. R. N. Longenecker; Grand Rapids, Mich.: Eerdmans, 2005), 268–291, especially 269–274. On Thomas, see Stevan Davies, "The Christology and Protology of the Gospel of Thomas," *JBL* 111 (1992): 663–682.

2 So rightly, George MacRae, "Messiah and Gospel," in *Judaisms and Their Messiahs*, 170: "There have been extensive analyses of the distribution and syntax of *Christos* throughout the New Testament, but in some cases there is little agreement on how to interpret the word in specific contexts."

The Name-versus-Title Debate

In the case of χριστός in Paul, the particular uses of the word that have been deemed possible and significant are use as a title and use as a proper name.[3] As a result, scholarly discussion of the messiahship of Jesus in Paul has long centered on the question whether Paul uses χριστός as a title ("the Messiah") or a proper name ("Christ"), the critical assumption being that use of the word as a title would indicate a particularly messianic Christology, while use of the word as a proper name would indicate no such Christology or, indeed, nothing at all. Werner Kramer's statement of the question is representative: "It is uncertain to what extent *Christos* has the meaning of Messiah in Paul's writings, and to what extent it is simply the proper name of a particular person or of him who died and rose again for our salvation."[4]

A sizable majority of modern interpreters have ruled that Paul uses χριστός as a name, not a title, and that consequently the messiahship of Jesus plays little or no role in Paul's thought. There is some variety in the particular terminology used; χριστός in Paul is variously referred to as a name, a surname, a cognomen, a personal name, and most often a proper name. But the same category is almost invariably meant by all of these terms, a category defined by its contrast term—it is not a title. So, in his influential study, Nils Dahl concludes, "Paul's letters represent a strikingly advanced stage in the evolution that transformed *Christos* from a messianic designation to Jesus' second proper name."[5] Therefore, the frequency of the word notwithstanding, "Paul's christology can be stated almost without referring to the messiahship of Jesus."[6] Following Dahl, George MacRae comments, "*Christos* is never or virtually never used by Paul as a title in the sense of Messiah, but only as a proper name."[7] It follows, then, that for Paul "the Christian message does not hinge, at least primarily, on the claim that Jesus was or is the Messiah."[8] In fact, for Paul, "the Messiahship of Jesus is simply not an issue."[9] More recently, Andrew Chester has reasoned, "Paul uses Χριστός...almost entirely as a

---

3 See most recently, Douglas R. A. Hare, "When Did 'Messiah' Become a Proper Name?" *Expository Times* 121 (2009): 70–73, who upholds the conventional name-versus-title rubric but argues that "messiah" had already become a proper name in Judaism before Paul.

4 Kramer, *Christ, Lord, Son of God*, 203.

5 Dahl, "Messiahship of Jesus in Paul," 18.

6 Dahl, "Messiahship of Jesus in Paul," 15.

7 MacRae, "Messiah and Gospel," 171.

8 MacRae, "Messiah and Gospel," 172.

9 MacRae, "Messiah and Gospel," 170.

proper name (often in combination with Ἰησοῦς), not as a title as such."[10] To whatever extent the word is a proper name, "to this extent reference to the 'Messiah' drops out," so that "Paul appears to say almost nothing otherwise that is distinctly messianic."[11] This is to cite just a few leading lights on the subject; examples could be multiplied.[12]

Meanwhile, the minority who have argued for a robust account of the messiahship of Jesus in Paul have done so by staking out exactly the opposite position on the name-versus-title debate. Especially, N. T. Wright has argued in a number of places that "this consensus is wrong." Instead, Wright argues, "Χριστός in Paul should regularly be read as 'Messiah.' "[13] That is to say, "Χριστός still bears, for Paul, the titular sense."[14] Moreover, because it is a title, not a name, Wright contends, "the time is ripe for a re-assessment of Messiahship as a major category within Pauline theology."[15] Wright's former student S. A. Cummins, building on Wright's case for reading χριστός as a title in Paul, concludes that "Paul's understanding of Jesus as Messiah lies at the very heart of his theology, ecclesiology, and eschatology."[16]

It is essential to note that, for both sides of the debate, the interpretive question of the role of messiahship in Paul's thought takes as its starting point the philological question whether Paul uses χριστός as a title or as a name: If he uses the word as a title ("the Messiah"), then the messiahship of Jesus is

---

10 Chester, "Messianiasm, Mediators, and Pauline Christology," 382.

11 Chester, "Messianiasm, Mediators, and Pauline Christology," 383.

12 There is difference of opinion in the details, but the axiom that Paul's χριστός is a name, not a title, is likewise affirmed by Grundmann, *TDNT* 9:540; Werner Georg Kümmel, *The Theology of the New Testament according to Its Major Witnesses: Jesus-Paul-John* (trans. John E. Steely; Nashville: Abingdon, 1973), 154; Gaston, *Paul and the Torah,* 7; Marinus de Jonge, "The Earliest Christian Use of *Christos*: Some Suggestions," *New Testament Studies* 32 (1986): 321–322; Paula Fredriksen, *From Jesus to Christ: The Origins of the New Testament Images of Christ* (New Haven: Yale University Press, 2000), 56; Dunn, *Theology of Paul,* 197; Larry Hurtado, "Paul's Christology," in *Cambridge Companion to St. Paul* (ed. J. D. G. Dunn; Cambridge: Cambridge University Press, 2003), 191; Douglas Moo, "The Christology of the Early Pauline Letters," in *Contours of Christology,* 186; Zetterholm, "Paul and the Missing Messiah," 37.

13 N. T. Wright, "ΧΡΙΣΤΟΣ as 'Messiah' in Paul: Philemon 6," in *Climax,* 41–55, here 41; see also Wright, "Adam, Israel, and the Messiah," in *Climax,* 18–40; Wright, *Paul: In Fresh Perspective;* all of which develop ideas expressed earlier in Wright, "Messiah and the People of God."

14 Wright, *Climax,* 46.

15 Wright, *Climax,* 42.

16 Cummins, "Divine Life," 190. Although Cummins is the only recent scholar to build extensively on Wright's work on this question, other Paulinists have concurred with Wright's conclusions in other contexts. See, e.g., Hays, "Christ Prays the Psalms," 111n30; J. Ross Wagner, *Heralds of the Good News: Isaiah and Paul "in Concert" in the Letter to the Romans* (Supplements to Novum Testamentum 101; Leiden: Brill, 2002), 308n7.

a substantial part of his thought and is likely to bear on a number of other problems in Pauline theology. If, however, he uses the word as a proper name ("Christ"), then he is either unconsciously neglecting or consciously downplaying the messiahship of Jesus, which therefore plays no significant part in his thought.

Amid this debate, however, there have occasionally been hints in the secondary literature that something is amiss, that χριστός in Paul is not quite what scholars mean by "name" and not quite what scholars mean by "title." Nils Dahl, the most important twentieth-century advocate for taking χριστός in Paul as a proper name, actually qualifies his argument at a crucial point. He writes that although χριστός in Paul is a proper name, "it is not a colorless proper name, however, but an honorific designation, whose content is supplied by the person and work of Jesus Christ."[17] A name, but not a colorless one. This caveat depends, of course, on the assumption that names are generally colorless but titles colorful; therefore, Dahl has to make room for a different kind of name, a name that is not colorless. Similarly, Udo Schnelle accepts the name-versus-title rubric but is unable to conclude on one side or the other: "For Paul, Χριστὸς Ἰησοῦς is a titular name, both title and name.... When combined with Ἰησοῦς, Χριστός is thus to be understood as a cognomen (surname) that also always has the overtones of its original titular significance."[18]

However, these hints of discontent with the terms of the debate have not been adequately heeded even by those who have expressed them. The fact that interpreters are forced to invoke or invent awkward concepts like "not colorless names" and "titular names" should have suggested that something was wrong with the question itself. In fact, the question as commonly posed—Is χριστός in Paul a name or a title?—rests upon two questionable assumptions: one an assumption about what names and titles are and how they work and the other an assumption about the onomastic categories that were available to Paul. Both assumptions, it turns out, are false.

How Names and Titles Mean

The first faulty assumption is that titles communicate significant information about the persons to whom they are applied, whereas proper names do not, that titles are "colorful," names "colorless," to paraphrase Dahl. This

---

17 Dahl, "Crucified Messiah," 37.

18 Udo Schnelle, *Apostle Paul: His Life and Theology* (trans. M. Eugene Boring; Grand Rapids, Mich.: Baker Academic, 2005), 439.

assumption can be, and has been, expressed in various ways. In his major study, N. T. Wright defines the problem in terms of connotation and denotation: Titles connote, whereas names merely denote.[19] That is, a title carries with it a sense or set of senses, but a name does nothing more than refer to a thing in the world. Titles have sense, but names have only reference. In philosophical terms, names are indexicals; they point to things in the world but do not say anything about those things. Or yet again, in linguistic terms, titles speak, while names only name.[20]

This question of the precise function of proper names is a long-standing problem in the philosophy of language and in linguistics.[21] Philosophers have been interested in proper names because, for some, they seem to offer an example of purely referential language, that is, of words that point directly to things in the world and do nothing else. The classic statement of this view is that of John Stuart Mill: "Proper names are not connotative: they denote the individuals who are called by them; but they do not indicate or imply any attributes as belonging to those individuals....A proper name [is] a word which answers the purpose of showing what thing it is we are talking about, but not of telling anything about it.... These have, strictly speaking, no signification."[22]

Mill's account of proper names exercised considerable influence through the nineteenth and into the twentieth century. A variation of the Millian view was advocated, for example, by the Cambridge philosopher and economist John Neville Keynes, who defended it from ostensible counterexamples. "Proper names of course become connotative when they are used to designate

---

19 See, e.g., Wright, "Messiah and the People of God," 19: "Since for Paul 'Jesus,' 'Christ,' and 'Lord' have the same denotation, a considerable overlap in his usage is inevitable: but the evidence will show that the two titles...had connotations which marked them off from the proper name 'Jesus.' "

20 These several theoretical issues (sense and reference, connotation and denotation, indexicality, proper and common names) are separate but related issues in the philosophy of language, but they are all invoked by Pauline interpreters in the question before us.

21 There is, of course, a mountain of secondary literature on the subject. In addition to John Stuart Mill, *A System of Logic, Ratiocinative and Inductive* (London: Parker, 1843) (discussed later), see the classic treatments of Gottlob Frege, "Über Sinn und Bedeutung," *Zeitschrift für Philosophie und philosophische Kritik* 100 (1892): 25–50; Bertrand Russell, "On Denoting," *Mind* 14 (1905): 479–493; John R. Searle, "Proper Names," *Mind* 67 (1958): 166–173; John McDowell, "On the Sense and Reference of a Proper Name," *Mind* 86 (1977): 159–185; Saul Kripke, *Naming and Necessity* (Cambridge, Mass.: Harvard University Press, 1980). Among recent literature see Scott Soames, *Reference and Description* (Princeton, N.J.: Princeton University Press, 2005). Basil Cottle has given apt expression to the vexed state of the question. A proper name, Cottle says, is "anything that you can't use in Scrabble" (Basil Cottle, *Names* [London: Thames and Hudson, 1983], 65).

22 Mill, *System of Logic*, 1.2.5.

a certain type of person; for example, a Diogenes, a Thomas, a Don Quixote, a Paul Pry, a Benedick, a Socrates. But, when so used, such names have really ceased to be proper names at all; and they have come to possess all the characters of general names."[23] That is, proper names do not connote. If a name connotes, then by definition it is no longer a proper name.

However, this Millian account of proper names is by no means agreed upon by philosophers, and some linguists have objected especially strongly to it.[24] In the early twentieth century, Otto Jespersen mounted a sophisticated argument against the Millian account of proper names. Jespersen makes explicit the contrast between Mill's interest in purely referential language (what Jespersen calls the "dictionary value" of a name) and the linguist's concern with describing the actual use of names by speakers and writers:

> What in my view is of prime importance is the way in which names are actually employed by speakers and understood by hearers. Now, every time a proper name is used in actual speech its value to both speaker and hearer is that of denoting one individual only.... Mill and his followers lay too much stress on what might be called the dictionary value of the name, and too little on its contextual value in the particular situation in which it is spoken or written.... In Mill's terminology, but in absolute contrast to his view, I should venture to say that proper names (as actually used) "connote" the greatest number of attributes.[25]

In this connection, Jespersen points to a linguistic phenomenon that is sometimes invoked in discussions of χριστός in Paul, namely the transition of a word from name to title.[26] On Jespersen's account, names can become titles

23 John Neville Keynes, *Studies and Exercises in Formal Logic* (New York: Macmillan, 1884), 21.

24 For a recent statement of the linguistic objection, see Michael J. Evans and Rainer Wimmer, "Searle's Theory of Proper Names, from a Linguistic Point of View," in *Speech Acts, Meaning, and Intention: Critical Approaches to the Philosophy of John R. Searle* (ed. Armin Burkhardt; Berlin: de Gruyter, 1990), 259–278, here 260: "The purely referential function is not the only one that proper names have in a natural language. Other aspects of these names are important for linguists...but philosophers...do not pay much attention to them."

25 Otto Jespersen, *The Philosophy of Grammar* (London: Allen & Unwin, 1924), 65–66.

26 Jespersen, *Philosophy of Grammar*, 66–67: "If proper names as actually understood did not connote many attributes, we should be at a loss to understand or explain the everyday phenomenon of a proper name becoming a common name.... In this way Caesar became the general name for Roman emperors, German Kaisers, and Russian tsars."

and vice versa because in actual use both have connotative value.[27] They are not, in fact, altogether different kinds of words. On the contrary:

> No sharp line can be drawn between common and proper names, the difference being one of degree rather than kind.... If the speaker wants to call up the idea of some person or thing, he has at his command in some cases a name specially applied to the individual concerned, that is, a name which in this particular situation will be understood as referring to it, or else he has to piece together by means of other words a composite denomination which is sufficiently precise for his purpose.[28]

In short, the difference between titles and names, common names and proper names, is relative, not absolute, and it lies in the speaker's deployment of the words, not in the nature of the words themselves.

Of course, this account may be more or less applicable to any particular language, depending on that language's own conventions of nomenclature.[29] The present majority opinion among students of ancient Greek onomastics is that it does apply there, that Greek nomenclature from the classical through the late antique period attested the convention of "appropriate names." Michael Crawford's recent comment is representative: "Names that are appropriate, that speak as well as name, are a feature already of Homer and the Old Comedy, for instance, and are indeed explicitly referred to by Aristophanes; there is thereafter a long tradition of discussion of such names, from Aristotle and Aristophanes of Byzantium, via Plautus, to Pliny the Elder and Donatus."[30]

---

27 Authors of fiction sometimes exploit this feature of language, as in the case of the "appropriate" names of characters in Anthony Trollope's *Chronicles of Barsetshire* series: Captain Cuttwater, Mr. Chaffanbrass, Mr. Hardlines, Mr. Oldeschole, Dr. Fillgrave, Mr. Gitemthruet, and so on. Such names, while apparently pleasing to readers, were not always so to critics (see "Mr. Trollope's Novels," *National Review* [October 1858], 416–435; repr. in *Anthony Trollope: The Critical Heritage* [ed. Donald Smalley; London: Routledge, 1996], 80–89).

28 Jespersen, *Philosophy of Grammar,* 70–71. But cf. Evans and Wimmer, "Searle's Theory of Proper Names," 26: "The common opinion of linguists...[is that] proper names are types of linguistic units, and part of the lexicon of a language, but are semantically different from so-called appellative words (roughly corresponding to common nouns), so that we need different techniques and kinds of description for the meanings of proper names versus appellatives."

29 Jespersen himself was a Dane who specialized in English linguistics.

30 Michael Crawford, "Mirabilia and Personal Names," in *Greek Personal Names: Their Value as Evidence* (ed. Simon Hornblower and Elaine Matthews; Proceedings of the British Academy 104; Oxford: Oxford University Press, 2000), 145–148, here 145.

In particular, it has been well documented that many ancient Greek names functioned to classify their bearers in one of a number of meaningful ways. Anna Morpurgo Davies has written about the ancient Greek evidence, "The primary role of personal names is to identify individuals, but personal names are also endowed with a strong classificatory function."[31] That is, Greek names related a variety of relevant demographic data about their bearers. As Anne Thompson has commented, "Personal names offer a picture of ancient Greek society, reflecting as they do language, landscape, population movement and mixture, family tradition and relations, the highest professions and humblest trades, historical events, local mythology and cults, politics, cultural values, physical and mental attributes."[32]

Doubtless, in ancient Greek as in other languages, a degree of de-etymologization will have occurred; personal names will have lost some of their original geographical, ethnic, family, or professional sense.[33] It is unclear, though, just in what cases and to what extent this process will have taken place. By way of comparison, Peter Fraser comments on some English geographic names—Blackstone, Browning, Greenhill—that they "seem very remote from their roots. We accept them without further thought, simply as surnames." Fraser suggests, however, that this was not the case for ancient Greek ethnic and geographic names. "We know very little about the psychological impact of names in the Greek world, but one or two passages enable us to see that in some cases the ethnic name was deliberate, and had not lost its specific content.... I feel it likely that the ethnic or topical link made more impact on the mind of the ancient Greek than it does with us in the [English] examples."[34]

---

31 Anna Morpurgo Davies, "Greek Personal Names and Linguistic Continuity," in *Greek Personal Names*, 15–40, here 20; citing the modern parallel of S. Smith-Bannister, *Names and Naming Patterns in England 1538–1700* (Oxford: Oxford University Press, 1997), 15: "Names can classify a person according to his or her sex, ethnic origin, family status, social status, and, in those societies which give different names to children at different stages in their life cycle, by age."

32 Anne Thompson, "Ancient Greek Personal Names," in *A History of Ancient Greek*, 677–692, here 687. The value of Greek personal names for social history has been widely recognized since the programmatic statement of J.-A. Letronne, "Observations philologiques et archéologiques sur l'étude des noms propres grecs," *Annales de l'Institut Archéologique* 17 (1845): 251–346.

33 But de-etymologization, even when it happens, is almost never complete. It sometimes leads to fascinating reuses, as with "the prohibition of titles of nobility in the USA, leading to such titles used as baptismal names, e.g., Duke Ellington" (Evans and Wimmer, "Searle's Theory of Proper Names," 271). As John Anderson has shown, "Surnames and titles illustrate that a name may contain a sense-bearing element.... De-etymologization doesn't lead to a complete loss of sense, but substitution of the limited sense [for the fuller one]" (John Mathieson Anderson, *The Grammar of Names* [Oxford: Oxford University Press, 2007], 93).

34 Peter M. Fraser, "Ethnics as Personal Names," in *Greek Personal Names*, 149–158, here 152.

There is good reason to think that Fraser is right about Greek ethnics, but even if not, it is in any case clear that many ancient Greek names did, in actual use, connote certain attributes of their bearers. As Steve Mason has observed in a context nearer to Paul, "Orators—and Josephus—did not forfeit their right to exploit the literal meaning of someone's name for the purpose of word-play, whether friendly or hostile."[35] In sum, in linguistics generally and in ancient Greek in particular, it is not the case that titles "mean" while proper names merely "refer." In fact, there were a variety of conventions in ancient Greek whereby certain types of names could connote things. The problem of χριστός in Paul cannot be solved simply by ruling in favor of either name or title. A more thorough account of ancient Greek naming is necessary.

Other Onomastic Possibilities

The second faulty assumption made by Pauline interpreters is that χριστός in Paul must be either a name or a title, that is, that those two onomastic categories were the only ones available to Paul.[36] It may be that modern speakers of German and English, at least, are accustomed to thinking of naming in this binary way, although in fact the rubric does not hold even in those languages.[37] In any case, the binary rubric is entirely inappropriate to the known naming conventions of ancient Greek. While Greek naming did not conform

---

35 Steve Mason, *Life of Josephus*, vol. 9 of *Flavius Josephus: Translation and Commentary* (ed. Steve Mason; Leiden: Brill, 2001), 8n20. On this convention, see further E. S. McCartney, "Puns and Plays on Proper Names," *Classical Journal* 14 (1919): 343–358; C. J. Fordyce, "Puns on Names in Greek," *CJ* 28 (1932): 44–46; Anthony Corbeill, *Controlling Laughter: Political Humor in the Late Roman Republic* (Princeton, N.J.: Princeton University Press, 1996), 57–98. A famous Latin example is the pun on the name of Rupilius Rex in Horace, *Sat.* 1.7: *per magnos, Brute, Deos te oro, qui reges consueris tollere, cur non hunc Regem iugulas*, "By the great gods I entreat you, Brutus, who are accustomed to doing away with kings [*reges*], why do you not kill this 'king' [*regem*]?" (Latin text ed. C. Smart, *The Works of Horace* [2 vols; Philadelphia: Whetham, 1836]).

36 There is irony in this, since New Testament interpreters have spent a great deal of creative energy mining Roman onomastics for categories pertinent to Paul's own name. See, e.g., G. A. Harrer, "Saul Who Is Also Called Paul," *Harvard Theological Review* 33 (1940): 19–34; A. N. Sherwin-White, *Roman Society and Roman Law in the New Testament* (Oxford: Clarendon, 1963), 153–154; F. F. Bruce, *Paul: Apostle of the Heart Set Free* (Exeter: Paternoster, 1977), 38; Colin J. Hemer, "The Name of Paul," *Tyndale Bulletin* 36 (1985): 179–183; T. J. Leary, "Paul's Improper Name," *NTS* 38 (1992): 467–469; Stephen B. Chapman, "Saul/Paul: Onomastics, Typology, and Christian Scripture," in *The Word Leaps the Gap: Essays on Scripture and Theology in Honor of Richard B. Hays* (ed. J. Ross Wagner et al.; Grand Rapids, Mich.: Eerdmans, 2008), 214–243.

37 On the diverse categories of German nomenclature see Adolf Bach, *Deutsche Namenkunde* (2d ed.; 3 vols; Heidelberg: Winter, 1952–1956), especially vol. 1, *Die deutschen Personennamen*. On English, see Elsdon C. Smith, *The Story of Our Names* (New York: Harper, 1950).

to as strict a pattern as the Roman *tria nomina*, it nevertheless had a number of standard features.[38]

In keeping with the Indo-European pattern and in contrast to Roman practice, a single name was the norm for Greeks, both male and female. In classifying Greek names, modern historians follow the precedent of the Peripatetic Clearchus of Soli (fourth–third centuries B.C.E.), who distinguishes between simple and compound names (ἁπλᾶ and σύνθετα ὀνόματα) and between theophoric and secular names (θεοφόρα and ἄθεα ὀνόματα).[39] Morphologically, a Greek name could be either simple or compound. If simple, it could be identical to a noun or an adjective or derived from one by means of a suffix (so the adjective θρασύς, "bold," yields the names Θράσυς, Θρασίων, Θράσυλλα, etc.). If compound, the possibilities are myriad (e.g., Θρασύ-τιμος/η/εία, Τιμο-θράσυς/ιων/υλλα). "Compound names could, with certain exceptions, take their elements in either order.... [The elements] combined to create thousands of different name-forms, some occurring in more than 50 different forms."[40]

Etymologically, a Greek name could be either theophoric or secular, that is, deriving from the name of a god or not doing so (Clearchus cites the examples of Διονύσιος and Κλεώνυμος, respectively). Theophoric names are a justly famous and numerous class, but so-called secular names in fact derive

---

38 The following account closely follows the programmatic statement of Elaine Matthews, "names, personal, Greek," in *Oxford Classical Dictionary* (3d ed.; Oxford: Oxford University Press, 2003), 1022–1024. The classic study on the subject is still Friedrich Bechtel, *Die historischen Personennamen des Griechischen bis zur Kaiserzeit* (Halle: Niemeyer, 1917). The first modern lexicon of Greek names is W. Pape and G. E. Benseler, *Wörterbuch der griechischen Eigennamen* (Braunschweig: 1863–1870), which covers only epigraphic evidence and only that collected in *Corpus inscriptionum graecarum* (4 vols.; Berlin, 1828–1877). Friedrich Preisigke, *Namenbuch* (Heidelberg: self-published, 1922) catalogs the papyrological evidence, and Rudolf Münsterberg, *Die Beamtennamen auf dem griechischen Munzen* (3 vols; New York: Hildesheim, 1911–1927), the numismatic evidence. The exhaustive work in progress of Peter M. Fraser and Elaine Matthews, eds., *A Lexicon of Greek Personal Names* (Oxford: Oxford University Press, 1987–) promises to supersede all of these.

39 The relevant passage (Clearchus frg. 86, apud Athenaeus, *Deipnosophistae* 10.448e) runs as follows: ἐν ὀνόματι δέ, οἷον ἐροῦμεν ὀνόματα ἁπλᾶ ἢ σύνθετα δισύλλαβα, οὗ μορφή τις ἐμφαίνεται τραγικὴ ἢ πάλιν ταπεινή, ἢ ἄθεα ὀνόματα, οἷον Κλεώνυμος, ἢ θεοφόρα, οἷον Διονύσιος; "[The γρῖφοι or riddles] also pertain to names, such as when we speak simple names or complex two-part names, by which some tragic or humble figure is meant, either secular names like Cleonymus or theophoric ones like Dionysius" (Greek text ed. Georg Kaibel, *Athenaei Naucratitae deipnosophistarum libri* xv [3 vols; Leipzig: Teubner, 1887–1890]).

40 Matthews, "names, personal, Greek," 1023; cf. the Roman naming system, where praenomina in the late Republican period, for example, comprised a pool of fewer than twenty names.

from a multitude of diverse etymological sources.[41] Matthews concedes, "It is not possible to do more than hint at the enormous range of concepts drawn on to form names," citing as examples animals (e.g., Λεοντίσκος), weapons (e.g., Θωρακίδης), body parts (e.g., Κεφαλίων), plants (e.g., Ἀμπελίς), rivers (e.g., Ἀσώπιος, from the Asopus river in Boetia), leadership (e.g., Δήμαρχος), militarism (e.g., Ἀγέστρατος), civic organization (e.g., Ἀρχέπολις), saving or defending (e.g., Ἀλεξίδημος), strength (e.g., Κράτιππος), beauty or nobility (e.g., Καλλίξενος), honor (e.g., Φιλοτίμη), reputation (e.g., Κλεομήδης), abstract nouns (especially in women's names: e.g., Ἀρέτη), and some curious instances of undesirable physical characteristics (e.g., Αἰσχρος).[42]

In addition to the personal name, ancient Greek knew of a number of secondary onomastic categories by which persons could be identified under special circumstances. The most important of these is the patronymic, the father's name, usually in the genitive (e.g., Ἀλέξανδρος Φιλίππου, "Alexander [son] of Philip") but also sometimes in an adjectival form ending in -ιος or -εια (e.g., Φιλίννα Ἀριστάρχεια, "Philinna [daughter] of Aristarchus"), which was commonly appended to a name for identification in public affairs.[43] By a similar logic, the demotic designated a person by his native deme in cities that were organized in that way (e.g., Δημοσθένης [ὁ] Παιανιεύς, "Demosthenes from the deme of Paiania"), and the ethnic designated a person by his native city or region when abroad (e.g., Φίλων [ὁ] Ἀλεξανδρεύς, "Philo the Alexandrian," or Φίλων [ὁ] Ἰουδαῖος, "Philo the Jew").[44]

Other types of names, however, fall under none of these standard headings; they are neither personal nor family nor geographical, and they are often expressly flagged when used (ὁ ἐπικαλούμενος, etc.). Elaine Matthews proposes an umbrella category of "secondary names" that were used of some persons: "Secondary names given in the Classical and Hellenistic periods to

---

41 On theophoric names see recently Robert Parker, "Theophoric Names and the History of Greek Religion," in *Greek Personal Names*, 53–80.

42 Matthews, "names, personal, Greek," 1023; this last category is amply attested in the Jewish onomasticon of the same period, discussed later.

43 Similar but less common are the matronymic (mother's name) and papponymic (grandfather's name); see B. H. McLean, *An Introduction to Greek Epigraphy of the Hellenistic Periods* (Ann Arbor: University of Michigan Press, 2002), 93–96.

44 However, on the thorny problems surrounding the ethnic Ἰουδαῖος, see Shaye J. D. Cohen, "Ioudaios, Iudaeus, Judaean, Jew," in *The Beginnings of Jewishness* (Berkeley: University of California Press, 2001), 69–106; Steve Mason, "Jews, Judaeans, Judaizing, Judaism: Problems of Categorization in Ancient History," *Journal for the Study of Judaism* 38 (2007): 457–512; and Daniel R. Schwartz, "'Judaean' or 'Jew'? How Should We Translate IOUDAIOS in Josephus?" in *Jewish Identity in the Greco-Roman World* (ed. Jorg Frey et al.; Arbeiten zur Geschichte des antiken Judentums und des Urchristentums 71; Leiden: Brill, 2007), 3–27.

public figures such as politicians, courtesans, and kings, usually linked by ὁ/ἡ, ὁ/ἡ ἐπικαλούμενος/η, etc., did not break this rule [i.e., the one-name rule], since they were nicknames and were not handed down in the family."[45] Paul's χριστός, if it is a Greek name, is patently not a birth name, a patronym, an ethnic, or a demotic. It may be, then, that it falls somewhere within this category of secondary names, a possibility to which I return later.

This survey of ancient Greek onomastics goes a long way toward clarifying the possibilities open to Paul, but Paul, as a Greek-speaking Jew in the eastern Roman Empire, operated under multiple cultural influences.[46] Jewish naming in the Hellenistic and Roman periods had certain characteristic features of its own.[47] Tal Ilan classifies Jewish names under six etymological headings: biblical names, Greek names, Latin names, Persian names, nonbiblical Semitic names in Hebrew characters, and nonbiblical Semitic names in Greek characters.[48] In the land of Israel, the most popular names by far are names of members of the Hasmonean dynasty, especially Simon, Judah, and Eleazar for males, and with just two names—Mariam and Salome—accounting for some 48 percent of all female names in the corpus.[49] Interestingly, Ilan also shows that "the names of Hellenistic monarchs who visited or resided in the east gained some ascendancy among Palestinian Jews," citing instances of Ἀλέξανδρος, Ἀντίγονος, Ἀντίοχος, Πτολεμαῖος, Φίλιππος, Βερενίκη, and Κλεοπάτρα.[50]

---

45 Matthews, "names, personal, Greek," 1022. Cf. the explanation of McLean, *Introduction to Greek Epigraphy,* 99–100: "Perhaps under Roman influence, Greek began to adopt surnames in official documents, especially in Egypt, Syria, and Anatolia.... The surname was connected to the personal name with the ὁ καί construction, or, less commonly, with ὁ ἐπικαλούμενος, ὁ λεγόμενος, or ὁ ἐπίκλησις, and was used to indicate ancestry, disambiguate homonymous persons, or include an indigenous name."

46 On the complexities of Paul's overlapping cultural contexts, see especially Wayne A. Meeks, *The First Urban Christians: The Social World of the Apostle Paul* (2d ed.; New Haven: Yale University Press, 2003).

47 The authoritative resource is Tal Ilan, ed., *Lexicon of Jewish Names in Late Antiquity: Part I: Palestine 330 BCE–200 CE* (TSAJ 91; Tübingen: Mohr Siebeck, 2002), which, however, covers only names attested in the land of Israel. Cf. the older and still invaluable collections *Corpus papyrorum judaicorum* (3 vols; ed. Victor A. Tcherikover and Alexander Fuks; Cambridge, Mass.: Harvard University Press, 1957–1964); and *Corpus inscriptionum judaicarum* (ed. Jean-Baptiste Frey; New York: Ktav, 1975).

48 Ilan, *Lexicon,* 4–16. The largest classes are Greek names and nonbiblical Hebrew names, each of which accounts for roughly 29 percent of all names in the corpus.

49 Ilan, *Lexicon,* 4–9. One exception to this pattern is the biblical name Joseph, which is second only to Simon in popularity.

50 Ilan, *Lexicon,* 11.

Most relevant to our question, whether Paul uses χριστός as a personal name, is the phenomenon of second or alternative names among Jews in antiquity. "Second names were not very common among Palestinian Jews at the time. However, under the influence of foreign cultures, which sometimes induced Jews to adopt a second name, and particularly under Roman influence where two, three and even more names were the rule, we sometimes find Jews bearing double names."[51] Ilan provides a rough taxonomy of types of Jewish second names. "Family (or sur)names were unknown in ancient Judaism."[52] But papponyms and patronyms were common (e.g., Bar Timaeus), and geography (e.g., Eleazar of Narot) and sectarian affiliation (e.g., Simon the Zealot) were also sources of second names.[53] On another proposed type, Ilan comments, "Much has been made of the supposed double names that Jews bore—Greek corresponding to Hebrew according to sound," citing as examples שמעון/Σίμων, ישוע/Ἰάσων, and ברכה/Βερενίκη. Ilan, though, actually turns up no other instances of Hebrew/Greek homophonous names than these three often-cited examples, suggesting that the phenomenon was not prevalent after all.[54] She also documents several standardized types of name pairs: Hebrew-Greek translation equivalent pairs (e.g., Thomas Didymus), biblical name plus Greek second name (e.g., Judah Aristobulus), biblical name plus Latin second name (e.g., Saul Paul), and given name plus nickname (e.g., Eleazar Goliath).[55] Most interestingly for our purposes, Ilan notes several instances of what she calls "titles" that are used as second names, namely סבא/זקן/πρεσβύτερος, "the elder"; קטן/νεοτέρας, "the younger"; אבא, "father"; אמא, "mother"; בהן, "the priest."[56]

Ilan's *Lexicon* covers only Jewish names attested in Palestine, and no comparable collection yet exists for Jewish names in the Diaspora. Margaret Williams has contributed substantially toward this end, however.[57] Williams documents the

---

51 Ilan, *Lexicon*, 47.

52 Ilan, *Lexicon*, 46. She qualifies, however, "Only families of importance had a name, which was carried by its members after their first name. Sometimes this was the name of an ancient ancestor, but usually this cannot be proven. Most of the time a family name appears in the form 'son of x,' making it hardly distinguishable from a father's name, or a nickname."

53 Ilan, *Lexicon*, 32–34.

54 Ilan, *Lexicon*, 11.

55 Ilan, *Lexicon*, 47.

56 Ilan, *Lexicon*, 33; cf. the enduring use of Cohen as a Jewish surname in a number of modern languages.

57 See Margaret H. Williams, "The Jews of Corycus: A Neglected Diasporan Community from Roman Times," *JSJ* 25 (1994): 274–286; Margaret H. Williams, "Exarchon: An Unsuspected Jewish Liturgical Title from Ancient Rome," *JJS* 51 (2000): 77–87; Margaret H. Williams, "Jewish Festal Names in Antiquity: A Neglected Area of Onomastic Research," *JSJ* 36 (2005): 21–40; Margaret H. Williams, "The Use of Alternative Names by Diaspora Jews in Late Antiquity," *JSJ* 38 (2007):

use of alternative names by Diaspora Jews in antiquity and concludes that "the practice was much less frequent than has been claimed and…that the most likely reason for that is that Jews, unlike Egyptians, did not use onomastics very much to maintain and assert their 'ethnic' identity."[58] In particular, Williams shows, among Diaspora Jews there are virtually no instances of the derogatory nicknames that are relatively common among Palestinian Jews of the same period.[59] Williams suggests a threefold taxonomy of reasons for which some Diaspora Jews did take alternative names: (1) "cases where the need to distinguish homonymous members of the community was present," (2) "cases where context is likely to have been the key determinant," and (3) "religious conversion as the reason for the adoption of an alternative name."[60] This general pattern seems to have held until the early Byzantine period, "when, in reaction to certain Christian naming practices, a distinctively Jewish onomasticon, in which undeclined Hebrew names of a patriotic character bulked large, started to take shape."[61]

The Romans, too, had their own naming conventions, quite distinct from the Greek and wider Indo-European pattern, which (for freeborn male Roman citizens) comprised the well-known *tria nomina*: the praenomen or personal name, the nomen (*gentilicium*) or clan name, and the cognomen.[62] The pool of praenomina was quite small. For males in the late republic and early empire, it comprised only eighteen names, with just five of these accounting for most

---

307–327; Margaret H. Williams, "Semitic Name-Use by Jews in Roman Asia Minor and the Dating of the Aphrodisias Stele Inscriptions," in *Old and New Worlds in Greek Onomastics* (ed. Elaine Matthews; PBA 148; Oxford: Oxford University Press, 2007), 173–197.

58 Williams, "Alternative Names," 323.

59 Ilan, *Lexicon*, 46, cites as an example שמעון בן גנס, "Simon son of Midget." In *Life* 3–4, Josephus numbers among his ancestors Σίμων ὁ Ψελλὸς ἐπικαλούμενος, "Simon called the Stutterer," and Ματθίας ὁ Κυρτὸς ἐπικληθείς, "Matthias called Humpback." Steve Mason suggests that such nicknames may have been used in priestly families like Josephus's to identify nonserving priests with reference to their disqualifying blemishes and that Josephus may have used them to "Romanize" his ancestry by analogy to the blemish-related cognomina held by some Roman nobility (Mason, *Life of Josephus*, 7–8n20).

60 Williams, "Alternative Names," 314–323.

61 Williams, "Alternative Names," 313–314; Williams, "Semitic Name-Use by Jews in Roman Asia Minor," 196–197, cites examples of such "heritage names" attested from the stele at Aphrodisias: Beniamin, Eussabathios, Iael, Iako, Iakob, Ioph, Ioseph, Eioseph, Ioudas, Eioudas, Iesseos, Iosoua, Ioses, Sabathios, Samouel.

62 So Gaius Julius Caesar had the personal name Gaius, belonged to the *gens Julia* (or the *Julii*), and also had his father's cognomen. In Caesar's case, actually, his name was identical to his father's in all three terms. My sketch of Roman naming follows that of Heikki Solin, "names, personal, Roman," *OCD*, 1024–1026. His *OCD* article condenses the findings of Heikki Solin, *Namenpaare: Eine Studie zur römischen Namengebung* (Helsinki: Societas Scientiarum Fennica, 1990). Cf. also the classic study of Theodor Mommsen, "Die römischen Eigennamen," in *Römische Forschungen* (2 vols; Berlin: Weidmann, 1864), 1:3–68.

persons.[63] The nomen probably corresponds to the single hereditary name of the Indo-European pattern and represents the most ancient Italian practice, as some archaic Latin inscriptions suggest.[64] The cognomen is the most complicated part of the Roman naming system, coming into use relatively late and changing in significance over time. "Originally unofficial surnames for individuals, thus complementing the function of the praenomina, the early cognomina of the Roman nobility became for the most part hereditary, designating a branch of a larger *gens*."[65]

It is often pointed out that some cognomina seem to have been derived from nicknames (e.g., Cicero, "chickpea"; Catulus, "puppy"; Scaurus, "swollen ankles"). In such cases, however, the etymologies usually lie in the distant past. "Chickpea" was not the nickname of Marcus Tullis Cicero but rather his hereditary family name, although it presumably was at first a nickname of some unknown ancestor of his. This historical obscurity is the reason that ancient biographers often relate speculative etymologies for the cognomina of important Romans.[66] A related phenomenon occurs when modern writers

---

63 Solin, "names, personal, Roman," 1024. The five most common are Gaius, Lucius, Marcus, Publius, and Quintus. The other male praenomina are Aulus, Decimus, Gnaeus, Manius, Numerius, Servius, Sextus, Spurius, Tiberius, Titus, and the Oscan names Salvius, Statius, and Vibius.

64 Solin, "names, personal, Roman," 1024. Romulus and Remus are sometimes invoked as analogies, but already the eighth-century B.C.E. king Numa Pompilius is known by a double name.

65 Solin, "names, personal, Roman," 1024. On the complex history of the cognomen, see Bruce A. Marshall, "Crassus and the Cognomen Dives," *Historia* 22 (1973): 459–467, here 459–460:

> There are three basic applications [of the term], and the Republican writers refer to all of them as cognomina. The original use was as a "nick-name" following the praenomen and *gentilicium*, and this is what later writers distinguished by the term agnomen.... However, individual agnomina came to be transmitted to children, and thus came to be used to designate a familia within a gens. This is the origin of the Roman third name, and is the commonest use of the cognomen.... The third application of cognomen is a slight extension of this: that is the case where an agnomen becomes a family cognomen and provides a fourth, and sometimes even a fifth, name.

66 See, e.g., Plutarch, *Cicero* 1.3–6 (trans. Bernadotte Perrin; LCL; Cambridge, Mass.: Harvard University Press, 1919):

> The first member of the family who was surnamed Cicero seems to have been worthy of note, and for that reason his posterity did not reject the surname, but were fond of it, although many made it a matter of raillery. For *cicer* is the Latin name for chickpea, and this ancestor of Cicero, as it would seem, had a faint dent in the end of his nose like the cleft of a chickpea, from which he acquired his surname. Cicero himself, however, whose Life I now write, when he first entered public life and stood for office and his friends thought he ought to drop or change the name, is said to have replied with spirit that he would strive to make the name of Cicero more illustrious than such names as Scaurus or Catulus. Moreover, when he was quaestor in Sicily and was dedicating to the gods a piece of silver plate, he had his first two names inscribed thereon, the Marcus and the Tullius, but instead of the third, by way of jest, he ordered the artificer to engrave a chickpea in due sequence. This, then, is what is told about his name.

simply confuse ancient nicknames with cognomina. For example, Caligula ("little boots") was not the cognomen of the third emperor of Rome but rather a true nickname.[67] Caligula's cognomen was Caesar, his full personal name Gaius Julius Caesar Augustus Germanicus.[68]

As Caligula's nomenclature illustrates, the imperial period witnessed the advent of so-called agnomina or supernomina, roughly nicknames, a development that was probably occasioned by the fixing of cognomina as hereditary names.[69] Some well-known agnomina are, for example, Pius, "virtuous"; Superbus, "haughty"; and Pulcher, "handsome."[70] An agnomen was sometimes appended to the name with the marker *qui/quae et* or *sive* (cf. Greek ὁ καί). A similar convention is the use of the so-called *signa*, which were appended to the name with the marker *signo* (e.g., Trebius Iustus signo Asellus). Unlike the venerable *tria nomina*, the *signa* "are attested from the end of the 2nd cent. AD and also characterized the lower classes."[71] The so-called detached *signa* in Latin inscriptions from the later imperial period possibly "derived from Greek acclamations," but this is contested.[72]

Grammarians of the imperial period also include under the heading "agnomina" the *cognomina ex virtute*, or victory titles, that is, honorifics corresponding to the place names of successful campaigns by military leaders (e.g.,

---

67　For this mistake see, e.g., H. F. Pelham, *Outlines of Roman History* (4th ed.; London: Rivingtons, 1905), 437n5.

68　The agnomen Germanicus he took from his biological father (the general Germanicus Julius Caesar), and the honorific Augustus from his adoptive father (the emperor Tiberius).

69　Solin, "names, personal, Roman," 1025. Agnomina are either identical with or a subset of supernomina, depending on the author's usage of the term. On the category see M. Lambertz, "Zur Ausbreitung des Supernomen oder Signum im römischen Reiche," *Glotta* 4 (1913): 78–143; 5 (1914): 99–169; Iiro Kajanto, *Supernomina: A Study in Latin Epigraphy* (Helsinki: Societas Scientarum Fennica, 1966).

70　For ancient witnesses to this practice see Pseudo-Probus, *Instituta artium* (ed. Heinrich Keil, *Grammatici latini*, IV, 119, 31–33): *propria hominum nomina in quattuor species dividuntur, praenomen nomen cognomen agnomen: praenomen, ut puta Publius, nomen Cornelius, cognomen Scipio, agnomen Africanus*; "People's personal names are divided into four types: praenomen, nomen, cognomen and agnomen: praenomen, for example, Publius, nomen Cornelius, cognomen Scipio, and agnomen Africanus." Likewise, Marius Victorinus's commentary on Cicero, *De inventione* (ed. Karl Halm, *Rhetores latini*, 215, ll. 2–5): *Iam agnomen extrinsecus venit, et venit tribus modis, aut ex animo aut ex corpore aut ex fortuna: ex animo, sicut Superbus et Pius, ex corpore, sicut Crassus et Pulcher, ex fortuna, sicut Africanus et Creticus*; "The agnomen comes from without and in three ways: either from character or from body or from circumstance: from character, so Superbus and Pius; from body, so Crassus and Pulcher; or from achievements, so Africanus and Creticus."

71　Solin, "names, personal, Roman," 1025.

72　See Solin, "names, personal, Roman," 1025; but cf. Lloyd B. Urdahl, review of Kajanto, *Supernomina*, in *CJ* 63 (1967): 140–141.

Africanus, Britannicus, Germanicus, Creticus).[73] So, as in Pseudo-Probus's example, Publius Cornelius Scipio was granted the victory title Africanus for his defeat of Hannibal at the battle of Zama near Carthage in the Second Punic War. This ought not to be confused with an ethnic; the sense is not "Scipio the African" but "Scipio the victor in Africa." So significant was this victory title that Scipio came to be referred to most of all by his cognomen plus agnomen: Scipio Africanus. Despite the English rendering "victory title," these are not really titles (either of office or of competence) but names (hence *cognomina ex virtute*). As such, they present an interesting parallel to some Greek secondary names.

It is important to note, however, that Greek and Jewish second names are not cognomina simply by virtue of their occurring in the Roman period. The Roman onomasticon's influence on Greek naming was significant but not total. "In the Roman, and especially the imperial period, significant changes in [Greek] nomenclature took place....A Greek with Roman citizenship would usually record the praenomen and nomen...and retain the Greek name in the cognomen," resulting in formulations like Τίτος Φλάβιος Ἀλκιβιάδης. Nevertheless, "practice was very varied. In absorbing Roman citizenship into their nomenclature Greeks showed as much ingenuity and license as they had in forming their own names."[74] Meanwhile, Roman influence on Jewish naming was not nearly as great as Greek influence had been. "Latin names, which were borne by Roman officials in the East, did catch on occasionally.... [But] very rarely can such distinctions [viz. praenomen, nomen, cognomen] be made with relationship to Jews who bore Latin names. Most of them were not Roman citizens, and thus did not belong to any of the Roman *gens* [sic]."[75] Whether or not Paul himself was a Roman citizen (cf. Acts 16:37–38; 22:25–29; 25:10–11), he would have had no reason to think that Jesus of Nazareth had been a Roman citizen or that χριστός was the latter's cognomen, strictly speaking.

Personal Names in Paul

If Paul did refer to Jesus with a real double name, it would be a striking exception to Paul's own general practice. In the seven undisputed letters, Paul names

---

73 On victory titles see Peter Kneissl, *Die Siegestitulatur der römischen Kaiser: Untersuchungen zu d. Siegerbeinamen d. 1. u. 2. Jahrhunderts* (Hypomnemata 23; Göttingen: Vandenhoeck & Ruprecht, 1969), 91–96.

74 Matthews, "names, personal, Greek," 1023.

75 Ilan, *Lexicon*, 13.

some fifty-five people, and he almost invariably uses a single personal name for each, never an alternate name or a combined form.[76] Paul's single-named persons are the following: Phoebe (Rom 16:1), Prisca (Rom 16:3; 1 Cor 16:19), Aquila (Rom 16:3; 1 Cor 16:19), Epenetus (Rom 16:5), Mary (Rom 16:6), Andronicus (Rom 16:7), Junia (Rom 16:7), Ampliatus (Rom 16:8), Urbanus (Rom 16:9), Stachys (Rom 16:9), Apelles (Rom 16:10), Aristobulus (Rom 16:10), Herodion (Rom 16:11), Narcissus (Rom 16:11), Tryphena (Rom 16:12), Tryphosa (Rom 16:12), Persis (Rom 16:12), Rufus (Rom 16:13), Asyncritus (Rom 16:14), Phlegon (Rom 16:14), Hermes (Rom 16:14), Patrobas (Rom 16:14), Hermas (Rom 16:14), Philologus (Rom 16:15), Julia (Rom 16:15), Nereus (Rom 16:15), Olympas (Rom 16:15), Timothy (Rom 16:21; 1 Cor 4:17; 16:10; 2 Cor 1:1, 19; Phil 1:1; 2:19; 1 Thess 1:1; 3:2, 6; Phlm 1), Lucius (Rom 16:21), Jason (Rom 16:21), Sosipater (Rom 16:21), Sosthenes (1 Cor 1:1), Chloe (1 Cor 1:11), Apollos (1 Cor 1:12; 3:4, 5, 6, 22; 4:6; 16:12), Stephanas (1 Cor 1:16; 16:15, 17), Barnabas (1 Cor 9:6; Gal 2:1, 9, 13), James (1 Cor 15:7; Gal 1:19; 2:9, 12), Fortunatus (1 Cor 16:17), Achaicus (1 Cor 16:17), Silvanus (2 Cor 1:19; 1 Thess 1:1), Titus (2 Cor 2:13; 7:6, 13, 14; 8:6, 16, 23; 12:18; Gal 2:1, 3), Aretas (2 Cor 11:32), John (Gal 2:9), Epaphroditus (Phil 2:25; 4:18), Euodia (Phil 4:2), Syntyche (Phil 4:2), Philemon (Phlm 1), Apphia (Phlm 2), Archippus (Phlm 2), Onesimus (Phlm 10), Epaphras (Phlm 23), Demas (Phlm 23), Aristarcus (Phlm 24), and Luke (Phlm 24).[77]

---

76 Cf. Acts, where double names appear with some frequency. These include several Roman names (the proconsul Sergius Paulus [Acts 13:7], the God-worshiper Titius Justus [Acts 18:7], the commander Claudius Lysias [Acts 23:26], and the governor Porcius Festus [Acts 24:27]); an Aramaic-Greek double name (Tabitha/Dorcas [Acts 9:36]); a Hebrew-Latin double name (John/Mark [Acts 15:36]); an agnomen (Simeon called Niger [Acts 13:1]); and an ethnic (Lucius of Cyrene [Acts 13:1]).

77 I exclude from this list two marginal cases: σύζυγος (Phil 4:3), which has yet to be attested anywhere else as a Greek personal name ("Syzygus") and so is better understood as a common noun ("yokefellow"), and Καῖσαρ in the phrase ἐκ τῆς Καίσαρος οἰκίας, "those from the household of Caesar" (Phil 4:22), since this is probably a technical reference to the *familia Caesaris* (on which see P. R. C. Weaver, *Familia Caesaris: A Social Study of the Emperor's Freedmen and Slaves* [Cambridge: Cambridge University Press, 1972]). The same pattern generally holds in the disputed Pauline letters: Tychicus (Eph 6:21; Col 4:7; 2 Tim 4:12; Titus 3:12), Timothy (Col 1:1; 2 Thess 1:1; 1 Tim 1:2, 18; 6:20; 2 Tim 1:2), Epaphras (Col 1:7; 4:12), Onesimus (Col 4:9), Aristarchus (Col 4:10), Mark (Col 4:10; 2 Tim 4:11), Barnabas (Col 4:10), Luke (Col 4:14; 2 Tim 4:11), Demas (Col 4:14; 2 Tim 4:10), Nympha (Col 4:15), Archippus (Col 4:17), Silvanus (2 Thess 1:1), Hymenaeus (1 Tim 1:20; 2 Tim 2:17), Alexander (1 Tim 1:20; 2 Tim 4:14), Lois (2 Tim 1:5), Eunice (2 Tim 1:5), Phygelus (2 Tim 1:15), Hermogenes (2 Tim 1:15), Onesiphorus (2 Tim 1:16; 2 Tim 4:19), Philetus (2 Tim 2:17), Crescens (2 Tim 4:10), Titus (2 Tim 4:10; Titus 1:4), Carpus (2 Tim 4:13), Prisca (2 Tim 4:19), Aquila (2 Tim 4:19), Erastus (2 Tim 4:20), Trophimus (2 Tim 4:20), Eubulus (2 Tim 4:21), Pudens (2 Tim 4:21), Linus (2 Tim 4:21), Claudia (2 Tim 4:21), Artemas (Titus 3:12), Zenas (Titus 3:13), and Apollos (Titus 3:13). But cf. Jesus who is called Justus (Col 4:11), and Pontius Pilate (1 Tim 6:13).

There is only one exception to this pattern.[78] Paul names Cephas eight times (1 Cor 1:12; 3:22; 9:5; 15:5; Gal 1:18; 2:9, 11, 14) and speaks of Peter twice (in quick succession: Gal 2:7, 8), but he never uses the two together as a double name.[79] This, together with the interpretive problems posed by the so-called Antioch incident, has led some interpreters to suppose that by "Peter" and "Cephas" Paul means two different persons, the former the apostle and the latter someone else.[80] This remains a minority position, however, and the evidence is better accounted for on the assumption that Paul knows and uses both the translated and the transliterated form of Peter's name.[81]

Altogether different from Cephas/Peter are the few persons for whom Paul uses one name form and Acts another. These are as follows: Prisca (Rom 16:3; 1 Cor 16:19; cf. Priscilla in Acts 18:2, 18, 26), Sosipater (Rom 16:21; cf. Sopater in Acts 20:4), Apollos (1 Cor 1:12; 3:4, 5, 6, 22; 4:6; 16:12; cf. Apollonius in Acts 18:24), and Silvanus (2 Cor 1:19; 1 Thess 1:1; cf. Silas in Acts 15–18). However, these are differences between Paul and Acts, not alternate names within the Pauline letters themselves.[82]

---

78 Epaphroditus of Philippi (Phil 2:25; 4:18) and Epaphras of Colossae (Phlm 23), although the forms of their names are related, are different persons, and so do not constitute an exception. Similarly, Udo Borse ("Timotheus und Titus, Abgesandte Pauli im Dienst des Evangeliums," in *Der Diakon: Wiederentdeckung und Erneuerung seines Dienstes* [ed. J. G. Ploger and H. J. Weber; Freiburg: Herder, 1980], 27–43) and Richard G. Fellows ("Was Titus Timothy?" *JSNT* 81 [2001]: 33–58) have suggested that Timothy and Titus in the undisputed Pauline letters, because of their similar prosopographic features, are alternate names for the same person. The positive evidence for this hypothesis, however, is too meager.

79 Cf. John 1:42, where the two are used together: Κηφᾶς, ὃ ἑρμηνεύεται Πέτρος, "Cephas, which is translated Peter."

80 So already Clement of Alexandria, *Hyp.* 5, apud Eusebius, *Hist. eccl.* 1.12.2, who suggests that the Cephas of Galatians 1–2 is not the apostle Peter but one of the Seventy (Luke 10:1–24); see also Kirsopp Lake, "Simon, Cephas, Peter," *HTR* 14 (1921): 95–97; and the response of George La Piana, "Cephas and Peter in the Epistle to the Galatians," *HTR* 14 (1921): 187–193; and more recently Bart D. Ehrman, "Cephas and Peter," *JBL* 109 (1990): 463–474; and the response of Dale C. Allison, "Cephas and Peter: One and the Same," *JBL* 111 (1992): 489–495.

81 Among recent treatments, see especially Markus Bockmuehl, "Simon Peter's Names in the Jewish Sources," *JJS* 55 (2004): 58–80, especially 76:

Even in the Aramaic-speaking churches of first-century Judaea, it was this unique appellation [viz. Cephas] that most clearly distinguished Peter. This realisation may in turn explain why Paul retains this nomenclature as his own preferred usage, after visiting "the churches of Judaea that are in Christ" deliberately in order to "make the acquaintance of Cephas" (Gal 1:18, 22).

82 On this phenomenon see the comment of W. M. Ramsay, *St. Paul the Traveller and the Roman Citizen* (London: Hodder & Stoughton, 1895), 268: "Luke regularly uses the language of conversation, in which the diminutive forms were usual; and so he speaks of Priscilla, Sopatros and Silas always, though Paul speaks of Prisca, Sosipatros and Silvanus"; see also the form Apollonius (Acts 18:24) for Apollos, which is probably not a diminutive, however.

With the significant exception of titles for God and Jesus, Paul actually uses titles for persons very rarely. He certainly does so at 2 Cor 11:32, where he refers to an unnamed ἐθνάρχης, "ethnarch" or "governor," and to Aretas ὁ βασιλεύς, "the king." The mention of Phoebe as a προστάτις (Rom 16:2) is best understood thus, as meaning "patron."[83] Erastus the οἰκονόμος τῆς πόλεως (Rom 16:23) has been much discussed, and the designation is probably best understood as a Greek translation equivalent for a level of the municipal *cursus honorum* at Corinth, perhaps quaestor.[84] Καῖσαρ in the expression οἱ ἐκ τῆς Καίσαρος οἰκίας (Phil 4:22; cf. Latin *familia Caesaris*) is functionally a title of office, "emperor," even if it was the cognomen of the Julio-Claudian emperors.[85] With terms for particular church leaders, it is sometimes difficult to distinguish polite designations from proper titles of office.[86] The latter, however, might include διάκονός (Rom 16:1) and ἀπόστολος (Rom 16:7; Gal 1:19).

In sum, then, Paul uses titles of office quite rarely, and he uses single rather than double names almost without exception. It is significant, though, that most of the named persons in the letters are members of the churches, and most of the uses of their names are in the form of address (especially, "Greet Aquila," etc.). That Paul addresses his people by their Greek single names, including transliterations of some Latin praenomina, is probably further evidence of what Wayne Meeks has called fictive kinship language in the Pauline churches.[87] Like the characteristic vocative ἀδελφοί and the mentions of Paul's being a father to his churches, the familiar use of single names reinforces the corporate perception of kinship among the Pauline believers. As for "Jesus

---

83 And so equivalent to Greek εὐεργέτις and Latin *patrona*; see E. A. Judge, "The Early Christians as a Scholastic Community," *Journal of Religious History* 1 (1960): 4–15, 125–137, especially 128–129; also Meeks, *First Urban Christians*, 60.

84 So Gerd Theissen, "Soziale Schichtung in der korinthischen Gemeinde," *Zeitschrift für die neutestamentliche Wissenschaft und die Kunde der älteren Kirche* 65 (1974): 232–272; also Meeks, *First Urban Christians*, 58–59.

85 See Meeks, *First Urban Christians*, 21–22.

86 By polite designations I mean Pauline commonplaces such as ἀδελφός, "brother or sister"; κοινωνός, "partner"; and συνεργός, "coworker."

87 See Meeks, *First Urban Christians*, 86–89:

> Especially striking is the language that speaks of members of the Pauline groups as if they were a family. They are children of God and also of the apostle. They are brothers and sisters; they refer to one another as "beloved." ... [This] is a vivid way of portraying what a modern sociologist might call the resocialization of conversion. The natural kinship structure into which the person has been born and which previously defined his place and connections with the society is here supplanted by a new set of relationships.

More recently, see Philip A. Harland, "Familial Dimensions of Group Identity: 'Brothers' (ΑΔΕΛΦΟΙ) in Associations of the Greek East," *JBL* 124 (2005): 491–513.

Christ," if it is a real double name for Paul, then it would be the only instance of a double name anywhere in his letters. This fact does not decide the question, but it does raise further doubts about the majority opinion that takes χριστός in Paul as a straightforward second name.

Christ as a Nickname?

One minority report has explained the fact that χριστός in Paul seems to be neither quite a name nor quite a title by appealing to one of the secondary ancient onomastic categories mentioned earlier, the nickname or byname.[88] In his Bampton Lectures for 1980, A. E. Harvey argued that the name χριστός was first attached to Jesus not at or after his death but during his lifetime, specifically, as a nickname conferred by his own friends.[89] Harvey points to the formula Ἰησοῦς ὁ λεγόμενος χριστός, "Jesus called Anointed" (Matt 1:16; 27:17, 22), citing as parallels Σίμων ὁ λεγόμενος Πέτρος, "Simon called Rock" (Matt 10:2), Θωμᾶς ὁ λεγόμενος Δίδυμος, "Thomas called Twin" (John 11:16; 20:24; 21:2), and Ἰησοῦς ὁ λεγόμενος Ἰοῦστος, "Jesus called Just" (Col 4:11). Harvey concludes, "In each of these cases the additional name is something approaching what we could call a nickname—Rock, Twin, the Just One—that is to say, a name given by others to a person in view of a particular quality, characteristic or accident of birth, distinguishing him from other men of the same official or family name."[90]

One advantage of this thesis, Harvey claims, is that it explains the allegedly colorless Pauline usage of the word. "Jesus was known by this additional name in his lifetime... [so that] Paul will have known this name, and used it without further discussion."[91] That is, Harvey concurs with the majority opinion that the term χριστός is not christologically significant for Paul, but he explains this phenomenon by means of the category of nickname. The argument rests especially on a controversial claim about what χριστός would have suggested to Jesus's contemporaries, namely, not an eschatological royal son of David ("Messiah") but rather the range of functions attributed to the figure who is "anointed by the Lord" in the songs of Second Isaiah.[92] Harvey explains:

---

88 I.e., what the ancients called agnomina or supernomina (see earlier; also Thompson, "Ancient Greek Personal Names," 682–683).

89 A. E. Harvey, *Jesus and the Constraints of History* (Philadelphia: Westminster, 1982), 80–82.

90 Harvey, *Constraints of History*, 81.

91 Harvey, *Constraints of History*, 139.

92 See especially Isa 61:1: "The spirit of the Lord YHWH is upon me, because YHWH anointed me (MT רוח אדני יהוה עלי יען משח יהוה אתי; LXX πνεῦμα κυρίου ἐπ᾽ ἐμέ, οὗ εἵνεκεν ἔχρισέν με) to bring good news to the afflicted; he sent me to bind up the brokenhearted, to proclaim liberty to the captives, and release to those who are bound."

Followers of Jesus, who had observed both the range and the primary emphasis of his teaching and healing, would have instinctively summed it all up in a few sentences from Isaiah [viz. Isaiah 42:1; 61:1], and have described him by means of the striking phrase contained in those texts: Jesus was the one "anointed" or "appointed" to preach the kingdom, to bring good news to the poor, to cure the blind, the deaf and the lame. He was—Christ.[93]

This account is marked by a certain ingenuity, to be sure, but there are reasons to question its logic.[94] For one thing, it depends on an unconventional and finally unpersuasive reconstruction of the semantic range of the word χριστός in the period, to which I responded in chapter 2. Even if we grant, though, that χριστός might have suggested the Isaianic servant rather than the Davidic king of the Psalter, it is still a stretch to claim, as Harvey does, that this association would have been obvious or instinctive to Jesus's contemporaries. Granted, this connection is made in Luke 4:16–21, but it is not attested widely in early Christian sources, and much less can it be assumed to have been obvious to people who have not left us any literary record. In addition, Harvey reasons from the formula ὁ λεγόμενος, which occurs with Jesus's name only in Matthew, to explain its use throughout the Jesus tradition. What is more, Harvey's strong distinction between the formulae ὁ ἐπικαλούμενος, "literally 'surnamed,'" and ὁ λεγόμενος, "'called' or 'known as,'" is not borne out in the documentary and epigraphic evidence.[95] In fact, both formulae were used to signal various additions to the personal name.[96] Last of all, Harvey's theory does not actually offer an explanation of the Pauline evidence; it simply assumes the classic "proper name, not title" hypothesis and provides that hypothesis with a bit more historical-onomastic detail.

Merrill Miller has recently proposed an interesting variation on Harvey's theory, suggesting that "the evidence that is best explained by his [Harvey's] suggestion can be found [not in the Gospels but] in Paul's letters. Initial use as a byname would explain why we have many instances in Paul's letters where it is difficult to determine whether it carries connotations of an honorific

---

93 Harvey, *Constraints of History*, 141–142.

94 See the review by Ben F. Meyer in *JBL* 103 (1984): 652–654, here 654: "Historical inference moves, not from possibility to actuality (as Harvey's method implies), but simply from the known to the unknown."

95 Harvey, *Constraints of History*, 80.

96 See Matthews, "names, personal, Greek," 1022.

or a title or is merely a proper name."[97] Despite their different terminology, Harvey and Miller are appealing to the same onomastic category; Harvey's "nickname" is Miller's "byname." However, whereas Harvey argues that the nickname "Anointed" was applied to Jesus by his followers during the course of his ministry, Miller suggests that it was added only retrospectively by the Jesus movement as a way of lending theocratic legitimacy to the fledgling group.[98] The movement will have chosen this word not because it had royal or eschatological resonance but because "the broad connotations of the term would have been those conveying divine authorization for a role of leadership."[99] More specifically still, by appealing to the many nicknamed philosophers attested in Diogenes Laertius's third-century C.E. *Lives of Eminent Philosophers,* Miller identifies a social setting for the use of the term. "The appropriate analogues for thinking about *christos* as a byname may not be found in figures of expectation, nor in popular royal claimants, but in schools where teachers and disciples are compared and values and authority are sorted out by means of nicknames and honorifics."[100]

Miller's thesis represents an improvement upon the name-versus-title stalemate in that it appeals to another known ancient onomastic category. However, as in the case of Harvey, the application of these categories presents problems. In a valuable survey of the particular nicknames attested in Diogenes Laertius's *Lives,* Barry S. Crawford notes two ways in which Miller's χριστός does not fit their pattern. First, in every known case, the philosopher's nickname corresponds to some feature or other of the person himself. "Plato himself was (or was thought to be) in some sense 'broad,' Democritus 'wise,' Lyco 'sweet-voiced,' and so forth."[101] Miller, however, contends that this was not the case with the use of χριστός for Jesus. Second, in all but two cases,

---

97 Miller, "Messianic Conception of Jesus," in *Redescribing Christian Origins,* 301–336, here 316; and Miller, "Anointed Jesus," in *Redescribing Christian Origins,* 375–416. Miller's work, together with several responses to it, are part of the work of the SBL Seminar on Redescribing Christian Origins, published as *Redescribing Christian Origins.*

98 "The general significance of the use of *mašiah/christos* in Jewish literatures outside the Bible, at least until the latter part of the first century C.E., is to give theocratic grounding to each of the institutions considered essential to the proper functioning of the life of the people" (Miller, "Anointed Jesus," 408). In this particular kind of sociological approach to early Christian history, Miller is deeply and expressly indebted to Burton L. Mack, *A Myth of Innocence: Mark and Christian Origins* (Philadelphia: Fortress, 1988), on which see chapter 1.

99 Miller, "Anointed Jesus," 408. Here Miller leans heavily on the argument of Karrer, *Der Gesalbte,* on which see chapter 2.

100 Miller, "Messianic Conception of Jesus," 327.

101 Barry S. Crawford, "*Christos* as Nickname," in *Redescribing Christian Origins,* 337–348, here 347.

the nicknamed philosophers received their nicknames during their own life-times, not after their deaths.[102] On Miller's account, though, χριστός was used of Jesus only after his death and for reasons having to do entirely with the self-perception of the movement. So if Miller is right about those two points, then the appeal to Greek nicknames is actually proportionally less convincing.

There is also the matter of Miller's claim, which mirrors Harvey's, that the word χριστός would have had no "messianic" associations in the period in question. Apart from the fundamental question whether this generalization is true to the evidence, Willi Braun has challenged the logic of Miller's argument at this point. "Given the highly contestatory mood of the formational activities of early Christians everywhere, I tend to think that brand names, especially *christos*, were chosen precisely because they were already heavily greased with allusionary and connotative oil.... What good is a brand name that does not evoke anything?"[103] That is, if χριστός is empty of any biblical connotations, then how does it render theocratic legitimacy at all? In fact, Miller's sociological account might fare better on the older account of the meaning of the word. In sum, then, the arguments on offer for understanding χριστός as an ancient Greek nickname are so far unconvincing. The search for a contemporary onomastic category that fits the Pauline evidence, however, is certainly worthwhile.

Christ as an Honorific

Nickname is not the appropriate ancient Greek onomastic category for Paul's χριστός, but there is such a category, namely the honorific.[104] Unfortunately, this category goes under a confusing variety of names in the secondary literature, including at least honorific, title, epithet, surname, and cult name. Historians use these various terms to denote the illustrious second terms added to the personal names of certain public figures. Perhaps the best-known example is provided

---

102 Crawford, "*Christos* as Nickname," 348.

103 Willi Braun, "Smoke Signals from the North: A Reply to Burton Mack's 'Backbay Jazz and Blues,'" in *Redescribing Christian Origins*, 433–442, here 434. Braun concludes:

> [We would need much more evidence] on the basis of which we could then cogently speculate the emergence of a grouping from whom the nontitular, nonmessianic chris-tos would compel itself (to the exclusion of other possible heroic or godly cognomina) as brand name for the start of something "novel" in terms of social regrouping and iden-tification.... Not that Miller's scenario sounded implausible, just that it is so vague as to be able to stand as a supposed scenario for almost anything. (Braun, "Smoke Signals from the North," 435)

104 A subset of Matthews's "secondary names" (Matthews, "names, personal, Greek," 1022).

by the Hellenistic kings, whom we typically designate by Roman numerals denoting their order of succession (e.g., Antiochus I, II, III). They and their contemporaries, however, instead used a system of honorific second names.

Alexander III of Macedon has been called Μέγας Ἀλέξανδρος, "Alexander the Great," from antiquity to the present but not, so far as we know, in his own lifetime.[105] The Diadochi ("successors") after him, however, used similar honorifics as a matter of course. The Seleucid kings in Syria appended honorifics to their personal names, yielding the forms familiar to us: Σέλευκος Νικάτωρ, "Seleucus [I] the Victor"; Ἀντίοχος Σωτήρ, "Antiochus [I] the Savior"; Ἀντίοχος Μέγας, "Antiochus [III] the Great"; Ἀντίοχος Ἐπιφανής, "Antiochus [IV] [God] Manifest"; and so on. The Ptolemaic dynasty in Egypt did likewise, with some overlap in terms with their Seleucid neighbors:[106] Πτολεμαῖος Σωτήρ, "Ptolemy [I] the Savior"; Πτολεμαῖος Εὐεργέτης, "Ptolemy [III] the Benefactor"; Πτολεμαῖος Ἐπιφανής, "Ptolemy [V] [God] Manifest"; Πτολεμαῖος Θεός Φιλοπάτωρ, "Ptolemy [XIII] the Father-loving God"; and so on.[107] For reasons that are not clear, the Antigonid rulers seem not to have used honorifics with their personal names, although they did disambiguate dynasts with more mundane nicknames, as with Ἀντίγονος ὁ Μονόφθαλμος, "Antigonus [I] the One-Eyed."[108]

In the course of use, a system of syntactical conventions developed for these honorifics. Like Greek secondary names generally, honorifics are

---

105 But not for lack of hubris on his part. Although the details are much debated, it is certain that Alexander accepted divine obeisance in a number of cities in the eastern part of his empire (see F. W. Walbank, "Monarchies and Monarchic Ideas," in *The Cambridge Ancient History* [14 vols; 2d ed.; Cambridge: Cambridge University Press, 1970–2005], 7.1:62–100).

106 But the Ptolemaic honorifics in particular may in some cases have been Greek equivalents of ancient pharaonic titles.

107 The system sometimes resulted in extravagant combinations, like that of Κλεοπάτρα Φιλομήτωρ Σώτειρα Δικαιοσύνη Νικηφόρος, "Cleopatra [III] the Mother-loving Savior, Righteous One, Bringer of Victory," who probably also bore the nickname Kokke, "Scarlet" (see Strabo 17.1.8).

108 See C. Ehrhardt, "Demetrius ὁ Αἰτωλικός and Antigonid Nicknames," *Hermes* 106 [1978]: 251–253; here 252–253:

Honorific epithets of other sorts are common in Hellenistic times for the Seleucids and Ptolemies, as well as for lesser dynasties—e. g. "Soter," "Philadelphus," "Euergetes," "Nicator," "Theos," "Callinicus," etc.—but are unknown among the Antigonids: their nicknames are either commonplace to the point of insult, or unintelligible to us which suggests they were unflattering, for complimentary epithets are seldom obscure. The first Antigonus was "Monophthalmus," which was made worse by the change to "Cyclops"; the byname of the second, "Gonatas," has baffled scholarship but may mean "Knock-kneed"; the third had three epithets, "Epitropus," i. e., the steward or guardian; "Doson," for which Plutarch suggests one meaning, and the *Etymologicum Magnum* a different and incompatible one; and the totally unintelligible "Phuscus."

sometimes marked by a variation of the formula "who is called" (ὁ λεγόμενος/ ὁ ἐπικαλούμενος/ὁ προσαγορευθείς), which distinguishes them from personal names on the one hand and titles of office on the other (so Ἀντίοχος ὁ προσαγορευθεὶς Ἐπιφανής [2 Macc 4:7; 10:9]).[109] In the absence of such formulae, however, honorifics have their own characteristic syntax whereby they admit of a variety of combinations.[110] So Antiochus IV Epiphanes was sometimes called Ἀντίοχος Ἐπιφανής (e.g., 1 Macc 1:10), sometimes ὁ Ἐπιφανὴς Ἀντίοχος (e.g., Josephus, *J.W.* 5.460). By the same token, Antiochus V Eupator is referred to variously as Ἀντίοχος ὁ Εὐπάτωρ (2 Macc 13:1), the inverse ὁ Εὐπάτωρ Ἀντίοχος (2 Macc 10:10), simply Ἀντίοχος (1 Macc 7:2), or simply Εὐπάτωρ (1 Macc 6:17; 2 Macc 10:13). All of these are distinct from his title of office, βασιλεύς, "king," as on his coins, which are stamped ΒΑΣΙΛΕΩΣ ΑΝΤΙΟΧΟΥ, "belonging to King Antiochus."

An episode related in 1 Maccabees 6 provides a window into the process whereby honorifics were assumed by their royal bearers. There the narrator explains how it was that Εὐπάτωρ, "of a noble father," came to be applied to Antiochus V: καὶ ἐπέγνω Λυσίας ὅτι τέθνηκεν ὁ βασιλεὺς καὶ κατέστησεν βασιλεύειν Ἀντίοχον τὸν υἱὸν αὐτοῦ ὃν ἐξέθρεψεν νεώτερον καὶ ἐκάλεσεν τὸ ὄνομα αὐτοῦ Εὐπάτωρ, "When Lysias learned that the king [viz. Antiochus IV Epiphanes] had died, he set up his [Epiphanes's] son Antiochus to reign, whom he [Lysias] had raised as a youth, and he called his name Eupator" (1 Macc 6:17). The honorific, here called an ὄνομα, is assumed at the time of accession to the throne, and in this instance, because the king is a minor, the honorific is assigned by his caretaker.

That the etymological force of an honorific was sometimes clearly perceived is evident in the case of 2 Maccabees, in which Antiochus IV Epiphanes is the arch villain of the story.[111] The anti-Seleucid epitomist, or perhaps Jason of Cyrene before him, exploits the king's honorific for polemical purposes by

---

109 Cf. the names of the five sons of Mattathias in 1 Macc 2:2–5, all with second names marked by ὁ καλούμενος (and in one case ὁ ἐπικαλούμενος): Ιωαννης ὁ ἐπικαλούμενος Γαδδι, Σιμων ὁ καλούμενος Θασσι, Ιουδας ὁ καλούμενος Μακκαβαῖος, Ελεαζαρ ὁ καλούμενος Αυαραν, and Ιωναθης ὁ καλούμενος Απφους.

110 On the many possible permutations, see the thorough catalog provided by Robert Dick Wilson, "Royal Titles in Antiquity: An Essay in Criticism, Article Four: The Titles of the Greek Kings," *Princeton Theological Review* 3 (1905): 238–267.

111 To take another example from the literature on Antiochus IV, it was the currency of the honorific Ἐπιφανής as a means of referring to him that made possible the popular pun attested in Polybius 26.1.1: Ἀντίοχος ὁ Ἐπιφανὴς μὲν κληθείς, Ἐπιμανὴς δ᾽ ἐκ τῶν πράξεων ὀνομασθείς, "Antiochus called Epiphanes [god manifest], but nicknamed Epimanes [madman] on account of the things he did" (Greek text ed. Theodorus Büttner-Wobst, *Polybii historiae* [4 vols; Leipzig: Teubner, 1893–1905]).

ironically using the cognate noun ἐπιφανεία, "manifestation" or "appearance," throughout for the wondrous acts of God by which the wicked Seleucid rulers are laid low.[112] In a telling introductory statement, the epitomist purports to tell of "the wars against Antiochus Epiphanes [Ἀντίοχον τὸν Ἐπιφανῆ] and his son Eupator, and the epiphanies that came from heaven [τὰς ἐξ οὐρανοῦ γενομένας ἐπιφανείας] for those who for the sake of Judaism nobly played the man" (2 Macc 2:20–21).[113]

Not coincidentally, a similar pattern of nomenclature is attested in the case of the Jewish rival to Seleucid dominance in Palestine, Judah ben Mattathias, or Judah Maccabee. His personal name was Judah, and apart from the acclaim that he gained in the revolt, he likely would have been further designated by his patronym (Judah ben Mattathias) or toponym (Judah of Modein). In the course of the revolt, however, he took the honorific Maccabee, Μακκαβαῖος, probably from Aramaic מקבא/Hebrew מקבת, "hammer," for his famous military might.[114] Like the Seleucid kings, Judah's second name is sometimes flagged with ὁ καλούμενος, "who was called," or equivalents: Ιουδας ὁ καλούμενος Μακκαβαῖος (1 Macc 2:4; 3:1), Ιουδας ὁ καὶ Μακκαβαῖος (1 Macc 8:20; 2 Macc 5:27; 8:1; Josephus, *Ant.* 12.286). However, he is very often called by the double name Ιουδας [ὁ] Μακκαβαῖος (1 Macc 2:66; 5:24), or just the one name or the other—Ιουδας (1 Macc 3:11; 2 Macc 2:14), or Μακκαβαῖος (1 Macc 5:34; 2 Macc 8:5, 16; 10:1), but never in the order Μακκαβαῖος Ιουδας.

After Judah Maccabee, the Hasmonean, and later the Herodian, dynasts in Palestine continued the trend of using onomastic conventions that were

---

112 See 2 Macc 2:21; 3:24; 5:4; 12:22; 14:15; 15:27; cf. similar uses of the cognate adjective ἐπιφανής at 2 Macc 6:23; 15:34.

113 On 2 Maccabees as a collection of ἐπιφανείαι, see Arnaldo Momigliano, "The Second Book of Maccabees," *Classical Philology* 70 (1975): 81–88, especially 86; on the book's peculiar style of polemic, see Martha Himmelfarb, "Judaism and Hellenism in 2 Maccabees," *Poetics Today* 19 (1998): 19–40.

114 See, e.g., the encomium to Judah at 1 Macc 3:3–9: "Like a giant he put on his breastplate; he bound on his armor of war and waged battles, protecting the camp by his sword.... He searched out and pursued those who broke the law; he burned those who troubled his people" (NRSV). Historians have pointed to the analogy of the eighth-century Frankish ruler Charles Martel (from Latin *martulus*, "hammer"), who gained his honorific at his victory in the battle of Tours. While this is the most likely etymology, others are possible. מקבן, "having a hammer-shaped head," is attested as an epithet for a physical blemish (*m. Bek.* 7:1; cf. *b. Bek.* 43b, which paraphrases דדמי רישיה למקבא [see Jastrow, 829; Sokoloff, 701]). Schürer-Vermes (*History,* 1:158n49) argue in favor of a dual etymology: "A nickname originally indicating a bodily peculiarity could easily have acquired, in changed circumstances, the meaning 'hammer (of God).'" Less likely, the honorific might derive from Hebrew מקביהו (from the root נקב), "appointed by YHWH," in connection with the choice of Judah as leader in 1 Macc 2:66 (see Mathias Delcor, "The Apocrypha and Pseudepigrapha of the Hellenistic Period," in *The Cambridge History of Judaism* [3 vols; ed. W. D. Davies and Louis Finkelstein; Cambridge: Cambridge University Press, 1984], 2:456).

current among their Hellenistic and Roman counterparts.[115] Despite this general trend, however, few actual honorifics appear among the Hasmoneans and Herodians. The name "Herod the Great" is actually a much later way of referring to Herod.[116] The form Ἡρῴδης ὁ Μέγας occurs only in Josephus, *Ant.* 18.130–136, where it means "Herod the Elder," to distinguish the patriarch from his several homonymous progeny.[117] The proper name Ἡρῴδης, which derives from the noun ἥρως, "hero, warrior, demigod," is attested in Greek sources well before the common era.[118] In the context of the Herodian dynasty, however, this proper name may have come to function as a dynastic title, as Caesar did for the Roman emperors.[119]

In any case, and perhaps not coincidentally, the honorific proper is again attested at the time of the Second Jewish Revolt against Rome in the 130s C.E. That war was led, on the Jewish side, by one Shimon bar Kosiba, who, like Judah Maccabee before him, played a role in the revolt that occasioned the introduction of a new name, this one based on a wordplay: Shimon bar *Kosiba*, "son of Kosiba," became Shimon bar *Kokhba*, "son of the star."[120] "Star" in the name is an allusion to the oracle in Num 24:17: דרך כוכב מיעקב, "A star goes forth from Jacob."[121] The rabbinic literature, however, uniformly refers to him with the derogatory wordplay [Bar/Ben] Kozeba, "liar," even in passages that

---

115 E.g., Eusebius and Jerome explain the name of John Hyrcanus as a victory title: "John the victor over the Hyrcanians" (ed. Alfred Schöne, *Die Weltchronik des Eusebius in ihrer Bearbeitung durch Heironymus* [Berlin: Weidmann, 1900], 2:130–131: Ὑρκανοὺς νικήσας Ὑρκανὸς ὠνομάσθη; *adversum Hyrcanos bellum gerens Hyrcani nomen accepit*). Against this, however, is the fact that the name Hyrcanus is attested among Jews before John Hyrcanus (see 2 Macc 3:11; Josephus, *Ant.* 12.186–236), and so more likely originated as a geographic at the time of the Persian deportations, designating a Jew from Hyrcania (see Schürer-Vermes, *History*, 1:201–202n2).

116 Cf. the earlier comment in this chapter on the name "Alexander the Great."

117 See Schürer-Vermes, *History*, 1:329 and n167.

118 See *CIG*, index p. 92; Pape-Benseler, *Wörterbuch*, s.v. Ἡρῴδης.

119 So Harold W. Hoehner, *Herod Antipas* (Society for New Testament Studies Monograph Series 17; Cambridge: Cambridge University Press, 1972), 105–109. As Hoehner points out, this may explain why, prior to *J.W.* 2.167, Josephus always calls Antipas "Antipas," and after he always calls him "Herod," because that passage narrates the deposition of Archelaus and the accession of Philip and Antipas; it is here that Antipas becomes "Herod" (Ἡρῴδης ὁ κληθεὶς Ἀντίπας). If "Herod" was indeed used as a dynastic title, one wonders whether it was so used in part because of its etymological resonance ("hero, warrior," etc.).

120 On Bar Kokhba and the Second Revolt generally, see especially Peter Schäfer, *Der Bar Kokhba-Aufstand: Studien zum zweiten jüdischen Krieg gegen Rom* (TSAJ 1; Tübingen: Mohr Siebeck, 1981).

121 This midrashic connection is most explicit in *y. Taʿan.* 4:8/27: "R. Shimon b. Yohai taught, 'R. Akiba used to expound, "A star will go forth from Jacob": Kozeba goes forth from Jacob.'"

preserve higher views of him.[122] He was Bar Kokhba to his supporters and Bar Kozeba to his later rabbinic detractors, but the documentary and numismatic record preserves his actual patronym, שמעון בר כוסבה, Shimon bar Kosiba.[123]

Ancient Christian sources know and transliterate the Aramaic honorific Bar Kokhba, so בר כוכבא is rendered with Greek Βαρχωχέβας and Latin Chochebas.[124] Transliteration, though, does not imply ignorance of the meaning of the name. Eusebius calls him Βαρχωχέβας, then explains, ὃ δὴ ἀστέρα δηλοῖ, "which plainly means 'star,'" and he further exploits the etymology by criticizing Bar Kokhba for posturing ὡς δὴ ἐξ οὐρανοῦ φωστὴρ αὐτοῖς κατεληλυθὼς, "as if he were a luminary that had come down from heaven" (Hist. eccl. 6.4.2).

Bar Kokhba is of course not a given name, but neither is it a title. His own preferred title, it appears from the coins and papyri, was נשיא על ישראל, "prince over Israel."[125] In the rabbinic literature, though, the title used in connection with him is Hebrew משיח, "messiah," or Aramaic מלכא משיחא, "king messiah." So, famously, at y. Ta'an. 4:8/27, R. Akiba says when he sees him, דין הוא מלכא משיחא, "This is the king messiah."[126] The title is forcibly denied him by rabbinic tradition generally, but "king messiah" is always the title in question. "Bar Kokhba," then, is neither a personal name nor a title but an honorific. It is assumed, not given at birth; its laudatory force is immediately evident, but it is not predicated of its bearer; and it can stand in for the personal name of its bearer.

It is clear, however, that Jewish honorifics like Maccabee and Bar Kokhba are for the most part a linguistic convention held in common with other antique civilizations, not one unique to Judaism.[127] This observation is apt in light of a strand in the secondary literature that would connect Paul's χριστός very closely to Semitic-language parallels rather than Greek ones. Martin Hengel, for example, comments in this connection, "Particularly in the Semitic sphere the transformation of what were originally titles into proper names is

---

122 See Lam. Rab. 2:4: "R. Yohanan said, 'Rabbi used to expound, "A star will go forth from Jacob": do not read "star" [כוכב] but "liar" [כוזב].'"

123 For the papyrus documents, see Yigael Yadin et al., The Finds from the Bar Kokhba Period in the Cave of Letters (3 vols; Jerusalem: Israel Exploration Society, 1963–2002). For the coins, see Leo Mildenberg, The Coinage of the Bar Kokhba War (Zurich: Schweizerische Numismatische Gesellschaft, 1984).

124 On the morphology of the name, see Schürer-Vermes, History, 2:543–544.

125 For an example, see P.Yadin 54, ll. 1–2: שמעון בר כוסבה הנסי על ישראל ליהונתן ולמסבלה סלם, "Shimon bar Kosiba, prince over Israel, to Yehonathan and to Mesabalah, peace."

126 See also b. Sanh. 93b, where Bar Kokhba himself says to the rabbis, אנא משיח, "I am the messiah."

127 In particular, Jewish usage is indebted to the conventions current in the Hellenistic kingdoms.

not uncommon in religious terminology," citing as examples the names of the demons שׂטן, "adversary," Satan in Job; משׂטמה, "hatred" or "enemy," Mastema in *Jubilees*; בליעל, "ruin" or "destroyer," Belial in 1QM.[128] Along similar lines, Klaus Berger has suggested that Paul's χριστός (from Aramaic משׁיחא) for Jesus works on the analogy to πέτρος (from Aramaic כיפא) for Simon the disciple.[129] These parallels may be apt, but they are not uniquely Semitic in any case.

Nearer to Paul's own time, similar honorifics are attested in the Latin nomenclature for the Roman emperor. Augustus is the first and best case since his personal nomenclature attests several remarkable developments during the course of his own adult life. Born Gaius Octavius Thurinus, he underwent the customary change of name at the time of his adoption by Julius Caesar, becoming Gaius Julius Caesar Octavianus (taking the *tria nomina* of his adopted father and appending an adjectival form of the nomen of his family of origin). However, after Caesar's assassination and Octavian's accession to power, the latter underwent several unconventional changes of name, as well.

First, Octavian took the title *imperator*, which in the Republican period had been a victory title for successful military commanders, as his actual praenomen, the *praenomen imperatoris*.[130] Both Cassius Dio and Suetonius attribute the innovation of the *praenomen imperatoris* to the reign of Julius Caesar, but epigraphic and numismatic evidence attests it only of Octavian.[131] The latter actually dropped his praenomen and *gentilicium* altogether and assumed the personal name Imperator Caesar divi filius.[132]

The second pertinent development in Octavian's nomenclature was his assumption of the name Augustus after defeating Antony and Cleopatra at

---

128 Hengel, "'Christos' in Paul," 75.

129 Klaus Berger, "Zum traditionsgeschichtlichen Hintergrund christologischer Hoheitstitel," *NTS* 17 (1971): 391–425, especially 391–392: "Sowohl 'Christus' als auch 'Petrus' sind eschatologische Eigennamen.... Der Name Petros ist nicht als zweiter Name aufzufassen, sondern ... als Amtsname für eine einmalige eschatologische Funktion." But this is to appeal to a category of names otherwise unknown in antiquity.

130 For the older use of the title, cf. the Italian word, now brought over into English, "generalissimo." The *praenomen imperatoris* is an important contemporary illustration of the slippage between personal names and titles, owing to the meaning potential of both types of words.

131 See Dio 43.44.2–5.; Suet. *Jul*. 76.1. However, in coins of and inscriptions to Julius Caesar, *imperator* customarily appears after his *tria nomina* at the head of his titles: C. Julius Caesar Imp. Pont. Dict. Perpetuo, and so on.

132 The cognominal divi filius became possible after the divinization of Julius Caesar by decree of the Roman Senate in 42 B.C.E. So during the Second Triumvirate, Octavian's name ran as follows: Imperator Caesar divi filius iii vir R.P.C. (i.e., *triumvir rei publicae constituendae*); during the principate it was Imperator Caesar divi filius Augustus (see further Henry Furneax's introduction to his edition of *Tacitus: Cornelii Taciti Annalium Ab Excessu Divi Augusti Libri* [Oxford: Clarendon, 1884], 1:63–66).

Actium in 27 B.C.E. Although he maintained the *praenomen imperatoris*, in actual use he was overwhelmingly designated as Caesar Augustus from that point on.[133] As J. A. Crook has noted, the magnitude of this onomastic change can scarcely be overestimated:

> On 16 January [27 B.C.E.] Caesar was heaped with new honours pro-
> posed by his adherents, above all with the name "Augustus"; and that was
> a fantastic novelty, the impact of which is blunted for us by two millennia
> of calling him by that name. No human person had been called it before,
> and its symbolic range was very large. The sources preserve a tale that
> Caesar, or some of his advisers, or both, had first thought of "Romulus."
> Some scholars doubt, others think that "Augustus" was a second-best
> imposed by the strength of opposition; but it came to the same thing.[134]

The analogy to Romulus, whatever the history behind the legend, shows that the new epithet was not another title of office (like pontifex, triumvir, etc.) but an actual name. As Sir Ronald Syme rightly noted, "In spite of the tricks and permutations, the house of the Caesars submits after all to rules of nomenclature. The man of destiny himself, the 'Divi Filius,' though porten-tous and unexampled, is not unexplained: as 'Imp. Caesar Augustus' he owns to '*tria nomina*.'"[135] The force of the new name, however, was no doubt felt by Octavian's subjects, as it was surely intended to be.[136]

---

133 See Donald McFayden, *The History of the Title Imperator under the Roman Empire* (Chicago: University of Chicago Press, 1920), 40–41: "After 27 B.C. the Praenomen Imperatoris was no longer felt to be his distinctive title. In such references he is spoken of as Caesar, Caesar Augustus, Augustus, or, more rarely, Augustus Caesar—a clear indication that he was thought of, and wished to be thought of, primarily as the great man and god-sent savior of society, not as the Imperator."

134 J. A. Crook, "Political History, 30 B.C. to A.D. 14," *CAH,* 10:70–112, here 79; citing Suet. *Aug.* 7.2; Dio 53.16.6–8.

135 Ronald Syme, "Imperator Caesar: A Study in Nomenclature," *Historia* 7 (1958): 172–188, here 187.

136 See H. Galsterer, "A Man, a Book, and a Method: Sir Ronald Syme's *Roman Revolution* after Fifty Years," in *Between Republic and Empire: Interpretations of Augustus and His Principate* (ed. Kurt A. Raaflaub and Mark Toher; Berkeley: University of California Press, 1993), 1–20, here 15:

> The emperor's full name after 27 B.C. was *Imperator Caesar divi filius Augustus,* while other Romans were simply called, for example, *Marcus Tullius Marci filius Cicero.* Thus in his titulature—which had almost supplanted the personal name—Augustus was rep-resented as son of a new god and as such "holy" and venerable himself. Even assuming the upper classes at Rome, enlightened skeptics (like [historian Sir Ronald] Syme him-self) did not take it seriously, there must have been a target group for this type of propa-ganda: presumably the mass of citizens and noncitizens throughout the empire.

The reception of the honorific Augustus into Greek is instructive in this regard. As in most modern languages, ancient personal names were customarily transliterated across languages (Flavius/Φλάβιος, etc.), and so Augustus often appears as Αὔγουστος in Greek sources. However, almost as common as this transliteration is the translation Σεβαστός, "venerable," for the name Augustus, which shows that the etymology of the name was widely perceived.[137] Pausanias, for example, explains the equivalency for his Greek readers: τὸ δὲ ὄνομα ἦν τούτῳ Αὔγουστος, ὃ κατὰ γλῶσσαν δύναται τὴν Ἑλλήνων σεβαστός, "His name was 'Augustus,' which in the Greek language means 'venerable'" (Paus. 3.11.4). So it is that Luke the evangelist can sometimes use Αὔγουστος with Καῖσαρ (Luke 2:1) and sometimes Σεβαστός with Καῖσαρ (Acts 25:21; cf. 25:25; 27:1).[138] The same translation dynamics obtain in the case of Greek χριστός for Hebrew משׁיח (Aramaic משׁיחא). One sometimes reads Μεσσίας (as in John 1:41; 4:25), but the prevailing custom is rather to translate meaningfully (χριστός, "anointed one") even if the idiom does not carry over smoothly into the target language.

By way of summary, then, Paul's ostensibly idiosyncratic use of χριστός is not really idiosyncratic, at least not in a formal sense. Granted, it is neither a proper name nor a title of office, but it is not therefore an onomastic innovation. Rather, it fits a known onomastic category from antiquity, namely the honorific. Honorifics, which are amply attested in Greek, Latin, and Hebrew in the Hellenistic and Roman periods, were typically borne by rulers. An honorific was taken by or bestowed on its bearer, usually in connection with military exploits or accession to power, not given at birth. It was formally a common noun or adjective (e.g., hammer, star, savior, manifest, august, anointed), not a proper noun. In actual use, it could occur in combination with the bearer's proper name or stand in for that proper name. It was not a uniquely Semitic-language convention but one shared among ancient

---

137 *TLG* turns up some 728 instances of Αὔγουστος, 507 of Σεβαστός in Greek literary sources. Although the Latin adjective *augustus* is very ancient, the transliteration αὔγουστος never occurs before the Roman principate and is occasioned only by the assumption of the honorific by Octavian. Moreover, σεβαστός, "venerable," is a cognate of the very ancient σέβομαι word group, but the adjective is unattested before the principate, when Dionysius of Halicarnassus uses it for Numa's temple to the divine Πίστις (οὕτω γοῦν σεβαστόν τι πρᾶγμα καὶ ἀμίαντον ἐνομίσθη τὸ πιστόν [*Ant. Rom.* 2.75.3]). Otherwise, it, like Αὔγουστος, is almost exclusively associated with eponymous Roman emperors.

138 But never Αὔγουστος and Σεβαστός together. Luke 2:1 has the double-name formula Καῖσαρ Αὔγουστος: "A decree went out from Caesar Augustus" (referring here to Octavian). In Acts 25:21, Σεβαστός and Καῖσαρ stand in apposition to one another: τοῦ δὲ Παύλου ἐπικαλεσαμένου τηρηθῆναι αὐτὸν εἰς τὴν τοῦ Σεβαστοῦ διάγνωσιν, ἐκέλευσα τηρεῖσθαι αὐτὸν ἕως οὗ ἀναπέμψω αὐτὸν πρὸς Καίσαρα, "But when Paul appealed to be held until the decision of *Augustus* ['the emperor' in NRSV], I ordered that he be held until I could send him to *Caesar*" (referring here to Nero).

Table 3.1

Title	Name	Cognomen
Κύριος	Ἰησοῦς	Χριστός
Βασιλεὺς	Πτολεμαῖος	Σωτήρ
Βασιλεὺς	Ἀντίοχος	Ἐπιφανής
Αὐτοκράτωρ	Καῖσαρ	Σέβαστος
Imperator	Caesar	Augustus

Mediterranean cultures and even translated from one language to another. It is not coincidental that these are the very features of Paul's use of χριστός that have so vexed his modern interpreters.

I am not the first to suggest the analogy between Paul's χριστός and other Greek honorifics; other interpreters have done so in other contexts.[139] However, no one, to my knowledge, has yet made a full and convincing case for the classification. To date, arguably the best treatment of the comparison is that of Martin Hengel.[140] Hengel writes, "The traditional form of the name, ὁ κύριος Ἰησοῦς Χριστός...has a similar form to that of the Roman ruler...or Hellenistic kings.... [In that form] Jesus was the real proper name, 'Christos' the cognomen and 'Kyrios' the title."[141] On Hengel's model, these parallel name forms line up as shown in table 3.1.[142]

The details of this scheme present certain problems. Most important, the category of cognomen is strictly applicable only in the context of the Roman

---

139 See, e.g., Earl Richard, *Jesus, One and Many: The Christological Concept of New Testament Authors* (Wilmington, Del.: Glazier, 1988), 326: "Roman usage of imperial titles offers interesting parallels (e.g., 'Imperator Caesar Augustus' as contrasted to 'Lord Jesus Christ') and confirms the close connection which existed between certain titles and proper names. Indeed, some titles, while retaining their titular force...could also be used as surnames"; Donald Dale Walker, *Paul's Offer of Leniency (2 Cor 10:1): Populist Ideology and Rhetoric in a Pauline Letter Fragment* [WUNT 2/152; Tübingen: Mohr Siebeck, 2002], 163n256: "Imperial nomenclature is no less confusing [than Paul's use of χριστός]. We might compare the evolution of Caesar from name to title. Even more complex is the shift of Augustus from title to name—and back to title"; Walker, *Paul's Offer of Leniency,* 164n260: "Though it obscures a legitimate question, 'honorific designation' is a better way of describing Paul's use of χριστός than 'name' or 'title.' Familiarity should not blind us to the respect accorded by compound appellations."

140 Hengel, "'Christos' in Paul."

141 Hengel, "'Christos' in Paul," 68.

142 Modified from Hengel, "'Christos' in Paul," 68.

tria nomina. It assumes a praenomen and nomen, too, which are lacking in Paul's nomenclature for Jesus, and in the nomenclature of the Hellenistic kings, for that matter. It also assumes Roman citizenship, which is likewise not pertinent to the present case. We have seen, too, that Imperator (Αὐτοκράτωρ), although originally and usually a title, is actually a praenomen in the case of Augustus at least. However, if we set aside the peculiar strictures of the Roman system and use the corresponding Greek categories instead—titles, personal names, and honorifics—then the analogy is actually quite close.

Still, despite his argument for the analogy to royal honorifics and perhaps because of the confusion with the Roman system, later on in the same essay Hengel expresses frustration with all of the available categories. "In fact 'Christos' seems to be a word with a character all its own. It was neither one name among many, like Jesus, nor was it a customary Greek title, an honorific designation like βασιλεύς, κύριος, or δεσπότης.... [Instead] Χριστός expresses the 'inalienable uniqueness' of Jesus."[143] Here Hengel is right in what he denies but wrong in what he affirms. It is true that χριστός in Paul is neither a personal name nor a title, but it does not follow that it is *sui generis*. If Paul intends to express the inalienable uniqueness of Jesus, he does not do so by using an unparalleled onomastic category. Paul's χριστός is an honorific, and it works according to the syntactical rules that govern that onomastic category.[144] That is to say, Paul's χριστός differs in kind, not in evolutionary stage, from names on the one hand and titles on the other. In the following chapter I show more precisely how this is the case.

---

143 Hengel, "'Christos' in Paul," 74; citing with approval Grundmann, *TDNT* 9:540: "By means of this commonly used name the unmistakable uniqueness of Jesus is emphasised."

144 My argument in this chapter finds an interesting point of contact with Horbury, *Jewish Messianism and the Cult of Christ,* who has argued for the influence of the Hellenistic ruler cult on the development of Jewish messianism and its Christian counterpart, although, for his part, Horbury does not comment on the linguistic analogy between the names of the Hellenistic kings and Roman emperors and the names of Jesus. In any case, my linguistic claim is narrower than and independent of Horbury's history-of-religions thesis.

4

Christ Phrases in Paul

HAVING CONSIDERED THE history of the question, the problem of the meaningfulness of ancient messiah language, and the onomastic categories available to Paul, we are now in a position to analyze the Pauline evidence proper. A large part of the discussion of χριστός in Paul has proceeded, as such things usually do, by way of interpretation of passages in which he comments more or less directly on the point in question; I discuss these passages in chapter 5. It is a peculiar feature of this discussion, however, that an equally large part of it has focused not on interpretation of Paul's prose in context but rather on a few ostensibly significant phrases. A principal influence in this trend has been a 1953 essay by Nils Dahl, in which he makes several negative philological observations about the use of χριστός in Paul:

1. In the Pauline letters *Christos* is never a general term but always a designation for the one Christ, Jesus.
2. *Christos* is never used as a predicate; Paul never says, "Jesus is the Christ," or the like.
3. A genitive is never added; Paul does not say "the Christ of God."
4. The form *Iēsous ho Christos* is not to be found in the earliest text of the epistles.[1]

Since Dahl's essay, many subsequent interpreters have taken his philological observations as axiomatic in the discussion.[2] Some, too, have made additional philological observations that are taken to bear on the question in one way

---

1 Dahl, "Messiahship of Jesus in Paul," here 15–16.

2 See, e.g., Hengel, "'Christos' in Paul," 67: "Dahl's four basic philological observations speak for themselves"; also Gaston, *Paul and the Torah*, 6–7; Wright, *Climax*, 41–42; Dunn, *Theology of Paul*, 197–199; Cummins, "Divine Life," 200; Zetterholm, "Paul and the Missing Messiah," 39–40, 131n37.

or another.³ The purpose of the present chapter is to examine each of the Pauline χριστός phrases that have been identified as relevant to the question of messianism and to decide whether, and if so in what way, each of them in fact is.

"Jesus Christ" and "Christ Jesus"

First, to round out the argument advanced in chapter 3, it is necessary to give an account of the double forms Ἰησοῦς Χριστός and Χριστὸς Ἰησοῦς. Paul uses Ἰησοῦς Χριστός some 57 times, of 135 instances of the phrase spread throughout the New Testament. He uses the inverse form Χριστὸς Ἰησοῦς only slightly less frequently (49 times), with the remaining 46 New Testament instances of that form appearing almost entirely in the disputed Pauline letters.⁴ As a result, interpreters have spoken of "Christ Jesus" as a characteristically Pauline inversion of the original double name "Jesus Christ."⁵ What, though, would the reason have been for this inversion?

At the beginning of the twentieth century, Ernst von Dobschütz made the influential suggestion that Paul, noticing the ambiguity of the word Ἰησοῦς in the oblique cases (declining, as it does, nominative Ἰησοῦς, genitive Ἰησοῦ, dative Ἰησοῦ, accusative Ἰησοῦν), chose to put "Christ" (genitive Χριστοῦ, dative Χριστῷ) before "Jesus" in the genitive and the dative in order to avoid confusing his readers.⁶ Despite the popularity of the explanation, however, there are significant problems with it. Most important, Paul is far from consistent in his application of Dobschütz's rule. On the one hand, he sometimes

---

3 In particular, Conzelmann, "Christenheit"; Kramer, *Christ, Lord, Son of God;* Cullmann, *Christology of the New Testament;* Wright, "Messiah and the People of God"; Wright, *Climax,* 41–55; Wright, *Paul: In Fresh Perspective,* 42–50. Their philological criteria are discussed later.

4 In the disputed Pauline letters: Eph 1:1; 2:6, 7, 10, 13, 20; 3:1, 6, 11, 21; Col 1:1, 4; 2:6; 4:12; 1 Tim 1:1, 2, 12, 14, 15, 16; 2:5; 3:13; 4:6; 5:21; 6:13; 2 Tim 1:1, 2, 9, 10, 13; 2:1, 3, 10; 3:12, 15; 4:1; Titus 1:4. Outside the *corpus Paulinum:* Acts 3:20; 5:42; 18:5, 28; 24:24; 1 Pet 5:10.

5 A formidable obstacle to certainty, however, is presented by the textual tradition, in which the two orders are frequently confused. "Only in two thirds of the instances is the textual witness unequivocal" (Grundmann, *TDNT* 9:541).

6 Ernst von Dobschütz, *Die Thessalonicher-Briefe* (Göttingen: Vandenhoeck & Ruprecht, 1909), 60–61, in an excursus titled "Paulinische Formeln für Gott und Christus," here 61: "Schon hieraus ergibt sich als Motiv der Umstellung lediglich das grammatische: die Undeutlichkeit der casus obliqui von Ἰησοῦς." In 1962 Werner Kramer reinforced this theory for another generation of interpreters: "We can only conclude that his purpose in doing so [i.e., writing 'Christ Jesus' in the genitive and dative] really was to avoid the ambiguity which would have resulted if he had allowed Jesus to precede" (Kramer, *Christ, Lord, Son of God,* 206).

uses the order in cases that do not require it.[7] On the other hand, he also frequently uses the allegedly confusing genitive form that he is supposed to have wanted to avoid.[8]

Inconsistency aside, there is also the question whether the ambiguous form would have actually confused readers or auditors of Paul's Greek. After all, the declensions of many Greek words include ambiguous forms that authors generally do not go out of their way to avoid.[9] As for the offending forms Ἰησοῦ Χριστοῦ and Ἰησοῦ Χριστῷ, a reader would have to read only as far as the second word to have the ambiguity resolved. Moreover, in some oblique-case instances of the phrase, Paul uses a preceding case-specific preposition, which resolves the issue before it even arises.[10] In short, Dobschütz's explanation leaves too much evidence unexplained.

Other interpreters have suggested that Paul inverted the order of the terms precisely to highlight the messiahship of Jesus. Oscar Cullmann argues that the double formula Χριστὸς Ἰησοῦς, in that order, signals that Paul is summoning the titular force of χριστός. Otherwise, Cullmann concedes the majority view that "already the letters of Paul, the oldest Christian writings we possess, have a tendency to fix the word Christ as a proper name." Not so in the phrase Χριστὸς Ἰησοῦς, however: "The passages in which Paul writes 'Christ' before 'Jesus' (i.e., 'Christ Jesus') serve as a reminder that he is still aware of its real meaning."[11] Grundmann and Dunn, among others, have taken the same view.[12] Ironically, though, it is actually possible to argue in the

---

7 So "Christ Jesus" occurs in the accusative at Rom 6:3; 15:5; Gal 2:16; 4:14; and perhaps in the nominative at Rom 8:34 (so it is in P46 ℵ A C F G L ψ 6 33 81 104 365 1505 sy^h lat bo; but cf. B D et al. and the majority text, which lack Ἰησοῦς).

8 Genitive Ἰησοῦ Χριστοῦ occurs at Rom 1:4, 6, 7, 8; 3:22; 5:1, 11, 15, 17, 21; 7:25; 15:6, 30; 16:25, 27; 1 Cor 1:2, 3, 7, 8, 9, 10; 6:11; 15:57; 2 Cor 1:2, 3; 4:6; 8:9; 13:13; Gal 1:1, 3, 12; 2:16; 3:22; 6:14, 18; Phil 1:2, 11, 19; 2:21; 4:23; 1 Thess 1:3; 5:9, 23, 28; Phlm 3, 25. However, dative Ἰησοῦ Χριστῷ only occurs once (1 Thess 1:1), and that in the phrase κυρίῳ Ἰησοῦ Χριστῷ.

9 For a case study in the probable capacity of ancient Greek readers to distinguish ambiguous forms, see Ashton Waugh McWhorter, "A Study of the So-Called Deliberative Type of Question," *Transactions and Proceedings of the American Philological Association* 41 (1910): 157–168, especially 165–167.

10 E.g., ἐν … κυρίῳ Ἰησοῦ Χριστῷ (1 Thess 1:1); διὰ Ἰησοῦ Χριστοῦ (Rom 1:8; 5:21; 7:25; 16:27; Gal 1:1; Phil 1:11). This point is well made by Wright, "Messiah and the People of God," 272n68.

11 Cullmann, *Christology of the New Testament*, 112. Cullmann is not explicit, however, about why this should be the case. Presumably the rationale is that reversing the "normal" order to put χριστός in front is meant to draw attention to that word.

12 Grundmann, *TDNT* 9:542: "The element of dignity is imported into the proper name [Jesus] by it [Christ]. This is particularly clear when χριστός comes first." More recently Dunn, *Theology of Paul*, 199: "It is just possible that the distinctively Pauline use of the double name 'Christ Jesus' (as against 'Jesus Christ') is a direct translation equivalent of 'Messiah Jesus,' with *Christos* still bearing its titular force."

opposite direction, that the form Ἰησοῦς Χριστός is actually the one that signals an especially messianic sense, as Martin Hengel has suggested.[13]

By and large, though, neither of these explanations has commanded wide assent because most interpreters are not convinced that there is any consistency to the contexts in which the one form or the other appears. That is, it is not the case that Χριστὸς Ἰησοῦς occurs in recognizably messianic contexts while Ἰησοῦς Χριστός does not, or vice versa. As a result, the majority opinion to date is that Paul simply uses the two forms indiscriminately.[14] They are functionally interchangeable, and this is possible because both individual terms, "Jesus" and "Christ," are mere proper names.[15]

This explanation has certain advantages over the others, but the appeal to proper names is deeply problematic. In fact, the interchangeability of the two forms actually counts against the axiom that χριστός is a proper name for Paul. Real double personal names have a fixed order: The name is Julius Caesar, not Caesar Julius; Simon bar Jonah, not Bar Jonah Simon.[16] This is patently not the case, though, with Paul's use of "Jesus" and "Christ." Hans Lietzmann, noticing this, insisted that χριστός must at some time have been an appellative for Paul to use it so.[17] This is saying too little, however. Vernon McCasland rightly points out, "[Lietzmann] overlooks the fact that 'Christ'

---

13 It is generally acknowledged that the Greek Ἰησοῦς Χριστός will have derived from Aramaic ישוע משיחא, or perhaps Hebrew ישוע משיח. Hengel ("'Christos' in Paul," 75) makes the point that this early Aramaic form would have been not a name but a confession, that is, with a suppressed verb of being: not "Jesus the messiah" but "Jesus [is] the messiah." Greek Ἰησοῦς Χριστός does not typically function in this way but rather as a compound noun. Hengel wonders, though, whether Paul's use of the terms in this order may suggest a recollection of that early confession, which would have had a strong messianic sense.

14 Or perhaps he uses them as he does in the interest of euphony. As Wright has noted, however, it is not clear why one of these forms should be thought to sound better than the other (see Wright, *Climax*, 45). It is conceivable that a particular instance of either phrase might play into a pattern of alliteration in its near context, but examples are not forthcoming.

15 So Kramer, *Christ, Lord, Son of God*, 40: "Christ and Jesus can only be interchanged when both have become proper names for the one person. Only in the Gentile Christian church is this stage reached."

16 The real double name Pontius Pilate, for example, is always written in the order Πόντιος Πιλᾶτος (Luke 3:1; Acts 4:27; 1 Tim 6:13); but cf. the interchangeable forms Ἡρῴδης ὁ βασιλεύς (Matt 2:1; Luke 1:5; Acts 12:1) and ὁ βασιλεὺς Ἡρῴδης (Matt 2:3; Mark 6:14), or again Καίσαρος Αὐγούστου (Luke 2:1) and Τιβερίου Καίσαρος (Luke 3:1). On these examples see S. Vernon McCasland, "Christ Jesus," *JBL* 65 (1946): 382–383; cf. also my treatment of honorifics in chapter 3.

17 Hans Lietzmann, *Einführung in die Textgeschichte der Paulusbriefe: An die Römer* (Handbuch zum Neuen Testament 8; Tübingen: Mohr Siebeck, 1928), 23: "Aber auch hier ist Christus Eigenname, denn was es als Appellativ besagen würde, kommt ja in κύριος zum Ausdruck....Aber die Umstellung wäre doch nicht möglich, wenn Χριστός nicht ursprünglich Appellativum wäre und 'der Messias' hieße."

must still be an appellative in order to permit the inversion.... So long as a writer feels free to write either Ἰησοῦς Χριστός or Χριστὸς Ἰησοῦς, Χριστός is still in his mind an appellative."[18]

Dahl explains this anomaly in chronological and evolutionary terms: χριστός is "not completely fixed as a proper name" yet, but Paul's usage attests "a strikingly advanced stage in the evolution" to such a state of affairs.[19] However, Dahl's objection to the proper-name hypothesis on the grounds of flexible word order is independent of his evolutionary explanation, and in fact other explanations are more compelling. It is better to say, as I argued in chapter 3, that Paul's χριστός is different in kind, not in evolutionary stage, from names on the one hand and titles on the other. The forms Ἰησοῦς Χριστός and Χριστὸς Ἰησοῦς are interchangeable because χριστός here is being used as an honorific, and that is how honorifics are written.

Appellative

Having addressed the inverse double forms, I turn next to the four phrases identified by Dahl. His first philological observation is that for Paul "*Christos* is never a general term but always a designation for the one Christ, Jesus."[20] By "general term," Dahl means what is traditionally called an appellative, that is, a noun that refers to a class, not to an individual only.[21] Dahl cites by way of contrast Acts 17:3, where Paul reasons from the scriptures with the Thessalonian Jews that τὸν χριστὸν ἔδει παθεῖν καὶ ἀναστῆναι ἐκ νεκρῶν, "it was necessary for the Christ to suffer and to be raised from the dead," and in addition that οὗτός ἐστιν ὁ χριστὸς Ἰησοῦς ὃν ἐγὼ καταγγέλλω ὑμῖν, "this Jesus whom I announce

---

18 McCasland, "Christ Jesus," 382. So also Dahl, "Messiahship of Jesus in Paul," 16: "The name 'Christ' is not completely fixed as a proper name. The interchangeability of the forms *Christos Iēsous* and *Iēsous Christos* is already an indication of this."

19 Dahl, "Messiahship of Jesus in Paul," 16, 18; anticipated by William Sanday and Arthur C. Headlam, *A Critical and Exegetical Commentary on the Epistle to the Romans* (International Critical Commentary; Edinburgh: T. & T. Clark, 1977 [1896]), 3–4.

20 Dahl, "Messiahship of Jesus in Paul," 15. Likewise Hengel, "'Christos' in Paul," 67: "In Paul Χριστός is...always simply the designation for one particular person, i.e., Jesus."

21 For a classic definition, see A. I. Silvestre de Sacy, *Principles of General Grammar* (trans. David Fosdick; New York: Leavitt, 1834), 24–25:

> Nouns may be divided into several classes. Some designate beings by the idea of their individual nature, that is to say, in such a manner that this designation is applicable only to a single thing, to a single individual [citing as examples "Paris," "Rome," "Alexander," and "Vespasian"].... These nouns are called proper nouns. Other nouns designate beings by the idea of a nature common to all the individuals of a species [citing as examples "man," "horse," and "cat"].... These nouns, applicable to all the individuals of a species, are called appellative nouns.

to you is the Christ." Here χριστός is a genuine appellative, a noun referring not to an individual but to a class. Paul argues from scripture that the Christ, whoever he may be, would have to suffer and be raised and, further, that Jesus of Nazareth is a member (the only member, in this case) of the class "Christ."[22] For Dahl, as for most interpreters since, use of χριστός as an appellative is taken to be evidence of a messianic sense. If, on the other hand, χριστός refers only to Jesus, not to a class of which he may or may not be a member, then the word is taken to be nonconnotative.

It is actually not the case, however, that all titular forms are appellatives. In other words, a noun can refer to a single individual only and nevertheless bear titular force. Up to and through his lifetime, "Augustus" applied to no one but Octavian, but it is no less connotative a word for this having been the case. Likewise, "Bar Kokhba" ("son of the star") applied only to Shimon bar Kosiba, but its honorific force is undisputed. So in the case of χριστός in Paul, its not being an appellative does not imply that it has somehow lost its conventional sense.

Moreover, there are exigencies of Paul's own context that are pertinent to his use of χριστός, quite apart from whether the word has a messianic sense for him. The Gospels reflect a milieu in which there is knowledge of a category "messiah" that Jesus may or may not fit. In the Acts of the Apostles, likewise, it is an open question in the synagogue scenes whether or not Jesus the individual fits the category "messiah." Not so Paul's letters. Both the apostle and his churches are already convinced of the messiahship of Jesus; other things are at issue in the letters.[23] If any of them previously thought of "Christ" as a class that may or may not have particular members, they do so no longer. That the messiahship of Jesus is agreed upon, however, does not mean that it is unimportant.[24] On the contrary, as James Dunn has rightly pointed out, "What is characteristic and central to someone's theology need not be distinctive; what

---

22 Dahl also cites Acts 26:23, part of Paul's defense of himself before Festus and Agrippa, where he claims to have preached nothing other than what Moses and the prophets had said, namely: εἰ παθητὸς ὁ χριστός, εἰ πρῶτος ἐξ ἀναστάσεως νεκρῶν φῶς μέλλει καταγγέλλειν τῷ τε λαῷ καὶ τοῖς ἔθνεσιν, "the Christ would suffer, be the first of the resurrection of the dead, and proclaim light both to the people and to the Gentiles." But whether χριστός is actually an appellative here is not entirely clear.

23 This is not simply a factor of the majority-Gentile makeup of the Pauline churches. Even entirely Jewish-Christian churches could operate on the basis of the same shared assumption. In other words, this fact ought not be taken by itself as evidence of hellenization.

24 Interpreters, however, too often find Paul "downplaying" or "undermining" things that in fact he is simply not intending to write about in a given context. For examples of this tendency in the literature see Chester, "Messiahs, Mediators and Pauline Christology"; Zetterholm, "Paul and the Missing Messiah."

is fundamental can also be shared, and as shared, little referred to; what is axiomatic is often taken for granted."[25]

This is not to say that Paul never knew or used χριστός as an appellative. It is possible, as Alan Segal has suggested, that before his revelation Paul had highly developed ideas about the messiah.[26] If so, then he would have used χριστός as an appellative, before and apart from his association of the term with Jesus. Whether Paul did in fact have a developed messianism before his revelation cannot, in my view, be answered with any confidence from the sources available to us.[27] In any case, as we have seen, even if Paul used the word χριστός only of Jesus, never as an appellative, this would not by any means be evidence that the word was empty of connotation for him.

Predicate of the Verb "To Be"

Dahl's second philological observation is that "*Christos* is never used as a predicate; Paul never says 'Jesus is the Christ,' or the like."[28] Had Paul said such a thing, it would have been evidence of messiah Christology, but he did not, so such evidence is proportionately lacking. George MacRae, following Dahl, concludes, "The important point is that he [Paul] does not discuss the issue [messiahship] in his writings, making no effort to prove or demonstrate the messianic identity of Jesus."[29] It is important to note the line of reasoning

---

25 James D. G. Dunn, "How Controversial Was Paul's Christology?" in *The Christ and the Spirit: Collected Essays* (Grand Rapids, Mich.: Eerdmans, 1998), 221.

26 Alan F. Segal, "Paul's Jewish Presuppositions," in *Cambridge Companion to St. Paul,* 159–172, here 169:

> Did Paul become messianic because he became a Christian or was messianism a part of his Judaism before his conversion? It seems to me quite improbable that the Pharisees before the Amoraim were devoid of messianism and that Paul found it only when he became a Christian. Paul, then, is again the earliest Pharisaic evidence of the existence of messianic beliefs among the Pharisees, even if that belief was perhaps greatly augmented and quickened by his later Christian faith.

27 Which is not to say that nothing can be known about his pre-Christian views. When Paul describes that period, however, he emphasizes his zeal for the Torah (e.g., Gal 1:13–14: "zealous for my ancestral traditions"; Phil 3:4–6: "as for zeal persecuting the church, blameless with respect to the righteousness of the Torah"); he never mentions anything about his views of the messiah.

28 Dahl, "Messiahship of Jesus in Paul," 15. Likewise Hengel, "'Christos' in Paul," 67: "Nowhere is Χριστός a predicate. In contrast to the account of his preaching in Acts, in the letters Paul no longer has to affirm 'Jesus is the Messiah.'" See more recently Zetterholm, "Paul and the Missing Messiah," 37: "Jesus is never explicitly called 'the Messiah,' that is, Paul never uses 'Christ' as a predication of Jesus in formulations, such as 'Jesus is the Christ.'"

29 MacRae, "Messiah and Gospel," 172.

followed here: Paul does not say, "Jesus is the messiah"; therefore, Paul is uninterested in the messiahship of Jesus.

There are several points to be made on this matter. First of all, it is actually not the case that χριστός is never a predicate in Paul. It is, of course, frequently a predicate in the traditional grammatical sense when it occurs in the accusative case as a direct object.[30] But the interpreters cited earlier mean "predicate" in the sense used in formal logic and linguistic semantics, that is, as a property that can be true of something, or, in grammatical terms, as a predicate of the verb "to be."[31] It is this particular usage of χριστός that is found to be absent from Paul.

Even this usage is not entirely absent, however. In the difficult account of the wilderness wandering in 1 Corinthians 10, Paul says that the ancestors all drank from the same spiritual rock and that ἡ πέτρα δὲ ἦν ὁ χριστός, "the rock was Christ" (1 Cor 10:4).[32] Similarly, in his interpretation of the promise to Abraham in Galatians 3, Paul quotes the phrase καὶ τῷ σπέρματί σου, "and to your seed," drawing attention to the singular form σπέρματί, "seed," which, he explains, ἐστιν χριστός, "is Christ" (Gal 3:16).[33] In fact, then, contrary to the received wisdom, Paul actually does predicate messiahship. He does so, however, not of Jesus but rather of these ciphers from the ancient stories of the patriarchs and the exodus.[34]

It does not follow that Paul does not think Jesus is the messiah, just that Paul has other aims than the ones his interpreters set for him. The exceptions presented by 1 Cor 10:4 and Gal 3:16 to the often-cited rule that χριστός in Paul is never a predicate show that what interpreters have in mind are clauses of the precise form: subject Ἰησοῦς, verb εἰμι, predicate χριστός. That is, there

---

30 E.g., at Rom 13:14; 1 Cor 1:23; 10:9; 15:15; 2 Cor 4:5; 5:16; Gal 3:27; Phil 1:15, 17; 3:8, 20.

31 On the basics of predicate logic, see Jens Allwood et al., *Logic in Linguistics* (Cambridge: Cambridge University Press, 1977), 58–95.

32 Dahl grants 1 Cor 10:4 as one of a few "places … where the careful reader would detect messianic connotations" ("Messiahship of Jesus in Paul," 17). On this verse see further E. Earle Ellis, "Χριστός in 1 Corinthians 10.4, 9," in *From Jesus to John: Essays on Jesus and the New Testament Christology in Honour of Marinus de Jonge* (ed. Martinus C. de Boer; JSNTSup 84; Sheffield: JSOT Press, 1993), 168–173.

33 On which see Richard B. Hays, *Echoes of Scripture in the Letters of Paul* (New Haven: Yale University Press), 85: "This exegesis is less perverse than it might appear, depending as it surely does on the linkage of the catchword seed to God's promise to David in 2 Sam. 7:12–14.… This [latter] passage treats the singular noun seed not as a collective term, but as a reference to a specific royal successor to David; thus, it bears evident potential for messianic interpretation."

34 Hays may be right that Paul's scriptural hermeneutic is more often ecclesiocentric than christocentric (see Hays, *Echoes,* 84–87), but as Hays himself has subsequently shown, in not a few passages Paul gives expressly christocentric interpretations of certain scriptural oracles (see Hays, "Christ Prays the Psalms"; also Juel, *Messianic Exegesis,* 80–81, 85–87, 90).

is an assumption widely held among interpreters that the sentence "Jesus is the Christ" is precisely the form of sentence that would count as evidence of a messiah Christology.

Sentences of that form are indeed a commonplace in early Christian literature of a variety of genres.[35] Central to the story line of the Synoptic Gospels is a controversy over Jesus's identity, in response to which Peter's confession, σὺ εἶ ὁ χριστός, "You are the Christ," is commended by the evangelists (Mark 8:29; Matt 16:16; Luke 9:20).[36] John's Gospel differs drastically from the others in some respects, but it shares with them the axiom that Jesus is the Christ. The purpose of the Gospel, according to the epilogue at the end of chapter 20, is ἵνα πιστεύητε ὅτι Ἰησοῦς ἐστιν ὁ χριστὸς ὁ υἱὸς τοῦ θεοῦ, "that you might believe that Jesus is the Christ, the son of God" (John 20:31).[37] Related to this theme in the Gospel is the controversy in the First Epistle of John over the claim Ἰησοῦς ἐστιν ὁ Χριστός, "Jesus is the Christ": the person who believes it is a child of God (1 John 5:1), but the person who denies it is a liar and an antichrist (1 John 2:22).[38] The same statement appears repeatedly in the Acts of the Apostles as the content of the missionary message.[39] So, for example, in Acts 9 the newly baptized Saul confounds the Damascene Jews by showing them that οὗτός ἐστιν ὁ χριστός, "This man [Jesus] is the Christ" (Acts 9:22).[40] More examples

---

35 The evidence is capably surveyed by MacRae, "Messiah and Gospel."

36 Cf. the refrain τίς ἐστιν οὗτος, "Who is this?" (Mark 4:41; Matt 21:10; Luke 5:21; 7:49, 9:9); also Jesus's prophecy about the latter-day deceivers who will say ἐγώ εἰμι ὁ χριστός, "I am the Christ" (Matt 24:5; cf. Mark 13:21; Matt 24:23: ἰδοὺ ὧδε ὁ χριστός); and the trial narratives, in which Peter's confession reappears word for word as a question on the lips of the high priest: σὺ εἶ ὁ χριστός, "Are you the Christ?" (Mark 14:61; Matt 26:63; on which see Dahl, "Crucified Messiah").

37 Cf. the Samaritan woman's question: οὗτός ἐστιν ὁ χριστός, "Is this man the Christ?" (John 4:29). Likewise, some among the crowds say, οὗτός ἐστιν ὁ χριστός, "This man is the Christ" (John 7:41). The criterion for expulsion from the synagogue is the confession: ἐάν τις αὐτὸν ὁμολογήσῃ χριστόν, ἀποσυνάγωγος γένηται, "If anyone should confess him as Christ, he would be put out of the synagogue" (John 9:22). It is an important Johannine corollary, too, that John the Baptizer is not the Christ (John 1:20; 3:28; cf. 1:25).

38 Cf. the parallel phrases Ἰησοῦς ἐστιν ὁ υἱὸς τοῦ θεοῦ, "Jesus is the son of God" (1 John 4:15; 5:5); Ἰησοῦν Χριστὸν ἐν σαρκὶ ἐληλυθότα, "Jesus Christ having come in flesh" (1 John 4:2); Ἰησοῦν Χριστὸν ἐρχόμενον ἐν σαρκί "Jesus Christ coming in flesh" (2 John 7). This theme in 1 John is perhaps more related to the messiahship of Jesus than it is to putative proto-Gnosticism in the Johannine community (so rightly Horbury, *Messianism among Jews and Christians*, 332), *pace* Raymond E. Brown, *The Community of the Beloved Disciple* (New York: Paulist, 1979).

39 Albeit always in contexts of discussion with Jews.

40 Again in Acts 17, Saul, now called Paul, declares to the "synagogue of the Jews" at Thessalonica, οὗτός ἐστιν ὁ χριστὸς Ἰησοῦς ὃν ἐγὼ καταγγέλλω ὑμῖν, "This Jesus whom I announce to you is the Christ" (Acts 17:3). Later still, Paul in Corinth, and Apollos in Ephesus, reason with the Jews from the scriptures εἶναι τὸν χριστὸν Ἰησοῦν, "that Jesus is the Christ" (Acts 18:5, 28).

could be cited, but the point is clear enough: Predication of messiahship of Jesus is one well-attested form of early Christian reflection on messiahship.

In the Pauline letters, though, the nearest analogy is the predication κύριος Ἰησοῦς, "Jesus is lord." In fact, as a number of interpreters have pointed out, if there was a characteristic confession in the Pauline churches, it was probably this and not χριστὸς Ἰησοῦς, "Jesus is the Christ."[41] Paul uses the former phrase several times in expressly confessional contexts.[42] For example, he writes, ἐὰν ὁμολογήσῃς ἐν τῷ στόματί σου κύριον Ἰησοῦν...σωθήσῃ, "If you confess with your mouth Jesus as lord...you will be saved" (Rom 10:9).[43] This and other similar references suggest that the confession κύριος Ἰησοῦς was indeed a hallmark of the Pauline churches, even if there is no evidence that Paul was advocating this confession, κύριος Ἰησοῦς, over against the other, χριστὸς Ἰησοῦς.[44]

What reason is there, though, for thinking that statements of the form "Jesus is the Christ" are the only, or even the best, evidence of a concern for messiahship on the part of an ancient author? In other words, why should that particular syntactical construction rather than any other be regarded as the criterion *par excellence* for messiah Christology? As far as I have been able to tell, this assumption goes almost entirely unexamined in the secondary literature.[45] It may be that it derives from a deep-seated and unconscious inheritance from the centuries-long *adversus Judaeos* tradition, in which a dominant question was: Is Jesus the messiah or not?[46] Pauline interpreters, and histo-

---

41 See Hengel, "'Christos' in Paul," 67: "κύριος Ἰησοῦς and not Ἰησοῦς ὁ χριστός was Paul's basic confession"; citing Cerfaux, *Christ in Paul;* also Lietzmann, *An die Römer,* 23.

42 A point emphasized by Conzelmann ("Christenheit," 64) and Kramer (*Christ, Lord, Son of God,* 65–84), who draw the further form-critical conclusion that the acclamation κύριος Ἰησοῦς was the characteristic "homologia" of the Pauline churches, made possible by their origin on Gentile rather than Jewish "soil."

43 Also 1 Cor 12:3: οὐδεὶς ἐν πνεύματι θεοῦ λαλῶν λέγει· Ἀνάθεμα Ἰησοῦς, καὶ οὐδεὶς δύναται εἰπεῖν Κύριος Ἰησοῦς, εἰ μὴ ἐν πνεύματι ἁγίῳ, "No one speaking in the spirit of God says, 'Jesus be anathema,' and no one can say 'Jesus is lord' except in the holy spirit"; and Phil 2:11, where God exalts the risen Jesus so that πᾶσα γλῶσσα ἐξομολογήσηται ὅτι κύριος Ἰησοῦς Χριστὸς εἰς δόξαν θεοῦ πατρός, "every tongue might confess that Jesus Christ is lord, to the glory of God the father."

44 As Zetterholm, "Paul and the Missing Messiah," suggests: "To present Jesus as the Messiah of Israel...would have contributed to the continuation of the ethnic confusion that Paul is trying to correct" (51).

45 The exception is the work of some early twentieth-century Jewish historians who criticize their Christian counterparts for their interest in only those Jewish messiah texts and traditions that closely mirror well-known Christian ones (see, e.g., Klausner, *Messianic Idea,* 3, in response to Drummond, *Jewish Messiah*).

46 For an early and paradigmatic example, see Justin, *Dialogue with Trypho.* In the modern period, cf. the famous comment of Gershom Scholem, "The Messianic Idea," 1: "Any discussion of the problems relating to Messianism is a delicate matter, for it is here that the essential conflict between Judaism and Christianity has developed and continues to exist."

rians of early Judaism and Christianity generally, have an intuition that that really is the issue and that any early Christian author who talked about messiahship would have had to talk about it in just this way.

This is only an intuition, however, not a warranted belief. As I have shown in chapter 2, both Jewish and Christian texts that comment on messiah figures do so in a vast variety of ways, only one of which is predication of messiahship of particular persons. Statements of the form "[name] is the Christ" account for just a small part of ancient literature about messiah figures. That Paul never writes "Jesus is the Christ" does not mean that he is not interested in messiahship. It means only that his interests are different from those represented in the texts that do make such statements.

Genitive Modifiers

Dahl's third philological observation is: "A genitive is never added; Paul does not say 'the Christ of God.' "[47] The second clause of this statement is really to the point. Dahl and his bibliographical successors are not looking for just any genitive modifier; they are looking for the biblical expression χριστὸς κυρίου, "the Lord's Christ," or χριστὸς θεοῦ, "the Christ of God." Hengel, for example, writes more directly, "In contrast to pre-Christian Old Testament and Jewish tradition it is never governed by a genitive (θεοῦ, κυρίου, etc.) or a possessive pronoun."[48]

Indeed, if one looks in Paul for this particular form, the results are admittedly meager. This observation should not be overinterpreted, however. For one thing, as I noted in chapter 2, there is actually considerable diversity in the use of χριστός in the Greek Jewish scriptures themselves. The idiom χριστὸς κυρίου, or χριστός with an equivalent genitive personal pronoun, is frequent in 1–2 Samuel (Greek 1–2 Kingdoms) and the Psalter and also occurs at a few places in the Prophets and Chronicles.[49] However, χριστός is also common and always adjectival in Leviticus;[50] and it occurs twice in the

---

47 Dahl, "Messiahship of Jesus in Paul," 15.

48 Hengel, " 'Christos' in Paul," 67.

49 See χριστὸς κυρίου (1 Sam 16:6; 24:7 [*bis*], 11; 26:9, 11, 16, 23; 2 Sam 1:14, 16; 2:5 LXX; 19:22; Lam 4:20; 2 Chron 22:7 LXX), χριστὸς θεοῦ (2 Sam 23:1), χριστὸς αὐτοῦ (1 Sam 2:10; 12:3, 5; Amos 4:13 LXX; Ps 2:2; 20:7 [19:7 LXX]; 28:8 [27:8 LXX]; 89:52 [88:52 LXX]); χριστὸς μου (1 Sam 2:35; Ps 132:17 [131:17 LXX]; Isa 45:1), χριστὸς σου (Ps 84:10 [83:10 LXX]; 89:38, 52 [88:39, 52 LXX]; 132:10 [131:10 LXX]; 2 Chron 6:42; Hab 3:13).

50 See ὁ ἱερεὺς ὁ χριστός, "anointed priest" (Lev 4:5, 16; 6:15; cf. 2 Macc 1:10); τὸ ἔλαιον τὸ χριστόν, "anointing oil" (Lev 21:10, 12).

absolute in Daniel.[51] In other words, it is not the case that the biblical "Christ" is always "the Christ of God," grammatically speaking. In light of this diversity of biblical usage, it is not surprising that many early Jewish texts that are widely and rightly taken to refer to messiah figures do not use the formula משיח יהוה/χριστὸς κυρίου.[52] There is, then, no reason for thinking that Paul's failure to use this formula renders his use of χριστός nonmessianic.

The formulaic "Christ of God," while it is not a fixed feature of Jewish messiah texts generally, does happen to be characteristic of Luke-Acts, and this may explain why interpreters expect to find it in Paul's letters and judge Paul to be nonmessianic for not using it.[53] It is well established that Luke's use of χριστός is closely modeled on the "Lord's anointed" of 1–2 Samuel and the Psalter.[54] For example, in a uniquely Lukan scene in the infancy narrative, Simeon the prophet is told that he will not see death before he sees τὸν χριστὸν κυρίου, "the Lord's Christ" (Luke 2:26).[55] In the Acts of the Apostles, when Peter and John are released from their arrest, the believers pray the words of Ps 2:1–2: The rulers gather together κατὰ τοῦ κυρίου καὶ κατὰ τοῦ χριστοῦ αὐτοῦ, "against the Lord and against his Christ" (Acts 4:26).[56] This usage is certainly evidence of a messiah Christology, but it is only one of the possible kinds of such evidence. In fact, "Christ of God" language turns out to be something of a Lukan idiosyncrasy, albeit one with an estimable biblical pedigree; it is not a fixed feature of ancient Jewish messiah language generally. That Paul for the most part does not use it only means that his usage is non-Lukan in this respect, not that it is nonmessianic.

Second, the absence of genitive qualifiers for χριστός in Paul should not be overstated. The fact that he does not use the phrase χριστὸς κυρίου is to be

---

51 See χριστός, "anointed one" (Dan 9:25, 26).

52 The phrase משיח יהוה is nowhere in the sectarian scrolls from Qumran, to recall just one significant example from chapter 2.

53 Per scholarly convention, I use "Luke" to refer to the author of Luke-Acts, without thereby making any claim about the identity of that author.

54 See Strauss, *Davidic Messiah in Luke-Acts*.

55 Similarly, in Luke Peter confesses Jesus to be τὸν χριστὸν τοῦ θεοῦ, "the Christ of God" (Luke 9:20); cf. the parallels at Mark 8:29 and Matt 16:16, which lack the "Christ of God" formula. Also, in Luke the rulers mock Jesus on the cross saying, "Let him save himself, if he is ὁ χριστὸς τοῦ θεοῦ ὁ ἐκλεκτός, "the Christ of God, the chosen one" (Luke 23:35); cf. the parallels at Mark 15:32 and Matt 27:40, which again lack the "Christ of God" formula.

56 The text of the citation in Acts 4:25–26 is identical to the text of Ps 2:1–2 LXX (ed. Rahlfs, *Psalmi cum Odis*): ἵνα τί ἐφρύαξαν ἔθνη/καὶ λαοὶ ἐμελέτησαν κενά/παρέστησαν οἱ βασιλεῖς τῆς γῆς/καὶ οἱ ἄρχοντες συνήχθησαν ἐπὶ τὸ αὐτὸ/κατὰ τοῦ κυρίου καὶ κατὰ τοῦ χριστοῦ αὐτοῦ. Cf. also Peter's first speech in Jerusalem, which uses χριστός with the genitive personal pronoun for God: τὸν χριστὸν αὐτοῦ, "his Christ" (Acts 3:18).

expected since for Paul the title κύριος applies, for the most part, not to God but to Jesus.[57] As for χριστὸς θεοῦ, while its general absence from Pauline usage is noteworthy, there is an interesting exception at 1 Cor 3:23—χριστὸς δὲ θεοῦ, "Christ is God's"—albeit a predicate, not an attributive, relation. Here, against certain Corinthian believers whom he censures for boasting in human beings (1:21), Paul counters, "All things are yours, and you are Christ's, and Christ is God's" (1:22–23). In this passage we find not only the elusive χριστὸς θεοῦ in Paul but also the parallel phrase ὑμεῖς χριστοῦ, evidence that the notion of "the people of the messiah" is not entirely absent from Paul.[58] Also relevant here is the appositional phrase at 1 Cor 1:24: Χριστὸν θεοῦ δύναμιν καὶ θεοῦ σοφίαν, "Christ, the power of God and the wisdom of God," where again Christ is "of God," but this time with intervening abstract nouns of apposition.[59]

It is true that, these exceptions aside, Paul does not relate Christ and God with this particular genitive formula, but it is necessary to note the other syntactical ways in which he does relate them.[60] Especially, Paul uses the converse genitive construction ὁ θεὸς καὶ πατὴρ τοῦ κυρίου ἡμῶν Ἰησοῦ Χριστοῦ, "the God and father of our lord Jesus Christ" (Rom 15:6; 2 Cor 1:3; cf. Eph 1:3; 1 Pet 1:3), where God and Christ are in genitive-construct relation, but the other way around from the pattern of 1–2 Samuel and the Psalter. It is

---

57 See Werner Foerster, "κύριος," *TDNT* 3:1088–1094; David B. Capes, *Old Testament Yahweh Texts in Paul's Christology* (WUNT 2/47; Tübingen: Mohr Siebeck, 1992). In more than a few cases, the referent of the title in context is stubbornly ambiguous, which may be intentional on Paul's part.

58 Schweitzer, *Mysticism,* and Wright, "Messiah and the People of God," especially, make a great deal of this latter notion, but clear, substantial evidence for it is slim. I discuss this further later on.

59 Understandably, discussion of this passage has tended to focus on the appositives δύναμιν and σοφίαν rather than on the genitive θεοῦ, especially as they pertain to questions of "wisdom Christology." Among the secondary literature, see the early treatment of Davies, *Paul and Rabbinic Judaism*, 147–176, under the heading "the old and the new Torah: Christ the wisdom of God."

60 Genitive constructions aside, also relevant are those places in which God and Christ appear as a pair, especially in the grace wish χάρις ὑμῖν καὶ εἰρήνη ἀπὸ θεοῦ πατρὸς ἡμῶν καὶ κυρίου Ἰησοῦ Χριστοῦ, "grace and peace to you from God our father and the lord Jesus Christ" (Rom 1:7; 1 Cor 1:3; 2 Cor 1:2; Gal 1:3; Phil 1:2; Phlm 3; cf. Eph 1:2; 2 Thess 1:2). A similar pairing of Christ and God is evident at 1 Cor 8:6, where Paul confesses εἷς θεὸς ὁ πατὴρ... καὶ εἷς κύριος Ἰησοῦς Χριστός, "one God the father... and one lord Jesus Christ"; likewise Gal 1:1, where Paul's apostleship comes through Ἰησοῦ Χριστοῦ καὶ θεοῦ πατρὸς τοῦ ἐγείραντος αὐτὸν ἐκ νεκρῶν, "Jesus Christ and God the father who raised him from the dead"; and also 1 Thess 1:1, the address to τῇ ἐκκλησίᾳ Θεσσαλονικέων ἐν θεῷ πατρὶ καὶ κυρίῳ Ἰησοῦ Χριστῷ, "the church of the Thessalonians that is in God the father and the lord Jesus Christ." In all of these cases, Christ is Christ in near relation to God, even if he is not "the Christ of God." Also relevant in this connection is "son of God" language in Paul (on which see Wright, *Climax,* 43–44; cf. Wright, *Paul: In Fresh Perspective,* 48).

not χριστὸς θεοῦ but θεὸς χριστοῦ, not "the Christ of God" but "the God of Christ."[61] So also, in the difficult passage about the covering of Corinthian women's heads, Paul writes, κεφαλὴ δὲ τοῦ Χριστοῦ ὁ θεός, "God is the head of Christ" (1 Cor 11:3), the grammatical converse of "Christ the power of God and wisdom of God" in 1 Cor 1:24.[62] Otherwise, Paul actually uses θεός with a genitive modifier very rarely. When he does so, it is customarily in a benediction formula (e.g., "the God of peace be with you"), where the genitive is an abstract noun for a virtue that characterizes God.[63]

In sum, the fact that χριστός in Paul does not take the formulaic genitive modifiers κυρίου and θεοῦ counts neither for nor against its bearing its conventional sense. Use of the idiom χριστὸς κυρίου, of which Luke-Acts is a standout example, is evidence of a particular sort of messianism, namely one that borrows heavily from the royal ideology of Samuel-Kings and the Greek Psalter. However, as twentieth-century research into Jewish messiah texts has made abundantly clear, there is more than one way to use biblical messiah language.[64] To rule against Paul's χριστός having a definite sense because it is not followed by κυρίου or θεοῦ is to confuse Pauline usage with its Lukan counterpart.

The Definite Article

The most frequently invoked grammatical reason for thinking that χριστός in Paul is a name, not a title, is the fact that Paul most often uses the word without an accompanying definite article. By my count, of the 269 instances of χριστός in the undisputed Pauline letters, 220 (i.e., 82 percent) lack the

---

61 It is worth noting that, unlike some of his early twenty-first-century interpreters, Paul never actually calls God "the God of Israel" (a point well made by Beverly Roberts Gaventa, "On the Calling-into-Being of Israel: Romans 9:6–29," in *Between Gospel and Election: Explorations in the Interpretation of Romans 9–11* [ed. Florian Wilk et al.; WUNT 257; Tübingen: Mohr Siebeck, 2010], 255–269). (For examples of the phrase used in connection with Paul, see Hays, *Echoes*, 69; Wright, *What Saint Paul Really Said*, 93; and recently J. R. Daniel Kirk, *Unlocking Romans: Resurrection and the Justification of God* [Grand Rapids, Mich.: Eerdmans, 2008], 4.) This is not to say that the phrase is not apt, just that it is not Paul's way of naming God (but cf. Ἰσραὴλ τοῦ θεοῦ, "the Israel of God," at Gal 6:16).

62 On κεφαλὴ δὲ τοῦ Χριστοῦ ὁ θεός in 1 Cor 11:3, see Dale B. Martin, *The Corinthian Body* (New Haven: Yale University Press, 1999), 232, who rightly notes that, a mountain of secondary literature notwithstanding, the force of the argument rests not on the precise sense of κεφαλή but rather on the analogies Christ:man:: man:woman:: God:Christ.

63 So especially ὁ θεὸς τῆς εἰρήνης, "the God of peace" (Rom 15:33; 16:20; Phil 4:9; 1 Thess 5:23); also ὁ θεὸς τῆς ὑπομονῆς καὶ τῆς παρακλήσεως, "the God of endurance and of encouragement" (Rom 15:5); ὁ θεὸς τῆς ἐλπίδος, "the God of hope" (Rom 15:13); and ὁ θεὸς τῆς ἀγάπης καὶ εἰρήνης, "the God of love and peace" (2 Cor 13:11).

64 On this point, see chapter 2.

definite article, while 49 (i.e., 18 percent) have it. This is the point of Dahl's fourth philological observation: "The form *Iēsous ho Christos* is not to be found in the earliest text of the epistles."[65] That is, the anarthrous name "Jesus" followed by articular title "the Christ" is not a Pauline expression. When Paul uses the two words together, both are always anarthrous, suggesting for Dahl that both are meant as names. Along the same lines, Dunn comments, "Of some 269 occurrences of 'Christ' only 46 (17%) speak of 'the Christ.'" Dunn concludes that "the title...has been elided into a proper name, usually with hardly an echo of the titular significance."[66] The absence of the definite article implies the absence of titular significance for the word.

On the other hand, those interpreters who argue in favor of a titular sense of χριστός in Paul often appeal to the instances where the apostle does use the definite article. Some such interpreters grant that the anarthrous forms have no titular force but insist that the relatively fewer articular forms do have such force. Hans Conzelmann writes: "Jesus trägt weiter den Messiastitel. 'Christus' hat da titularen Sinn, wo der bestimmte Artikel steht."[67] Other interpreters extrapolate from the articular forms to argue that the anarthrous forms, too, retain their titular force.[68]

The appeal to the definite article in this matter is actually a commonplace in research into ancient texts about messiah figures generally.[69] As for

---

65 Dahl, "Messiahship of Jesus in Paul," 16, citing the Textus Receptus of 1 Cor 3:11 as the sole later instance of the form, on which see the later discussion.

66 Dunn, "How Controversial?" 214–215.

67 Conzelmann, "Christenheit," 65.

68 See Wright, *Climax,* especially 43. However, more recently he has cautioned, "The use of the definite article, in relation to *Christos,* though important, doesn't get us very far, because Greek uses the article in subtly different ways to English. We must beware of easy but false assumptions at this point" (Wright, *Paul: In Fresh Perspective,* 43).

69 For example, Charlesworth comments in his *ANRW* article on the messiah in the Pseudepigrapha:

> We are usually uncertain that a noun is a title, since the original languages of the documents—notably Hebrew, Aramaic, Syriac, and Greek—did not clarify when a term should be capitalized in English and in our conceptions, and no morphological or grammatical clue helps us to separate non-titular from titular usages. Some of the pseudepigrapha are preserved solely or primarily in Syriac, which has no clear means to denote the definite article. (Charlesworth, "Messiah in the Pseudepigrapha," *ANRW* 2.19.1:196)

In modern English usage, capitalization and the definite article are widely recognized signals that a noun is being used as a title. Capitalization, though, was not for the most part a feature of any of the ancient languages in question, and the definite article in this period is notoriously difficult to handle across languages. Greek has a completely inflected article, Hebrew an uninflected one. Aramaic lacks the definite article but has an emphatic or determined state that exercises the same function. Latin and Syriac lack the article altogether, but exigencies of translation sometimes resulted in the appropriation of other features of those languages ancient Greek, it is true that, as a rule, it does not employ the definite article with personal names. Smyth summarizes, "Names of persons and places are individual and therefore omit the article unless previously mentioned or specially marked as well known."[70] While Greek names are generally anarthrous, though, not all anarthrous nouns are names. In particular, it is well known that some appellatives, especially titles, are characteristically anarthrous, too. Smyth comments, "Several appellatives, treated like proper names, may omit the article."[71] The same pattern holds in early Christian Greek, as well.[72] Paul's own practice corresponds to this general flexibility in the language. He customarily uses anarthrous forms of personal names (as, for example, in all of the greetings in Romans 16), but not always so;[73] and he frequently uses the title χριστός without the article in a manner analogous to a personal name. In all this he is well within standard conventions for the use of the definite article.

Dahl emphasizes that the exact form Ἰησοῦς ὁ χριστός, "Jesus the Christ" (that is, anarthrous Ἰησοῦς followed by articular χριστός), does not occur anywhere in the earliest text of the Pauline letters.[74] Not much should be made of this fact, however. In fact, that form does not occur anywhere at all in the Greek New Testament, according to the text of NA27.[75] Presumably, Dahl has in mind several similar forms that do occur, like Ἰησοῦν τὸν κύριον ἡμῶν, "Jesus our lord" (1 Cor 9:1; 2 Pet 1:2), and Ἰησοῦν τὸν υἱὸν τοῦ θεοῦ, "Jesus the son of God" (Heb

---

to compensate (on the Greek definite article in Syriac translation, see Theodor Nöldeke, *Compendious Syriac Grammar* [trans. James A. Crichton; Winona Lake, Ind.: Eisenbrauns, 2001], §228).

70 Smyth §1136. If it is objected that χριστός is exceptional because cultic, it is also the case that "names of deities omit the article, except when emphatic…or when definite cults are referred to" (Smyth §1137).

71 Smyth §1140, citing as examples "βασιλεύς king of Persia" and "πρυτάνεις the Prytans."

72 See BDF §260. In the case of χριστός, BDF read the articular instances as titles and the anarthrous instances as names: "Χριστός is properly an appellative=the Messiah, which comes to expression in the Gospels and Acts in the frequent appearance of the article; the Epistles usually (but not always) omit the article" (§260), following Bernhard Weiss, "Der Gebrauch des Artikels bei den Eigennamen," *Theologische Studien und Kritiken* 86 (1913): 349–389.

73 Excluding instances that appear in LXX citations and borderline cases like Satan, Caesar, Israel, and Pharaoh, there are twenty or so instances in which Paul uses articular forms of personal names (namely Adam, Moses, Hosea, Jesus, Cephas, and Stephanas). See Rom 4:9, 13; 8:11; 9:15, 25; 1 Cor 1:16; 9:9; 10:2; 15:22; 2 Cor 4:10, 11; Gal 2:14; 3:8, 14, 29; 6:17; 1 Thess 4:14.

74 He notes, however, the exception at 1 Cor 3:11 (θεμέλιον γὰρ ἄλλον οὐδεὶς δύναται θεῖναι παρὰ τὸν κείμενον, ὅς ἐστιν Ἰησοῦς [ὁ] Χριστός, "For no one can lay any other foundation than the one that has been laid, which is Jesus [the] Christ"), where NA27, with all the early papyrus and majuscule witnesses, reads Ἰησοῦς Χριστός, but the majority text has an intervening article (Dahl, "Messiahship of Jesus in Paul," 16). This is significant if only as evidence that a tradent of the text of 1 Corinthians thought that Paul wrote, or ought to have written, an intervening article.

75 But cf. Ἰησοῦς ὁ λεγόμενος χριστός (Matt 1:16; 27:17, 22).

4:14).[76] Of these similar forms, though, only one is Pauline, and that only in a single instance (Ἰησοῦν τὸν κύριον ἡμῶν in 1 Cor 9:1). Paul does not characteristically write Ἰησοῦς ὁ κύριος, and yet the signification of κύριος in Paul is not in question, and rightly so because interpreters recognize that use of the form "[anarthrous name] [articular appellative]" is not otherwise a proper criterion for knowing whether the second term signifies something or not.

In many instances, furthermore, the presence or absence of the definite article with χριστός in Paul is simply *pro forma* and contributes nothing to the question whether the word signifies something, as both Dahl and Kramer have shown.[77] Especially, the use of the genitive forms χριστοῦ and τοῦ χριστοῦ depends on whether the governing noun has the article or not; the genitive will match its governing noun in this respect.[78] Nominative, dative, and accusative forms of χριστός usually lack the article in Pauline usage.[79] Some of the articular instances are simply anaphoric, referring to a preceding instance of the same word. When the presence or absence of the article is determined by formal factors like these, it cannot reasonably be taken as evidence for any particular theory as to whether or what the word signifies.[80]

In short, the presence or absence of the article is not determinative of the class of noun being used.[81] Both names and appellatives may take the arti-

---

76 Other similar forms include Ἰησοῦς ὁ Ναζαρηνός, "Jesus the Nazarene" (Mark 10:47; Luke 24:19); Ἰησοῦς ὁ Ναζωραῖος, "Jesus the Nazarene" (Matt 26:71; Luke 18:37; John 18:5, 7; Acts 2:22; 6:14; 22:8; 26:9); Ἰησοῦς ὁ Ναζωραῖος ὁ βασιλεὺς τῶν Ἰουδαίων, "Jesus the Nazarene, the king of the Jews" (John 19:19); Ἰησοῦς ὁ βασιλεὺς τῶν Ἰουδαίων, "Jesus the king of the Jews" (Matt 27:37).

77 Dahl, "Messiahship of Jesus in Paul," 16; Kramer, *Christ, Lord, Son of God*, 206–212.

78 Per the so-called Canon of Apollonius (see Dahl, "Messiahship of Jesus in Paul," 16; Kramer, *Christ, Lord, Son of God*, 207). For an excellent example, see both forms in 1 Cor 6:15: οὐκ οἴδατε ὅτι τὰ σώματα ὑμῶν μέλη Χριστοῦ ἐστιν; ἄρας οὖν τὰ μέλη τοῦ Χριστοῦ ποιήσω πόρνης μέλη; "Do you not know that your bodies are parts of Christ? Will I therefore take the parts of Christ and make them parts of a prostitute?" There is a single exception at Phil 2:30: διὰ τὸ ἔργον Χριστοῦ μέχρι θανάτου ἤγγισεν, "He [Epaphroditus] was near death for the sake of the work of Christ"; the majority text has the articular τοῦ Χριστοῦ, which is almost certainly a correction.

79 In the nominative, anarthrous χριστός forty times but articular ὁ χριστός seven times (Rom 9:5; 15:3, 7; 1 Cor 1:13; 10:4; 11:3; 12:12). In the dative, anarthrous χριστῷ fifty-nine times but articular τῷ χριστῷ four times (Rom 14:18; 1 Cor 15:22; 2 Cor 2:14; 11:2). In the accusative, anarthrous χριστόν twenty-four times but articular τὸν χριστόν six times (1 Cor 10:9; 15:15; 2 Cor 11:3; Phil 1:15, 17; 3:7).

80 The seven instances of nominative χριστός with the definite article but unaccompanied by Ἰησοῦς (namely, Rom 9:5; 15:3, 7; 1 Cor 1:13; 10:4; 11:3; 12:12) have tended to be at the center of the discussion of messiahship in Paul. If interpreters grant any titular uses of χριστός at all, they are usually among these seven texts. I comment on several of these passages in their contexts in chapter 5.

81 As Kramer, *Christ, Lord, Son of God*, 212, concedes: "As time went on *Christ* came to be regarded increasingly as a proper name, yet in spite of this the article was still used with it here and there. This was possible because the pattern had already been formed, but equally because it was quite possible to use the article with the proper name."

cle or not. Especially, a significant group of appellatives follow the same rules for articles that names do. In Grundmann's words, "Since proper names are used with the article, χριστός with the article can have the same sense as χριστός without it.... Use of the article does not help us to decide when χριστός is a title and when it is a name."[82] The apparent parallel with the English definite article does not hold up under scrutiny. The many anarthrous instances of χριστός in Paul are not evidence that for him the word is merely a name, but neither are the articular instances evidence that it is a title.

Subject of a Sentence

Dahl's four philological observations identify forms that, if present, would count as evidence of a messianic use of χριστός. Their general absence from Pauline usage, then, is taken to count against messiahship in Paul's thought. Since Dahl's influential essay, other interpreters have suggested several phrases that Paul does use that might be taken as evidence for a messianic χριστός. One such form, advocated by Hans Conzelmann in the 1950s, is Paul's use of χριστός as the subject of a sentence. Conzelmann writes, "'Christus' hat da titularen Sinn... wo 'Christus' (ohne den Namen 'Jesus') Subjekt eines Satzes ist. 'Christus' heisst Jesus mit Vorliebe dann, wenn er als der Vollbringer des geschichtlichen Heilswerkes beschrieben werden soll: 'Christus ist gestorben und auferstanden.'"[83]

It is true that, of the relatively few instances of χριστός alone as the nominative subject of a Pauline sentence, many appear in contexts that are widely regarded as confessional, often mentioning Jesus's dying or rising.[84] This pattern is surely significant even if it cannot be proved, as Kramer undertakes

---

82 Grundmann, *TDNT* 9:540; also Hengel, "'Christos' in Paul," 69: "There is no demonstrable connection in principle between the use of the article and a rudimentary significance as a title."

83 Conzelmann, "Christenheit," 65.

84 See Rom 5:6: Χριστὸς...ὑπὲρ ἀσεβῶν ἀπέθανεν, "Christ died for the impious"; Rom 5:8: Χριστὸς ὑπὲρ ἡμῶν ἀπέθανεν, "Christ died for us"; Rom 6:4: ἠγέρθη Χριστὸς ἐκ νεκρῶν, "Christ was raised from the dead"; Rom 6:9: Χριστὸς ἐγερθεὶς ἐκ νεκρῶν οὐκέτι ἀποθνῄσκει, "Christ, raised from the dead, no longer dies"; Rom 14:9: Χριστὸς ἀπέθανεν καὶ ἔζησεν, "Christ died and lived again"; Rom 14:15: Χριστὸς ἀπέθανεν, "Christ died"; 1 Cor 5:7: τὸ πάσχα ἡμῶν ἐτύθη Χριστός, "Christ our passover was sacrificed"; 1 Cor 8:11: Χριστὸς ἀπέθανεν, "Christ died"; 1 Cor 15:3: Χριστὸς ἀπέθανεν ὑπὲρ τῶν ἁμαρτιῶν ἡμῶν κατὰ τὰς γραφάς, "Christ died for our sins according to the scriptures"; 1 Cor 15:20: Χριστὸς ἐγήγερται ἐκ νεκρῶν, "Christ has been raised from the dead"; Gal 2:20: ζῇ δὲ ἐν ἐμοὶ Χριστός, "Christ lives in me." Cf., however, 1 Thess 4:15 (Ἰησοῦς ἀπέθανεν καὶ ἀνέστη), where it is "Jesus," not "Christ," who is the subject of these verbs.

to do, that all of these Pauline sayings derive genetically from the primitive *Pistisformel* preserved in 1 Cor 15:3–4: Χριστὸς ἀπέθανεν...καὶ ἐγήγερται.[85] Against Conzelmann's generalization, however, in several instances of this sentence form, dying and rising are not mentioned, and if they are implied, it is only very obliquely.[86] Nevertheless, exceptions aside, Conzelmann's rule of thumb—"'Christus' heisst Jesus mit Vorliebe dann, wenn er als der Vollbringer des geschichtlichen Heilswerkes beschrieben werden soll"—is not without exegetical warrant.

This pattern of usage does not necessarily imply that χριστός means "messiah" in such formulae, however. It is possible that it is just the name that Paul happens to use in such statements. At this point the argument begins to break down. Conzelmann imagines that Paul's auditors will have caught this special use of χριστός, but Kramer objects, "For Gentile Christians this was not possible, for they had no knowledge or understanding of the titular significance of *Christ* or of its religious background in Judaism."[87] Even if one should grant this claim, there is the fact that Paul himself, at least, would have known the conventional sense of the word.[88] This may be true in general, Kramer grants, but the question "how Paul himself understood *Christ* in the context of the pistis-formula... is not a question which can be answered with great clarity....At all events there is nothing in the text to warrant such an assumption."[89] In sum, Conzelmann is right to notice an interesting pattern of usage, but his christological conclusion does not follow from this pattern. The argument fails to find traction; the use of χριστός as the subject of a sentence cannot be invoked as evidence that the word has a special messianic sense in such phrases.

---

85 Kramer, *Christ, Lord, Son of God,* especially 19–44; followed by Zetterholm, "Paul and the Missing Messiah," 37–38.

86 See Rom 15:3: ὁ Χριστὸς οὐχ ἑαυτῷ ἤρεσεν, "Christ did not please himself"; Rom 15:7: ὁ Χριστὸς προσελάβετο ὑμᾶς, "Christ received you"; 1 Cor 1:17: οὐ γὰρ ἀπέστειλέν με Χριστὸς βαπτίζειν ἀλλὰ εὐαγγελίζεσθαι, "Christ sent me not to baptize but to preach the gospel"; Gal 3:13: Χριστὸς ἡμᾶς ἐξηγόρασεν ἐκ τῆς κατάρας τοῦ νόμου, "Christ redeemed us from the curse of the law"; Gal 5:1: Τῇ ἐλευθερίᾳ ἡμᾶς Χριστὸς ἠλευθέρωσεν, "Christ freed us for freedom."

87 Kramer, *Christ, Lord, Son of God,* 213. Kramer's confidence notwithstanding, the question of the background knowledge of Paul's Gentile auditors is a very complicated one, especially with respect to the possibility of knowledge of Judaism via synagogue sympathization.

88 See Morna D. Hooker, *Paul: A Short Introduction* (Oxford: Oneworld, 2003), 47: "Gentiles, it is argued, would not have understood the significance of the word, but it is Paul who is writing and he certainly understood its significance!"

89 Kramer, *Christ, Lord, Son of God,* 213. Of course, if it is impossible to know what Paul thought, how much more so his anonymous auditors. In fact, both author-centered and audience-centered theories of meaning, at least in their strong forms, tend to obscure the actual use of language in linguistic communities (on which see chapter 2).

"Jesus," "Christ," and "Lord"

Beginning in the 1980s and up to the present, N. T. Wright has pointed to a number of Pauline patterns of speech that, Wright suggests, trade on the full titular sense of χριστός. One such pattern is Paul's varied use of the words Ἰησοῦς, χριστός, and κύριος, each by itself and also in various combinations, to speak of Jesus.[90] Wright has argued that Paul's choice among these terms is very deliberate and confirms the titular sense of χριστός:

> Though both words *denote* the same human being, Paul uses Ἰησοῦς to refer to that man as Jesus, the man from Nazareth, who died on a cross and rose again as a human being, and through whose human work, Paul believed, Israel's God had achieved his long purposes; and he uses χριστός to refer to that same man, but this time precisely as Israel's Messiah in whom the true people of God are summed up and find their identity.[91]

Wright cites Werner Foerster and Walter Schmithals in support of this line of argument. There is something to this bibliographical appeal since both Foerster and Schmithals strongly distinguish Ἰησοῦς from κύριος in Pauline usage.[92] Their reasons for making these distinctions are very different from Wright's, however, and in any case neither one is concerned with χριστός in particular.[93]

---

90 Ἰησοῦς alone 11 times, χριστός alone 153 times, κύριος alone 116 times (but many of these in LXX quotations), Ἰησοῦς χριστός 57 times, χριστὸς Ἰησοῦς 49 times, κύριος Ἰησοῦς 26 times, but never κύριος χριστός (ironically, in light of the title of Bousset's famous monograph, but cf. Col 3:24).

91 Wright, *Climax*, 46; italics in the original. Elsewhere Wright appeals especially to passages in which Paul switches from speaking of "Jesus" to speaking of "Christ" and back again: "There are also several passages in which Paul moves sure-footedly between *Christos*, the representative of his people, and *Iēsous*, the man Jesus of Nazareth. Though in several other passages the titular use appears dormant, its emergence here shows that it has not disappeared," citing as examples 1 Corinthians 12 and Rom 8:1–11, in which Ἰησοῦς "undoubtedly means 'the man Jesus'" and χριστός "is indubitably incorporative" (Wright, "Messiah and the People of God," 20).

92 See Werner Foerster, "Ἰησοῦς," *TDNT* 3:284–286; Walter Schmithals, *Gnosticism in Corinth* (trans. John E. Steely; Nashville: Abingdon, 1971), 131–132. Foerster argues for a distinction between Ἰησοῦς and κύριος in Pauline usage. On his account Paul uses κύριος to refer to the risen lord, the object of Christian faith, and Ἰησοῦς to refer, only rarely and in passing, to the historical Jesus (see Werner Foerster, "Ἰησοῦς," *TDNT* 3:284–293; Werner Foerster, "κύριος," *TDNT* 3:1088–1094; Werner Foerster, *Herr ist Jesus: Herkunft und Bedeutung des urchristlichen Kyrios-Bekenntnisses* [Gütersloh: Bertelsmann, 1924]). For Schmithals, Ἰησοῦς in Paul refers not to the historical Jesus *simpliciter* but rather to the earthly manifestation of the heavenly man, drawn from the pre-Christian Gnostic redeemer myth, whom Paul calls "Christ" (see Schmithals, *Gnosticism*, especially 130–132: "Excursus: Paul's Use of the Name 'Jesus,'" but on the problems with the Gnostic redeemer myth see Karen L. King, *What Is Gnosticism?* [Cambridge, Mass.: Harvard University Press, 2005], 137–148).

93 E.g., Foerster, *TDNT* 3:1091: "There is no set pattern for the distribution of Χριστός and κύριος.... There is a certain freedom of use."

Altogether different and generally more representative of the majority view is Kramer's conclusion. Contrary to Foerster and Schmithals before him and Wright after him, Kramer contends that Paul uses Ἰησοῦς and χριστός basically indiscriminately:

> We may say that in terms of their content *Jesus, Christ,* and *Jesus Christ* have exactly the same meaning in the Paulines. All are summary expressions indicating the one in whom the saving events, the death and the resurrection, took place.... Definite and clearly distinguished christological conceptions are not invariably associated with these designations.[94]

This question is a difficult one to settle concisely, but on balance it is best to say that, on the one hand, Kramer mistakenly irons over the actual variety of Pauline usage, while, on the other hand, Wright and his predecessors reify the several designations in a way that Paul himself does not. One example is Paul's use of κύριος to name Jesus in those few places where he cites dominical sayings.[95] In such contexts, if anywhere, one might expect Paul to use "Jesus" on the criteria proposed by Foerster, Schmithals, and Wright, yet in these very contexts he uses "lord" instead. But he uses "lord" consistently in these cases, not indiscriminately, as Kramer suggests. Furthermore, the fact that Paul uses the preposition ἐν not only with χριστός but also frequently with κύριος suggests, *pace* Wright, that the former word does not have a uniquely incorporative sense.[96] On the other hand, Paul never writes ἐν Ἰησοῦ (cf. Eph 4:21; Acts 4:2; Rev 1:9), so his choice of objects of the preposition is not random. Furthermore, Paul's custom is to write about the "faith of Christ," which Wright reasonably takes to mean "the faithfulness of the messiah *qua* messiah";[97] but in Rom 3:26 he writes instead about the "faith of Jesus," which breaks an otherwise elegant pattern. The implication of these examples is that christological categories do not map quite so neatly onto these Pauline words as Foerster, Schmithals, or Wright suggest. On the other hand, contra Kramer,

---

94 Kramer, *Christ, Lord, Son of God,* 202. Here as elsewhere in his study, Kramer takes a logically minimalist approach, assuming that there is no difference in meaning among the various words unless understanding them thus generates a nonsense reading. Because the latter almost never happens, Kramer takes it that his assumption is vindicated.

95 1 Cor 7:10: "not I but the lord says"; 7:12: "not the lord but I say"; 7:25: "I have no command of the lord"; 9:14: "the lord commanded"; 1 Thess 4:15: "we tell you this in a saying of the lord"; cf. also Gal 1:19: "James the brother of the lord."

96 On the phrase ἐν χριστῷ see the later discussion.

97 On the phrase πίστις χριστοῦ see the later discussion.

a pattern of usage is discernible; Paul's choices of words in these settings is not indiscriminate.[98]

The words Ἰησοῦς, χριστός, and κύριος, because they are different words, have their own respective ranges of meaning. It is true that their joint association with the person Jesus sometimes will have led to conflation of different degrees and kinds in certain Christian authors, but it is not the case that Christian authors simply redefined all of the terms to mean "Jesus." Paul certainly does not do so. He does, though, use χριστός as an honorific (see chapter 3), and this allows for some variability in usage: Jesus can be called "Jesus" or "Christ," just as the Seleucid king could be called "Antiochus" or "Epiphanes." This is not to say, though, that the two terms mean exactly the same thing. To put it differently, Paul has reasons for using χριστός when he does, but it is not the case that every instance of the word can be glossed with a maximalist definition of "messiah."[99]

"In Christ"

The characteristically Pauline prepositional phrase ἐν χριστῷ has a cottage industry of New Testament research unto itself.[100] Its many problems notwithstanding, my only concern here is the relation of the phrase to the question of messiah Christology. It is possible, first of all, to distinguish several syntactical uses of the phrase. It is sometimes adverbial (e.g., Gal 2:17: ζητοῦντες δικαιωθῆναι ἐν Χριστῷ, "seeking to be justified in Christ"), other times adjectival (e.g., Rom 16:3: τοὺς συνεργούς μου ἐν Χριστῷ Ἰησοῦ, "my coworkers in Christ Jesus"), still other times substantive (e.g., Rom 8:1: τοῖς ἐν Χριστῷ Ἰησοῦ, "those who are in Christ Jesus") or complementary to a verb (e.g., 1 Cor 15:19:

---

98 These few examples are enough to make the basic point; see chapter 5 for discussion of the crucial passages.

99 On this last point cf. Wright, *Climax*, 41: "I want now to suggest that…Χριστός in Paul should regularly be read as 'Messiah'; and that one of the chief significances which this word then carries is *incorporative*, that is, that it refers to the Messiah as the one in whom the people of God are summed up" (italics in the original). For my part, I am advocating an approach like that taken by Leander E. Keck, "'Jesus' in Romans," *JBL* 108 (1989): 443–460, who documents the different linguistic patterns without also identifying each one with a discrete christological concept. See Keck's methodological warning: "What moderns refer to when they speak of Jesus must be distinguished clearly from the 'Jesus' to whom Paul refers" (443).

100 This is presumably because the phrase "utterly defies definite interpretation" (BDF §219), an understandable overstatement. The phrase itself (either ἐν Χριστῷ or ἐν Χριστῷ Ἰησοῦ) occurs fifty-two times in the undisputed letters, at Rom 3:24; 6:11, 23; 8:1, 2, 39; 9:1; 12:5; 15:17; 16:3, 7, 9, 10; 1 Cor 1:2, 4, 30; 3:1; 4:10, 15, 17; 15:18, 19, 31; 16:24; 2 Cor 2:17; 3:14; 5:17, 19; 12:2, 19; Gal 1:22; 2:4, 17; 3:14, 26, 28; Phil 1:1, 13, 26; 2:1, 5; 3:3, 14; 4:7, 19, 21; 1 Thess 2:14; 4:16; 5:18; Phlm 8, 20, 23; cf. in the disputed letters Eph 1:1, 3; 2:6, 7, 10, 13; 3:6, 21; 4:32; Col 1:2, 4, 28; 1 Tim 1:14; 3:13; 2 Tim 1:1, 9, 13; 2:1, 10; 3:12, 15; also 1 Pet 3:16; 5:10, 14. The articular ἐν τῷ Χριστῷ occurs only at 1 Cor 15:22; 2 Cor 2:14; but cf. Eph 1:10, 12, 20; 3:11.

ἐν Χριστῷ ἠλπικότες ἐσμέν, "we have hoped in Christ").[101] This taxonomy is preferable to more speculative theological ones like that of Dunn, who distinguishes between objective, subjective, and hortatory instances of the phrase.[102]

Much, perhaps most, of the secondary literature has been concerned with parsing the precise sense of this dative, that is, just what sort of "in" relationship is meant.[103] In a survey of and a response to this tradition of research, A.J.M. Wedderburn catalogs the many types of ἐν-plus-dative relationships that have been suggested, citing eight discrete uses culled from several standard New Testament Greek grammars.[104] Classical Greek grammars, though, do not distinguish so many or such exotic categories.[105] Wedderburn rightly worries, "When it is argued that their sense is, for instance, 'historical,' then this decision

---

101 To anticipate my conclusion a bit, these differences should not be exaggerated, as if they implied that the phrase itself means something different in each case. All of these uses are "an extension of language, but still a quite intelligible one. There is, for instance, no reason to segregate these phrases as a separate class when they are used with verbs.... Other uses may be more striking and novel, but we should not too easily isolate them from normal uses of this preposition" (A. J. M. Wedderburn, "Some Observations on Paul's Use of the Phrases 'In Christ' and 'With Christ,'" *Journal for the Study of the New Testament* 25 [1985]: 88). So also Sanders, *Paul and Palestinian Judaism,* 459: "'In Christ' and related phrases cannot be quite so neatly parcelled out to parenetic and polemical contexts as 'in the Spirit,' 'one body' and related phrases."

102 Dunn, *Theology of Paul,* 396–401.

103 Adolf Deissmann (*Die neutestamentliche Formel "In Christo Jesu" untersucht* [Marburg: Elwert, 1892]) famously interpreted the phrase in a "mystical" sense, as meaning "in the sphere of" Christ or "under the power of" Christ, an interpretation that was followed in the twentieth century by Ernst Lohmeyer, Hans Lietzmann, Martin Dibelius, Rudolf Bultmann, and others. Scholarly work on the phrase peaked in the early 1960s with the monographs of Fritz Neugebauer, *In Christus: Eine Untersuchung zum paulinischen Glaubensverständnis* (Göttingen: Vandenhoeck & Ruprecht, 1961), and Michel Bouttier, *En Christ: Étude d'exégèse et de théologie pauliniennes* (Études d'histoire et de la philosophie religieuses 54; Paris: Presses Universitaires de France, 1962). Neugebauer proposes a "historical" interpretation of the phrase in place of Deissmann's mystical one, while Bouttier argues that ἐν χριστῷ is a dominant Pauline motif and that the several related prepositional phrases represent specifications of it. Valuable work has been done on the subject since, but none on the scale of Neugebauer's and Bouttier's. In 1983 Udo Schnelle commented that it was time for a new monograph on the subject (Udo Schnelle, *Gerechtigkeit und Christusgegenwart: Vorpaulinische und paulinische Tauftheologie* [Göttingen: Vandenhoeck & Ruprecht, 1983], 107, 225n4), but none has yet been written.

104 Wedderburn, "Observations," 83–97. They are the following: instrumental, temporal, local, sociative or modal, relation or respect (all in BDF), descriptive (C. F. D. Moule, *An Idiom Book of New Testament Greek* [Cambridge: Cambridge University Pres, 1963]), "in the power of" (W. W. Goodwin, *Greek Grammar* [rev. C. B. Gulick; Boston: Ginn, 1930, 1955]), and "in the presence of" (J. H. Moulton and G. Milligan, *The Vocabulary of the Greek Testament* [London: Hodder & Stoughton, 1949]). If these were not enough, N. Turner even has a category of "peculiarly Christian usages" of ἐν plus dative (*A Grammar of New Testament Greek III: Syntax* [Edinburgh: T. & T. Clark, 1963]).

105 See Smyth §1687, who has just three uses: local, temporal, and instrument/means/cause/manner; and the latter two are simply figurative uses of the first.

is likely to have been reached on the basis of an overall interpretation of Paul's theology, into which the interpretation of these ἐν phrases is then fitted."[106]

In reality, this is not the way prepositions work in ancient Greek or in other languages, for that matter. There is no authoritative list of discrete uses according to which every instance of a form must, or can, be classified.[107] That interpreters are endlessly coining new uses is evidence that this is the case. On the contrary, "Such grammatical categories as place, manner, etc., are the result of a modern analysis and they should not be regarded as watertight compartments; these are distinctions of which the writers and readers of ancient texts may have been largely unconscious as they freely wandered to and fro across the frontiers that modern grammarians have detected."[108]

Granted that this is the case, there are then the further questions where this pattern of speech comes from and what its analogies in the language are. In his major study on "Christ-mysticism" in Paul, Schweitzer presses this question: "On what lines, then, does he work out this assumption? In some way or other he must call to his aid the conception that those who are elect to the Kingdom stand in a relationship of fellowship with Christ."[109] In other words, the "in Christ" motif cannot have sprung fully formed from Paul's head; he must have been drawing on some available form of thought.[110] It is both significant and problematic that Schweitzer appeals to sources of thought rather than patterns of speech. If, however, we approach the problem in terms

---

106 Wedderburn, "Observations," 87, referring here to the theory of Neugebauer, *In Christus.*

107 On the logic of Greek prepositions, see Smyth §§1636–1637: "All prepositions seem to have been adverbs originally and mostly adverbs of place.... The prepositions express primarily notions of space, then notions of time, and finally are used in figurative relations to denote cause, agency, means, manner, etc."

108 Wedderburn, "Observations," 86. He adds, "It is better to say that ἐν χριστῷ and other such expressions "are not likely to be 'formulae,' but rather characteristic, and versatile, phrases of Paul's" (87). Furthermore, "Paul's usage is *sui generis*, but not, I think, incomprehensible on the basis of Greek usage if due allowance is made for the flexibility of that language" (89–90). But this concedes too much. If the language really is that flexible, then Paul's usage is not *sui generis* in any significant sense.

109 Schweitzer, *Mysticism*, 101.

110 There is a venerable tradition of explaining the phrase under the rubric of "corporate personality" (for theoretical discussions of the notion see J. R. Porter, "The Legal Aspects of the Concept of 'Corporate Personality' in the Old Testament," *VT* 15 [1965]: 361–380; J. W. Rogerson, "The Hebrew Conception of Corporate Personality: A Re-examination," *JTS* 21 [1970]: 1–16; A. J. M. Wedderburn, "The Body of Christ and Related Concepts in 1 Corinthians," *Scottish Journal of Theology* 2 [1971]: 74–96, especially 83–85). Wright, for one, argues for the perpetuation of the concept in the present case (*Climax,* 46n17). Wedderburn has strongly criticized the notion, however, allowing for its use only "provided that the limitations and ambiguities of this phrase are recognized...and perhaps recognized as a good reason why it should not be used at all" ("Observations," 97n52).

of linguistics rather than the history of ideas, it becomes an interesting and perhaps an answerable question.

For Schweitzer, ἐν χριστῷ is immediately intelligible in terms of its plain lexical sense, "in the messiah": "In point of fact, eschatology offers such a conception. It is that of the preordained union of those who are elect to the Messianic Kingdom with one another and with the Messiah which is called 'the community of the Saints.'"[111] On Schweitzer's model, there is a uniform Jewish eschatology attested in the apocalypses of the Hellenistic and Roman periods that includes a fixed notion of a messiah with whom God's elect are predestined to be united. As has been well documented since, substantiating this theory from the sources presents serious problems.[112] Nevertheless, Schweitzer believed that it was there, and on this assumption Paul's ἐν χριστῷ has an immediate and exact conceptual source.[113]

W. D. Davies, who stands very much in the Schweitzerian tradition of interpreting Paul in his Jewish context, takes an entirely different view. Although for Davies the messiahship of Jesus is axiomatic for many aspects of Paul's thought, this is not the case with the phrase ἐν χριστῷ.[114] In fact, in response to Schweitzer's view that ἐν χριστῷ means something like "in predestined union with the messiah," Davies cites H. A. A. Kennedy's assessment that this interpretation is "grotesque."[115] For Davies, ἐν χριστῷ does not mean "in the messiah" but rather "in Israel" or, better, "in the new Israel."[116] Accordingly, he draws an extensive analogy with the Passover liturgy preserved in Mishnah *Pesaḥim*, wherein, on the model of Ex 13:8, the festival celebrants ritually

---

111 Schweitzer, *Mysticism*, 101.

112 See the essays collected in Neusner et al., *Judaisms and Their Messiahs;* Charlesworth, *Messiah;* and my treatment in chapter 2.

113 For Schweitzer, this argument is part of a larger polemic about what constitutes the center of Paul's thought, namely Christ-mysticism and not justification by faith (the latter being a *Nebenkrater* in relation to the former).

114 Davies, *Paul and Rabbinic Judaism,* 324: "It was at this one point that Paul parted company with Judaism, at the valuation of Jesus of Nazareth as the Messiah with all that this implied."

115 H. A. A. Kennedy, *St. Paul and the Mystery Religions* (London: Hodder & Stoughton, 1913), 295; Davies, *Paul and Rabbinic Judaism,* 98: "It is difficult not to agree." Davies's objection seems to have to do with Schweitzer's emphasis on predestination in particular: "The mechanical conception of Christian life it involves does not do justice to the centrality of Faith in Paul."

116 Davies, *Paul and Rabbinic Judaism,* 102: "If for Paul, as for Jesus, the community of Christians was a New Israel, then entry into it would have some analogy with entry into the Old Israel. In other words, the process by which a man became ἐν Χριστῷ, and died and rose again with Christ, may be illuminated for us by the process through which membership in the Jewish community was, ideally at least, achieved."

narrate the events of the exodus as having happened to themselves.[117] This, Davies suggests, is what Paul intends by speaking figuratively of being "in Christ": membership in his community.

This is not impossible, but at the linguistic level, at least, ἐν χριστῷ in Paul functions in much more complicated ways than ἐν Ισραηλ does in the LXX. A more plausible linguistic parallel has been suggested by Wright, who points to the expression, which occurs several times in both MT and LXX Samuel-Kings, "in David" or "in the king." The first instance of this phrase comes soon after the death of Absalom, when the estranged tribal militias of Judah and Israel quarrel over their respective claims on King David. The Judahites claim, קרוב המלך אלי, "The king is near [of kin] to us" (2 Sam 19:43), an appeal to David's own Judahite lineage.[118] The Israelites, though, retort, עשר ידות לי במלך וגם בדוד אני ממך, "We have ten shares in the king, indeed, we have more in David than you" (2 Sam 19:44), an appeal to the number of their ten tribes over against the Judahites' two.[119] In short, the Israelites stake their claim on the ground that they have a part "in David" or "in the king."

The same idiom can be employed negatively, too, as in the next chapter, when Sheba, son of Bichri, launches his ill-fated revolt with the watchword אין לנו חלק בדוד ולא נחלה לנו בבן ישי, "We have no part in David; we have no inheritance in the son of Jesse" (2 Sam 20:1).[120] Later in 1 Kings 12, when the northern tribes rise up against Reheboam, son of Solomon, they use an almost identical slogan, מה לנו חלק בדוד ולא נחלה בבן ישי, "What part have we in David? Indeed, we have no inheritance in the son of Jesse" (1 Kgs 12:16).[121] If "having a share in David" (2 Sam 19:44) is a claim to the king's favor or support, then "having no part in David" (2 Sam 20:1; 1 Kgs 12:16) is effectively a declaration of secession. People identify themselves as "in" or "not in" the king. In Wright's words, "Their membership in David's people is expressed graphically

---

117 See *m. Pesaḥ* 10:5 (trans. Danby): "In every generation a man must so regard himself as if he came forth himself out of Egypt"; cf. Ex 13:8: "You shall tell your son on that day, 'It is because of what YHWH did for me when I went out from Egypt.'"

118 Rendered closely in the LXX: ἐγγίζει πρός με ὁ βασιλεύς. But ἐγγίζει may suggest that the translator read קרוב or קרב rather than MT's קרוב.

119 Where יד is clearly used in the idiomatic sense of "part" or "share" (BDB, s.v. יד; cf. Gen 47:24; 2 Kgs 11:7; Neh 11:1), but rendered in a word-for-word fashion with χείρ in the LXX. The LXX closely renders both clauses: δέκα χεῖρές μοι ἐν τῷ βασιλεῖ...καί γε ἐν τῷ Δαυιδ εἰμὶ ὑπὲρ σέ, but it also has an intervening plus: καὶ πρωτότοκος ἐγὼ ἢ σύ, "We are firstborn before you," probably an appeal to Reuben's precedence in birth order over Judah.

120 LXX: οὐκ ἔστιν ἡμῖν μερὶς ἐν Δαυιδ, οὐδὲ κληρονομία ἡμῖν ἐν τῷ υἱῷ Ιεσσαι.

121 LXX: τίς ἡμῖν μερὶς ἐν Δαυιδ; καὶ οὐκ ἔστιν ἡμῖν κληρονομία ἐν υἱῷ Ιεσσαι.

by this incorporative idiom."[122] Most important, the phrases "in David" and "in the king," in the logic of Samuel-Kings, are conceptually very close to "in the anointed one."

Against the putative parallel, however, are several considerations. First, while ἐν τῷ Δαυιδ and ἐν τῷ βασιλεῖ are striking phrases, they do not provide a pre-Pauline instance of ἐν χριστῷ itself. As often as it appears in the LXX, especially in 1–4 Kingdoms, χριστός is never a dative object of the preposition ἐν. Second, the idiom in Samuel-Kings is specifically "to have a [share, part, inheritance] in the king," not simply "in the king." According to the pattern, the prepositional phrase modifies an immediately preceding noun (יד, χείρ, "share"; חלק, μερίς, "part"; נחלה, κληρονομία, "inheritance"), which is not the case in the Pauline expression.[123] Third, the idiom is relatively obscure, occurring in just a single stratum of the biblical tradition and apparently without currency in Jewish literature of the Hellenistic and Roman periods. Wright himself concedes that these few references in Samuel-Kings are an inadequate basis for a claim of direct intertextuality with the Pauline ἐν χριστῷ.[124] He maintains, however, that they constitute positive literary evidence of a widespread ancient conception of kingship on which Paul draws.[125]

Wedderburn has argued for a different biblical precedent for Paul's use of ἐν χριστῷ, one that is not subject to these objections.[126] Wedderburn points to the citation in Gal 3:8 of God's promise to Abraham: ἐνευλογηθήσονται ἐν σοὶ πάντα τὰ ἔθνη, "In you all the nations will be blessed," which Paul takes to refer to the present justification of the Gentiles.[127] Here, as with ἐν χριστῷ, one finds ἐν with a personal dative object.[128] Moreover, ἐν χριστῷ itself occurs

---

122 Wright, *Climax,* 47.

123 But ἐν τῷ Δαυιδ εἰμὶ ὑπὲρ σέ (2 Kgdms 19:44) is an exception.

124 Wright, *Climax,* 47: "While these texts are not sufficient in and of themselves to suggest that such language was familiar in the first century, it does at least suggest a matrix of ideas out of which a fresh incorporative usage could grow, namely, that of the king representing the people."

125 Wright, *Climax,* 46: "Why should 'Messiah' bear such an incorporative sense? Clearly, because it is endemic in the understanding of kingship, in many societies and certainly in ancient Israel, that the king and the people are bound together in such a way that what is true of the one is true in principle of the other."

126 Wedderburn, "Observations."

127 The citation in Gal 3:8 is nearly identical to Gen 18:18 LXX (ἐνευλογηθήσονται ἐν αὐτῷ πάντα τὰ ἔθνη τῆς γῆς), except for the second-person singular ἐν σοί, which may be harmonized to LXX Gen 12:3 (ἐνευλογηθήσονται ἐν σοὶ πᾶσαι αἱ φυλαὶ τῆς γῆς) or may simply be a result of Paul's adjusting the citation to fit the context of his own argument (on the latter practice, see Christopher D. Stanley, *Paul and the Language of Scripture: Citation Technique in the Pauline Epistles and Contemporary Literature* [SNTSMS 74; Cambridge: Cambridge University Press, 1992], especially 338–360).

128 Albeit a personal pronoun rather than a personal name per se.

just a few lines later in a parallel expression, where Paul writes, ἵνα εἰς τὰ ἔθνη ἡ εὐλογία τοῦ Ἀβραὰμ γένηται ἐν χριστῷ Ἰησοῦ, "in order that in Christ Jesus the blessing of Abraham might come to the nations" (Gal 3:14).[129] Here, significantly, ἐν χριστῷ Ἰησοῦ takes the place of ἐν σοὶ in Gal 3:8, as the adverbial phrase expressing the means by which the blessing comes.

Two verses later, Paul makes the further point that the promise just cited was made to Abraham and his seed, quoting the form of the same promise in Gen 22:18: ἐνευλογηθήσονται ἐν τῷ σπέρματί σου πάντα τὰ ἔθνη τῆς γῆς, "In your seed all the nations will be blessed." Paul exploits the singular form, making a point of the fact that it is not τοῖς σπέρμασιν σου but τῷ σπέρματί σου, adding finally, ὅς ἐστιν χριστός. That is, "the seed" of the promise "is Christ." So the parallel between the biblical ἐν σοὶ and ἐν τῷ σπέρματί σου and the Pauline ἐν χριστῷ is not only a formal one but also an explicit theological one.[130] What is more, at least one of the other participationist Pauline phrases, σὺν χριστῷ, also has a near parallel in this passage, at Gal 3:9, where Paul writes, οἱ ἐκ πίστεως εὐλογοῦνται σὺν τῷ πιστῷ Ἀβραάμ, "Those who are of faith are blessed together with faithful Abraham."[131] Wedderburn concludes, "Abraham provides an analogy to, though not, of course, a source of, the ἐν χριστῷ and the σὺν χριστῷ language of Paul....Abraham and Christ are viewed as representative figures through whom God acts toward the human race."[132]

---

129 Where the expression ἡ εὐλογία τοῦ Ἀβραάμ is apparently taken from Gen 28:4 LXX.

130 Just here, Wedderburn's close exegesis actually fills out a connection that has been suggested by other interpreters. See Dahl, "Adequate Reward for the Akedah?" 146: "The interpretation of Genesis 22 presupposes that Jesus was identified not only as the Messiah but was also predicated Son of God, in accordance with 2 Samuel 7:14 and Psalm 2:7. By way of analogy, not only 'offspring of David' but also 'offspring' of Abraham was taken to refer to Jesus as the Messiah"; likewise Juel, *Messianic Exegesis,* 87: "The connections established among the various scriptural texts that underlie Paul's arguments in Galatians and Romans...depend upon the identification of Jesus as the 'seed.' That identification, in turn, depends upon messianic oracles like 2 Sam. 7:10–14, which could be applied to Jesus because he was confessed as the Christ"; and more recently still Jon D. Levenson, *The Death and Resurrection of the Beloved Son: The Transformation of Child Sacrifice in Judaism and Christianity* (New Haven: Yale University Press, 1993), 211: "The beloved son to whom and about whom the ancient promises were made is no longer Isaac but Jesus, no longer the Israelite patriarch in whom the future of the nation is prefigured but the messiah of Christian belief."

131 The parallel is not quite exact, however, since it is not σὺν Ἀβραάμ but rather σὺν τῷ πιστῷ Ἀβραάμ, as Wedderburn concedes ("Observations," 88).

132 Wedderburn, "Observations," 91. If so, then "the analogy casts doubt on some religio-historical explanations of Paul's usage, particularly those which appeal to the background of a supposed theology of the Hellenistic mystery-cults; for there can be little justification for treating Abraham as a mystery-god, let alone a dying and rising one" (91).

By way of comparison, Wright gives greater weight to the closer semantic parallel.[133] In the absence of any pre-Pauline instance of ἐν χριστῷ itself, ἐν τῷ Δαυιδ and ἐν τῷ βασιλεῖ in 1–4 Kingdoms are the closest analogies to the notion "in the anointed one." Even so, if Wright has the closer semantic parallel on his side, Wedderburn has the closer syntactical one on his. Although Abraham, unlike David, is not the "christ" in biblical tradition, nevertheless Paul's "in Abraham" phrases are structurally closer to his "in Christ" phrases than anything else is. Because Paul directly cites the Abrahamic promises in this connection but not the relatively obscure "a share in David" references and because of the explicit interpretive move at Gal 3:16 ("the seed [of Abraham] is Christ"), the latter explanation is in the end a more compelling one.[134] Paul uses the phrase ἐν χριστῷ on analogy to the tremendously influential biblical phrases ἐν σοί and ἐν τῷ σπέρματί σου.

This realization, in turn, goes some way toward answering the long-standing question of what kind of dative phrase ἐν χριστῷ is. So far from being a uniquely Christian "mystical" or "historical" or "realistic" dative, the Abrahamic "in your seed" is a conventional figurative use of the locative ἐν with dative.[135] In Abraham's seed—that is, by means of or through the agency of Abraham's seed—all the Gentiles will be blessed. Most instances of ἐν χριστῷ in Paul likely ought to be read along the same lines.[136] To borrow Leander Keck's turn of phrase, "Everything about Paul that matters and everything that Christians are and hope for pivot on this figure 'in' whom and 'through' whom God effects salvation. That is, Paul refers to him 'adverbially'—to specify and qualify God's act."[137]

---

133 Wright (*Climax,* 45–46) has objected to Wedderburn: "Not very likely are the theories which explain (for instance) the ἐν Χριστῷ formula on the analogy of 'in Adam' or 'in Abraham,' and then extrapolate from these into the other apparently 'incorporative' phrases."

134 Here I agree with Dahl, Juel, Hays, and Levenson that the identification of "Christ" with "seed" warrants, for Paul, the conflation of Abrahamic traditions with Davidic ones. It is this interpretive move, not a generic concept of corporate personality, that underlies Paul's line of reasoning (see chapter 5).

135 Per Smyth §1687, ἐν with dative is locative, expressing place at which, and from it derive two figurative uses: time at which and means by which.

136 Cf. the social-linguistic account of Richard B. Hays, *The Faith of Jesus Christ: The Narrative Substructure of Galatians 3:1–4:11* (2d ed.; Biblical Resource Series; Grand Rapids, Mich.: Eerdmans, 2002), 214: "In the case of a story that becomes foundational for the self-understanding of a community, the identification of community members with the protagonist may be so comprehensive that it can be spoken of as 'participation' in the protagonist's destiny." This theoretical account is consistent with, but does not necessarily follow from, the grammatical explanation offered here.

137 Keck, "'Jesus' in Romans," 449. This is true in most but not all instances of the phrase. Paul's "in Christ" modifies not only verbs of which God is the subject (e.g., "God was in Christ

"The People of Christ"

In further support of his claim that χριστός in Paul is always to be read "the Messiah," Wright also invokes those instances of the genitive [τοῦ] χριστοῦ, "of Christ," where the governing noun is a collective personal noun or pronoun (e.g., "the people of Christ").[138] He comments, "One of the clearest indications of the titular sense of 'Christ' is the genitive *Christou*, when used not for Christ as the possessor of things or qualities but as the one to whom people belong."[139] Elsewhere, Wright glosses the Pauline τοῦ χριστοῦ in this way: "The church is 'Messiah's,' the people of the Messiah."[140]

Wright's best examples are the two instances of the phrase οἱ τοῦ Χριστοῦ, "those who are Christ's" or "the people of the messiah." One such instance appears in the discussion of resurrection in 1 Corinthians 15, where Paul explains, "Just as in Adam all die, so also in Christ all will be made alive," specifying: Ἕκαστος δὲ ἐν τῷ ἰδίῳ τάγματι ἀπαρχὴ χριστός, ἔπειτα οἱ τοῦ Χριστοῦ ἐν τῇ παρουσίᾳ αὐτοῦ, "But each in his own order: Christ the firstfruits, then, at his coming, the people of Christ" (1 Cor 15:23). The second instance follows immediately on the fruit of the spirit discourse in Galatians 5. There Paul writes, οἱ δὲ τοῦ Χριστοῦ τὴν σάρκα ἐσταύρωσαν σὺν τοῖς παθήμασιν καὶ ταῖς

---

reconciling the world to himself" [2 Cor 5:19]) but also sometimes verbs of which human beings are the subjects, not only passive verbs of which God is the implied agent (e.g., "we seek to be justified in Christ" [Gal 2:17]) but also active ones (e.g., "I speak the truth in Christ" [Rom 9:1]). Another exception is 1 Cor 1:30 (ἐξ αὐτοῦ δὲ ὑμεῖς ἐστε ἐν Χριστῷ Ἰησοῦ, "[God], by whose agency you are in Christ Jesus"), where God himself is referred to adverbially. As Wright has noted, the Pauline phrase εἰς χριστόν, especially with reference to baptism (Rom 6:3; Gal 3:27), is related to but not identical to ἐν χριστῷ (Wright, *Climax*, 44–45, 54).

138 In "Messiah and the People of God," 27–31, Wright separately adduces σῶμα Χριστοῦ, "the body of Christ" (Rom 7:4; 12:5; 1 Cor 10:16; 12:27) as evidence that χριστός means "messiah": "If ... Paul wished to speak of the crucified and risen Messiah and his people, God's eschatological Israel, on the analogy of David and his people, he would refer to them not as his 'flesh' but as his 'body'.... The church is the 'body' of Christ in the same sense as the Jews are his flesh" (27). This line of reasoning, while interesting, is also speculative.

139 Wright, "Messiah and the People of God," 19–20; citing as examples Rom 8:17; 1 Cor 1:12; 3:23; 15:23; 2 Cor 10:7 [*bis*]; Gal 3:29; 5:24; cf. Rom 14:8 with "lord" rather than "Christ."

140 Wright, *Climax*, 44. With this phrase, as with ἐν χριστῷ, Wright offers an exegetically sophisticated variation on Schweitzer's concept of "the preordained union of those who are elect to the Messianic Kingdom with one another and with the Messiah" (Schweitzer, *Mysticism*, 101). For Schweitzer, this concept is an axiom of all Jewish eschatology and therefore would have been both obvious and important to any ancient person who subscribed to that way of thinking: "Since both Jesus and Paul move in an eschatological world of thought, the concept of this 'Community of the Saints,' in which by the predestination of God the Saints are united with one another and with the Messiah as the Lord of the Elect, is to them perfectly familiar" (*Mysticism*, 104). Wright does not take the concept for granted in the way that Schweitzer does; rather, he undertakes to demonstrate its presence in Paul's own characteristic patterns of language.

ἐπιθυμίαις, "The people of Christ crucified the flesh along with the passions and the desires" (Gal 5:24).[141] These references are at least suggestive of a formulaic way of speaking. I have already commented on 1 Cor 3:22–23: πάντα ὑμῶν, ὑμεῖς δὲ Χριστοῦ, Χριστὸς δὲ θεοῦ, "All things are yours, and you are Christ's, and Christ is God's." This passage is striking in that it contains both expressions in parallel—"the people of Christ" and "the Christ of God"—although both genitives are in predicate, not attributive, position, so that an intervening verb "to be" is implied. Nevertheless, this passage might be counted alongside the two just cited as representative of a kind of "people of the messiah" motif.[142]

Other passages are not as amenable to this reading, however. Wright also cites Rom 8:17: κληρονόμοι μὲν θεοῦ, συγκληρονόμοι δὲ Χριστοῦ, "heirs of God, and fellow-heirs of Christ," where the latter phrase probably has the sense of "joint heirs with Christ" (NRSV). If, though, the genitive Χριστοῦ is here part of an idiom with συγκληρονόμοι, then it cannot really be adduced as evidence of a "people of the messiah" motif. Likewise problematic is 1 Cor 1:12, where Paul scolds his audience for saying things like ἐγὼ μέν εἰμι Παύλου, ἐγὼ δὲ Ἀπολλῶ, ἐγὼ δὲ Κηφᾶ, ἐγὼ δὲ Χριστοῦ, " 'I am Paul's,' and 'I am Apollos's,' and 'I am Cephas's,' and 'I am Christ's.' " Here, per Wright's criterion, the genitive Χριστοῦ occurs governed by a personal pronoun, but ἐγὼ Χριστοῦ is an exact parallel to three other phrases in the verse. Wright contends that the genitive χριστοῦ with a personal noun or pronoun has a unique incorporative sense, but here it is simply another factionalist slogan. The expression works equally well with the personal names Παύλος, Ἀπολλῶς, and Κηφᾶς.[143] Finally, Rom 14:8 presents an interesting variation on this pattern. "Whether we live or die," Paul writes, τοῦ κυρίου ἐσμέν, "we are of the lord." Here is an implied first-person plural pronoun governing a genitive, but the genitive is κυρίου, not χριστοῦ. If Paul can use other designations for Jesus in this expression, though, then it is proportionately less likely that the expression trades on a unique sense of χριστός.

Similarly, Wright has pointed to the forms τοὺς ἐκ τῶν Ἀριστοβούλου, "those from among Aristobulus's people" (Rom 16:10) and τοὺς ἐκ τῶν Ναρκίσσου,

---

141 οἱ δὲ τοῦ Χριστοῦ is the reading attested by P46 D F G 0122*² and the majority text, but ℵ A B C P ψ 0122¹. 0278. 33. 104*. 1175. 1241ˢ. 1739 (1881) l 249 have οἱ δὲ τοῦ Χριστοῦ Ἰησοῦ, "the people of Christ Jesus," which, if original, would, of course, be pertinent to Wright's thesis. NA27 prints the text οἱ δὲ τοῦ Χριστοῦ [Ἰησοῦ], ruling in favor of the authenticity of Ἰησοῦ but with a high degree of uncertainty.

142 Unless it simply refers back to 1 Cor 1:12 ("Each of you says, 'I am of Paul,' " etc.)

143 On the interpretation of this verse in relation to the purpose of the letter, see Margaret M. Mitchell, *Paul and the Rhetoric of Reconciliation: An Exegetical Investigation of the Language and Composition of 1 Corinthians* (Louisville, Ky.: Westminster John Knox, 1993), 83–99.

"those from among Narcissus's people" (Rom 16:11) as parallels. He writes, "The parallel with the implicit *hoi tou Aristoboulou* and *hoi tou Narkissou* behind Rom 16.10f... indicates that a 'corporate' (i.e., 'family' or 'household') solidarity could thus be linked even with a proper name, becoming *a fortiori* easier with a title."[144] Here, first of all, as Wright notes, the form οἱ ἐκ τῶν [name in the genitive] is one step removed from Paul's actual expression; a more immediate parallel is ἐδηλώθη γάρ μοι... ὑπὸ τῶν Χλόης, "It has been reported to me by Chloe's people" (1 Cor 1:11).[145] Second and more important, though, in each of these parallel instances the term in the genitive is a personal name. This fact raises an obvious problem for the claim that the Pauline phrase οἱ [τοῦ] χριστοῦ is evidence that he uses χριστός as a title, not a personal name.

At this point Wright introduces an argument from the lesser to the greater: "A 'corporate'... solidarity could thus be linked even with a proper name, becoming *a fortiori* easier with a title."[146] This argument, though, depends on an implied premise, namely, that corporate solidarity is more associated with titles than it is with personal names. This premise might possibly be true, but at any rate it goes unsubstantiated. In fact, it turns out that one is hard pressed to find near parallels with titles rather than proper names in their genitive terms, which suggests that the implied premise is probably false. In other words, if all of the nearest parallels to the phrase οἱ [τοῦ] χριστοῦ have personal names, not titles, in their genitive terms, then this is actually evidence against, not for, taking χριστός as a title in such constructions.[147]

"The Faith of Christ"

As is well known, there is a longstanding and spirited debate concerning the Pauline phrase πίστις Ἰησοῦ Χριστοῦ, "faith of Jesus Christ," and variations.[148]

---

144 Wright, "Messiah and the People of God," 272n61.

145 Wright, "Messiah and the People of God," 272n61. In addition to 1 Cor 1:11, Wright adduces several other putative parallels: Phil 3:12: κατελήμφθην ὑπὸ Χριστοῦ, "I have been overtaken by Christ," but because of the preposition, this is not actually a parallel; Mark 9:41: Ὅς γὰρ ἂν ποτίσῃ ὑμᾶς ποτήριον ὕδατος ἐν ὀνόματι ὅτι Χριστοῦ ἐστε, "whoever gives you a cup of water in the name because you are Christ's"; and 1 Chron 12:19, which works in the MT (לְךָ דָוִיד וְעִמְּךָ בֶן יִשַׁי, "[We are] yours, O David, and [we are] with you, O son of Jesse") but not as well in the LXX (πορεύου καὶ ὁ λαός σου Δαυιδ υἱὸς Ιεσσαι, "Go, and your people, O David son of Jesse") since the translator has taken לְךָ not as the preposition לְ plus 2ms suffix ("yours") but rather as an imperative form of the verb הלך ("go").

146 Wright, "Messiah and the People of God," 272n61.

147 As I argue in chapter 3, it is better still not to talk in terms of "name or title" at all.

148 In addition to the long form πίστις Ἰησοῦ Χριστοῦ (Rom 3:22; Gal 2:16; 3:22), we find the shorter forms πίστις Ἰησοῦ (Rom 3:26; cf. Rev 14:12) and πίστις Χριστοῦ (Gal 2:16; Phil 3:9).

The secondary literature on the subject is voluminous and ranges far beyond the concerns of the present study.[149] At several crucial points, however, the interpretation of the phrase has been taken to bear directly on issues of Pauline Christology, in particular the question of the messiahship of Jesus.[150] It is incumbent on us to consider this possibility here. For all its notoriety, actually only six instances of the phrase appear in the Pauline letters.[151] There are a number of issues involved in interpreting the phrase in its several contexts, but the debate has centered on the important question whether χριστοῦ here is better understood as a subjective genitive ("the faithfulness that Christ showed") or an objective genitive ("human faith in Christ").[152]

In his 1981 Emory dissertation, Richard Hays makes a forceful case for understanding it primarily as a subjective genitive over against the objective interpretation that had been dominant to that point.[153] More specifically, for

149 Still essential reading is the provocative monograph of Hays, *Faith of Jesus Christ*. Among shorter treatments, especially noteworthy are Arland J. Hultgren, "The *Pistis Christou* Formulation in Paul," *NovT* 22 (1980): 248–263; Luke Timothy Johnson, "Rom 3:21–26 and the Faith of Jesus," *CBQ* 44 (1982): 77–90; Sam K. Williams, "Again *Pistis Christou*," *CBQ* 49 (1987): 431–447; Morna D. Hooker, "ΠΙΣΤΙΣ ΧΡΙΣΤΟΥ," *NTS* 35 (1989): 321–342; Richard B. Hays, "Πίστις and Pauline Christology: What Is at Stake?" in *Pauline Theology*, vol. 4, *Looking Back, Pressing On* (SBLSS 4; ed. David M. Hay and E. Elizabeth Johnson; Atlanta: Scholars Press, 1997), 35–60; James D. G. Dunn, "Once More, ΠΙΣΤΙΣ ΧΡΙΣΤΟΥ," in *Pauline Theology*, vol. 4, 61–81. The most recent major contributions are Karl Friedrich Ulrichs, *Christusglaube: Studien zum Syntagma pistis Christou und zum paulinischen Verständnis von Glaube und Rechtfertigung* (WUNT 2/227; Tübingen: Mohr Siebeck, 2007); and *The Faith of Jesus Christ: Exegetical, Biblical and Theological Studies* (ed. Michael F. Bird and Preston M. Sprinkle; Peabody, Mass.: Hendrickson, 2009).

150 The importance of the πίστις Χριστοῦ debate for Christology is highlighted by Hays, "Πίστις and Pauline Christology: What Is at Stake?"

151 Namely: Rom 3:22: δικαιοσύνη θεοῦ πεφανέρωται... δικαιοσύνη δὲ θεοῦ διὰ πίστεως Ἰησοῦ Χριστοῦ εἰς πάντας τοὺς πιστεύοντας; Rom 3:26: ὃν προέθετο ὁ θεὸς ἱλαστήριον... πρὸς τὴν ἔνδειξιν τῆς δικαιοσύνης αὐτοῦ ἐν τῷ νῦν καιρῷ, εἰς τὸ εἶναι αὐτὸν δίκαιον καὶ δικαιοῦντα τὸν ἐκ πίστεως Ἰησοῦ; Gal 2:16: οὐ δικαιοῦται ἄνθρωπος ἐξ ἔργων νόμου ἐὰν μὴ διὰ πίστεως Ἰησοῦ Χριστοῦ, καὶ ἡμεῖς εἰς Χριστὸν Ἰησοῦν ἐπιστεύσαμεν, ἵνα δικαιωθῶμεν ἐκ πίστεως Χριστοῦ καὶ οὐκ ἐξ ἔργων νόμου, ὅτι ἐξ ἔργων νόμου οὐ δικαιωθήσεται πᾶσα σάρξ; Gal 3:22: ἀλλὰ συνέκλεισεν ἡ γραφὴ τὰ πάντα ὑπὸ ἁμαρτίαν, ἵνα ἡ ἐπαγγελία ἐκ πίστεως Ἰησοῦ Χριστοῦ δοθῇ τοῖς πιστεύουσιν; Phil 3:9: ἡγοῦμαι πάντα ζημίαν... εὑρεθῶ ἐν αὐτῷ, μὴ ἔχων ἐμὴν δικαιοσύνην τὴν ἐκ νόμου ἀλλὰ τὴν διὰ πίστεως Χριστοῦ, τὴν ἐκ θεοῦ δικαιοσύνην ἐπὶ τῇ πίστει; cf. similar forms at Gal 2:20; Eph 3:12; Rev 14:12. A few other passages that lack the phrase have been adduced in order to explain it, e.g., Rom 1:17 (Desta Heliso, Pistis *and the Righteous One: A Study of Romans 1:17 against the Background of Scripture and Second Temple Jewish Literature* [WUNT 2/235; Tübingen: Mohr Siebeck, 2007]) and Rom 5:12–21 (Johnson, "Rom 3:21–26 and the Faith of Jesus").

152 So these two grammatical categories are sometimes taken to correspond roughly to "christological" and "anthropological" interpretations of the phrase itself.

153 This was the effect in terms of trends in the history of interpretation. In fact, though, Hays grants a considerable amount of ambiguity in the phrase: "Paul's language may sometimes be ambiguous by design, allowing him to speak in one breath of Christ's faith and our faith" (Hays, *Faith of Jesus Christ*, 161).

Hays, "the faithfulness of Christ" is a shorthand reference to a particular story about Jesus's obedient, self-giving death, a story that is presupposed by Paul's argument in Galatians 3–4. More specifically still, this story casts Jesus in the role of messiah in particular.[154] It is important to note that Hays's argument is not about Christology per se, but it bears on Christology nonetheless. That is, if one takes the view that the phrase πίστις χριστοῦ implies an underlying narrative about Jesus's obedient death, then the notion that χριστός in that phrase means "messiah" rather than just "Jesus" becomes more plausible. Paul's use of the phrase πίστις χριστοῦ, on Hays's interpretation of that phrase, implies that Paul thinks of Jesus specifically as messiah.[155]

A similar conclusion is reached by N. T. Wright, but by a different route. Wright has argued in a number of publications and for a number of reasons that χριστός in Paul should everywhere be understood in the "full titular sense" as meaning "messiah." Wright adduces a variety of arguments toward this end, one of which is an interpretation of πίστις χριστοῦ after Hays's model. So in his Hulsean Lectures for 2005 Wright writes, "This theme [viz. the messiahship of Jesus] makes it very likely, in my view, that when Paul speaks in Galatians and Romans of *pistis Christou*, he normally intends to denote the *faithfulness of the Messiah to the purposes of God*.... Precisely as Messiah, he offers God that representative faithfulness to the plan of salvation through which the plan can go ahead at last."[156] The logic here is the reverse of Hays's. For Wright, if one is convinced for other reasons that χριστός in Paul means "messiah," then a subjective genitive reading of the Pauline πίστις χριστοῦ makes sense within and further confirms this interpretive scheme.

The πίστις χριστοῦ debate will no doubt continue apace, with those who favor a subjective rendering being generally more open to the possibility that χριστός in the phrase should be read as "messiah." There is, however, no necessary correlation between these positions on their respective questions.

---

154 See Hays, *Faith of Jesus Christ,* 140–141: "Paul's Gospel is founded upon the story of a Messiah who is vindicated (='justified') by God through faith. This Messiah (Jesus Christ) is not, however, a solitary individual whose triumph accrues only to his own benefit; he is a representative figure in whom the destiny of all God's elect is embodied. Thus, all are justified through *his* faith" (italics in the original).

155 For a relatively early statement of this connection, see Markus Barth, "The Faith of the Messiah," *Heythrop Journal* 10 (1969): 363–370. Both Barth and Hays make this connection, and many who have followed them on πίστις χριστοῦ have been similarly inclined.

156 Wright, *Paul: In Fresh Perspective,* 48; italics in the original. In his earlier work on the subject, however, Wright seems not to have pointed to πίστις χριστοῦ as evidence of messiah Christology in Paul, whether because he took it as an objective genitive or because he did not find it relevant to the question of messiahship, I do not know.

Table 4.1

2 Sam 23:1 MT	2 Kgdms 23:1
ואלה דברי דוד האחרנים	καὶ οὗτοι οἱ λόγοι Δαυιδ οἱ ἔσχατοι
נאם דוד בן ישי	πιστὸς Δαυιδ υἱὸς Ιεσσαι
ונאם הגבר הקם על	καὶ πιστὸς ἀνήρ ὃν ἀνέστησεν κύριος ἐπὶ
משיח אלהי יעקב	χριστὸν θεοῦ Ιακωβ
ונעים זמרות ישראל	καὶ εὐπρεπεῖς ψαλμοὶ Ισραηλ

One could read πίστις χριστοῦ, on the one hand, as "faith in the messiah *qua* messiah"—that is, objective genitive with messianic χριστός—or, on the other hand, as "the faithfulness of the person whose name happens to be Christ"—that is, subjective genitive with nonmessianic χριστός. In light of this range of options, πίστις χριστοῦ should not be invoked as evidence in the messiahship question in a manner independent of the wider debate.

It is possible, however, to make one observation that bears on both discussions and may contribute in a small way to their mutual resolution. There is an interesting verbal connection in the Greek scriptures between the virtue of πίστις and David's role as the χριστός that I have not yet found addressed anywhere in the secondary literature on πίστις χριστοῦ in Paul.[157] It is clearest in the heading to the testament of David in 2 Samuel 23.[158] The text of that verse, in the MT and LXX, respectively, is shown in table 4.1.[159]

The most striking difference between the MT and the LXX is the double occurrence of the Greek adjective πιστός, "faithful," in place of the Hebrew noun נאם, "utterance." It is possible that this difference reflects a deliberate change or that the translator has simply confused by metathesis נאם, "utterance," for אמן, "faithful," since the two words share all three

---

157 But 2 Sam 23:1 is cited, at least, by Barth, "Faith of the Messiah," 365, in support of his more general comment: "In the O.T., a faithful servant chosen by the faithful God is the instrument by which God carries out the salvation and restoration of his people to obedience and faith."

158 Cf. also 1 Kgdms 26:23, where David explains his resolution not to harm Saul: καὶ κύριος ἐπιστρέψει ἑκάστῳ τὰς δικαιοσύνας αὐτοῦ καὶ τὴν πίστιν αὐτοῦ, ὡς παρέδωκέν σε κύριος σήμερον εἰς χεῖράς μου καὶ οὐκ ἠθέλησα ἐπενεγκεῖν χεῖρά μου ἐπὶ χριστὸν κυρίου, "The Lord repays each person for his righteous acts and his faithfulness; so the Lord handed you over into my hands today, and I was not willing to lay my hand on the Lord's anointed." Here χριστός refers not to David but to Saul, although, as the reader knows, David is already the *messias designatus* (1 Kgdms 16:1–13). In any case, the words appear together again in close connection.

159 For 1–4 Kingdoms I follow the Greek text of Rahlfs, *Septuaginta*. To date, no major critical edition of 1–4 Kingdoms (whose text is notoriously difficult) has appeared, which also means that my comments here are necessarily provisional.

radicals.[160] More likely, the translator's *Vorlage* read, or the translator took it to read, נאמן, which the translator vocalized as a niphal ms participle—נֶאֱמָן— for which the adjective πιστός is a common equivalency in 1–4 Kingdoms (1 Kgdms 2:35 [*bis*]; 3:20; 22:14; 25:28; 3 Kgdms 11:38).[161] The result is that Greek Kingdoms has passed on a verbal association between the roots πίστις and χριστός, an association susceptible of reuse by later readers of the Greek scriptures.[162]

Paul never cites 2 Kgdms 23:1, so no claim of express literary dependence can be made. He does, however, cite 2 Kgdms 22:50 (=Ps 17:50 LXX), a phrase from the end of a song of David that immediately precedes our verse. That citation, moreover, comes in a passage that is widely recognized as Davidic-messianic.[163] This suggests that the near context was available to Paul at least. It is possible, though not demonstrable, that Paul's association of the words πίστις, χριστός, and κύριος derives in part from this particular strand in the Greek scriptures. In that scriptural context, χριστός is specifically Davidic, and πιστός has the sense of "faithful." If Paul's usage reflects familiarity with this language, then it tends to lend some additional weight to the suggestion that πίστις χριστοῦ be read as "the faithfulness of the messiah."

Conclusion

Having examined the several Pauline phrases that are invoked in the discussion of χριστός in Paul, we are in a position to draw some conclusions. First,

---

160 Against the latter possibility, the translators of 1–4 Kingdoms do not otherwise stumble over נאם, but consistently render it with the Greek verbs λέγω and φημί, "to say" (1 Kgdms 2:30 [*bis*]; 4 Kgdms 9:26 [*bis*]; 19:33; 22:19).

161 So Frank Moore Cross et al., DJD XVII: 189–190, in their notes on 4QSam^a (4Q51), which unfortunately has a lacuna at this point in the verse (frgs. 155–158, l. 23).

162 The Greek plus κύριος in the third line is also noteworthy. Whereas MT has הקם, "raised up," a hophal form of קום, "to arise," the Greek translator opts for an active-voice verb, ἀνέστησεν, and then supplies the implied subject, κύριος, so that in Greek the line reads "the faithful man whom the Lord raised on high." The result of this translation choice is that the words πίστις, χριστός, and κύριος occur together in close connection, as they sometimes do in Paul (see Rom 5:1: Δικαιωθέντες οὖν ἐκ πίστεως εἰρήνην ἔχομεν πρὸς τὸν θεὸν διὰ τοῦ κυρίου ἡμῶν Ἰησοῦ Χριστοῦ, "Therefore, having been rightwised by faithfulness, we have peace with God through our lord Jesus Christ"; 1 Cor 1:9: πιστὸς ὁ θεός, δι' οὗ ἐκλήθητε εἰς κοινωνίαν τοῦ υἱοῦ αὐτοῦ Ἰησοῦ Χριστοῦ τοῦ κυρίου ἡμῶν, "God is faithful, through whom you were called into fellowship with his son Jesus Christ our lord"; also 1 Cor 4:17; 1 Thess 1:3; and cf. Eph 6:23; 1 Tim 1:2, 12, 14).

163 Rom 15:9: διὰ τοῦτο ἐξομολογήσομαί σοι ἐν ἔθνεσιν, καὶ τῷ ὀνόματί σου ψαλῶ, "Therefore I will confess you among the Gentiles, and I will sing to your name." The Greek text of 2 Kgdms 22:50 differs only in a one-word plus: διὰ τοῦτο ἐξομολογήσομαί σοι κύριε ἐν τοῖς ἔθνεσιν, καὶ ἐν τῷ ὀνόματί σου ψαλῶ. On Rom 15:7–13, see chapter 5; also Matthew V. Novenson, "The Jewish Messiahs, the Pauline Christ, and the Gentile Question," *JBL* 128 (2009): 373–389.

to round out the argument begun in chapter 3, the varied Pauline usage of the forms "Jesus," "Christ," "Jesus Christ," and "Christ Jesus" falls within the syntactical conventions of Greek honorifics. In particular, the fact that the order of the two terms is interchangeable strongly suggests that it is not a true double name but rather a combination of personal name plus honorific. If χριστός in Paul seems to be not quite a title and not quite a name, this is not because it is on an evolutionary path from the one category to the other but because it is generically something else.[164] If χριστός in Paul is an honorific, then, this reopens the question of its possible range of signification.

Second, it is clear that several philological features that have been taken to exclude the possibility of messiahship in Paul's thought do not in fact do so at all. Especially, the facts that χριστός is not an appellative, that it is not a predicate of a copulative sentence of which Ἰησοῦς is the subject, that it is not modified by the genitive κυρίου or θεοῦ, and that it is often anarthrous are no evidence that it does not connote messiahship.[165] Interestingly, some of the proposed philological criteria for identifying messiahship in Paul turn out to be just characteristically Lukan phrases, not criteria derived from any other larger set of messiah texts.[166]

Third, however, the converse is also true: The relatively few instances where Dahl's criteria are met in Paul are not special evidence of the role of messiahship in his thought.[167] Moreover, if Dahl's negative philological observations do not exclude the possibility of messianism in Paul, neither do Wright's positive philological observations prove it. That is, neither the use of χριστός as the subject of a sentence, nor the careful use of the different designations for Jesus, nor the particular phrases "in Christ," "the people of Christ," or "the faithfulness of Christ" implies any maximalist definition of "messiah" in every, or even in any particular, use of the word. As Dahl already pointed out, none of the instances of χριστός in Paul absolutely must be translated as "messiah." Nor is it the case that, methodologically speaking, several possibly significant phrases jointly add

---

164 *Pace* Dahl, "Messiahship of Jesus in Paul."

165 *Pace* Dahl, "Messiahship of Jesus in Paul."

166 Here I am reminded of Robert Morgan's imaginary conversation between Paul and Rudolf Bultmann, in which Paul complains that Bultmann has insisted that he sound just like John (see Robert Morgan, "Introduction: The Nature of New Testament Theology," in *The Nature of New Testament Theology: The Contribution of William Wrede and Adolf Schlatter* [ed. and trans. Robert Morgan; SBT 2/25; London: SCM, 1973], 49). Paulinists have likewise insisted that Paul sound like Luke in order to be counted as a messianic thinker.

167 *Pace* Wright, *Climax*, 41–49.

up to one certainly significant conclusion. In short, the sense of χριστός cannot be read directly off the syntax of the phrases in which Paul uses it.

This observation raises the crucial question of the relation between semantics and syntax. Kramer, for example, examines every grammatical form in which χριστός appears in Paul to show that in no case is it necessary to take the word as bearing its lexical sense of "anointed" or "messiah." This is true enough. That it is not necessary, however, does not mean that it is not possible or probable.[168] Kramer's conclusion raises the question why Paul bothered using that word at all. Or, to paraphrase John Collins, if his 270 uses of the Greek word for "messiah" are not evidence that Paul means "messiah," then what would we accept as evidence? Semantics (the meanings of words) are never independent of syntax (the arrangement of words in sentences), but at the same time, syntax does not render semantics empty. In all but the most exceptional cases, syntax molds and specifies semantics; it does not undo them. In the end we are left with the question why Paul used this word rather than any other so predominantly.

That question can finally be answered only by means of attentive reading.[169] This is the case because linguistic communication actually takes place not at the level of letters and words but at the level of sentences and paragraphs. James Barr's reminder about theological language applies equally well to language generally: "The linguistic bearer of the theological statement is usually the sentence and the still larger literary complex and not the word or the morphological and syntactical mechanisms."[170] The question of meaning, then, "has to be settled at the sentence level, that is, by the things the writers say, and not by the words they say them with."[171] This procedural rule, however, is too little followed in the secondary literature on our question.[172] More than a

---

168 And, after all, it is probability, not necessity, that is the historian's proper purview.

169 See Dahl, "Messiahship of Jesus in Paul," 17: "Only contextual exegesis can decide to what degree the notion of the messiahship is found in a particular passage." Kramer, too, finally concedes that the meaning of χριστός in Paul "is only found by examining the context very thoroughly. It can never be found simply by applying general criteria based on formal, grammatical considerations" (Kramer, *Christ, Lord, Son of God*, 214). But cf. the criticism of Wright, "Messiah and the People of God," 276n128: "The arguments of these passages, as well as their detailed formulations, are all-important: Kramer's claim to have studied contexts as well as details must be accounted a failure."

170 Barr, *Semantics of Biblical Language*, 269.

171 Barr, *Semantics of Biblical Language*, 270.

172 Wright is a notable exception to this trend. His philological arguments, to which I have responded here, are accompanied by thorough exegetical arguments, to which I respond in chapter 5.

few studies proceed by raising the question, citing Dahl or Kramer on a few philological points, and concluding that χριστός in Paul is a proper name that signifies nothing.[173] Such an approach is clearly unsatisfactory. It remains for us, therefore, to give close attention to the crucial Pauline passages in their respective contexts.

---

173 Lloyd Gaston's conclusion is radical, but his approach is quite conventional in this respect: "Dahl and Kramer have convincingly demonstrated that *Christos* is for Paul a proper name and is not to be translated 'Messiah.' ... There nowhere appears a sentence in which Jesus is the subject and Christ part of the predicate, and Christ is never followed by a genitive. ... Jesus is then for Paul not the Messiah" (Gaston, *Paul and the Torah*, 7).

5

Christ Passages in Paul

THE PREVIOUS CHAPTER examined those set phrases that have been taken to count either for or against χριστός meaning "messiah" in Paul and concluded that the question of meaning cannot be settled by formal grammar alone. Instead, as Barr insists, questions like this one must be settled "at the sentence level, that is, by the things the writers say, and not by the words they say them with."[1] In terms of the rubric presented in chapter 2—messiah language at the close syntactical level and at the wider literary level—it remains for us to consider the latter in the case of Paul. Although Paul never writes in the mode of what we call Christology strictly speaking, in a number of passages he indicates the notion that underlies his use of the word χριστός.[2] Accordingly, the purpose of this chapter is to comment in some detail on nine such passages. The focal question in the exegesis that follows is this: At the level of sentences and paragraphs, do these passages participate in the type of discourse that I am calling messiah language?[3]

First, a word on the rationale for the selection of these passages is in order. Among those scholars who entertain the possibility of messiah Christology in Paul's use of χριστός, a common approach has been to concede that the word is generally a sense-less proper name but to identify a few passages in which one

---

1 Barr, *Semantics of Biblical Language*, 270.

2 A point well made by Larry Hurtado, *Lord Jesus Christ: Devotion to Jesus in Earliest Christianity* (Grand Rapids, Mich.: Eerdmans, 2003), 98. Cf. the apt distinction between "theology" and "theologizing" represented by Jouette M. Bassler, "Paul's Theology: Whence and Whither?" in *Pauline Theology*, vol. 2, *1 & 2 Corinthians* (ed. David M. Hay; Minneapolis: Fortress, 1993), 3–17; and James D. G. Dunn, "In Quest of Paul's Theology: Retrospect and Prospect," in *Pauline Theology*, vol. 4, 95–115.

3 It is beyond the scope of this study to offer a thorough commentary on each passage, but I do comment on the particular ways in which the issue of messiahship bears on the larger contextual concerns of each passage.

may discern titular significance.[4] As I showed in chapter 3, however, χριστός in Paul is best conceived neither as a sense-less proper name nor as a title of office but rather as an honorific, a word that can function as a stand-in for a personal name but part of whose function is to retain its supernominal associations. Consequently, we ought not to imagine Paul habitually writing χριστός as if it signified nothing, then occasionally, suddenly recalling its scriptural associations and subtly redeploying it. We ought rather to think of Paul using the honorific throughout his letters and occasionally, for reasons of context, clarifying one or more aspects of how he means the term.[5] In other words, these passages warrant particular attention not because they are the only ones in which Paul uses χριστός to mean "messiah" but because they are ones in which Paul indicates the range of meaning within which he uses the term throughout.

The chapter has two main parts. The first part comprises treatments of several illustrative passages that meet the criteria for messiah language proposed in chapter 2: They comment on a figure called χριστός in patterns of speech drawn from the Jewish scriptures. The second part comprises treatments of several passages that have been taken to show that Paul ignores or repudiates messiahship as a theological category.[6] My claim is twofold: that Paul does all that we normally expect any ancient Jewish or Christian text to do to count as a messiah text and that in no case does he ever disclaim the category of messiahship. First, then, it is necessary to consider several illustrative Pauline messiah texts.

Gal 3:16: "Abraham's Seed, Which Is Christ"

One noteworthy feature of the secondary literature on messiah Christology in Paul is a concern for sorting out the particular biblical characters to whom Paul appeals by way of confirmation of his gospel. The logic of this approach is that, insofar as early Jewish messiah traditions tend to be closely associated with some biblical characters and not others, Paul's choices of biblical characters for comment in his letters will be a reliable indicator of his interest—or

---

4 E.g., Dahl, "Messiahship of Jesus in Paul," 17: "There are other places as well where the careful reader would detect messianic connotations"; further Dahl, "Messiahship of Jesus in Paul," 24nn11–12. Dahl's approach has often been cited approvingly in subsequent treatments. The same approach was taken earlier by Dobschütz, *Die Thessalonicher-Briefe*, 60–61.

5 Per chapter 2, this is just the way other Jewish and Christian messiah texts typically work: At appropriate places, they clarify how they intend the polysemous word "messiah," usually by using the language of one cluster of scriptural texts or another.

6 In fact, there is some overlap between these two sets of texts, but the distinction will be helpful for organizational purposes.

not—in messiahship as a theological category. Lloyd Gaston represents one form of this approach: "Though the Jerusalem church spoke of Jesus as the Messiah, Paul never does. For Paul, Jesus relates neither to David nor to Moses but to Adam and to Abraham."[7] This claim is doubly mistaken, however. For one thing, as I showed in chapter 2, while all ancient messiah texts draw on scriptural linguistic resources, the David tradition is only one of a number of such resources. For another, as I argue later, Paul actually does not dissociate Jesus from traditions about the house of David even if his explicit David references are few (Rom 1:3; 15:12; cf. Rom 15:3, 9; 1 Cor 15:25).

It is possible to say still more, however. One might think that Paul does in fact make a few messianic David references alongside his many better-known nonmessianic Abraham references.[8] In Galatians 3, however, Paul gives an indication that the matter is more complicated still and that he actually interprets the Abrahamic promises through David, as it were. In the admittedly difficult argument that comprises Gal 3:1–4:11, Paul is concerned to show that Christ's law-cursed death is the means by which the blessing that God promised to Abraham has at last come upon the ἔθνη ("nations" in Genesis, "Gentiles" for Paul).[9] He makes this connection by means of a grammatical analysis of the text of the promise. At Gal 3:16 Paul writes:

> τῷ δὲ Ἀβραὰμ ἐρρέθησαν αἱ ἐπαγγελίαι καὶ τῷ σπέρματι αὐτοῦ. οὐ λέγει· καὶ τοῖς σπέρμασιν, ὡς ἐπὶ πολλῶν ἀλλ᾽ ὡς ἐφ᾽ ἑνός·καὶ τῷ σπέρματί σου, ὅς ἐστιν Χριστός.

> The promises were spoken to Abraham and to his seed. It does not say *and to seeds*, as if concerning many, but rather as concerning one, *and to your seed*, which is Christ.

Paul alludes to scripture frequently throughout his letters, and he cites it explicitly almost as often, but for all his intertextual comings and goings, it is exceptional for Paul to parse the language of the scriptural text as he does here.[10] The

---

7 Gaston, *Paul and the Torah,* 114–115.

8 This is roughly the position taken, e.g., by Christopher G. Whitsett, "Son of God, Seed of David: Paul's Messianic Exegesis in Rom 1:3–4," *JBL* 119 (2000): 661–681.

9 The argument is hard to follow, but strong explications in recent research include Hays, *Faith of Jesus Christ,* 163–208; Wright, *Climax,* 137–174; and J. Louis Martyn, *Galatians: A New Translation with Introduction and Commentary* (Anchor Bible 33A; New York: Doubleday, 1997), 281–418.

10 But cf. 1 Cor 15:27 (see later discussion).

exact citation—καὶ τῷ σπέρματί σου—actually occurs four times in the Greek text of God's promises to Abraham in Genesis 12–25.[11] Paul's provocative exegetical move is to insist that in this instance the grammatical number of the Greek word—a singular noun—entails the individuality of its referent and then to identify that referent.[12] One strand in the secondary literature has been concerned with pointing out that Paul's exegesis here is mistaken, that in Gen 13:15 and parallels the word σπέρμα does not refer to the messiah.[13] This is simultaneously true and beside the point. Most Pauline scriptural interpretation and indeed most early Jewish and Christian scriptural interpretation can be called "mistaken" in this sense, but early Jewish and Christian scriptural interpretation had a kind of logic of its own, a set of "rules of the game" by which ancient interpreters proceeded and which they found compelling.[14] This is not to say that Paul's interpretation of σπέρμα in Gen 13:15 is not an "interested" one or that his contemporaries would have agreed with it. It is the case, though, that Paul's contemporaries would have recognized what he was doing.

On this aspect of the Gal 3:16 citation, Richard Hays comments as follows:

> This exegesis is less perverse than it might appear, depending as it surely does on the linkage of the catchword *seed* to God's promise to David in 2 Sam. 7:12–14. . . . This passage treats the singular noun *seed* not as a collective term, but as a reference to a specific royal successor to David;

---

11 Gen 13:15: πᾶσαν τὴν γῆν ἣν σὺ ὁρᾷς σοὶ δώσω αὐτὴν καὶ τῷ σπέρματί σου ἕως τοῦ αἰῶνος, "All the land that you see I will give to you *and to your seed* forever"; 17:8: δώσω σοι καὶ τῷ σπέρματί σου μετὰ σὲ τὴν γῆν ἣν παροικεῖς, "I will give to you *and to your seed* after you the land in which you sojourn"; 22:18: ἐνευλογηθήσονται ἐν τῷ σπέρματί σου πάντα τὰ ἔθνη τῆς γῆς, "*In your seed* all the nations of the earth will be blessed"; 24:7: σοὶ δώσω τὴν γῆν ταύτην καὶ τῷ σπέρματί σου, "To you *and to your seed* I will give this land" (per the text of J. W. Wevers, ed., *Genesis* [Septuaginta 1; Göttingen: Vandenhoeck & Ruprecht, 1974]).

12 For the standard collective sense of σπέρμα (which, of course, Paul knows [Rom 4:13, 16; 9:7, 8; 2 Cor 11:22; Gal 3:29]), see BDAG, s.v. σπέρμα, 2a.

13 E.g., H. St. J. Thackeray, *The Relation of St. Paul to Contemporary Jewish Thought* (London: Macmillan, 1900), 69–70: "The argument by which he seeks to establish a Messianic reference in Genesis must be considered extremely fanciful and sophistical"; likewise Heikki Räisänen, *Paul and the Law* (Tübingen: Mohr, 1987), 73; but cf. J. B. Lightfoot, *The Epistle of St. Paul to the Galatians* (Grand Rapids, Mich.: Zondervan, 1971), 142–143.

14 The term "rules of the game" comes from Juel, *Messianic Exegesis*, 31–57, an excellent summary treatment of a subject that boasts a mountain of secondary literature. Among this literature, important treatments include Geza Vermes, *Scripture and Tradition in Judaism: Haggadic Studies* (2d ed.; Leiden: Brill, 1973); Geza Vermes, *Post-Biblical Jewish Studies* (Leiden: Brill, 1975); James L. Kugel and Rowan A. Greer, *Early Biblical Interpretation* (Philadelphia: Westminster, 1986); James L. Kugel, *The Bible as It Was* (Cambridge, Mass.: Harvard University Press, 1999).

Table 5.1

Gen 17:7 LXX	2 Kgdms 7:12
καὶ <u>στήσω</u> τὴν διαθήκην μου ἀνὰ μέσον ἐμοῦ καὶ ἀνὰ μέσον σοῦ καὶ ἀνὰ μέσον <u>τοῦ σπέρματός σου μετὰ σὲ</u> εἰς γενεὰς αὐτῶν εἰς διαθήκην αἰώνιον, εἶναί σου θεὸς καὶ τοῦ <u>σπέρματός σου μετὰ σέ</u>.	καὶ ἔσται ἐὰν πληρωθῶσιν αἱ ἡμέραι σου καὶ κοιμηθήσῃ μετὰ τῶν πατέρων σου, καὶ <u>ἀναστήσω τὸ σπέρμα σου μετὰ σέ</u> ὃς ἔσται ἐκ τῆς κοιλίας σου, καὶ ἑτοιμάσω τὴν βασιλείαν αὐτοῦ.

thus, it bears evident potential for messianic interpretation...and it authorizes, by means of the device of *gezerah shawah*, a messianic reading of other promissory texts in which the key word seed appears.[15]

The appeal to *gezerah shawah* (גזרה שוה, "same category") is problematic since that hermeneutical rule is a rabbinic convention. According to tradition, it was one of the *middot* of Hillel (*t. Sanh.* 7:11);[16] but even so one cannot assume that Paul knew this *middah* as a *middah*. The principle, however, is the same: In cases in which scriptures share a phrase in common, the interpreter is justified in reading the one scripture in light of the other.[17] The phrase "your [singular] seed" is remarkably prominent in God's several promises to Abraham.[18] Outside Genesis it is quite rare, but it occurs again in God's promise to David in 2 Sam 7:12, whence it is recounted in Ps 89:3–4 and 1 Chron 17:10–14. The Greek texts of the Abraham and David promises have in common not only this conspicuous phrase but several other verbal links as well, as a comparison of Gen 17:7 LXX and 2 Kgdms 7:12 demonstrates (see table 5.1).

Genesis 17:7 LXX shares with 2 Kgdms 7:12 not only the key phrase τὸ σπέρμα σου, "your seed" but also the adjectival phrase μετὰ σέ, "[your seed] after you,"

---

15 Hays, *Echoes*, 85. In favor of this connection see further Dennis C. Duling, "The Promises to David and Their Entry into Christianity," *NTS* 20 (1973): 55–77; Max Wilcox, "The Promise of the 'Seed' in the New Testament and the Targumim," *JSNT* 5 (1979): 2–20; Juel, *Messianic Exegesis*, 85–87; Martyn, *Galatians*, 340 and n161.

16 Cf. the similar lists of the *middot* of R. Ishmael (introduction to *Sifra* [ed. Friedmann, 17–23]) and the *middot* of R. Eliezer (*Mishnat de R. Eliezer*).

17 On *gezerah shawah*, see further Schürer-Vermes, *History*, 2:344; H. L. Strack and Günter Stemberger, *Introduction to the Talmud and Midrash* (trans. Markus Bockmuehl; Edinburgh: T. & T. Clark, 1991), 18–19. Examples in the Mishnah include *m. Bez.* 1:6; *m. Arakh.* 4:4 (both with the phrase גזרה שוה).

18 It occurs some fourteen times in the Abraham cycle alone (Gen 12:7; 13:15, 16; 15:5, 13, 18; 16:10; 17:7, 8, 9, 10, 12; 22:17, 18), nearly a quarter of all the instances of the phrase in the Hebrew Bible. This may account for the plural ἐπαγγελίαι, "promises," in Gal 3:16 (cf. Rom 9:4) (so, e.g., Lightfoot, *Galatians*, 142; Martyn, *Galatians*, 339).

and a first-person singular future form of the verb ἵστημι, so that in both God promises "I will establish." Because of the confluence of these factors, Paul is able to read the scriptures in such a way that the seed of Abraham actually is the seed of David, the Christ.[19] In other words, there is a very particular logic to Paul's choice of the word χριστός here. For Paul, "Abraham's seed" may be Jesus, but it is not "Jesus." Rather it is "Christ."[20]

As with the other passages in this chapter, Paul's messianic interpretation in Gal 3:16 was neither inevitable nor necessary.[21] Nothing in the scriptures prescribed it; Paul need not have made it; other ancient interpreters did not in fact make it; and some who heard it may well have disagreed with it.[22] Other members of the linguistic community, however, would have understood what Paul was doing when he made this interpretation; they would have "known what the words meant." Galatians 3:16 shows that, for Paul, it is not the case that Jesus is the seed of Abraham on the one hand (e.g., as he pertains to Gentiles) and the seed of David on the other (e.g., as he pertains to Jews), as if those were different christological offices.[23] On the contrary, Jesus's messiahship is axiomatic for Paul in such a way that other, nonmessianic scriptural testimonies apply to him through his messiahship, not alongside it and certainly not in spite of it.[24]

---

19 The "seed of David" and the "Christ" are expressly identified in the so-called song of David (2 Sam 22:51=Ps 18:50), from which Paul himself quotes in Rom 15:9 (see the earlier discussion). If Martyn, *Galatians,* is right about the views of "the Teachers" in the Galatian churches (Martyn, *Galatians,* 13–42, especially 28–29), then Paul's counterintuitive messianic interpretation might have had a particular polemical edge: "The Galatians are sure to have learned of the expression 'seed of Abraham' from the Teachers, and the Teachers will have used it in its collective sense… [but] Paul hears in Gen 17:8 a messianic prophecy.… Paul might have been ready to defend his reading of Gen 17:8 by referring to 2 Sam 7:12–14" (Martyn, *Galatians,* 340 and n161).

20 Per the discussion in chapter 4, the words Ἰησοῦς, κύριος, and χριστός are not simply interchangeable.

21 *Pace* Schweitzer, *Mysticism,* 266, who comments on Gal 3:16: "Since they refer to the Times of the End, the single person can be no other than Christ."

22 Here I differ from Wright, who argues that this kind of messianic reading was largely fixed by the shape of scripture and presaged widely in Judaism before Paul (*Climax,* 21–26, 46–49, 162–168; *The New Testament and the People of God* [London: SPCK, 1992], 307–320). See, e.g., *Climax,* 46: "Why should 'Messiah' bear such an incorporative sense? Clearly, because it is endemic in the understanding of kingship, in many societies and certainly in ancient Israel, that the king and the people are bound together in such a way that what is true of the one is true in principle of the other."

23 Much less is it the case that Paul's Jesus is the seed of Abraham and not the seed of David at all, contra Gaston, *Paul and the Torah,* 7, 33.

24 Cf. the selective theological history of Israel at Rom 9:4–5, discussed later.

1 Cor 15:20–28: "When He Hands Over the Kingdom to God"

One Pauline passage that has often been cited even in discussions of ancient Jewish messianism is the fascinating text about Christ handing over the kingdom to God in 1 Cor 15:20–28.[25] This passage is not a pericope unto itself but rather is part of an extended *apologia* for the resurrection of the dead that runs from 15:12 ("How can some of you say that there is no resurrection of the dead?") through 15:57 ("Thanks be to God, who gives us the victory").[26] Beginning in 15:20, Paul makes the point that Christ's own resurrection guarantees the future resurrection of his people (οἱ τοῦ Χριστοῦ [15:23]).[27] Then, beginning in 15:24, he goes on to narrate what happens after the resurrection (εἶτα [v. 24]):[28]

εἶτα τὸ τέλος, ὅταν παραδιδῷ τὴν βασιλείαν τῷ θεῷ καὶ πατρί, ὅταν καταργήσῃ πᾶσαν ἀρχὴν καὶ πᾶσαν ἐξουσίαν καὶ δύναμιν. δεῖ γὰρ αὐτὸν βασιλεύειν ἄχρι οὗ θῇ πάντας τοὺς ἐχθροὺς ὑπὸ τοὺς πόδας αὐτοῦ. ἔσχατος ἐχθρὸς καταργεῖται ὁ θάνατος· πάντα γὰρ ὑπέταξεν ὑπὸ τοὺς πόδας αὐτοῦ. ὅταν δὲ εἴπῃ ὅτι πάντα ὑποτέτακται, δῆλον ὅτι ἐκτὸς τοῦ ὑποτάξαντος αὐτῷ τὰ πάντα. ὅταν δὲ ὑποταγῇ αὐτῷ τὰ πάντα, τότε [καὶ] αὐτὸς ὁ υἱὸς ὑποταγήσεται τῷ ὑποτάξαντι αὐτῷ τὰ πάντα, ἵνα ᾖ ὁ θεὸς [τὰ] πάντα ἐν πᾶσιν.

Then the end comes, when he hands over the kingdom to the God and father, when he has undone every rule and every authority and power. For he must reign until *he puts all his enemies under his feet* [Ps 110:1]. Death is undone as the last enemy. For *he subjected all things under his feet* [Ps 8:7]. But when it says *all things were subjected* [Ps 8:7], it

---

25 Schweitzer, *Mysticism*, 66–68, takes 1 Corinthians 15, together with Revelation 20–21, *4 Ezra* 7, and *2 Baruch* 30, as representing an outline of the messianic idea in Judaism, but cf. the objection of Davies, *Paul and Rabbinic Judaism*, 290. More recently, MacRae, "Messiah and Gospel," 172, echoes Schweitzer: "That Paul sometimes thinks of Jesus in messianic terms may also be inferred from his use of inherited apocalyptic imagery in such passages as 1 Corinthians 15:23–28.... The association of Christ with an eschatological kingdom, albeit a temporary one, is strikingly reminiscent of the main lines of Jewish royal messianism"; but cf. Collins, *Scepter and the Star*, 199.

26 Among the vast bibliography on this passage, especially relevant for my purposes are the treatments of Jan Lambrecht, "Paul's Christological Use of Scripture in 1 Cor 15:20–28," *NTS* 28 (1982): 502–527; C. E. Hill, "Paul's Understanding of Christ's Kingdom in 1 Cor 15:20–28," *NovT* 30 (1988): 297–320; Martinus C. de Boer, *The Defeat of Death: Apocalyptic Eschatology in 1 Corinthians 15 and Romans 5* (JSNTSup 22; Sheffield: JSOT Press, 1988), 93–140; Horbury, *Messianism among Jews and Christians*, 189–226.

27 On the phrase οἱ τοῦ Χριστοῦ, see chapter 4.

28 I cite the text per NA27, including the editors' bracketed [καὶ] and [τὰ] in v. 28. The text is generally quite stable.

is clear that the one who subjected all things to him is excluded. But when all things have been subjected to him, then the son himself will be subjected to the one who subjected all things to him, so that God may be all in all.

The word χριστός does not occur in this paragraph, but it does occur four times in the preceding one and is the understood subject of the verbs in v. 24, so in context this is a messiah text strictly speaking. According to the scenario Paul sketches here, Christ has been delegated authority over God's kingdom until such time as he successfully subdues all of the hostile powers, last of all death itself.[29] Only then will he return the kingdom to God the father.[30] This affirmation of the ultimate kingship of God (ἵνα ᾖ ὁ θεὸς πάντα ἐν πᾶσιν [15:28]) is the point of the apparently pedantic explanation in v. 27b: "But when it says *all things were subjected* [Ps 8:6], it is clear that the one who subjected all things to him is excluded." Christ is God's delegate, whose job it is to subdue all of the hostile powers that oppose God in the present evil age. Talk of the ὑποτάξις, "subjection," of ἀρχαί, "rulers," ἐξουσίαι, "authorities," and δυνάμεις, "powers" occurs elsewhere in Paul (cf. Rom 8:38) and comes from the late-biblical apocalyptic tradition of Daniel.[31] Having painted this scene, Paul justifies it by quoting—without introductory formulae—from Ps 110 and Ps 8 in turn, which have in common language of things being put "under one's feet."[32]

---

29 In all the undisputed letters, Paul uses the word βασιλεία, "kingdom," just eight times: six in the expression βασιλεία θεοῦ, "kingdom of God" (Rom 14:17; 1 Cor 4:20; 6:9, 10; 15:50; Gal 5:21), and twice by itself (1 Cor 15:24; 1 Thess 2:12) (cf. 126 instances of βασιλεία in the canonical Gospels); but cf. the verb βασιλεύω in Rom 5:14, 17, 21; 6:12, where, for reasons closely related to 1 Cor 15:20–28, the hostile powers (sin and death) are the subjects of the verb (on this connection see Boer, *Defeat of Death*).

30 It is contested whether Christ's delegated reign in 1 Cor 15:20–28 ought to be understood as future relative to Paul (so, e.g., Horbury, *Messianism among Jews and Christians*, 218–223) or present relative to Paul (so, e.g., Hill, "Paul's Understanding of Christ's Kingdom"). I find the latter view more compelling in light of the striking differences between 1 Cor 15:20–28 and Rev 20:1–6 (on which see Boer, *Defeat of Death*, 134–135).

31 Cf. Dan 7:27: καὶ τὴν βασιλείαν καὶ τὴν ἐξουσίαν καὶ τὴν μεγαλειότητα αὐτῶν καὶ τὴν ἀρχὴν πασῶν τῶν ὑπὸ τὸν οὐρανὸν βασιλειῶν ἔδωκε λαῷ ἁγίῳ ὑψίστου, βασιλεῦσαι βασιλείαν αἰώνιον, καὶ πᾶσαι αἱ ἐξουσίαι αὐτῷ ὑποταγήσονται καὶ πειθαρχήσουσιν αὐτῷ, "Their kingdom and authority and majesty, and the rule of all the kingdoms under heaven, he [God] gave to the holy people of the Most High, to rule an eternal kingdom, and all authorities were subjected to them and obeyed them." That 1 Cor 15:20–28 is apocalyptic, in content if not in form, is widely acknowledged (cf. ἀποκάλυψις, ἀποκαλύπτω in 1 Cor 1:7; 3:13), although the details of its relation to other Jewish apocalypses are contested. With Davies (*Paul and Rabbinic Judaism*, 285–290), contra Schweitzer (*Mysticism*, 65–68, 92–93), the sequence of events in 1 Cor 15:20–28 does not correspond exactly to those in *4 Ezra* or *2 Baruch*, nor does it need to do so.

32 Both of these psalms are frequently cited in the New Testament (Ps 8 in Matt 21:16; 1 Cor 15:27; Eph 1:22; Heb 2:6–7; Ps 110 in Matt 22:44; Mark 12:36; Luke 20:42–43; Acts 2:34–35;

Table 5.2

Ps 109:1 LXX	1 Cor 15:25
θῶ τοὺς ἐχθρούς <u>σου</u>	θῇ <u>πάντας</u> τοὺς ἐχθροὺς
ὑπο<u>πόδιον</u> τῶν ποδῶν σου	ὑπὸ τοὺς πόδας αὐτοῦ

Table 5.3

Ps 8:7 LXX	1 Cor 15:27
πάντα ὑπέταξας	πάντα <u>γὰρ</u> ὑπέταξεν
ὑπο<u>κάτω</u> τῶν ποδῶν αὐτοῦ	ὑπὸ τοὺς πόδας αὐτοῦ

At 1 Cor 15:25 Paul writes, δεῖ γὰρ αὐτὸν βασιλεύειν ἄχρι οὗ θῇ πάντας τοὺς ἐχθροὺς ὑπὸ τοὺς πόδας αὐτοῦ, "For he must reign until he *puts all his enemies under his feet* [Ps 110:1]." The citation is close to the text of the Greek Psalter (see table 5.2; differences underlined). Immediately following on this citation, at 1 Cor 15:26–27 Paul writes, ἔσχατος ἐχθρὸς καταργεῖται ὁ θάνατος·πάντα γὰρ ὑπέταξεν ὑπὸ τοὺς πόδας αὐτοῦ, "Death is undone as the last enemy. For *he subjected all things under his feet* [Ps 8:7]." This citation, too, follows the text of the Greek Psalter (see table 5.3; differences underlined). Both citations follow the LXX text reasonably closely, and the differences are best explained as modifications made by Paul to fit the context of his argument.[33]

With the exception of the key phrase "under his feet," the two source texts are quite different from one another. Psalm 110 is a parade example of a royal

---

1 Cor 15:25; Heb 1:3, 13; 5:6, 10; 7:17, 21), and the two psalms appear side by side in Hebrews 1–2, as well as in 1 Corinthians 15. Elsewhere in Paul, cf. Phil 3:21: τὴν ἐνέργειαν τοῦ δύνασθαι αὐτὸν καὶ ὑποτάξαι αὐτῷ τὰ πάντα, "the power by which he [Christ] is able even to subject all things to himself." On the reception of Ps 110 in early Christianity, the major study is David M. Hay, *Glory at the Right Hand: Psalm 110 in Early Christianity* (Society of Biblical Literature Monograph Series 18; Nashville: Abingdon, 1973); also Juel, *Messianic Exegesis*, 135–150.

33 In the Ps 110 citation: Whereas in the psalm God speaks in the first person, Paul narrates in the third person, so the 1s verb θῶ becomes the 3s θῇ. For the same reason, where the psalm twice reads the 2ms pronoun σου, Paul lacks the first instance and renders the second with the 3ms αὐτοῦ. MSS A, F, G, 33, 104, 629, and some versional and patristic witnesses have αὐτοῦ in the first instance as well, but this reading is likely secondary. Paul also reads πάντας where the LXX does not, which is likely an assimilation to the Ps 8 citation (πάντα γὰρ ὑπέταξεν) and to the surrounding context of 1 Corinthians 15 (cf. πάς in 1 Cor 15:22, 24, 25, 27, 28). In the Ps 8 citation: Paul has the 3s verb ὑπέταξεν in place of the 2s verb ὑπέταξας since the psalmist is addressing God, but Paul is narrating in the third person. Paul also includes a γάρ to connect the citation to the previous clause. On these modifications see further Dietrich-Alex Koch, *Die Schrift als Zeuge des Evangeliums: Untersuchungen zur Verwendung und zum Verständnis der Schrift bei Paulus* (Beiträge zur historischen Theologie 69; Tübingen: Mohr Siebeck, 1986), 19–20, 244–245; and Stanley, *Paul and the Language of Scripture*, 206–207.

enthronement psalm, in which God promises the newly seated king victory over all his enemies.[34] Psalm 8, on the other hand, is a hymn to God in praise of the human creature.[35] In Ps 110:1 God vows to put all the king's enemies "under your [the king's] feet," while in Ps 8:7 the psalmist praises God for putting all of nonhuman creation "under his [humanity's] feet." Paul's collocation of the two psalms is occasioned primarily by this shared phrase, and it is abetted by the fact that both are psalms of David (τῷ Δαυιδ [Pss 8:1; 109:1 LXX]).[36] Here as virtually everywhere in the letters, Paul is not out to make the point that Jesus is the messiah.[37] He has other pressing rhetorical goals—in this case, to demonstrate that the general resurrection is a necessary consequence of Christ's resurrection and reign. By way of making his argument, however, Paul appeals to psalms of David as if they are straightforwardly about Christ, as for him they are.[38] This association is admittedly tendentious, but it is not random; the psalms of David are about "Christ" because they are first about "christ."[39] The Davidic messiahship of Jesus is not the point of 1 Cor 15:20–28, but it is axiomatic for the argument of the passage.

2 Cor 1:21–22: "Anointed into the Anointed One"

If most of the passages treated in this chapter have received considerable attention in the secondary literature, one has received very little, although a few interpreters have pointed to it as a potentially important contribution to

---

34 On this psalm type see Sigmund Mowinckel, *The Psalms in Israel's Worship* (trans. D. R. Ap-Thomas; 2 vols; Grand Rapids, Mich.: Eerdmans, 2004 [1962]), 1:42–80.

35 On this aspect of Ps 8 see Hans-Joachim Kraus, *Theology of the Psalms* (trans. Keith Crim; Minneapolis: Fortress, 1992), 148–150.

36 On Paul's association of psalms of David with Jesus, see the later discussion. In addition to this feature, Ps 8 LXX includes in its superscription the phrase εἰς τὸ τέλος, "for the end" (for Hebrew למנצח), which may also have contributed to Paul's interpretation (cf. εἶτα τὸ τέλος, "then the end" [1 Cor 15:24]).

37 On this point, see chapter 4.

38 Cf. Acts 2:25–36; 13:33–37, where the author argues that the psalms of David cited are in fact not about David but about Jesus. Paul, by contrast, assumes the connection rather than arguing for it.

39 Cf. *Midr. Pss.* 18 §29: "R. Yudan said in the name of R. Hama: In the time-to-come, when the Holy One, blessed be he, seats the lord Messiah at his right hand, as it is said, The Lord saith unto my lord, *Sit thou at my right hand* [Ps 110:1]" (trans. Braude, 1:261). *Midrash Tehillin* is, of course, much later than Paul (perhaps eighth century C.E.), but as far as we know it is independent of the Christian interpretive tradition (see further Strack-Stemberger, *Introduction*, 322–323). The point is that both 1 Corinthians 15 and *Midrash Tehillin* attest the use of the language of Ps 110, a psalm of David, to talk about a messiah.

the question.[40] In 2 Corinthians 1, in the midst of a defense of his reasons for not yet having come to Corinth, Paul writes:

ὁ δὲ βεβαιῶν ἡμᾶς σὺν ὑμῖν εἰς Χριστὸν καὶ χρίσας ἡμᾶς θεός, ὁ καὶ σφραγισάμενος ἡμᾶς καὶ δοὺς τὸν ἀρραβῶνα τοῦ πνεύματος ἐν ταῖς καρδίαις ἡμῶν.

It is God who establishes us with you into the <u>anointed one</u> ["Christ"] and <u>anointed</u> ["christened"] us, who moreover sealed us and gave us the collateral of the spirit in our hearts. (2 Cor 1:21–22)

This passage is significant not because it comprises a sustained discourse on Christology—it does not—but rather because in it Paul gives an indication of the range of meaning within which he uses the word χριστός. This is the only instance in the Pauline corpus of the verb χρίω, "anoint," which here follows immediately upon its cognate χριστός, "anointed one."[41] Unlike the verb, of course, the noun is extremely common in the Pauline corpus. Paul's use of the two cognates together in close proximity but not in a standard cognate construction is an instance of paronomasia, in this case a play on their common root.[42] Martin Hengel, one of the few who comment on this feature of the passage, rightly notes, "How very conscious Paul is of the actual meaning in the name χριστός—which implies God's acting on, and with, Jesus—can be seen in the word play of 2 Cor. 1:21.... He uses [the word χρίω] to show the connection between those 'anointed' with God's Spirit and him who is *the* 'Christos,' that is, the Anointed *par excellence*."[43]

Hengel is surely right, over against his interlocutors, that Paul is "conscious of the actual meaning" of the word χριστός. What is more, the paronomasia in 2 Cor 2:21 shows not just lexical awareness but literary artifice. Paul deploys the word here in a play on its multiple senses: God anoints the believers and

---

40 See the brief comments of Hengel, "Jesus, the Messiah of Israel," 5–6; Wright, *Climax*, 49; Cummins, "Divine Life," 200.

41 Beyond this verse, χρίω occurs only four other times in the New Testament, always with God as the subject and Jesus as the object (Luke 4:18 [citing Isa 61:1]; Acts 4:27; 10:38; Heb 1:9).

42 On this linguistic aspect of the verse, see Victor Paul Furnish, *II Corinthians* (AB 32A; Garden City, N.Y.: Doubleday, 1984), 137. Wordplays like this are different from simple cognate constructions (e.g., Rom 9:32: προσέκοψαν τῷ λίθῳ τοῦ προσκόμματος, "They stumbled over the stumbling-stone"; 1 Cor 10:4: πάντες τὸ αὐτὸ ἔπιον πόμα, "They all drank the same drink").

43 Hengel, "Jesus, the Messiah of Israel," 6; italics in the original.

establishes them in the anointed one.[44] N. T. Wright comments on this verse: "There could hardly be a better indication of Paul's intention to mean 'the anointed one,' i.e. 'the Messiah,' when he says Χριστός, or of the incorporative significance that the word then carries."[45] While Paul's use of the word here is not determinative of his use of it elsewhere, it nevertheless indicates an aspect of the range of meaning within which he takes χριστός to function.

This Pauline connection between the anointing of believers and the anointed Jesus is unusual in the New Testament. The only analogy is 1 John 2:18–27, where it is those who have the χρῖσμα, "anointing" (1 John 2:20, 27), who know that Jesus is the χριστός, "anointed one" (1 John 2:22). Conversely, the person who lacks the χρῖσμα denies that Jesus is the χριστός and therefore is himself an ἀντίχριστος (1 John 2:18, 22). Outside the New Testament, this connection is reflected in several second-century patristic sources. Theophilus of Antioch explains the etymology of the label Χριστιανός, "Christian," with reference not to "Christ" but rather to the "christening" of believers: τοιγαροῦν ἡμεῖς τούτου εἵνεκεν καλούμεθα χριστιανοὶ ὅτι χριόμεθα ἔλαιον θεοῦ, "Therefore for this reason we are called 'Christians,' because we are 'christened' with the oil of God" (Autol. 1.12).[46] Likewise, Tertullian, in a passage on

44 This is not the only instance of such wordplay in the Pauline letters. He does something similar with the root ἔργον, "work," in Gal 3:5: ὁ οὖν ἐπιχορηγῶν ὑμῖν τὸ πνεῦμα καὶ <u>ἐνεργῶν</u> δυνάμεις ἐν ὑμῖν, ἐξ <u>ἔργων</u> νόμου ἢ ἐξ ἀκοῆς πίστεως; "Does he who supplies the spirit to you and <u>works</u> mighty deeds among you do so from <u>works</u> of the law or from the hearing of faith?" (and cf. the same root in Phil 2:12–13). It may be that πίστις in Gal 2:16 is another example: εἰδότες ὅτι οὐ δικαιοῦται ἄνθρωπος ἐξ ἔργων νόμου ἐὰν μὴ διὰ <u>πίστεως</u> Ἰησοῦ Χριστοῦ, καὶ ἡμεῖς εἰς Χριστὸν Ἰησοῦν <u>ἐπιστεύσαμεν</u>, ἵνα δικαιωθῶμεν ἐκ <u>πίστεως</u> Χριστοῦ καὶ οὐκ ἐξ ἔργων νόμου, "We know that a person is not justified from works of the law, except through the <u>faith</u> of Jesus Christ, and we <u>had faith</u> in Christ Jesus, in order that we might be justified from the <u>faith</u> of Christ and not from works of the law." On the objective-genitive interpretation of πίστις χριστοῦ, there is considerable redundancy here, but on the subjective-genitive hypothesis, the middle clause is a play on what comes before and after: "Because a person is justified from Christ's faith, we put our faith in Christ."

45 Wright, Climax, 49. For the difficult "incorporative" phrase εἰς Χριστόν, cf. Rom 16:5: ἀσπάσασθε Ἐπαίνετον τὸν ἀγαπητόν μου, ὅς ἐστιν ἀπαρχὴ τῆς Ἀσίας εἰς Χριστόν, "Greet my beloved Epaenetus, who is the firstfruits of Asia into Christ"; Phlm 6: ὅπως ἡ κοινωνία τῆς πίστεώς σου ἐνεργὴς γένηται ἐν ἐπιγνώσει παντὸς ἀγαθοῦ τοῦ ἐν ἡμῖν εἰς Χριστόν, "So that the fellowship of your faith may be effective in the knowledge of every good thing that is among us unto Christ." Probably related is the idiom βαπτίζω εἰς Χριστόν, "baptize into Christ" (Rom 6:3; Gal 3:27); cf. 1 Cor 1:13, 15: εἰς τὸ ὄνομα Παύλου ἐβαπτίσθητε, "Were you baptized into the name of Paul?"; 1 Cor 10:2: πάντες εἰς τὸν Μωϋσῆν ἐβαπτίσθησαν, "All were baptized into Moses"; ἡμεῖς πάντες εἰς ἓν σῶμα ἐβαπτίσθημεν, "We were all baptized into one body." On the difference between εἰς χριστόν and ἐν χριστῷ, see Wright, Climax, 54–55.

46 Greek text ed. Robert M. Grant, Ad Autolycum (Oxford Early Christian Texts; Oxford: Clarendon, 1970). Cf. the earlier reference to the origin of the term in Acts 11:26, which, however, offers no etymology: χρηματίσαι τε πρώτως ἐν Ἀντιοχείᾳ τοὺς μαθητὰς Χριστιανούς, "The disciples first bore the name 'Christians' in Antioch."

the rite of unction that accompanied Christian baptism, gives an etymology of the dominical name Christus:

> *Exinde, egressi de lavacro, perungimur benedicta unctione de pristina disciplina, qua ungi oleo de cornu in sacerdotium solebant. Ex quo Aaron a Moyse unctus est: unde Christus dicitur, a chrismate quod est unctio, quae Domino nomen accommodavit, facta spiritualis, quia spiritu unctus est a Deo Patre.*

Then, after exiting from the font, we are anointed all over with a blessed anointing, from the old discipline whereby they used to be anointed in the priesthood with oil from a horn, ever since Aaron was anointed by Moses. Whence he [Aaron] is called "Christ," from the "chrism," that is, the anointing, which, made spiritual, adapted a name for the Lord, because he was "anointed" with the Spirit by God the Father. (*Bapt.* 7 [PL 1206C-1207A])

More generally, one might point, as I did in chapter 3, to the relatively common ancient convention of wordplays on the meanings of names. Paul's purpose here is neither hostile nor humorous, but he nevertheless capitalizes on the etymology of the honorific Χριστός to make a point about his believers in Corinth. Jesus is the anointed one *par excellence*, but God also anoints all those who are "established into him." If we ask what range of meaning χριστός had for Paul, 2 Cor 1:21–22 supplies part of an answer.

Rom 9:1–5: "From the Israelites Comes the Christ"

There is one Pauline passage in which most interpreters grant that χριστός has the sense of "messiah," namely Rom 9:5.[47] In Rom 9:1–5 Paul voices his own "great pain and unceasing sorrow" on behalf of his Jewish kinfolk. The degree of Paul's sorrow corresponds to the tragedy of his people's situation, namely, that they have "stumbled" in God's sight despite their tremendous benefits, which Paul catalogues in vv. 4–5:

---

47 See, e.g., Dahl, "Messiahship of Jesus in Paul," 17: "There is at least one passage, Romans 9:5, where the result is unambiguous. Anyone who knows the original meaning of the name understands that the Christ belongs to Israel precisely as Messiah." To my knowledge, only Lloyd Gaston (*Paul and the Torah*, 139) insists that not even in Rom 9:5 does Paul entertain the idea that Jesus is the messiah.

οἵτινές εἰσιν Ἰσραηλῖται, ὧν ἡ υἱοθεσία καὶ ἡ δόξα καὶ αἱ διαθῆκαι καὶ ἡ νομοθεσία καὶ ἡ λατρεία καὶ αἱ ἐπαγγελίαι, ὧν οἱ πατέρες καὶ ἐξ ὧν ὁ Χριστὸς τὸ κατὰ σάρκα, ὁ ὢν ἐπὶ πάντων θεὸς εὐλογητὸς εἰς τοὺς αἰῶνας, ἀμήν.⁴⁸

They are the Israelites, theirs are the sonship and the glory and the covenants and the giving of the law and the temple service and the promises, theirs are the patriarchs, and from them, according to the flesh, comes the Christ. God who is over all be blessed forever, amen.

Most directly relevant to our question is the mention of χριστός in v. 5. In fact, this verse has received an inordinate amount of attention in the secondary literature, but not for reasons having to do with messiah Christology.⁴⁹ Rather, most scholarly attention has fallen on one aspect of the syntax of the verse, namely, whether ὁ ὢν ἐπὶ πάντων θεὸς commences a new sentence or stands in apposition to ὁ Χριστός.⁵⁰ If the former, then "God who is over all be blessed forever, amen"; if the latter, then "Christ, who is God over all, be blessed forever, amen."⁵¹ Whether or not Paul says here that Christ is God, it is at any rate clear that for him the word χριστός does not mean "God," so the semantic question remains. As mentioned earlier, many interpreters actually make a concession to messiah Christology for Rom 9:5.⁵² They do so, first, on the grounds of the articular nominative form ὁ χριστός, which many take to be a theologically significant grammatical anomaly, and second, because most

---

48 Aside from some confusion over singular and plural forms of διαθήκη and ἐπαγγελία in v. 4, the text of these verses is quite stable.

49 F. C. Burkitt wrote that "the punctuation [of Rom 9:5] has probably been more discussed than that of any other sentence in literature" ("On Romans IX.5 and Mark XIV.61," *JTS* 3 [1904]: 451).

50 See Bruce M. Metzger, "The Punctuation of Rom 9:5," in *Christ and the Spirit in the New Testament* (ed. Barnabas Lindars and Stephen S. Smalley; Cambridge: Cambridge University Press, 1973), 95–112, who distinguishes eight syntactical possibilities, each of which, however, is a variation on one or the other of these two basic options.

51 The theological stakes of this discussion are understandably high since this would be the only place in the undisputed letters at which Paul expressly identifies Jesus with God (but cf. Titus 2:13: τοῦ μεγάλου θεοῦ καὶ σωτῆρος ἡμῶν Ἰησοῦ Χριστοῦ, "our great God and savior Jesus Christ"). Absent punctuation, the syntax is genuinely ambiguous. I think it marginally more likely that a full stop is intended and that ὁ ὢν ἐπὶ πάντων θεὸς, etc. is a freestanding God benediction analogous to Rom 1:25; 2 Cor 1:3; 11:31.

52 E.g., MacRae, "Messiah and Gospel," 171: "One possible exception to this general [non-messianic] Pauline usage is Romans 9:5.... Here it would be very easy to understand a direct reference to the Messiah."

operate with a working idea of what a messianic reference would look like, and Rom 9:1–5 seems to fit that idea.[53]

In fact, it is true that χριστός in Rom 9:5 means "messiah," but not for these reasons. First of all, as chapter 4 showed, nothing about the form ὁ χριστός in Rom 9:5 makes the word mean something other than what it means when Paul uses it without the article or in another grammatical case. In particular, neither the article nor the nominative case has the power to render an otherwise meaningless proper name suddenly meaningful. Second, as chapter 2 showed, there was in antiquity no standard covenantal history of Israel to which Paul could appeal, whether in this passage or throughout his corpus. This is not to say that such a theologically interested history of Israel was inconceivable. It patently was conceivable since we know of a number of examples from the literature of the period.[54] My point, rather, is that there was no consensus about the shape of such a history.[55] Any author who would write one had to create it by selecting from and interpreting bits and pieces of the received biblical history of Israel. Or, to state the same point from a different angle, all such histories of Israel are constructions. In the case of Rom 9:4–5 and furthermore Rom 9:6–13 we should think of Paul as hinting at—although not actually narrating—one conceivable messianically oriented history of Israel, one that highlights their constitution as God's children (υἱοθεσία), the divine presence (δόξα), the covenants (διαθῆκαι), the giving of the law at Sinai (νομοθεσία), the temple service on Zion (λατρεία), the divine promises (ἐπαγγελίαι), the ancestors (πατέρες), and ultimately the messiah (χριστός).

Rom 15:3, 9: "Your Reproaches Fell on Me... I Will Praise Your Name"

Also of considerable importance for the question of messiah Christology but little discussed in the secondary literature are the places at which Paul quotes

---

53 For both arguments see Dahl, "Messiahship of Jesus in Paul," 17; Kramer, *Christ, Lord, Son of God*, 210; Juel, *Messianic Exegesis*, 9; Wright, *Climax*, 43; Dunn, *Theology of Paul*, 198.

54 E.g., Ben Sira 44–50; *Jubilees*; *1 Enoch* 85–90 (=the Animal Apocalypse); Pseudo-Philo, *Biblical Antiquities*; Acts 7:2–53; and Josephus, *Antiquities*, to name a few. I am concerned here only with the Hellenistic and Roman periods, but, of course, this phenomenon is attested already in ancient Israel and in the Tanakh itself, e.g., in the Chronicler's reworking of the events of the Deuteronomistic History (see Samuel Sandmel, "The Haggadah within Scripture," *JBL* 80 [1961]: 105–122; Fishbane, *Biblical Interpretation in Ancient Israel*).

55 Wright (*Climax*, 21–26, 46–49; *New Testament and the People of God*, 307–320) concedes this lack of consensus but nevertheless argues for several more or less agreed-upon biblical features of "the king that would come" (*New Testament and the People of God*, 307).

psalms of David as words spoken by Christ. Paul's interest in the Psalter as a source text is well documented; it ranks alongside Isaiah, Genesis, and Deuteronomy as one of his most frequently cited scriptural books.[56] He explicitly cites from Psalms twenty-one times: fifteen times in Romans, four times in 1 Corinthians, and twice in 2 Corinthians.[57] Among these Pauline Psalms citations, the psalms of David are disproportionately represented.[58] They account for half of the Psalter, but more than 80 percent (seventeen of twenty-one) of Paul's psalm citations.[59] In two of these David psalm citations but not in any non-David psalm citations, Paul interprets the psalmist's words not simply as a scriptural testimony about Christ but rather as words spoken by Christ himself.[60]

---

56 By my count, Paul cites Isaiah twenty-eight times, Psalms twenty-one times, Genesis fifteen times, and Deuteronomy fifteen times, while he cites no other scriptural book more than five times. It is interesting to compare the distribution of biblical scrolls found at Qumran, where Psalms (thirty-six MSS), Deuteronomy (twenty-nine MSS), and Isaiah (twenty-one MSS) are the most-attested biblical books (on this point see James C. VanderKam, *The Dead Sea Scrolls Today* [Grand Rapids, Mich.: Eerdmans, 1994], 30–32). On Paul's use of the Psalms in particular see Roy A. Harrisville, "Paul and the Psalms: A Formal Study," *Word and World* 5 (1985): 168–179; Sylvia C. Keesmaat, "The Psalms in Romans and Galatians," in *The Psalms in the New Testament* (ed. Steve Moyise and M. J. J. Menken; London: T. & T. Clark, 2004), 139–162; H. H. Drake Williams III, "The Psalms in 1 and 2 Corinthians," in *Psalms in the New Testament*, 163–180.

57 My numbers. The difference between a citation and an allusion can sometimes be slight, which accounts for the different tallies of citations in the secondary literature (cf. Koch, *Die Schrift als Zeuge*, 21–23; Hays, *Echoes*, 162; Stanley, *Paul and the Language of Scripture*, 33–37, 65–66).

58 The psalms of David are those seventy-three psalms in the MT Psalter (viz. Pss 3–9; 11–32; 34–41; 51–65; 68–70; 86; 101; 103; 108–110; 122; 124; 131; 133; 138–145) that bear the super-scription לְדָוִד, "of David," either by itself or in combination with a musical term, and in some cases also a reference to an event in the life of David. As a rule, the Greek Psalter renders לְדָוִד closely with τῷ Δαυιδ, but in Pss 122 and 124 it lacks any equivalency for לְדָוִד, and in some thirteen psalms (Pss 33; 43; 71; 91; 93–99; 104; 137) it has τῷ Δαυιδ where the MT lacks לְדָוִד. In addition, the Greek Psalter preserves the supernumerary Davidic Ps 151, which is also attested in Hebrew in the Qumran Psalms Scroll (11QPsᵃ). On this very ancient association of David with the psalms, see Brevard S. Childs, "Psalm Titles and Midrashic Exegesis," *Journal of Semitic Studies* 16 (1971): 137–150; James L. Mays, "The David of the Psalms," *Interpretation* 40 (1986): 143–155. On the reception of the superscriptions in the LXX, see Martin Rösel, "Die Psalmüberschriften des Septuaginta-Psalter," in *Der Septuaginta-Psalter: Sprachliche und theologische Aspekte* (ed. Erich Zenger; Herders biblische Studien 32; Freiburg: Herder, 2001), 125–148; and, rather differently, Albert Pietersma, "Septuagintal Exegesis and the Superscriptions of the Greek Psalter," in *The Book of Psalms: Composition and Reception* (ed. Peter W. Flint and Patrick D. Miller; VTSup 99; Leiden: Brill, 2005), 443–475.

59 Twice Paul cites psalms that lack David superscriptions in the MT but have them in the LXX, viz. Rom 3:14/Ps 9:28 LXX (=10:7 MT); 1 Cor 3:20/Ps 93:11 LXX (=94:11 MT).

60 Hays ("Christ Prays the Psalms," 108–109) argues for a third instance as well, viz. 2 Cor 4:13 (citing Ps 115:1 LXX): Ἔχοντες δὲ τὸ αὐτὸ πνεῦμα τῆς πίστεως κατὰ τὸ γεγραμμένον· ἐπίστευσα, διὸ ἐλάλησα, καὶ ἡμεῖς πιστεύομεν, διὸ καὶ λαλοῦμεν, "Because we have the same spirit of faith as that which is written, *I believed, therefore I spoke*, we also believe, therefore we speak." I am not persuaded, however, that Paul reads ἐπίστευσα, διὸ ἐλάλησα here as a word of Christ rather than simply as a word of scripture.

The first of these instances is Rom 15:3. Referring back to his discussion of the "weak in faith" in Romans 14, Paul urges in 15:1–2 that each person should seek not her own good but the good of her neighbor. In defense of this exhortation, he adds:

καὶ γὰρ ὁ Χριστὸς οὐχ ἑαυτῷ ἤρεσεν, ἀλλὰ καθὼς γέγραπται· οἱ ὀνειδισμοὶ τῶν ὀνειδιζόντων σε ἐπέπεσαν ἐπ᾽ ἐμέ.

For even Christ did not please himself; rather, as it is written, *The reproaches of those who reproached you fell upon me.*

The citation comes from Ps 68:10 LXX.[61] Although this psalm is a psalm of David, Paul does not cite the verse as a word of David, as he does elsewhere.[62] Nor, again, does he cite it as the testimony of scripture generally, as he does with many citations.[63] Rather, Paul reads Ps 69:9 as a word actually spoken by Christ. Having introduced Christ as the subject of the previous sentence—"Christ did not please himself"—he then explicates that claim not by narrating in the third person (as, e.g., in Rom 5:6: "Christ died for the impious") but rather by having Christ speak, in the first person, an apt word from scripture: "The reproaches of those who reproached you fell upon me."[64]

The second instance of this literary conceit comes just a few verses later in Rom 15:9. Unlike Rom 15:3, which is a freestanding citation, Rom 15:9 is the first in a chain of four scriptural citations (Ps 18:50; Deut 32:43; Ps 117:1; Isa 11:10) adduced in support of the claim that "Christ became a servant of the circumcision for the sake of God's truthfulness, in order to confirm the promises to the patriarchs, and for the sake of his mercy, in order that the Gentiles

---

61 The text of Paul's citation is identical to the text of Ps 68:10 LXX as we have it (see Rahlfs, *Psalmi cum Odis,* ad loc.).

62 Interestingly, at Rom 11:9 Paul cites a different part of this very same psalm (viz. Ps 68:23–24 LXX) as a word of David: Δαυὶδ λέγει, "David says." See also Rom 4:6 (citing Ps 31:1–2 LXX): Δαυὶδ λέγει τὸν μακαρισμὸν, "David speaks a blessing."

63 Cf. ἡ γραφὴ λέγει, "scripture says," in Rom 4:3; 9:17; 10:11; 11:2; Gal 4:30.

64 This scriptural word is apt in part because of the association of "Christ" with "reproaches" established by Ps 88:52 LXX: οὗ ὠνείδισαν οἱ ἐχθροί σου κύριε οὗ ὠνείδισαν τὸ ἀντάλλαγμα τοῦ χριστοῦ σου (see Juel, *Messianic Exegesis,* 109–110). Also possibly significant is the association, attested in the Gospel tradition, of other parts of Ps 69 with the passion of Jesus (Matt 27:34, 48; Mark 15:23, 36; Luke 23:36; John 15:25; 19:28).

might glorify God" (Rom 15:8–9).[65] On the heels of this claim Paul cites Ps 17:50 LXX almost exactly:[66]

διὰ τοῦτο ἐξομολογήσομαί σοι ἐν ἔθνεσιν, καὶ τῷ ὀνόματί σου ψαλῶ.

Therefore I will confess you among the Gentiles, and I will praise your name.

Paul's principal claim here is that the Gentiles will glorify God (15:9a), and the second and third citations in the catena are invitations to the Gentiles to do so (15:10, 11), but the first citation is the psalmist's declaration of his own intent to praise God in the presence of the Gentiles. Only this first citation has a first-person speaker, and in the context of Paul's argument, this speaker is best understood as Christ himself.[67] To paraphrase: "Christ became a servant of the circumcision in order that the Gentiles might glorify God, *as he says*: I will praise you among the Gentiles."[68] Here as in Rom 15:3, Paul

---

65 On the difficult syntax of this sentence see J. Ross Wagner, "The Christ, Servant of Jew and Gentile: A Fresh Approach to Romans 15:8–9," *JBL* 116 (1997): 473–485. As my translation here suggests, I follow Wagner in taking ὑπὲρ ἀληθείας θεοῦ and ὑπὲρ ἐλέους as parallel adverbial phrases modifying the infinitive γεγενῆσθαι, but I differ in taking τὰ δὲ ἔθνη not as an accusative of respect and a parallel to περιτομῆς but rather as the independent subject of the infinitive δοξάσαι.

66 The LXX text differs in just a single word: διὰ τοῦτο ἐξομολογήσομαί σοι ἐν ἔθνεσιν, κύριε, καὶ τῷ ὀνόματί σου ψαλῶ. It is possible that Paul's LXX text lacked κύριε, but there are no MSS in the Greek textual tradition that attest such a reading (see Rahlfs, *Psalmi cum Odis*, ad loc.). More likely, Paul has modified his source text to fit his own composition. This accords with the fact that Paul makes Christ the speaker here since, for Paul, Christ himself is the κύριος (cf. Mark 12:35–37 and parallels, which assume the same verbal quandary: "David calls the messiah 'lord' [κύριος], so how can he be his son?").

67 There is not consensus on this point (cf. Käsemann, *Romans*, 386, who suggests that Paul envisions himself as the speaker of this psalm), but it finds wide support among modern interpreters (e.g., Sanday and Headlam, *Romans*, 398; M.-J. Lagrange, *Saint Paul Épitre aux Romains* [Études bibliques; Paris: Lecoffre, 1916], 347; C. E. B. Cranfield, *A Critical and Exegetical Commentary on the Epistle to the Romans* [2 vols.; 6th ed.; ICC; Edinburgh: T. & T. Clark, 1975–1979], 2:745; Otto Michel, *Der Brief an die Römer übersetzt und erklärt* [Kritisch-exegetischer Kommentar über das Neue Testament; Göttingen: Vandenhoeck & Ruprecht, 1955], 359–360; Wagner, *Heralds of the Good News*, 311–315). Leander E. Keck, "Christology, Soteriology, and the Praise of God (Romans 15:7–13)," in *The Conversation Continues: Studies in Paul and John in Honor of J. Louis Martyn* (ed. Robert T. Fortna and Beverly Roberts Gaventa; Nashville: Abingdon, 1990), 85–97, rightly notes that this identification does not imply a reference to the ministry of Jesus.

68 The introductory formula γέγραπται, "it is written," underdetermines the rhetorical force of the citations. Depending on both content and context, the implied speaker of a citation preceded by γέγραπται might be Christ, as here, or God (e.g., Rom 9:13), or the saints (e.g., Rom 8:36), or no one in particular.

makes his point by having Christ speak, in the first person, an apt word from scripture.[69]

In both these passages, it is not just any word from scripture that Christ speaks; it is a psalm, and a psalm of David in particular. It is possible that this is a mere accident of citation, that Paul chose whatever scriptural sayings seemed to fit the point he wanted to make and that both happened to be psalms of David, but the more likely explanation is that there is a rationale behind his use of these scriptures for this purpose.[70] As Donald Juel has documented, the convention of citing psalms of David as words of Christ is actually broadly attested in the New Testament.[71] While Paul is the earliest literary witness to this phenomenon, the association of Jesus with David certainly did not originate with Paul, and the early Christian custom of reading psalms of David as words of Christ is probably pre-Pauline as well.[72] It is not clear, however, just how this custom came about. Juel suggests, appealing to the rabbinic exegetical rule of *gezerah shawah*, that Ps 89:51 provided the necessary keyword link to permit the practice.[73] Psalm 89 itself, however, is not cited anywhere in the New Testament, as one might reasonably expect it to be on Juel's hypothesis. For this reason it is more likely that a

---

69 Paul himself explains, in part, the reasoning behind these citations in Rom 15:4: ὅσα γὰρ προεγράφη, εἰς τὴν ἡμετέραν διδασκαλίαν ἐγράφη, "For whatever was written beforehand was written for our instruction."

70 On the role of the Psalter in early Christian Christology see Adela Yarbro Collins, "The Psalms and the Origins of Christology," in *Psalms in Community: Jewish and Christian Textual, Liturgical, and Artistic Traditions* (ed. Harold W. Attridge and Margot E. Fassler; SBLSS 25; Leiden: Brill, 2003), 113–124.

71 See Juel, *Messianic Exegesis*, 89–117; also Harold W. Attridge, "Giving Voice to Jesus: Use of Psalms in the New Testament," in *Psalms in Community*, 101–112. Examples include: John 2:17 citing Ps 69:9; Matt 27:46 and Mark 15:34 citing Ps 22:1; Luke 23:46 citing Ps 31:5; Heb 2:12 citing Ps 22:22; Heb 10:5–7 citing Ps 40:6–8. One such instance (Matt 26:38 and Mark 14:34 citing Ps 42:5, 11) is a psalm of the sons of Korah, not of David. It may be significant that this Korahite psalm, like all of the David psalms cited, has the LXX superscription εἰς τὸ τέλος (on which see the later discussion).

72 It is admittedly possible either that the Synoptic Gospels and Hebrews developed the same convention later than and independently of Paul or that those texts all adopted the convention secondhand from Paul. The simplest explanation, however, is that it was a pre-Pauline convention. With Dahl ("Crucified Messiah") and Juel (*Messianic Exegesis*), I think it likely that this convention owes to the identification of Jesus as messiah already at the crucifixion and resurrection.

73 Juel, *Messianic Exegesis*, 109–110. Psalm 89:51 (=88:51 LXX) expressly associates the "reproaches of God's enemies" with the "christ": οὗ ὠνείδισαν οἱ ἐχθροί σου κύριε οὗ ὠνείδισαν τὸ ἀντάλλαγμα τοῦ χριστοῦ σου. Per *gezerah shawah*, this association would warrant reading other lament psalms as pertaining to the christ. Of course, appealing to rabbinic *middot* in the interpretation of Paul presents chronological difficulties; on the other hand, one might think that this particular exegetical practice would have had some intuitive force prior to and independent of the rabbis.

general perceived correspondence between David the χριστός and Jesus the χριστός will have allowed for the psalms of David to be read as words of Christ.[74]

What is more, it is possible that this convention derives not from the David superscriptions alone but also from a concomitant accident of translation. Some fifty-five psalms in the MT Psalter begin with the superscription למנצח, "for the [music] leader" (piel participle of the verb נצח, "to be preeminent").[75] The Greek Psalter, however, invariably translates למנצח with εἰς τὸ τέλος, "for the end" (from the noun נצח, "perpetuity"). Most, but not all, of these εἰς τὸ τέλος psalms are also psalms of David, and both the ones that Paul cites as words of Christ are superscribed with both εἰς τὸ τέλος and τῷ Δαυιδ. We know that, in the Second Commonwealth, David was sometimes thought of as an eschatological figure;[76] and the phrase εἰς τὸ τέλος may have especially suggested such an association for Paul.[77] Whether or not this phrase played such a role, it is clear that Paul reads some psalms of David as words spoken by Christ. This hermeneutical strategy works for Paul because and insofar as he uses the word χριστός in such a way as to draw on its scriptural associations with David.

Rom 15:7–12: "The Root of Jesse Who Rises to Rule the Gentiles"

Interpreters have long noted that Rom 15:7–12, culminating in a citation of the "root of Jesse" oracle from Isa 11:10, is a conspicuous piece of evidence for messiah Christology in the Pauline letters.[78] The Isaiah reference is the last in

---

74 See Hays, "Christ Prays the Psalms," 110: "The earliest Christians...did not need to find an isolated sentence (like Ps 89:51) that spoke of the *christos* as the target of the scorn of God's enemies, because they read all the promises of an eternal kingdom for David and his seed typologically."

75 See BDB, s.v. נצח, who suggest that the preposition ל in למנצח "indicates not assignment [i.e., "for the director"]...but that these [psalms] were from an older major Psalter known as the Director's Collection [so "from the director"]."

76 Already in Ezek 34:23–34; 37:24–25. On this point see Collins, *Scepter and the Star*, 49–73.

77 See Hays, "Christ Prays the Psalms," 107. In favor of this possibility see Rom 10:4: τέλος γὰρ νόμου Χριστός, "Christ is the end of the law"; 1 Cor 10:11: ἡμῶν, εἰς οὓς τὰ τέλη τῶν αἰώνων κατήντηκεν, "Us on whom the end of the ages has come"; 1 Cor 15:24: εἶτα τὸ τέλος, ὅταν παραδιδῷ τὴν βασιλείαν τῷ θεῷ, "Then the end, when he [Christ] hands over the kingdom to God." On this last reference see the earlier discussion in this chapter.

78 Already in the nineteenth century, F. C. Baur (on whom see chapter 1), rightly perceiving that Rom 15:7–12 contradicted his anti-Judaic account of Paulinism, proposed a text-critical solution. Baur cites Origen's testimony to the effect that Marcion excised chapters 15–16 of Romans from his *Apostolicon* but suggests that, in fact, Marcion had a fourteen-chapter

a chain of four scriptural citations (Ps 18:49; Deut 32:43; Ps 117:1; Isa 11:10) that jointly explain Paul's claim that "Christ became a servant of the circumcision for the sake of God's truthfulness, in order to confirm the promises to the patriarchs, and for the sake of his mercy, in order that the Gentiles might glorify God" (Rom 15:8–9).[79] The four parts of the catena all have in common the mention of the ἔθνη in connection with the people of Israel. The first of these, Ps 18:49 (Ps 17:50 LXX), has messianic overtones insofar as it puts the words of David ὁ χριστός (Ps 17:51 LXX) in the mouth of Jesus ὁ χριστός (Rom 15:8).[80] What is allusive in Rom 15:9, however, becomes explicit in Rom 15:12:

καὶ πάλιν Ἡσαΐας λέγει
ἔσται ἡ ῥίζα τοῦ Ἰεσσαὶ
καὶ ὁ ἀνιστάμενος ἄρχειν ἐθνῶν,
ἐπ᾽ αὐτῷ ἔθνη ἐλπιοῦσιν.

And again, Isaiah says,
The root of Jesse shall [come],
even he who rises to rule the Gentiles;
in him the Gentiles shall hope.

In this citation Paul follows the text of LXX Isaiah almost exactly, departing from it only in the omission of the phrase ἐν τῇ ἡμέρᾳ ἐκείνῃ (see table 5.4).[81] It is significant, too, that Paul follows the LXX in particular rather than a proto-MT Hebrew text or a Greek version revised toward proto-MT since the LXX itself represents a departure from its putative Hebrew *Vorlage* (see table 5.5).[82] In Isa 11:10, the LXX differs from the MT in two significant respects.[83] First, the translator renders the prepositional phrase לְנֵס, "for a sign," with the Greek purposive infinitive ἄρχειν, "to rule," putting the Davidic

---

recension of Romans not because he truncated it but because Paul wrote it that way. In other words, the longer catholic recension of Romans is the corrupt one, the Marcionite recension the original (see Baur, *Paul the Apostle*, 1:370–372).

79 On the difficult syntax of this sentence and on my translation see the earlier discussion in this chapter.

80 On this citation see the earlier discussion in this chapter.

81 For LXX Isaiah I follow the text of Joseph Ziegler, ed., *Isaias* (Septuaginta 14; Göttingen: Vandenhoeck & Ruprecht, 1967), noting variants where relevant.

82 At Isa 11:10 LXX, MS 565 alone omits καὶ ὁ ἀνιστάμενος ἄρχειν ἐθνῶν, ἐπ᾽ αὐτῷ ἔθνη ἐλπιοῦσιν, which is almost certainly an instance of haplography due to homoioarcton, the scribe's eye having jumped from the first καί to the next.

83 In addition, the LXX opts for τιμή for כָּבוֹד, while the later Greek versions all use δόξα, but both of these are quite conservative equivalencies.

king in a more expressly dominant position in relation to the pagan nations.[84] Second, the translator renders the verb יִדְרֹשׁ, "they will seek," with ἐλπιοῦσιν, "they will hope," the only instance of this equivalency anywhere in the LXX.[85] Paul makes much of this rendering, following this citation with the prayer that ὁ θεὸς τῆς ἐλπίδος, "the God of hope," would fill the auditors with joy and peace so that they might abound ἐν τῇ ἐλπίδι, "in hope."

It is also significant that in Romans 15 Paul speaks again, as he did in Rom 1:5, of his apostolic commission to bring about the ὑπακοὴ ἐθνῶν, "the obedience of the Gentiles" (Rom 15:18; cf. 1:5; 16:26).[86] The ὑπακοὴ ἐθνῶν is not a Pauline innovation; it has a small but important place in the LXX tradition. There are two places in the LXX in which ὑπακοή, "obedience," and the ἔθνη, "Gentiles," are mentioned together in subject-verb relation.[87] Psalm 17 LXX (Ps 18 MT) is expressly Davidic and messianic, being superscribed "to David the servant of the Lord" (17:1) and ending with the praise of God, "who magnifies the deliverances of his king and works mercy for David his christ, and for his seed, forever" (17:51). In 17:44–45 the psalmist prays:

ῥύσῃ με ἐξ ἀντιλογιῶν λαοῦ,
καταστήσεις με εἰς κεφαλὴν <u>ἐθνῶν</u>
λαός ὃν οὐκ ἔγνων ἐδούλευσέν μοι
εἰς ἀκοὴν ὠτίου <u>ὑπήκουσέν</u> μοι.

You will deliver me from the disputes of the people,
you will establish me as head over the <u>Gentiles</u>;
a people whom I did not know served me,
at the hearing of the ear they <u>obeyed</u> me.[88]

---

84 Cf. the later Greek versions, all of which render לְנֵס more literally with σύσσημον. The LXX rendering may have resulted from a confusion of נָשִׂיא (sometimes written נְסִיא), "prince," with נֵס, "sign."

85 Interestingly, all three later Greek versions agree with the LXX in this. Both LXX and the later versions, either independently or together, may be reading intra-Isaianically with Isa 42:4: וּלְתוֹרָתוֹ אִיִּים יְיַחֵילוּ; LXX: καὶ ἐπὶ τῷ ὀνόματι αὐτοῦ ἔθνη ἐλπιοῦσιν; Aquila, Symmachus, Theodotion: καὶ τῷ νόμῳ αὐτοῦ ἔθνη ἐλπιοῦσιν; where all the Greek translators are apparently reading גּוֹיִם for אִיִּים (see Joseph Ziegler, *Untersuchungen zur Septuaginta des Buches Isaias* [Alttestamentliche Abhandlungen 12.3; Münster: Aschendorff, 1934], 140–141).

86 On this phrase and these verses see Paul S. Minear, *The Obedience of Faith: The Purposes of Paul in the Epistle to the Romans* (SBT 2/19; London: SCM, 1971), especially 1–45.

87 Significantly, however, nowhere else in Greek literature antecedent to Paul. Here again, per the argument of chapter 2, the point is not that Paul is commenting on Psalm 18 or Isaiah 11 (although where there are express citations, as in Romans 15, that would appear quite likely) but rather that the language he uses to talk about a messiah is drawn from the Jewish scriptures.

88 Or possibly, if we take εἰς to express result, "they obeyed me so as to listen with the ear" (so Wagner, *Heralds of the Good News*, 313).

Table 5.4

Isa 11:10 LXX	Rom 15:12
ἔσται <u>ἐν τῇ ἡμέρᾳ ἐκείνῃ</u> ἡ ῥίζα τοῦ Ιεσσαι καὶ ὁ ἀνιστάμενος ἄρχειν ἐθνῶν, ἐπ' αὐτῷ ἔθνη ἐλπιοῦσιν.	ἔσται ἡ ῥίζα τοῦ Ἰεσσαὶ καὶ ὁ ἀνιστάμενος ἄρχειν ἐθνῶν, ἐπ' αὐτῷ ἔθνη ἐλπιοῦσιν.

Table 5.5

Isa 11:10 MT	Isa 11:10 LXX
וְהָיָה בַּיּוֹם הַהוּא	ἔσται ἐν τῇ ἡμέρᾳ ἐκείνῃ
שֹׁרֶשׁ יִשַׁי	ἡ ῥίζα τοῦ Ιεσσαι
אֲשֶׁר עֹמֵד לְנֵס עַמִּים	καὶ ὁ ἀνιστάμενος <u>ἄρχειν</u> ἐθνῶν,
אֵלָיו גּוֹיִם יִדְרֹשׁוּ	ἐπ' αὐτῷ ἔθνη <u>ἐλπιοῦσιν</u>,
וְהָיְתָה מְנֻחָתוֹ כָּבוֹד	καὶ ἔσται ἡ ἀνάπαυσις αὐτοῦ τιμή.

Psalm 17 LXX ends with the ἔθνη, "nations, pagans, Gentiles" in a state of ὑπακοή, "obedience," to the Davidic king of Israel. In its most ancient context the psalm was surely a piece of Davidic royal ideology, which the superscription further expanded by associating it with the accession of David to the throne of Saul.[89] In the context of the Second Commonwealth, however, the psalm admits of use by authors, like Paul, who have in mind one or another latter-day χριστός, to whom the Gentiles are to be subjected.[90]

The obedience of the Gentiles also figures in Isa 11:13–14 LXX, a passage that follows immediately after the root of Jesse saying that is cited in Rom 15:12. On the day that the root of Jesse rises to rule the Gentiles (Isa 11:10), the Lord will also show his hand in order to claim the remnant of his people (Isa 11:11). When the exiles return, they will plunder the nations from which they depart, and those nations will be subjected to the children of Israel.

[κύριος] ἀρεῖ σημεῖον εἰς <u>τὰ ἔθνη</u> καὶ συνάξει τοὺς ἀπολομένους Ισραηλ καὶ τοὺς διεσπαρμένους τοῦ Ιουδα....καὶ ἐπὶ Μωαβ πρῶτον τὰς χεῖρας ἐπιβαλοῦσιν, οἱ δὲ υἱοὶ Αμμων πρῶτοι <u>ὑπακούσονται</u>.

---

89 On this psalm see further Frank Moore Cross and David Noel Freedman, "A Royal Psalm of Thanksgiving: II Samuel 22=Psalm 18," *JBL* 72 (1953): 15–34.

90 Cf. *Pss. Sol.* 17:22: ὑπόζωσον αὐτὸν ἰσχὺν, "Gird him [the christ] with strength"; citing Ps 17:33 LXX: ὁ θεὸς ὁ περιζωννύων με δύναμιν, "God who girds me [the christ] with power."

[The Lord] will raise a sign for <u>the Gentiles</u> and will gather the desolate of Israel and the scattered of Judah.... They will lay hands on Moab first, and the leaders of the Ammonites will <u>obey</u> them.

In this oracle the υἱοὶ Ἀμμων πρῶτοι, "leaders of the Ammonites" (v. 14), are representative of the ἔθνη (v. 13), who previously oppressed God's people. Their obedience to the reconstituted children of Israel (v. 14) is an instantiation of the Davidic king's rule over the Gentiles (v. 10).

It is striking that the two chapters in the Greek Bible that include references to the ὑπακοὴ ἐθνῶν, both of which are specifically messianic textual units ("to David his 'christ' and to his seed forever" [Ps 17:51 LXX]; "a scepter from the root of Jesse" [Isa 11:1]), are both cited in the same catena in Romans 15. Two conclusions follow. First, in the LXX itself, the ὑπακοὴ ἐθνῶν stands in a particular thematic connection with the rule of the χριστός; the Gentiles obey the anointed one. Second, the confluence of these several texts in Romans 15 is evidence that Paul's understanding of his commission to bring about the ὑπακοὴ ἐθνῶν (Rom 15:18; cf. 1:5; 16:26) is dependent on his conviction that Jesus is the χριστός spoken of in the scriptural oracles.[91] Here, as in the passages discussed earlier, Paul writes about the χριστός whom he preaches in language drawn from a particular strand of scriptural tradition. This much is clear enough. Despite Paul's use of the formal conventions of ancient Jewish messiah language, however, there are a few passages in which interpreters have taken Paul to demur from, repudiate, or even polemicize against messiahship as a theological category. It remains to consider three such passages. I argue that in none of them does Paul actually repudiate messiahship as a category and indeed that all three depend on χριστός bearing its conventional range of meaning.

1 Cor 1:23: "We Preach a Crucified Christ"

One frequently cited passage in discussions of messiah Christology in Paul is the well-known saying about the content of Paul's preaching in 1 Cor 1:23. Paul begins that letter by protesting the unseemly divisions among the Corinthian believers, to which baptism by particular apostles may have contributed (1 Cor 1:10–16).[92] For this reason Paul relativizes the importance of

---

91 For a more extended treatment see Novenson, "Jewish Messiahs, the Pauline Christ, and the Gentile Question."

92 This tantalizing reference was the impetus for F. C. Baur's early work on the Petrine and Pauline sects in early Christianity ("Die Christuspartei in der korinthischen Gemeinde"). Among recent treatments see Maria A. Pascuzzi, "Baptism-Based Allegiance and the Divisions in Corinth: A Reexamination of 1 Corinthians 1:13–17," *CBQ* 71 (2009): 813–829.

baptism in his apostolic commission: "For Christ did not send me to baptize but to preach the gospel, not in wisdom of speech, lest the cross of Christ be emptied" (1 Cor 1:17). He goes on to specify the content of this gospel that he preaches, again with reference to the terms "wisdom," "cross," and "Christ":[93]

ἐπειδὴ καὶ Ἰουδαῖοι σημεῖα αἰτοῦσιν καὶ Ἕλληνες σοφίαν ζητοῦσιν, ἡμεῖς δὲ κηρύσσομεν Χριστὸν ἐσταυρωμένον, Ἰουδαίοις μὲν σκάνδαλον, ἔθνεσιν δὲ μωρίαν, αὐτοῖς δὲ τοῖς κλητοῖς, Ἰουδαίοις τε καὶ Ἕλλησιν, Χριστὸν θεοῦ δύναμιν καὶ θεοῦ σοφίαν.

For Jews ask for signs and Greeks seek wisdom, but we preach a crucified Christ, a scandal to Jews and foolishness to Gentiles, but to those who are called, both Jews and Greeks, Christ the power of God and wisdom of God.

With respect to our question, the most important part of the passage is the phrase Χριστὸν ἐσταυρωμένον, "a crucified Christ."[94] In recent Pauline interpretation, as with most of the passages treated here, scholars have tended to say that χριστός in this expression is a meaning-less proper name (so "Christ crucified," not "a crucified messiah").[95] A bit further back in the history of interpretation, however, this passage was an important source for the modern distinction between "the Jewish messiah" and "the Christian messiah."[96] About this interpretive tradition Morton Smith writes, "This verse has been made the hair on which to hang a mountain of nonsense about Jewish resistance to the substitution of a spiritual Saviour for a military Messiah."[97] The

---

93 The text is quite stable, but significant variants include the following: The majority text reads Ἕλλησι in place of ἔθνεσιν in v. 23, which is almost certainly an assimilation to Ἕλλησιν in v. 24. P46 reads the final clause in the nominative rather than the accusative case, making it syntactically independent of what comes before: "For those who are called, both Jews and Greeks, Christ is the power of God and wisdom of God."

94 On which see E. Earle Ellis, "Christ Crucified," in *Reconciliation and Hope: New Testament Essays on Atonement and Eschatology Presented to L. L. Morris on His 60th Birthday* (ed. Robert Banks; Carlisle, UK: Paternoster, 1974), 69–75. Cf. the parallel expression in 1 Cor 2:2: Ἰησοῦν Χριστὸν καὶ τοῦτον ἐσταυρωμένον, "Jesus Christ and him crucified," on which see Wiard Popkes, "1 Kor 2,2 und die Anfänge der Christologie," *ZNW* 95 (2004): 64–83.

95 E.g., Kramer, *Christ, Lord, Son of God*, 133; Sanders, *Paul and Palestinian Judaism*, 444; but cf. Dahl, "Messiahship of Jesus in Paul," 24n12; Hengel, "'Christos' in Paul," 71.

96 E.g., Klausner, *Messianic Idea*, 519–531; Mowinckel, *He That Cometh*, 329; Fitzmyer, *One Who Is to Come*, 182–183.

97 Morton Smith, "The Reason for the Persecution of Paul and the Obscurity of Acts," in *Studies in Mysticism and Religion Presented to Gershom G. Scholem on His Seventieth Birthday* (ed. E. E. Urbach et al.; Jerusalem: Magnes, 1967), 263.

point is hyperbolically put, but it is not inaccurate. Paul says that the "crucified Christ" whom he preaches is a scandal to Jews, but he supplies no contrast term, no opposite "Jewish Christ" as a foil for his own Christ.[98] Still less is there any hint of a contrast here between a "spiritual" Christian messiah and a "political" Jewish one.[99]

It is instructive to compare the nearby parallel in 1 Cor 1:18, of which 1 Cor 1:22–24 is an expanded restatement. That verse reads as follows: Ὁ λόγος γὰρ ὁ τοῦ σταυροῦ τοῖς μὲν ἀπολλυμένοις μωρία ἐστίν, τοῖς δὲ σῳζομένοις ἡμῖν δύναμις θεοῦ ἐστιν, "The message of the cross is foolishness to those who are perishing, but to us who are being saved it is the power of God." In common with 1:22–24 are the terms σταυρός, "cross," μωρία, "foolishness," and δύναμις θεοῦ, "power of God." But where 1:23 has Χριστὸν ἐσταυρωμένον, "Christ crucified," 1:18 has ὁ λόγος τοῦ σταυροῦ, "the message of the cross," the latter being a shorthand for the former.[100] More important still, 1:18 does not distinguish Jews from Gentiles in their respective responses; it refers only to the ἀπολλυμένοις, "those who are perishing," and the σῳζομένοις, "those who are being saved."[101] Verse 18 further clarifies what is also the case in vv. 22–24: Paul's rhetorical contrast is not between Christians and Jews but rather between "the called" (both Jews and Greeks) on the one hand and "the perishing" (both Jews and Greeks) on the other. In short, "the Jewish messiah" of modern scholarship is not a character in 1 Cor 1:22–24.

While Paul supplies no equal and opposite counterpart to his crucified messiah, he seems to assume that the range of ways in which contemporary Jews understood the word "messiah" typically did not include the notion of crucifixion.[102] A number of recent interpreters have undertaken to say more

---

98 So rightly Dahl, "Messiahship of Jesus in Paul," 24n12: "In 1 Cor. 1:23 we certainly do not find any antithesis to a Messiah who is not crucified." Cf. Justin Martyr, *Dial.* 10.3: "This is what we are most at a loss about…that you, because you put your hopes in a crucified person [ἄνθρωπον σταυρωθέντα], hope to obtain some good from God, even though you do not do his commandments!" (Greek text ed. Edgar J. Goodspeed, *Die ältesten Apologeten* [Göttingen: Vandenhoeck & Ruprecht, 1915]), where the reference is simply to a "crucified person," and the real curiosity is the Christian failure to keep Torah. See further A. J. B. Higgins, "Jewish Messianic Belief in Justin Martyr's *Dialogue with Trypho*," *NovT* 9 (1967): 298–305.

99 On the liabilities of this distinction see chapter 2.

100 Cf. Gal 5:11, where Paul speaks of τὸ σκάνδαλον τοῦ σταυροῦ, "the offense of the cross"— again without explicit reference to it being the messiah's cross—as an alternative to the proclamation of circumcision (περιτομὴν κηρύσσω), which presumably does not cause offense.

101 Where the latter corresponds to the κλητοῖς, "the called," of 1 Cor 1:24.

102 On the literary evidence for Jewish perceptions of crucifixion in antiquity see Martin Hengel, *Crucifixion* (trans. John Bowden; Philadelphia: Fortress, 1997), 1–10; David W. Chapman, *Ancient Jewish and Christian Perceptions of Crucifixion* (WUNT 2/244; Tübingen: Mohr Siebeck, 2008).

precisely what about the claim "we preach a crucified messiah" would have constituted a scandal to ancient Jews. Wright echoes both Trypho and Paul himself in locating the offense in the particular mode of death.[103] James Dunn suggests that the offense to Paul's contemporary Jews lay not in the "crucified" nor in the "messiah" but rather in the "preaching."[104] Paula Fredriksen, echoing Martin Buber, finds the offense not in anything Paul says here but rather in the failure of the world to live up to Paul's claims.[105] Alan Segal offers a sophisticated version of the traditional contrast with a Jewish militant messiah.[106] All of these are worthwhile proposals, and probably at least some contemporary Jews will have objected to Paul's message for each of these reasons. All of them, however, are speculative in the sense that they claim more for 1 Cor 1:22–24 than Paul himself says. What the phrase Χριστὸν ἐσταυρωμένον, Ἰουδαίοις μὲν σκάνδαλον certainly means is that, whatever the conventional range of meaning of χριστός in Paul's linguistic community, from his perspective it generally did not include the notion of crucifixion. It does not follow that there was a single opposite meaning of "messiah" that rendered Paul's

---

103 Wright, *Climax*, 61: "The real scandal is not simply the death of the Messiah but the shameful and penal mode of that death, particularly in relation to the corporate significance of the Messiah." Cf. Gal 3:13: Χριστὸς ἡμᾶς ἐξηγόρασεν ἐκ τῆς κατάρας τοῦ νόμου γενόμενος ὑπὲρ ἡμῶν κατάρα, ὅτι γέγραπται ἐπικατάρατος πᾶς ὁ κρεμάμενος ἐπὶ ξύλου, "Christ redeemed us from the curse of the law, having become a curse for us, for it is written, *Cursed is everyone who is hung on a tree* [Deut 27:26]"; Justin Martyr, *Dial.* 90.1: "We know that [the Christ must] suffer and be led as a sheep [Isa 53:7]; but whether he must also be crucified and die so shamefully and dishonorably through a death cursed in the law, prove to us. For this we cannot even conceive."

104 Dunn, "How Controversial?" 218: "The offense for most Jews was not simply the message of a crucified Messiah, the fact that some other Jews (and Gentiles) believed and preached that Jesus, crucified and all, was Messiah. It was the prospect of accepting that claim for themselves which was the stumbling block."

105 Fredriksen, *From Jesus to Christ*, 167–168: "The message failed…because its central and motivating claim—that crucifixion actually confirmed Jesus' status as messiah—could not be accommodated to mainstream Jewish messianism, which linked the coming of the messiah to the coming of the messianic age.…A messiah, crucified or otherwise, was not a messiah in the eyes of Jewish tradition if after his coming the world continued as before." Cf. Martin Buber's letter to a newspaper editor (as cited by J. Louis Martyn, *Theological Issues in the Letters of Paul* [Edinburgh: T. & T. Clark, 1997], 279): "According to my faith, the Messiah has not appeared in a definite moment of history, but rather his appearance can only mark the end of history. In the perspective of my faith, the redemption of the world did not happen nineteen centuries ago. On the contrary, we still live in an unredeemed world."

106 Alan F. Segal, *Paul the Convert: The Apostolate and Apostasy of Saul the Pharisee* (New Haven: Yale University Press, 1990), 123: "The logic of this argument depends on knowing that the Jews believed in a messiah who would defeat their national enemies and usher in a period of tranquility. Such a concept virtually eliminated the possibility of a crucified messiah for Paul when he was a Pharisee."

usage offensive;[107] nor does it follow that the notion of a crucified messiah, once proposed, was inconceivable.[108] Paul simply used the linguistic resources available to him to say what he was sure was true about Jesus.[109] In so doing he certainly pushed the conventional boundaries of the word "messiah," but insofar as his contemporaries understood him clearly enough either to believe or to take offense, he did not break those boundaries.

2 Cor 5:16–17: "We No Longer Know Christ according to the Flesh"

Paul's provocative statement in 2 Cor 5:16–17 about "no longer knowing Christ according to the flesh" has been a theater for several disputes in the history of interpretation.[110] The context for this statement is a discourse on Paul's apostolic "ministry of reconciliation" (2 Cor 5:18), whose goal is to "persuade people" (2 Cor 5:11). It is with these people in view, for whom Christ died and was raised (2 Cor 5:14–15), that Paul writes:[111]

Ὥστε ἡμεῖς ἀπὸ τοῦ νῦν οὐδένα οἴδαμεν κατὰ σάρκα· εἰ καὶ ἐγνώκαμεν κατὰ σάρκα Χριστόν, ἀλλὰ νῦν οὐκέτι γινώσκομεν. ὥστε εἴ τις ἐν Χριστῷ, καινὴ κτίσις· τὰ ἀρχαῖα παρῆλθεν, ἰδοὺ γέγονεν καινά.

So then, from now on we know no one according to the flesh. Even if we have known Christ according to the flesh, now, at any rate, we no longer know [him so]. So then, if anyone is in Christ, new creation happens. The old things have passed away; behold, the new have come.

---

107 *Pace* Segal, *Paul the Convert,* 123: "The logic of this argument depends on knowing that the Jews believed in a messiah who would defeat their national enemies."

108 So rightly Fredriksen, *From Jesus to Christ,* 167: "A crucified messiah was evidently not inconceivable: Jews could and did conceive it."

109 Cf. Segal, *Paul the Convert,* 123: "Since Paul knows from his personal, visionary experience that Christ was crucified and rose…he transforms it into a new understanding of messiahship."

110 Three disputes, especially: first, the details of Paul's own preconversion and postconversion viewpoints; second, the relative importance of the historical Jesus for Pauline and Christian theology; and third, the role of Jewish messianism as a factor in Pauline Christology. For present purposes I am concerned only with the third of these.

111 The text of this passage is generally quite stable. There is some confusion about the beginning of the second clause; especially, the original hands of P46, ℵ, B, and D all read εἰ καί (so also NA27), but correctors to ℵ, C, and D, along with the Majority Text, read εἰ δὲ καί. With NA27 I follow the uncorrected reading. In addition, several minuscule MSS (6, 33, 81, 614, 630, 1241, 1505, 1881) read τὰ πάντα καινά, "all things [have become] new," in place of καινά, "the new things [have come]," but this reading is surely secondary and probably reflects assimilation to Rev 21:5: ἰδοὺ καινὰ ποιῶ πάντα.

Most of the interpretive disputes that have attended this passage have been concerned with the phrase κατὰ σάρκα Χριστόν, "Christ according to the flesh," and one of these disputes has to do with that phrase's possible associations with Jewish messiah traditions. F. C. Baur, in particular, interpreted the passage along these lines. He gives an extended paraphrase, speaking for Paul:

> If it were the case that formerly I knew no other Messiah than the Messiah of Judaism—such a one as all the peculiar prejudices and material inclinations of my nation presented to me; and if I were not prepared to raise myself to the new stage of spiritual life on which I now stand—where I live in Christ who died for me, as for all, yet now I do not any longer acknowledge this conception of the Messiah as the true one. I have freed myself from all prejudices, from all the material ideas and expectations which had naturally taken hold of me from my nationality—which had devolved upon me as a born Jew.[112]

For Baur, these verses are a polemical manifesto on the Jewish and Pauline notions of messiah. Baur takes κατὰ σάρκα adjectivally, as qualifying a kind of messiah, namely a fleshly, nationalistic, Jewish kind, in contrast to Paul's own higher, spiritual, Christian kind. If, as Baur has it, κατὰ σάρκα here is adjectival, then the verbs of "knowing" would seem to signify an act of choosing against the κατὰ σάρκα Christ and in favor of an alternate kind of Christ. That is to say, "we *no longer know* that Christ" means roughly "we *reject* that Christ." Baur's Paul repudiates messianism as a theological category altogether since it is a byproduct of Paul's own unfortunate ethnic Jewish heritage.[113] In so doing Paul "raises himself to a new level of spiritual life."

Like the mid-nineteenth-century Baur, early to middle twentieth-century interpreters tended to conclude that κατὰ σάρκα here is an adjectival phrase modifying Χριστόν and that Paul is rejecting a "Christ according to the flesh." Unlike Baur, however, they identified this "Christ according to the flesh" not with the Jewish messiah but rather with the historical Jesus. On this reading, the

---

112 Baur, *Paul the Apostle,* 1:283.

113 Aside from the problem of the adjectival reading of κατὰ σάρκα (on which see the later discussion), there are problems with Baur's identification of "fleshly" with "Jewish." Against this identification Paul very often uses κατὰ σάρκα simply to mean "genealogically," and in virtually all of these instances he has the Jewish family tree in view because he happens to be talking about David (Rom 1:3) or Abraham (Rom 4:1) or Jesus (Rom 9:5) or the ancient Israelites (1 Cor 10:18) or the contemporary Jews (Rom 9:3). However, this is not because κατὰ σάρκα means "Jewish"; it is simply an accident of context.

grammar of the passage works exactly as it does on Baur's account, but the lexical value of the key term is completely different. For Baur, what was "fleshly" about Jesus was his Jewishness, while for Heitmüller, Bousset, Schweitzer, Bultmann, and others, what was "fleshly" about Jesus was his mere *Historismus*.[114] By their lights, 2 Cor 5:16–17 is about Paul's rejection of the historical Jesus as a basis for theology and resolution to confess the risen Christ of faith instead.[115]

All such interpretations run aground, however, on the observation that the prepositional phrase κατὰ σάρκα is, in fact, not adjectival but adverbial, that it modifies not the noun Χριστόν, but rather the verb ἐγνώκαμεν.[116] As early as the 1920s, some interpreters recognized this and registered a minority report.[117] Later in the twentieth century, when the "problem of Paul and Jesus" was no longer such a dominant motif in research, what had been a minority report gradually gained traction in mainstream Pauline interpretation.[118] It is

114 The fact that such radically different lexical values have been accorded the same phrase raises questions about any approach that reads the passage as a polemic about a "fleshly Christ." Just so, 2 Cor 5:16–17 is a classic example of how a phrase or a passage from scripture can become a cipher for each generation's theological concerns. Cf. John W. Fraser, "Paul's Knowledge of Jesus: II Corinthians V.16 Once More," *NTS* 17 (1971): 293–313, here 307: "When so many varied interpretations of this verse have been given, when they are made to follow the current theological fashion, one suspects the text is used like a Lesbian rule."

115 E.g., Wilhelm Heitmüller, "Zum Problem Jesus und Paulus," *ZNW* 13 (1912): 320–337: "Quite decisively Paul says here [in 2 Cor 5:16–17] that the earthly Jesus, the human personality Jesus, has no meaning whatever for his religious life, for him as one who is 'in Christ' and thereby belongs to a higher reality than the earth....Paul knows the exalted Lord, the 'Christ according to the spirit'; he lives in Paul and Paul in him; by him Paul is filled. How could the earthly Jesus, the 'Christ according to the flesh,' be important to him?" (trans. Wayne A. Meeks, ed., *The Writings of St. Paul* [Norton Critical Editions; New York: Norton, 1972], 309); likewise Bousset, *Kyrios Christos*, 169; Schweitzer, *Mysticism*, 114; Bultmann, *Theology of the New Testament*, 1:238.

116 The syntax is not unequivocal, but for a number of contextual reasons (see the later discussion), the adverbial reading is the more compelling.

117 E.g., Friedrich Büchsel, *Der Geist Gottes im Neuen Testament* (Gütersloh: Bertelsmann, 1926), 278–279: "Aber Christus nach dem Fleisch kennen heisst nicht, Christus geschichtlich kennen....Das Fleisch Jesu und die geschichtliche Wirklichkeit Jesu decken sich nicht"; likewise A. E. J. Rawlinson, *The New Testament Doctrine of the Christ* (London: Longmans, 1926), 90n5: "What he is repudiating is not a fleshly kind of Christ but a fleshly kind of knowledge." Remarkably, Bultmann actually concedes the grammatical point but insists that it does not make any difference: "The latter [i.e., the adverbial reading] is the more probable, it seems to me. But this decision means nothing for the sense of the total context, for a 'Christ regarded in the manner of the flesh' is just what a 'Christ after the flesh' is" (*Theology of the New Testament*, 1:238–239).

118 See especially the 1967 study of J. Louis Martyn, "Epistemology at the Turn of the Ages," in *Theological Issues in the Letters of Paul*, 89–110, here 95: "He is saying that there are two ways of knowing, and that what separates the two is the turn of the ages, the apocalyptic event of Christ's death/resurrection." Since Martyn, the adjectival reading persists among only a minority, e.g., John Howard Schütz, *Paul and the Anatomy of Apostolic Authority* (SNTSMS 26; Cambridge: Cambridge University Press, 1975), 177; Boyarin, *Radical Jew*, 29–30: "There was a Christ according to the flesh ... —which corresponds to the literal, historical Jesus—and a Christ according to the spirit—the allegorical, risen Christ."

not "we knew Christ-according-to-the-flesh" but rather "we knew Christ in a fleshly way." That this is so is clear from the preceding clause, ἡμεῖς ἀπὸ τοῦ νῦν οὐδένα οἴδαμεν κατὰ σάρκα, "From now on we know no one in a fleshly way." That is, not only Jesus but other people, too, can be known both κατὰ σάρκα and otherwise.[119] The difference lies not in the object known but rather in the knower. For Paul, human knowers have undergone a drastic change of circumstances with the coming of Christ and the turn of the ages.[120] It is just this eschatological change of circumstances that is reflected in the following verse: ὥστε εἴ τις ἐν Χριστῷ, καινὴ κτίσις, "So that if anyone is in Christ, new creation happens." In no way, then, does 2 Cor 5:16–17 constitute a repudiation of messianism as a theological category.

Rom 1:3–4: "From the Seed of David according to the Flesh"

Romans 1:3–4 might initially seem to be positive evidence of messiah Christology in Paul, but its terminology and its placement have led some interpreters to conclude just the opposite. In the opening line of the Epistle to the Romans, Paul introduces himself as "an apostle set apart for the gospel of God, which he promised beforehand through his prophets in the holy scriptures" (Rom 1:1–2). This gospel of God, Paul clarifies, is a gospel περὶ τοῦ υἱοῦ αὐτοῦ…Ἰησοῦ Χριστοῦ τοῦ κυρίου ἡμῶν, "about his son…Jesus Christ our Lord." Paul then characterizes Christ with a pair of adjectival participial phrases whose syntax is mostly straightforward but whose interpretation has been beset with difficulties. Christ, Paul writes, τοῦ γενομένου ἐκ σπέρματος Δαυὶδ κατὰ σάρκα, "came from the seed of David according to the flesh," and τοῦ ὁρισθέντος υἱοῦ θεοῦ ἐν δυνάμει κατὰ πνεῦμα ἁγιωσύνης ἐξ ἀναστάσεως νεκρῶν, "was appointed son of God in power according to the spirit of holiness from the resurrection of the dead" (Rom 1:3–4).[121]

---

119 The indefinite "no one" here fits the immediately preceding context, where Paul's concern is the "people" whom he seeks to persuade (2 Cor 5:11) and for whom Christ died and was raised (2 Cor 5:18).

120 So rightly Martyn, "Epistemology at the Turn of the Ages." Schweitzer, *Mysticism,* 114, likewise highlights the turn of the ages but misidentifies the implication that 2 Cor 5:16–17 draws from this event.

121 The text of these verses is quite stable. Minuscule 61 (sixteenth c.) has γεννωμένου, "was born," in place of γενομένου, "came," and the Latin textual tradition has *praedestinatus* (perhaps reflecting Greek προορισθέντος [cf. Rom 8:29, 30; 1 Cor 2:7]), "foreordained," in place of ὁρισθέντος, "appointed." Both of these variants, however, are almost certainly secondary.

Table 5.6

2 Kgdms 22:51/Ps 17:51 LXX	Rom 1:3–4
μεγαλύνων [τὰς] σωτηρίας [τοῦ] βασιλέως αὐτοῦ καὶ ποιῶν ἔλεος τῷ χριστῷ αὐτοῦ τῷ Δαυὶδ καὶ τῷ σπέρματι αὐτοῦ ἕως αἰῶνος	τοῦ γενομένου ἐκ σπέρματος Δαυὶδ κατὰ σάρκα, τοῦ ὁρισθέντος υἱοῦ θεοῦ ἐν δυνάμει κατὰ πνεῦμα ἁγιωσύνης ἐξ ἀναστάσεως νεκρῶν, Ἰησοῦ Χριστοῦ

When Paul speaks of Jesus in Rom 1:3–4 as the "Christ from the seed of David," he is using the idiom of the song of David, which is preserved in both 2 Samuel 22 and Psalm 18, the only place in the Greek Jewish scriptures in which the words "christ," "seed," and "David" all occur together in close proximity (see table 5.6).[122] Paul may or may not have been conscious of the particular source of this expression.[123] The pertinent point is that, conscious or not, he uses a pattern of speech that does in fact come from the Jewish scriptures. That in this case Paul probably inherits this scriptural idiom secondhand from an antecedent tradition further illustrates my claim in chapter 2 that the scriptures functioned in ancient Judaism and Christianity not only as religious texts but also as a pool of linguistic resources. Romans 1:3–4 is a messiah text in the sense outlined there: It reflects on a messiah figure in language drawn from the Jewish scriptures.

The parallel terms σάρξ, "flesh," and πνεῦμα, "spirit," have been cause for some comment since those words occur elsewhere in Paul as a contrasting pair with heavy value judgments attached (Rom 8:4–13; 1 Cor 5:5; Gal 3:3; 4:29; 5:16–17; 6:8; Phil 3:3).[124] Some interpreters, following this exegetical lead, take Paul to be making a value-laden contrast in Rom 1:3–4, denigrating the fleshly Davidic descent of Jesus and advocating for a spiritual son-of-God Christology instead.[125] It is true that κατὰ σάρκα and κατὰ πνεῦμα often

---

122 The texts of the LXX parallels are virtually identical to one another, with the exception that the Psalm text has two definite articles (in square brackets here) where the 2 Kingdoms text does not. On the textual history of the psalm see further Cross and Freedman, "Royal Psalm of Thanksgiving."

123 *Prima facie*, there is no reason to assume that he would have been conscious of it, but the fact that he cites the verse preceding this one (i.e., 2 Kgdms 22:50/Ps 17:50 LXX) in Rom 15:9 (on which see the earlier discussion) may be reason to think that he was.

124 On the spirit-flesh contrast in Paul see especially Martyn, *Theological Issues in the Letters of Paul*, 111–124, 251–266.

125 E.g., Dahl, "Messiahship of Jesus in Paul," 20; Eduard Schweizer, "Römer 1,3f. und der Gegensatz von Fleisch und Geist vor und bei Paulus," *Evangelische Theologie* 15 (1955): 563–571; James D. G. Dunn, "Jesus: Flesh and Spirit: An Exposition of Romans 1:3–4," *JTS* 24 (1973): 40–68; MacRae, "Messiah and Gospel," 171. This interpretation is at least as old as Augustine,

signify different, competing spheres in Pauline usage.[126] In such cases, however, both phrases are normally adverbial to verbs of conduct (e.g., εἰμί, περιπατέω, φρονέω, ζάω); people "walk" or "live" either according to the flesh or according to the spirit (e.g., Rom 8:4–13; Gal 3:3; 5:16–17; 6:8; Phil 3:3). But this is not the case in Rom 1:3–4. On the contrary, the syntagm κατὰ σάρκα, when used in conjunction with a mention of an ancestor or ancestral people as it is in Rom 1:3, simply means "genealogically."[127] Therefore, ἐκ σπέρματος Δαυὶδ κατὰ σάρκα simply expresses Jesus's familial descent from David; it does not imply any value judgment thereon.[128]

More controversial than the meaning of this expression, however, is its relationship to the wider Pauline corpus. This is the only place in the undisputed Pauline letters where Jesus is said to be "from the seed of David."[129] This is also the only place where Paul uses the phrase πνεῦμα ἁγιωσύνης, "spirit of holiness."[130] In light of these anomalies, a large part of the literature on the passage has focused on the origin of the expression that comprises Rom 1:3–4. In

---

who supplies from 2 Cor 13:4 ("He was crucified from weakness, but he lives from the power of God") the phrase "in weakness" for Rom 1:3 to contrast with "in power" in Rom 1:4: *ut infirmitas pertineat ad David, vita vero aeterna ad virtutem dei*, "So weakness pertains to David, but eternal life to the power of God" (*ep. Rm. inch.* 1.5 [PL 35:2091]). As Charles Cousar rightly notes, however, in 2 Cor 13:4 the "weakness" is a feature of the crucifixion in particular, not of Jesus's humanity or genealogy (Charles B. Cousar, *A Theology of the Cross: The Death of Jesus in the Pauline Letters* [Overtures to Biblical Theology 24; Minneapolis: Fortress, 1990], 1).

126 Even when they occur together in Paul, however, the two words are not always contrast terms. See 2 Cor 3:3: ἐγγεγραμμένη…πνεύματι θεοῦ ζῶντος…ἐν πλαξὶν καρδίαις σαρκίναις, "inscribed…with the spirit of the living God…on tablets that are fleshy hearts"; and 2 Cor 7:1: καθαρίσωμεν ἑαυτοὺς ἀπὸ παντὸς μολυσμοῦ σαρκὸς καὶ πνεύματος, "Let us cleanse ourselves from every defilement of flesh and spirit."

127 See BDAG, s.v. σάρξ, 4. So it is in Rom 9:3: τῶν ἀδελφῶν μου τῶν συγγενῶν μου κατὰ σάρκα, "my brethren, my kinfolk according to the flesh"; Rom 9:5: ἐξ ὧν ὁ Χριστὸς τὸ κατὰ σάρκα, "from [the Israelites] comes Christ according to the flesh" (see the later discussion); 1 Cor 10:18: βλέπετε τὸν Ἰσραὴλ κατὰ σάρκα, "Consider Israel according to the flesh"; probably also Rom 4:1: Ἀβραὰμ τὸν προπάτορα ἡμῶν κατὰ σάρκα, "Abraham, our forefather according to the flesh" (but on this verse cf. Richard B. Hays, "'Have We Found Abraham to Be Our Forefather according to the Flesh?' A Reconsideration of Rom 4:1," *NovT* 27 [1985]: 76–98).

128 Also relevant in this connection is the fact that the two participial phrases are not separated by so much as a particle (e.g., δέ), much less a strong disjunction (e.g., ἀλλά). Syntactically, they are not opposites but complements (so rightly Schweitzer, *Mysticism*, 63).

129 But cf. Rom 15:12 (ἡ ῥίζα τοῦ Ἰεσσαί, "the root of Jesse"), on which see the earlier discussion. David appears by name elsewhere, but as a speaker of scripture, not an ancestor of Jesus (see Rom 4:6; 11:9: Δαυὶδ λέγει, "David says," followed by scriptural citations). Cf. 2 Tim 2:8, which may be dependent on Romans 1: Μνημόνευε Ἰησοῦν Χριστὸν ἐγηγερμένον ἐκ νεκρῶν, ἐκ σπέρματος Δαυίδ, κατὰ τὸ εὐαγγέλιόν μου, "Remember Jesus Christ, raised from the dead, from the seed of David, according to my gospel."

130 Cf. his customary expression πνεῦμα ἅγιον, "holy spirit" (Rom 5:5; 9:1; 14:17; 15:13, 16; 1 Cor 6:19; 12:3; 2 Cor 6:6; 13:13; 1 Thess 1:5, 6).

particular, interpreters have argued that part or all of the passage represents a pre-Pauline Christian confession that Paul chooses, for one reason or another, to quote at this point in the letter. In Bultmann's well-known formulation, "Though the title [son of David] is of no importance to him [Paul], he refers to it in Rom. 1:3, a sentence which is evidently due to a handed-down formula; he desires thereby to accredit himself to the unknown Roman Church as an apostle who advocates right doctrine."[131]

Despite its considerable influence, this approach has not gone uncontested. A minority have objected that the reasons commonly adduced for thinking that Rom 1:3–4 is a pre-Pauline fragment are not compelling, and in fact this objection is not without merit.[132] It is likely that Rom 1:3–4 does reflect a pre-Pauline tradition but not on account of the association with David, the uniqueness of which in the Pauline corpus has been overstated.[133] The phrase πνεῦμα ἁγιωσύνης, "spirit of holiness," however, is more significant in this respect. The Greek looks very much like a close rendering of the Hebrew idiom רוח קדש, "spirit of holiness" in the sense of "holy spirit" (Isa 63:10, 11; Ps 51:13), but the LXX translators consistently render that idiom with Greek τὸ πνεῦμα τὸ ἅγιόν.[134] What is interesting about the phrase πνεῦμα ἁγιωσύνης is not that it is not characteristically Pauline—that much is true of everything about which Paul writes only once—but that it is a variant form of an expression for which Paul has an otherwise entirely consistent form.[135]

---

131 Bultmann, *Theology of the New Testament*, 1:49. Cf. the source-critical proposals of Christoph Burger, *Jesus als Davidssohn: Eine traditionsgeschichtliche Untersuchung* (FRLANT 98; Göttingen: Vandenhoeck & Ruprecht, 1970), 25–27; Eta Linnemann, "Tradition und Interpretation in Röm 1,3f," *EvT* 31 (1971): 264–275; Heinrich Schlier, "Eine christologische Credoformel der römischen Gemeinde: Zu Röm 1,3f," in *Der Geist und Die Kirche: Exegetische Aufsätze und Vorträge* (4 vols.; Freiburg: Herder, 1980), 4:56–69; Robert Jewett, "The Redaction and Use of an Early Christian Confession in Romans 1:3–4," in *The Living Text: Essays in Honor of Ernest W. Saunders* (ed. Dennis E. Groh and Robert Jewett; Lanham, Md.: University Press of America, 1985), 99–122; among others. All agree that Paul is citing an earlier tradition; the discussion centers on which particular words and phrases comprise the pre-Pauline kernel and which are Pauline additions.

132 For this minority report see Vern S. Poythress, "Is Romans 1:3–4 a Pauline Confession after All?" *ExpTim* 87 [1976]: 180–183; Whitsett, "Son of God, Seed of David."

133 See the earlier discussion.

134 Independently of Paul, the Greek phrase πνεῦμα ἁγιωσύνης is attested only in *T. Levi* 18:11: καὶ δώσει τοῖς ἁγίοις φαγεῖν ἐκ τοῦ ξύλου τῆς ζωῆς, καὶ πνεῦμα ἁγιωσύνης ἔσται ἐπ᾽ αὐτοῖς, "And he will give the holy ones to eat from the tree of life, and the spirit of holiness will be upon them." But cf. Hebrew רוח קדש in 1QS 4.21; 8.16; 9.3; CD 2.12; 1QH 7.6–7; 9.32.

135 The undisputed Pauline letters contain hundreds of *hapax legomena*, most of which are not taken to suggest pre-Pauline tradition, and rightly so. It is generally recognized that lexical anomaly by itself is not a reliable guide in questions of tradition history.

Even if Rom 1:3–4 preserves a pre-Pauline tradition, however, it is still necessary to explain Paul's choice of the tradition for inclusion at this point in the letter. Let us grant that Rom 1:3–4 preserves a pre-Pauline formula; it does not at all follow from this that the view expressed is therefore non-Pauline in outlook. Quite the contrary. As a general rule, Paul's citations of antecedent texts and traditions function in such a way as to confirm Paul's own claims; indeed, in most cases this is precisely the rationale for the citations.[136] As for Bultmann's proposal that in Rom 1:3 Paul says something he does not mean in order to ingratiate himself with his audience, this account is less than plausible. Even in Romans, where presumably Paul is more than usually politic toward his audience, his rhetoric is not out-and-out disingenuous. In those instances where Paul really does not mean what he says—that is, where his prose is genuinely sarcastic or prosopopoetic—he typically makes this clear by means of certain conventional literary signals.[137] There are no such signals, however, in the near context of Rom 1:3–4, which is as one would expect since Paul's epistolary introductions are generally quite earnest in their tone.[138]

For these reasons, it is best to conclude that Paul speaks for himself when he composes Rom 1:3–4, even if he borrows the language from an antecedent tradition. As the subfield of redaction criticism has come to recognize, the viewpoint of an ancient author is conveyed not only in the places at which she differs from her sources but also in the places at which she cites those sources

---

136 This is most obvious in Paul's many citations of scripture (καθὼς γέγραπται, "as it is written," etc.), but it is also true of his occasional citations of antecedent Christian tradition (e.g., 1 Cor 15:3: "I delivered to you first of all what I also received, that Christ died for our sins according to the scriptures"). An exception to this rule is the well-known Corinthian "slogans" (e.g., 1 Cor 6:12=10:23 [πάντα [μοι] ἔξεστιν, "Everything is permitted"]; 6:13 [τὰ βρώματα τῇ κοιλίᾳ καὶ ἡ κοιλία τοῖς βρώμασιν, "Food for the belly, and the belly for food"]; 6:18 [πᾶν ἁμάρτημα ὃ ἐὰν ποιήσῃ ἄνθρωπος ἐκτὸς τοῦ σώματός ἐστιν, "Every sin that a person does is outside the body"]), which Paul cites in order to correct them (see Jerome Murphy-O'Connor, *Keys to First Corinthians: Revisiting the Major Issues* [Oxford: Oxford University Press, 2009], 20–31, 242–256).

137 E.g., Τί οὖν ἐροῦμεν; … μὴ γένοιτο, "What then shall we say? … Not at all!" (Rom 6:1–2; 7:7; 9:14); καθὼς βλασφημούμεθα καὶ καθώς φασίν τινες ἡμᾶς λέγειν, "As some slanderously say that we say" (Rom 3:8); κατὰ ἄνθρωπον λέγω, "I am speaking in a human manner" (Rom 3:5); γινώσκουσιν γὰρ νόμον λαλῶ, "I am speaking for those who know the law" (Rom 7:1). Granted, this methodological problem is much disputed in current Pauline research (see, e.g., the recent discussion surrounding Douglas A. Campbell, *The Deliverance of God: An Apocalyptic Rereading of Justification in Paul* [Grand Rapids, Mich.: Eerdmans, 2009]). My own view, which comprises one of my present research projects, is that there is a methodological control in the form of linguistic conventions like these, but of course this claim is not uncontroversial.

138 Cf. 2 Cor 1:1–7; Gal 1:1–5; Phil 1:1–11; 1 Thess 1:1–3; Phlm 1–7; but 1 Cor 1:1–9 is a possible exception. On the conventional tone of epistolary introductions in antiquity, see Stanley K. Stowers, *Letter Writing in Greco-Roman Antiquity* (Philadelphia: Westminster, 1986), 41–48, 51–57.

in implicit agreement. By the same logic, pre-Pauline traditions, once used by Paul, become functionally Pauline, and must be made sense of as meaningful parts of the texts in which they appear.[139] Paul's use of the "Christ from the seed of David" expression in Rom 1:3–4 is neither ironic nor merely rhetorical; it is his way of saying what he wants to say about Jesus.

Conclusion

From my treatment of these nine passages, it is possible to draw several conclusions, which, in turn, reinforce and clarify the findings of the previous four chapters. First, in these and other passages, Paul's prose does all that we normally expect any ancient Jewish or Christian text to do to count as a messiah text. He writes at length and in detail about a character whom he designates with the Septuagintal word χριστός, and he clarifies what he means by this polysemous term in the customary way—by citing and alluding to certain scriptural source texts rather than others. Paul's letters meet all of the pertinent criteria for early Jewish messiah language.[140]

Second, contrary to one influential strand in the history of interpretation, Paul does not repudiate messiahship as a theological category.[141] The "crucified messiah" whom Paul preaches in 1 Cor 1:23 is an offense to some Jews not because he is a non- or an anti- or a supra-messiah but because he is a crucified messiah, neither more or less. By the same token, when Paul writes that "we no longer know Christ according to flesh" (2 Cor 5:16), he is commenting on an eschatological change in the mode of human knowing, not a philosophical change of mind from a messianic Christology to a nonmessianic one. Because Paul does not repudiate messiahship as a theological category and because his prose meets all the usual criteria for messiah language, it is only by a double standard that Paul's letters would not count as early Jewish messiah texts.

---

139 This methodological point has been well made by Cousar, *Theology of the Cross*, 15–18, here 17:

> Is material taken from the pre-Pauline tradition necessarily to be given less importance than the material immediately from Paul? A creed might be quoted … precisely because it says what Paul wants to say and perhaps says it better. He may have intended it to be read emphatically, as if it were italicized. Or Paul may employ traditional material because it provides a common ground he shares with his audience and a basis from which to argue. In both cases, the traditional material has become "Pauline."

140 On these criteria, see chapter 2.

141 On this strand in the history of interpretation, see chapter 1. On the related proposals that Paul repudiates messianism either onomastically or grammatically, see chapters 3 and 4, respectively.

Third, as with other messiah texts, it is possible to trace the particular contours of Paul's messianism by noting which scriptural source texts he cites and what the logic is by which he interprets them. In Paul's case, his scriptural source texts are overwhelmingly associated with the house of David rather than, say, the Aaronic priesthood or Daniel's visions (but cf. Dan 7:27 and 1 Cor 15:24). This is not insignificant since other messiah texts, even Christian ones, go in quite different directions.[142] Paul's David texts include several of the David texts most frequently cited in other Jewish and Christian messiah texts (e.g., 2 Sam 7:12; Ps 110:1);[143] but within the pool of available source texts, Paul shows a particular affinity for passages that envision the Davidic king ruling over the Gentile nations (e.g., Isa 11:10; 2 Sam 22=Ps 18), probably for reasons having to do with Paul's Gentile mission. Moreover, there is some evidence that Paul conflates these Davidic messiah traditions with other scriptural traditions in certain contexts (e.g., Gen 17:7 in Gal 3:16). Like the examples I discussed in chapter 2, Paul takes his messiah language from the Jewish scriptures, both from explicitly "messianic" scriptures and non-"messianic" ones. In this and other respects his letters are invaluable examples of messiah language in ancient Judaism.

---

142 The Epistle to the Hebrews, to cite one Christian example (which was widely thought to be Pauline in antiquity), trades heavily on the "anointed [high] priest" language of Leviticus: Lev 4:3: ὁ ἀρχιερεὺς ὁ κεχρισμένος; Lev 4:5, 16; 6:15: ὁ ἱερεὺς ὁ χριστός; and cf. Heb 5:5: ὁ Χριστὸς οὐχ ἑαυτὸν ἐδόξασεν γενηθῆναι ἀρχιερέα; Heb 9:11: Χριστὸς δὲ παραγενόμενος ἀρχιερεύς.

143 On this common pool of scriptural source texts see chapter 2.

Conclusion

Summary of the Argument

I began this study with a history of the question (chapter 1), which showed how the discussion of χριστός in Paul has often been a subset of or a cipher for more urgent interpretive disputes and how Pauline interpreters have been confident that χριστός in Paul does not mean "messiah," even while scholars of ancient Judaism have reopened the question what "messiah" means. Chapter 2 traced the rise and fall of "the messianic idea" in Jewish studies and gave an alternative account of the meaningfulness of messiah language in antiquity: Messiah language worked, as a social-linguistic phenomenon, because there existed both an accessible pool of linguistic resources (namely, the Jewish scriptures) and a community of competent language users (namely, the Jewish community and their sympathizers). Chapter 3 responded to the claim that the normal rules for understanding χριστός do not apply to Paul because he uses the word as a proper name. It showed that is not the case that titles mean things but proper names do not, that ancient Greek admits of many more onomastic categories than just titles and names, and that χριστός in Paul functions for the most part as an honorific, comparable in form to Epiphanes, Augustus, or Bar Kokhba.

In chapter 4 I undertook a philological study of a number of set phrases (e.g., "Jesus Christ," "Christ Jesus," "in Christ," "the Christ of God") that have been taken as evidence that Paul either did or did not use χριστός in keeping with its conventional range of meaning and concluded that that question cannot be settled on the grounds of formal grammar alone. Chapter 5, finally, examined nine passages in the Pauline letters in which Paul comments directly on how he means χριστός. Those passages do all that we normally expect any Jewish or Christian text to do to count as a messiah text: They comment on a "messiah" in language borrowed from a particular set of scriptural source texts. In short, Christ language in Paul relates to messiah language in ancient Judaism not as a contrast term but as a sample. It remains now to comment briefly on the consequences of this conclusion for Pauline interpretation on the one hand and messianism research on the other.

Christ Language in Paul

At present, the secondary literature on Pauline Christology stands in an ironic position. On the one hand, mainstream Pauline studies has whole-heartedly embraced the post–World War II turn to the Jewish Paul, but many recent treatments of Pauline Christology perpetuate the early twentieth-century *religionsgeschichtliche* thesis that Paul actively downplays the messiah Christology of the earliest Jesus movement and advocates instead for a Gentile-accessible κύριος Christology. One result of my study is to bring the Pauline Christology discussion more closely in line with wider developments in Pauline interpretation. There are many interesting debates to be had about how Paul's different christological categories relate to one another and to his various audiences, but whether Paul conceives of Jesus as the messiah is not one of them. If I have succeeded in proving this point, then one historically significant and apparently still tempting cul-de-sac can be closed off once and for all.

If one cul-de-sac is closed off, however, many other avenues for research are opened up. Much interesting work remains to be done on the question how Paul's messiah Christology relates to his accounts of, say, God, Torah, faith, Gentiles, evil powers, or the state, to name just a few. In this connection it is noteworthy that the basic insight of this study—that χριστός in Paul means "messiah"—has been recognized by Pauline interpreters from diverse corners of the guild. This is the case because the claim itself is not allied exclusively with any one account of Paulinism, for example, an "apocalyptic" account such as Martyn's, or a "participationist eschatology" account such as Sanders's, or a "Gentile self-mastery" account such as Stowers's. To be sure, my conclusion strains against certain interpretive schemes that militate against messiahship as a theological category. But aside from the few outright anti-messianic accounts of Paul, with which this study has some irreconcilable differences, most of the major approaches to Paul currently on offer are open for fruitful dialogue with it. To put the same point differently, the conclusion of this study is not itself an answer to the larger question of the shape of Paul's thought. I take it that the messiahship of Jesus is one important aspect of Paul's thought, one that is likely to bear significantly on other aspects, but I am not proposing a "messianic" account of Paulinism over against other synthetic accounts. To do so would be to misunderstand the sort of thing Paul's messianism is.

As for those bibliographical predecessors who have made the case for the messiahship of Jesus in Paul's letters—in particular Schweitzer, Davies,

Dahl, and Wright—in my view, they are all basically right on this one important point of Pauline interpretation, although not necessarily on other points of Pauline interpretation. On the other hand, as chapter 2 implies, they all go astray in significant ways in their respective accounts of Jewish messianism. Schweitzer proposes that Jewish eschatology delivered categories over to Paul ready-made and that all contemporary Jews who were thinking about "the end" were thinking about it in just this way.[1] Davies proposes that once Paul confessed Jesus as messiah, a thousand theological consequences followed from that confession like so many dominoes falling.[2] Dahl argues that the messiahship of Jesus is axiomatic for Paul but proposes that it is a Christian messiahship rather than a Jewish one.[3] Wright, in a variation on Schweitzer and Davies, hypothesizes a widespread, coherent Jewish messianic worldview in which Paul's messianism is largely scripted for him.[4]

It is just here that approaching Paul's Christ language as a case study in early Jewish messiah language pays off. Contra Schweitzer, Davies, and Wright, there was nothing at all inevitable about the form that Paul's messiah language took. Like all authors of messiah texts, he had to construct his discourse from the linguistic resources available to him. Contra Dahl, however, Paul's messiah language is no less Jewish for this being the case. Ancient Jewish messiah language was quite flexible, indeed, flexible enough to allow Paul's anomalous usage. Indeed, it is precisely because of this flexibility that any text that uses such language must be taken into account as evidence of its possible range of meaning. In other words, Christ language in Paul is an invaluable example of messiah language in ancient Judaism.

Messiah Language in Ancient Judaism

As I wrote in the introduction to this book, strictly speaking this is a study not of Christ language in Paul but rather of messiah language in ancient Judaism, with Paul as a test case. Although Paul might appear to be a statistical outlier,

---

1 See Schweitzer, *Mysticism*, 101: "Eschatology offers such a conception. It is that of the preordained union of those who are elect to the messianic kingdom with one another and with the messiah."

2 See Davies, *Paul and Rabbinic Judaism*, 324: "It was at this one point that Paul parted company with Judaism, at the valuation of Jesus of Nazareth as the Messiah with all that this implied."

3 See Dahl, "Messiahship of Jesus in Paul," 17, 19.

4 See Wright, *Climax*, 21–26, 46–47, 162–168; Wright, *New Testament and the People of God*, 307–320.

by virtue of the volume of his messianic literary *oeuvre*, it turns out that he is valuably illustrative of a whole range of features that are otherwise attested only in a fragmentary way in the relatively few Jewish messiah texts from the Hellenistic and Roman periods.[5] Granted, Paul's letters differ from the non-Christian Jewish messiah texts in his axiomatic identification of Jesus as the messiah. This important exception aside, however, the Pauline messiah texts are like their Jewish counterparts in many ways that stand to shed valuable light on the latter.[6] Like the *Parables of Enoch*, Paul collocates a number of titles of exaltation in reference to a single messiah figure. Like the *Psalms of Solomon*, Paul conceives the messiah as a Davidide whose job it is to rule over the pagan nations. Like Josephus, Paul translates scriptural messiah language into other cultural idioms to make it more readily intelligible to Gentiles. Like the rabbinic accounts of Bar Kokhba, Paul reconciles scriptural messiah traditions with the actual career of a historical figure who was thought to have fit the role. The point is not that these parallels add up to a new synthesis of "the messianic idea" but that the Pauline letters provide a wealth of corroborating evidence—and some altogether new evidence—for the diverse strands of messianism in ancient Judaism.[7]

It is fitting, in conclusion, to recall W. D. Davies's provocative claim, "It was at this one point that Paul parted company with Judaism, at the valuation of Jesus of Nazareth as the Messiah with all that this implied."[8] Like all provocative claims, this one has garnered criticism from many quarters. On the New Testament studies side, E. P. Sanders objects, "The conclusions which, in the view of Davies and many others, Paul must have drawn from the fact

---

5 This represents a step toward Vermes's ideal "Schürer-type religious history of the Jews from the Maccabees to AD 500 that fully incorporates the New Testament data...a reliable guide to the diverse streams of post-biblical Judaism in all their manifestations and reciprocal influences" (Vermes, "Jewish Literature and New Testament Exegesis," 88).

6 So rightly, Stuckenbruck, "Messianic Ideas," 113n44: "If we allow for such diversity in both early Christian and Jewish communities, there is no reason to suppose that, beyond the reconciliation of 'Messiah' by Christians to the experiences of Jesus, Jewish and Christian ideas were necessarily very distinct from one another."

7 In this connection, James Charlesworth has proposed, "The gospels and Paul must not be read as if they are reliable sources for pre-70 Jewish beliefs in the Messiah" (Charlesworth, "From Messianology to Christology," 35). We may leave aside the Gospels, which were likely written after 70 C.E. and so have their own peculiar set of problems. As for Paul, however, he is a Jew, living before 70 C.E., writing about a χριστός. What other criteria do we expect him to meet? Charlesworth's rule is certainly right in the sense that Paul cannot be "mirror-read" for evidence of other Jews' messianic views, but surely Paul speaks for his own Jewish messianic views, and those ought to count as proper evidence for conventions regarding the use of messiah language in antiquity.

8 Davies, *Paul and Rabbinic Judaism*, 324.

that Jesus was the Messiah, he need not and seems not to have drawn."[9] This criticism is apt, but Sanders mistakenly infers from it that Paul took no interest in the messiahship of Jesus.[10] In fact, messiahship in ancient Judaism did not entail anything, strictly speaking; every messiah text drew its own creative conclusions. In this respect, Paul's letters are actually like other Jewish messiah texts, not unlike them.

Meanwhile, on the Jewish studies side, Samuel Sandmel objects to Davies: "Pauline Christianity and rabbinic Judaism share little more than a common point of departure, the Bible."[11] This criticism is also apt, but Sandmel mistakenly assumes that to share the Jewish scriptures as a common point of departure in antiquity was a small thing.[12] In fact, it was a thing whose importance can hardly be overstated. Indeed, the scriptures are one of a very few things that any ancient Jews shared in common with all other ancient Jews.[13] In this respect, too, then, Paul's letters are very much like other Jewish messiah texts, not unlike them. The last generation of scholarship has witnessed a welcome renewal of interest in Paul as a primary source for ancient Judaism; it is time to extend this courtesy to Paul's written reflections on the messiah, about whom he clearly had much to say.

---

9 Sanders, *Paul and Palestinian Judaism,* 514.

10 See Sanders, *Paul and Palestinian Judaism,* 514: "Paul's principal conviction was not that Jesus *as the Messiah* had come, but that God had appointed Jesus Christ *as Lord*" (italics in the original).

11 Sandmel, *Genius of Paul,* 59.

12 See further Sandmel, *Genius of Paul,* 59: "They use it [the Bible], of course, but in manners totally divergent—so much so that they might as well not have had the common point of origin."

13 On this difficulty see E. P. Sanders, *Judaism: Practice and Belief, 63 BCE–66 CE* (4th ed.; London: SCM, 2005); Cohen, *Beginnings of Jewishness.*

Bibliography

PRIMARY SOURCES

Aland, Kurt, Barbara Aland, Johannes Karavidopoulos, Carlo M. Martini, and Bruce M. Metzger, eds. *Novum Testamentum Graece.* 27th ed. Stuttgart: Deutsche Bibelgesellschaft, 1999.

Bardy, G., ed. *Eusèbe de Césarée: Histoire ecclésiastique.* 3 vols. Sources chrétiennes 31, 41, 55. Paris: Éditions du Cerf, 1952–1958.

Baumgarten, J. M., T. Elgvin, E. Eshel, E. Larson, M. R. Lehmann, S. Pfann, and L. H. Schiffman, eds. *Qumran Cave 4.XXV: Halakhic Texts.* Discoveries in the Judaean Desert 35. Oxford: Clarendon, 1999.

Bensly, R. L., ed. *The Fourth Book of Ezra: The Latin Version Edited from the MSS.* Texts and Studies 3.2. Cambridge: Cambridge University Press, 1895.

Berkowitz, L., and K. A. Squitier, eds. *Thesaurus linguae graecae: Canon of Greek Authors and Works.* 3d ed. Oxford: Oxford University Press, 1990.

Boeckh, A., ed. *Corpus inscriptionum graecarum.* 4 vols. Berlin: Reimer, 1828–1877.

Boissevain, U. P., ed. *Cassii Dionis Cocceiani historiarum Romanarum quae supersunt.* 3 vols. Berlin: Weidmann, 1895–1901.

Braude, W. G., trans. *The Midrash on Psalms.* 2 vols. Yale Judaica. New Haven: Yale University Press, 1959.

Brooke, G. J., J. J. Collins, P. Flint, J. Greenfield, E. Larson, C. Newsom, É. Puech, L. H. Schiffman, M. Stone, and J. Trebolle Barrera, eds. *Qumran Cave 4.XVII: Parabiblical Texts, Part 3.* Discoveries in the Judaean Desert 22. Oxford: Clarendon, 1996.

Buber, S., ed. *Midrasch Echa Rabbati: Sammlung aggadischer Auslegungen der Klagelieder.* Wilna, 1899.

Büttner-Wobst, Theodorus, ed. *Polybii historiae.* 4 vols. Leipzig: Teubner, 1893–1905.

Ceriani, A. M., ed. *Opuscula et fragmenta miscella magnam partem apocrypha.* Monumenta sacra et profana 5. Milan: Pogliani, 1868.

Charles, R. H., ed. *The Ethiopic Version of the Book of Enoch.* 2 vols. Anecdota Oxoniensia, Semitic Series 11. Oxford: Clarendon, 1906.

Charlesworth, James H., ed. *The Old Testament Pseudepigrapha.* 2 vols. Garden City, N.Y.: Doubleday, 1983.

Danby, Herbert, trans. *The Mishnah*. Oxford: Clarendon, 1933.

Diggle, J., ed. *Euripidis fabulae*. 3 vols. Oxford: Clarendon, 1984.

Elliger, K., and W. Rudolph, eds. *Biblia Hebraica Stuttgartensia*. Stuttgart: Deutsche Bibelgesellschaft, 1983.

Epstein, I., ed. *Hebrew-English Edition of the Babylonian Talmud*. 30 vols. London: Soncino, 1960–1990.

Fraser, Peter M., and Elaine Matthews, eds. *A Lexicon of Greek Personal Names*. Oxford: Oxford University Press, 1987.

Freedman, H., and Maurice Simon, eds. *Midrash Rabbah*. 10 vols. 3d ed. London: Soncino, 1983.

Frey, Jean-Baptiste, ed. *Corpus inscriptionum judaicarum*. New York: Ktav, 1975.

Friedmann, Meir, ed. *Sifra*. Breslau: Marcus, 1915.

Furneax, Henry, ed. *Cornelii Taciti Annalium ab excessu divi Augusti libri*. 2 vols. Oxford: Clarendon, 1884.

García Martínez, F., E. J. C. Tigchelaar, and A. S. van der Woude, eds. *Manuscripts from Qumran Cave 11 (11Q2–18, 11Q20–30)*. Discoveries in the Judaean Desert 23. Oxford: Clarendon, 1997.

Goodspeed, Edgar J., ed. *Die ältesten Apologeten*. Göttingen: Vandenhoeck & Ruprecht, 1915.

Grant, Robert M., ed. *Theophilus of Antioch: Ad Autolycum*. Oxford Early Christian Texts. Oxford: Clarendon, 1970.

Halm, Karl, ed. *Rhetores latini minores*. Leipzig: Teubner, 1863.

Ilan, Tal, ed. *Lexicon of Jewish Names in Late Antiquity: Part I: Palestine 330 BCE–200 CE*. Texte und Studien zum Antiken Judentum 91. Tübingen: Mohr Siebeck, 2002.

Jacoby, K., ed. *Dionysii Halicarnasei antiquitatum Romanarum quae supersunt*. 4 vols. Leipzig: Teubner, 1885–1905.

Kaibel, Georg, ed. *Athenaei Naucratitae deipnosophistarum libri xv*. 3 vols. Leipzig: Teubner, 1887–1890.

Keil, Heinrich, ed. *Grammatici latini*. 7 vols. Leipzig: Teubner, 1855–1880.

Knibb, Michael A., ed. *The Ethiopic Book of Enoch: A New Edition in Light of the Aramaic Dead Sea Fragments*. Oxford: Clarendon, 1978.

Meeks, Wayne A., ed. *The Writings of St. Paul*. Norton Critical Editions. New York: Norton, 1972.

Meineke, A., ed. *Strabonis geographica*. 3 vols. Leipzig: Teubner, 1877.

Münsterberg, Rudolf, ed. *Die Beamtennamen auf dem griechischen Munzen*. 3 vols. New York: Hildesheim, 1911–1927.

Nickelsburg, George W. E., and James C. VanderKam, trans. *1 Enoch: A New Translation*. Minneapolis: Fortress, 2004.

Niese, Benedictus, ed. *Flavii Josephi opera*. 7 vols. Berlin: Weidmann, 1885–1895.

Page, D. L., ed. *Aeschyli Septem Quae Supersunt Tragoedias*. Oxford: Clarendon, 1972.

Pape, W., and G. E. Benseler, eds. *Wörterbuch der griechischen Eigennamen*. 3rd ed. Braunschweig: 1863–1870.

Patrologia graeca. Edited by J.-P. Migne. 162 vols. Paris, 1857–1886.

Patrologia latina. Edited by J.-P. Migne. 217 vols. Paris, 1844–1864.

Plutarch. *Lives.* Translated by Bernadotte Perrin. 11 vols. Loeb Classical Library. Cambridge, Mass.: Harvard University Press, 1914–1926.

Preisigke, Friedrich, and Enno Littmann, eds. *Namenbuch.* Heidelberg: self-published, 1922.

Rabbinowitz, J., ed. *Mishnah Megillah.* Oxford: Oxford University Press, 1931.

Rahlfs, Alfred, ed. *Psalmi cum Odis.* Septuagina 10. Göttingen: Vandenhoeck & Ruprecht, 1931.

———, ed. *Septuaginta: Id est Vetus Testamentum graece iuxta LXX interpretes.* 2 vols. Stuttgart: Deutsche Bibelgesellschaft, 1979.

Schäfer, Peter, and Hans-Jürgen Becker, eds. *Synopse zum Talmud Yerushalmi.* 4 vols. Texte und Studien zum antiken Judentum 31, 33, 35, 47, 82–83. Tübingen: Mohr Siebeck, 1991–2001.

Schöne, Alfred, ed. *Die Weltchronik des Eusebius in ihrer Bearbeitung durch Heironymus.* Berlin: Weidmann, 1900.

Smart, C., ed. *The Works of Horace.* 2 vols. Philadelphia: Joseph Whetham, 1836.

Suetonius. *The Lives of the Caesars.* Translated by J. C. Rolfe. Loeb Classical Library. Cambridge, Mass.: Harvard, 1914.

Tacitus. *Histories.* Translated by Clifford H. Moore. Loeb Classical Library. Cambridge, Mass.: Harvard University Press, 1962–1963.

Tcherikover, Victor A., and Alexander Fuks, eds. *Corpus papyrorum judaicorum.* 3 vols. Cambridge, Mass.: Harvard University Press, 1957–1964.

Ulrich, E., F. M. Cross, R. E. Fuller, J. E. Sanderson, P. W. Skehan, and E. Tov, eds. *Qumran Cave 4.X: The Prophets.* Discoveries in the Judaean Desert 15. Oxford: Clarendon, 1997.

Ulrich, E., F. M. Cross, D. Parry, and R. Saley, eds. *Qumran Cave 4.XII: 1–2 Samuel.* Discoveries in the Judaean Desert 17. Oxford: Clarendon, 2005.

Wevers, J. W., ed. *Genesis.* Septuaginta 1. Göttingen: Vandenhoeck & Ruprecht, 1974.

Yadin, Yigael, ed. *The Finds from the Bar Kokhba Period in the Cave of Letters.* 3 vols. Jerusalem: Israel Exploration Society, 1963–2002.

Ziegler, Joseph, ed. *Isaias.* Septuagina 14. Göttingen: Vandenhoeck & Ruprecht, 1939.

———, ed. *Susanna, Daniel, Bel et Draco.* Septuagina 16.2. Göttingen: Vandenhoeck & Ruprecht, 1954.

SECONDARY SOURCES

Aejmelaus, Anneli. "Faith, Hope and Interpretation: A Lexical and Syntactical Study of the Semantic Field of Hope in the Greek Psalter." Pp. 360–376 in *Studies in the Hebrew Bible, Qumran, and the Septuagint Presented to Eugene Ulrich.* Edited by Peter W. Flint, Emanuel Tov, and James C. VanderKam. Supplements to Vetus Testamentum 101. Leiden: Brill, 2006.

Agamben, Giorgio. *The Time That Remains: A Commentary on the Letter to the Romans.* Translated by Patricia Dailey. Meridian: Crossing Aesthetics. Stanford: Stanford University Press, 2005.

Alexander, Philip S. "The King Messiah in Rabbinic Judaism." Pp. 456–473 in *King and Messiah in Israel and the Ancient Near East.* Edited by John Day. Journal for the Study of the Old Testament Supplement Series 270. Sheffield: Sheffield Academic, 1998.

Allison, Dale C. "Cephas and Peter: One and the Same." *Journal of Biblical Literature* 111 (1992): 489–495.

Allwood, Jens, Lars-Gunnar Andersson, and Östen Dahl. *Logic in Linguistics.* Cambridge: Cambridge University Press, 1977.

Alter, Robert. *The Pleasures of Reading in an Ideological Age.* New York: Norton, 1996.

Ameriks, Karl. "Introduction: Interpreting German Idealism." Pp. 1–17 in *The Cambridge Companion to German Idealism.* Edited by Karl Ameriks. Cambridge: Cambridge University Press, 2000.

———. "The Legacy of Idealism in the Philosophy of Feuerbach, Marx, and Kierkegaard." Pp. 258–281 in *The Cambridge Companion to German Idealism.* Edited by Karl Ameriks. Cambridge: Cambridge University Press, 2000.

Anderson, John Mathieson. *The Grammar of Names.* Oxford: Oxford University Press, 2007.

Attridge, Harold W. "Giving Voice to Jesus: Use of Psalms in the New Testament." Pp. 101–112 in *Psalms in Community: Jewish and Christian Textual, Liturgical, and Artistic Traditions.* Edited by Harold W. Attridge and Margot E. Fassler. Society of Biblical Literature Symposium Series 25. Leiden: Brill, 2003.

Bach, Adolf. *Deutsche Namenkunde.* 3 vols. 2d ed. Heidelberg: Winter, 1952–1956.

Baeck, Leo. "The Faith of Paul." *Journal of Jewish Studies* 3 (1952): 93–110.

Baird, William. *History of New Testament Research.* 2 vols. Minneapolis: Fortress, 1992–2003.

Baldermann, Ingo, Ernst Dassmann, and Ottmar Fuchs, eds. *Der Messias.* Jahrbuch für Biblische Theologie 8. Neukirchen-Vluyn: Neukirchener Verlag, 1993.

Barr, James. *The Semantics of Biblical Language.* Oxford: Oxford University Press, 1961.

Barth, Markus. "The Faith of the Messiah." *Heythrop Journal* 10 (1969): 363–370.

Bassler, Jouette M. "Paul's Theology: Whence and Whither?" Pp. 3–17 in *Pauline Theology.* Vol. 2, *1 & 2 Corinthians.* Edited by David M. Hay. Minneapolis: Fortress, 1993.

Bauer, Bruno. *Kritik der Evangelien und Geschichte ihres Ursprungs.* 4 vols. Berlin: Hempel, 1850–1851.

———. *Kritik der evangelischen Geschichte der Synoptiker.* 3 vols. Leipzig: Wigand, 1841–1842.

Baur, F. C. "Die Christuspartei in der korinthischen Gemeinde, der Gegensatz des paulinischen und petrinischen Christentums in der ältesten Kirche, den Apostel Petrus in Rom." *Tübinger Zeitschrift für Theologie* 4 (1831): 61–206.

———. *Paul the Apostle of Jesus Christ: His Life and Works, His Epistles and Teachings.* 2 vols. London: Williams & Norgate, 1845–1846. Reprint, Peabody, Mass.: Hendrickson, 2003. Translation of *Paulus, der Apostel Jesu Christi, sein Leben und Wirken, seine Briefe und seine Lehre.* Stuttgart: Becher und Müller, 1845.

———. *Die sogenannten Pastoralbriefe des Apostels Paulus.* Stuttgart: Cotta, 1835.

———. *Vorlesungen über neutestamentliche Theologie.* Edited by F. F. Baur. Leipzig: Fues, 1864.

Bechtel, Friedrich. *Die historischen Personennamen des Griechischen bis zur Kaiserzeit.* Halle: Niemeyer, 1917.

Becker, Adam H., and Annette Yoshiko Reed. *The Ways That Never Parted: Jews and Christians in Late Antiquity and the Early Middle Ages.* Texte und Studien zum Antiken Judentum 95. Tübingen: Mohr Siebeck, 2003.

Berger, Klaus. "Zum traditionsgeschichtlichen Hintergrund christologischer Hoheitstitel." *New Testament Studies* 17 (1971): 391–425.

Bertram, Georg. "Praeparatio Evangelica in der Septuaginta." *Vetus Testamentum* 7 (1957): 225–249.

Biale, David. *Gershom Scholem: Kabbalah and Counter-History.* 2d ed. Cambridge, Mass.: Harvard University Press, 1982.

Bird, Michael F., and Preston M. Sprinkle, eds. *The Faith of Jesus Christ: Exegetical, Biblical and Theological Studies.* Peabody, Mass.: Hendrickson, 2009.

Black, Matthew. "The Biblical Languages." Pp. 1–10 in *The Cambridge History of the Bible: From the Beginnings to Jerome.* Edited by P. R. Ackroyd and C. F. Evans. Cambridge: Cambridge University Press, 1970.

———. "The Messianism of the Parables of Enoch." Pp. 145–168 in *The Messiah: Developments in Earliest Judaism and Christianity.* Edited by James H. Charlesworth. Minneapolis: Fortress, 1992.

Blass, F., A. Debrunner, and R. W. Funk. *A Greek Grammar of the New Testament and Other Early Christian Literature.* Chicago: University of Chicago Press, 1961.

Boccaccini, Gabriele, ed. *Enoch and the Messiah Son of Man: Revisiting the Book of Parables.* Grand Rapids, Mich.: Eerdmans, 2007.

Bockmuehl, Markus. "Simon Peter's Names in the Jewish Sources." *Journal of Jewish Studies* 55 (2004): 58–80.

———, and James Carleton Paget, eds. *Redemption and Resistance: The Messianic Hopes of Jews and Christians in Antiquity.* London: T. & T. Clark, 2007.

Boer, Martinus C. de. *The Defeat of Death: Apocalyptic Eschatology in 1 Corinthians 15 and Romans 5.* Journal for the Study of the New Testament Supplement Series 22. Sheffield: JSOT Press, 1988.

Bornkamm, Günther. "Baptism and New Life in Paul." Pp. 71–86 in *Early Christian Experience.* Translated by Paul L. Hammer. New York: Harper and Row, 1969.

Borse, Udo. "Timotheus und Titus, Abgesandte Pauli im Dienst des Evangeliums." Pp. 27–43 in *Der Diakon: Wiederentdeckung und Erneuerung seines Dienstes.* Edited by J. G. Ploger and H. J. Weber. Freiburg: Herder, 1980.

Bouissac, Paul. "Saussure's Legacy in Semiotics." Pp. 240–260 in *The Cambridge Companion to Saussure.* Edited by Carol Sanders. Cambridge: Cambridge University Press, 2004.

Bousset, Wilhelm. *Kyrios Christos: A History of the Belief in Christ from the Beginnings of Christianity to Irenaeus.* Translated by John E. Steely. Nashville: Abingdon, 1970. Translation of *Kyrios Christos: Geschichte des Christusglaubens von den Anfängen des Christentums bis Irenaeus.* Göttingen: Vandenhoeck & Ruprecht, 1913.

Bouttier, Michel. *En Christ: Étude d'exégèse et de théologie pauliniennes.* Études d'histoire et de philosophie religieuses 54. Paris: Presses Universitaires de France, 1962.

Boyarin, Daniel. *A Radical Jew: Paul and the Politics of Identity.* Berkeley: University of California Press, 1994.

Braun, Willi. "Smoke Signals from the North: A Reply to Burton Mack's 'Backbay Jazz and Blues.'" Pp. 433–442 in *Redescribing Christian Origins.* Edited by Ron Cameron and Merrill P. Miller. Society of Biblical Literature Symposium Series 28. Atlanta: Society of Biblical Literature, 2004.

Brinton, Laurel J. *The Structure of Modern English.* Philadelphia: Benjamins, 2000.

Brown, F., S. R. Driver, and C. A. Briggs. *A Hebrew and English Lexicon of the Old Testament.* Oxford: Clarendon, 1907.

Brown, Raymond E. *The Community of the Beloved Disciple.* New York: Paulist, 1979.

Bruce, F. F. *Paul: Apostle of the Heart Set Free.* Exeter: Paternoster, 1977.

Büchsel, Friedrich. *Der Geist Gottes im Neuen Testament.* Gütersloh: Bertelsmann, 1926.

Bultmann, Rudolf. "Introductory Word to the Fifth Edition." Pp. 7–9 in *Kyrios Christos: A History of the Belief in Christ from the Beginnings of Christianity to Irenaeus,* by Wilhelm Bousset. Translated by John E. Steely. Nashville: Abingdon, 1970.

———. *Theology of the New Testament.* Translated by Kendrick Grobel. 2 vols. New York: Scribner's, 1951. Translation of *Theologie des Neuen Testaments.* 3 vols. Tübingen: Mohr, 1948–1953.

Burger, Christoph. *Jesus als Davidssohn: Eine traditionsgeschichtliche Untersuchung.* Forschungen zur Religion und Literatur des Alten und Neuen Testaments 98. Göttingen: Vandenhoeck & Ruprecht, 1970.

Burkitt, F. C. "On Romans IX.5 and Mark XIV.61." *Journal of Theological Studies* 3 (1904): 451–455.

Calvin, John. *Commentaries on the Epistle of Paul the Apostle to the Romans.* Grand Rapids, Mich.: Eerdmans, 1948.

Campbell, Douglas A. *The Deliverance of God: An Apocalyptic Rereading of Justification in Paul.* Grand Rapids, Mich.: Eerdmans, 2009.

Capes, David B. *Old Testament Yahweh Texts in Paul's Christology.* Wissenschaftliche Untersuchungen zum Neuen Testament. Second Series 47. Tübingen: Mohr Siebeck, 1992.

Carroll, Lewis. *Through the Looking Glass and What Alice Found There.* Philadelphia: Altemus, 1897.

Cameron, Ron, and Merrill P. Miller, eds. *Redescribing Christian Origins.* Society of Biblical Literature Symposium Series 28. Atlanta: Society of Biblical Literature, 2004.

Cerfaux, Lucien. *Christ in the Theology of St. Paul.* Translated by Geoffrey Webb and Adrian Walker. New York: Herder and Herder, 1959. Translation of *Christ dans la théologie de saint Paul.* Lectio divina 6. Paris: Éditions du Cerf, 1951.

Chabon, Michael. *The Yiddish Policemen's Union.* New York: HarperCollins, 2007.

Chapman, David W. *Ancient Jewish and Christian Perceptions of Crucifixion.* Wissenschaftliche Untersuchungen zum Neuen Testament. Second Series 244. Tübingen: Mohr Siebeck, 2008.

Chapman, Stephen B. "Saul/Paul: Onomastics, Typology, and Christian Scripture." Pp. 214–243 in *The Word Leaps the Gap: Essays on Scripture and Theology in Honor of Richard B. Hays.* Edited by J. Ross Wagner, C. Kavin Rowe, and A. Katherine Grieb. Grand Rapids, Mich.: Eerdmans, 2008.

Charlesworth, James H. "The Concept of the Messiah in the Pseudepigrapha." *ANRW* 2.19.1:188–218. Part 2, *Principat,* 19.1. Edited by H. Temporini and W. Haase. Berlin: de Gruyter, 1979.

———. "From Jewish Messianology to Christian Christology: Some Caveats and Perspectives." Pp. 225–264 in *Judaisms and Their Messiahs at the Turn of the Christian Era.* Edited by Jacob Neusner, William Scott Green, and Ernest Frerichs. Cambridge: Cambridge University Press, 1987.

———. "From Messianology to Christology: Problems and Prospects." Pp. 3–35 in *The Messiah: Developments in Earliest Judaism and Christianity.* Edited by James H. Charlesworth. Minneapolis: Fortress, 1992.

———, ed. *The Messiah: Developments in Earliest Judaism and Christianity.* Minneapolis: Fortress, 1992.

———. Hermann Lichtenberger, and Gerbern S. Oegema, eds. *Qumran-Messianism: Studies on the Messianic Expectations in the Dead Sea Scrolls.* Tübingen: Mohr Siebeck, 1998.

Chester, Andrew. "The Christ of Paul." Pp. 109–121 in *Redemption and Resistance: The Messianic Hopes of Jews and Christians in Antiquity.* Edited by Markus Bockmuehl and James Carleton Paget. London: T. & T. Clark, 2007.

———. *Messiah and Exaltation.* Wissenschaftliche Untersuchungen zum Neuen Testament 207. Tübingen: Mohr Siebeck, 2007.

———. "Messianism, Mediators and Pauline Christology." Pages 329–396 in *Messiah and Exaltation.* Wissenschaftliche Untersuchungen zum Neuen Testament 207. Tübingen: Mohr Siebeck, 2007.

———. "The Nature and Scope of Messianism." Pp. 191–327 in *Messiah and Exaltation.* Wissenschaftliche Untersuchungen zum Neuen Testament 207. Tübingen: Mohr Siebeck, 2007.

Childs, Brevard S. *Introduction to the Old Testament as Scripture.* Philadelphia: Fortress, 1979.

———. "Psalm Titles and Midrashic Exegesis." *Journal of Semitic Studies* 16 (1971): 137–150.

Clark, Elizabeth Ann. *History, Theory, Text: Historians and the Linguistic Turn.* Cambridge, Mass.: Harvard University Press, 2004.

Cohen, Shaye J. D. *The Beginnings of Jewishness: Boundaries, Varieties, Uncertainties.* Berkeley: University of California Press, 2001.

———. "Ioudaios, Iudaeus, Judaean, Jew." Pp. 69–106 in *The Beginnings of Jewishness: Boundaries, Varieties, Uncertainties.* Berkeley: University of California Press, 2001.

Collins, Adela Yarbro. "Jesus as Messiah and Son of God in the Letters of Paul." Pp. 101–122 in *King and Messiah as Son of God: Divine, Human, and Angelic Messianic Figures in Biblical and Related Literature,* by John J. Collins and Adela Yarbro Collins. Grand Rapids, Mich.: Eerdmans, 2008.

———. "The Psalms and the Origins of Christology." Pp. 113–124 in *Psalms in Community: Jewish and Christian Textual, Liturgical, and Artistic Traditions.* Edited by Harold W. Attridge and Margot E. Fassler. Society of Biblical Literature Symposium Series 25. Leiden: Brill, 2003.

Collins, John J., ed. *Apocalypse: The Morphology of a Genre.* Semeia 14. Missoula, Mont.: Scholars Press, 1979.

———. *Daniel: A Commentary on the Book of Daniel.* Hermeneia. Minneapolis: Fortress, 1993.

———. "Messiahs in Context: Method in the Study of Messianism in the Dead Sea Scrolls." Pp. 213–230 in *Methods of Investigation of the Dead Sea Scrolls and the Khirbet Qumran Site: Present Realities and Future Prospects.* Edited by Michael O. Wise, Norman Golb, John J. Collins, and Dennis G. Pardee. Annals of the New York Academy of Sciences 722. New York: New York Academy of Sciences, 1994.

———. "Messianism in the Maccabean Period." Pp. 97–110 in *Judaisms and Their Messiahs at the Turn of the Christian Era.* Edited by Jacob Neusner, William Scott Green, and Ernest Frerichs. Cambridge: Cambridge University Press, 1987.

———. "Mowinckel's *He That Cometh* in Retrospect." Pp. xv–xxiii in *He That Cometh: The Messiah Concept in the Old Testament and Later Judaism,* by Sigmund Mowinckel. Translated by G. W. Anderson. Grand Rapids, Mich.: Eerdmans, 2005.

———. Review of William Horbury, *Jewish Messianism and the Cult of Christ. Journal of Religion* 79 (1999): 657–659.

———. *The Scepter and the Star: The Messiahs of the Dead Sea Scrolls and Other Ancient Literature.* Anchor Bible Reference Library. New York: Doubleday, 1995.

———, and Adela Yarbro Collins. *King and Messiah as Son of God.* Grand Rapids, Mich.: Eerdmans, 2008.

Conzelmann, Hans. "Was glaubte die frühe Christenheit?" *Schweizerische theologische Umschau* 25 (1955): 61–74.

Corbeill, Anthony. *Controlling Laughter: Political Humor in the Late Roman Republic.* Princeton, N.J.: Princeton University Press, 1996.

Cottle, Basil. *Names.* London: Thames and Hudson, 1983.

Cousar, Charles B. *A Theology of the Cross: The Death of Jesus in the Pauline Letters.* Overtures to Biblical Theology 24. Minneapolis: Fortress, 1990.

Cranfield, C. E. B. *A Critical and Exegetical Commentary on the Epistle to the Romans.* 2 vols. 6th ed. International Critical Commentary. Edinburgh: T. & T. Clark, 1975–1979.

Crawford, Barry S. "*Christos* as Nickname." Pp. 337–348 in *Redescribing Christian Origins.* Edited by Ron Cameron and Merrill P. Miller. Society of Biblical Literature Symposium Series 28. Atlanta: Society of Biblical Literature, 2004.

Crawford, Michael. "Mirabilia and Personal Names." Pp. 145–148 in *Greek Personal Names: Their Value as Evidence.* Edited by Simon Hornblower and Elaine Matthews. Proceedings of the British Academy 104. Oxford: Oxford University Press, 2000.

Crook, J. A. "Political History, 30 B.C. to A.D. 14." Pp. 70–112 in vol. 10 of *The Cambridge Ancient History.* 14 vols. 2d ed. Cambridge: Cambridge University Press, 1970–2005.

Cross, Frank Moore, and David Noel Freedman. "A Royal Psalm of Thanksgiving: II Samuel 22=Psalm 18." *Journal of Biblical Literature* 72 (1953): 15–34.

Crossan, John Dominic, and Jonathan L. Reed. *In Search of Paul: How Jesus's Apostle Opposed Caesar's Empire with God's Kingdom.* New York: Harper, 2004.

Culler, Jonathan D. *Ferdinand de Saussure.* Rev. ed. Ithaca, N.Y.: Cornell University Press, 1986.

Cullmann, Oscar. *The Christology of the New Testament.* Translated by Shirley C. Guthrie and Charles A. M. Hall. Philadelphia: Westminster, 1963. Translation of *Christologie des Neuen Testaments.* Tübingen: Mohr, 1957.

Cummins, S. A. "Divine Life and Corporate Christology: God, Messiah Jesus, and the Covenant Community in Paul." Pp. 190–209 in *The Messiah in the Old and New Testaments.* Edited by Stanley E. Porter. Grand Rapids, Mich.: Eerdmans, 2007.

Dahl, Nils A. "The Atonement: An Adequate Reward for the Akedah?" Pp. 137–151 in *Jesus the Christ: The Historical Origins of Christological Doctrine.* Edited by Donald H. Juel. Minneapolis: Fortress, 1991.

———. "The Crucified Messiah." Pp. 27–47 in *Jesus the Christ: The Historical Origins of Christological Doctrine.* Edited by Donald H. Juel. Minneapolis: Fortress, 1991.

———. "The Crucified Messiah and the Endangered Promises." Pp. 65–79 in *Jesus the Christ: The Historical Origins of Christological Doctrine.* Edited by Donald H. Juel. Minneapolis: Fortress, 1991.

———. *Jesus the Christ: The Historical Origins of Christological Doctrine.* Edited by Donald H. Juel. Minneapolis: Fortress, 1991.

———. "The Messiahship of Jesus in Paul." Pp. 15–25 in *Jesus the Christ: The Historical Origins of Christological Doctrine.* Edited by Donald H. Juel. Minneapolis: Fortress, 1991. Reprint of "The Messiahship of Jesus in Paul." Pp. 37–47 in *The Crucified Messiah.* Minneapolis: Augsburg, 1974. Translation of "Die Messianität Jesu bei Paulus." Pp. 83–95 in *Studia Paulina in honorem Johannis de Zwaan septuagenarii.* Haarlem: Bohn: 1953.

————. "Sigmund Mowinckel: Historian of Religion and Theologian." *Scandinavian Journal of the Old Testament* 2 (1988): 8–22.

————. "Sources of Christological Language." Pp. 113–136 in *Jesus the Christ: The Historical Origins of Christological Doctrine.* Edited by Donald H. Juel. Minneapolis: Fortress, 1991.

Davies, Alan T., ed. *Antisemitism and the Foundations of Christianity.* New York: Paulist, 1979.

Davies, Anna Morpurgo. "Greek Personal Names and Linguistic Continuity." Pp. 15–40 in *Greek Personal Names: Their Value as Evidence.* Edited by Simon Hornblower and Elaine Matthews. Proceedings of the British Academy 104. Oxford: Oxford University Press, 2000.

Davies, Stevan. "The Christology and Protology of the Gospel of Thomas." *Journal of Biblical Literature* 111 (1992): 663–682.

Davies, W. D. *Paul and Rabbinic Judaism: Some Rabbinic Elements in Pauline Theology.* Philadelphia: Fortress, 1980.

Day, John, ed. *King and Messiah in Israel and the Ancient Near East.* Journal for the Study of the Old Testament Supplement Series 270. Sheffield: Sheffield Academic, 1998.

Decosimo, David. "Comparison and the Ubiquity of Resemblance." *Journal of the American Academy of Religion* 78 (2010): 226–258.

Deissmann, Adolf. *Die neutestamentliche Formel "In Christo Jesu" untersucht.* Marburg: Elwert, 1892.

————. *Paul: A Study in Social and Religious History.* Translated by William E. Wilson. 2d ed. New York: Harper, 1957.

Delcor, Mathias. "The Apocrypha and Pseudepigrapha of the Hellenistic Period." p. 409–503 in vol. 2 of *The Cambridge History of Judaism.* Edited by W. D. Davies and Louis Finkelstein. 3 vols. Cambridge: Cambridge University Press, 1984.

Delitzsch, Franz. *Paulus des Apostels Brief an die Römer: Aus dem griechischen Urtext auf Grund des Sinai-Codex in das Hebräischer übersetzt, und aus Talmud und Midrasch erläutert.* Leipzig: Dörffling und Franke, 1870.

Dobschütz, Ernst von. *Die Thessalonicher-Briefe.* Göttingen: Vandenhoeck & Ruprecht, 1909.

Drummond, James. *The Jewish Messiah: A Critical History of the Messianic Idea among the Jews from the Rise of the Maccabees to the Closing of the Talmud.* London: Longmans, Green, 1877.

Duling, Dennis C. "The Promises to David and Their Entry into Christianity." *New Testament Studies* 20 (1973): 55–77.

Dunn, James D. G. "How Controversial Was Paul's Christology?" Pp. 212–228 in *The Christ and the Spirit: Collected Essays.* Grand Rapids, Mich.: Eerdmans, 1998. Reprint of "How Controversial Was Paul's Christology?" Pp. 148–167 in *From Jesus to John: Essays on Jesus and the New Testament Christology in Honour of Marinus de Jonge.* Edited by Martinus C. de Boer. Journal for the Study of the New Testament Supplement Series 84. Sheffield: JSOT Press, 1993.

———. "In Quest of Paul's Theology: Retrospect and Prospect." Pp. 95–115 in *Pauline Theology.* Vol. 4, *Looking Back, Pressing On.* Edited by David M. Hay and E. Elizabeth Johnson. Society of Biblical Literature Symposium Series 4. Atlanta: Scholars Press, 1997.

———. "Jesus: Flesh and Spirit: An Exposition of Romans 1:3–4." *Journal of Theological Studies* 24 (1973): 40–68.

———. *Jesus, Paul, and the Law: Studies in Mark and Galatians.* Louisville, Ky.: Westminster John Knox, 1990.

———. "Once More, ΠΙΣΤΙΣ ΧΡΙΣΤΟΥ." Pp. 61–81 in *Pauline Theology.* Vol. 4, *Looking Back, Pressing On.* Society of Biblical Literature Symposium Series 4. Edited by David M. Hay and E. Elizabeth Johnson. Atlanta: Scholars Press, 1997.

———. *The Theology of Paul the Apostle.* Grand Rapids, Mich.: Eerdmans, 1998.

Eckardt, Regine, Klaus von Heusinger, and Christoph Schwarze, eds. *Words in Time: Diachronic Semantics from Different Points of View.* Berlin: de Gruyter, 2003.

Ehrhardt, C. Demetrius ὁ Αἰτωλικός and Antigonid Nicknames." *Hermes* 106 (1978): 251–253.

Ehrman, Bart D. "Cephas and Peter." *Journal of Biblical Literature* 109 (1990): 463–474.

Elliott, Neil. *Liberating Paul: The Justice of God and the Politics of the Apostle.* Maryknoll, N.Y.: Orbis, 1994.

Ellis, E. Earle. "Christ Crucified." Pp. 69–75 in *Reconciliation and Hope: New Testament Essays on Atonement and Eschatology Presented to L. L. Morris on His 60th Birthday.* Edited by Robert Banks. Grand Rapids, Mich.: Eerdmans, 1975.

———. "Χριστός in 1 Corinthians 10.4, 9." Pp. 168–173 in *From Jesus to John: Essays on Jesus and the New Testament Christology in Honour of Marinus de Jonge.* Edited by Martinus C. de Boer. Journal for the Study of the New Testament Supplement Series 84. Sheffield: JSOT Press, 1993.

Evans, Craig A. "Mishna and Messiah 'in Context': Some Comments on Jacob Neusner's Proposals." *Journal of Biblical Literature* 112 (1993): 267–289.

Evans, Michael J., and Rainer Wimmer. "Searle's Theory of Proper Names, from a Linguistic Point of View." Pp. 259–278 in *Speech Acts, Meaning and Intention: Critical Approaches to the Philosophy of John R. Searle.* Edited by Armin Burkhardt. Berlin: de Gruyter, 1990.

Fee, Gordon D. *Pauline Christology: An Exegetical-Theological Study.* Peabody, Mass.: Hendrickson, 2007.

Fellows, Richard G. "Was Titus Timothy?" *Journal for the Study of the New Testament* 81 (2001): 33–58.

Fishbane, Michael. *Biblical Interpretation in Ancient Israel.* Oxford: Oxford University Press, 1985.

Fitzmyer, Joseph A. *The One Who Is to Come.* Grand Rapids, Mich.: Eerdmans, 2007.

———. "The Use of Explicit Old Testament Quotations in Qumran Literature and in the New Testament." Pp. 3–58 in *Essays on the Semitic Background of the New Testament.* Missoula, Mont.: Scholars Press, 1974.

Foerster, Werner. *Herr ist Jesus: Herkunft und Bedeutung des urchristlichen Kyrios-bekenntnisses.* Gütersloh: Bertelsmann, 1924.

Fordyce, C. J. "Puns on Names in Greek." *Classical Journal* 28 (1932): 44–46.

Fraser, John W. "Paul's Knowledge of Jesus: II Corinthians V.16 Once More." *New Testament Studies* 17 (1971): 293–313.

Fraser, Peter M. "Ethnics as Personal Names." Pp. 149–158 in *Greek Personal Names: Their Value as Evidence.* Edited by Simon Hornblower and Elaine Matthews. Proceedings of the British Academy 104. Oxford: Oxford University Press, 2000.

Fredriksen, Paula. *From Jesus to Christ: The Origins of the New Testament Images of Christ.* New Haven: Yale University Press, 2000.

———. *Jesus of Nazareth: King of the Jews.* New York: Vintage, 1999.

———. "Judaism, the Circumcision of Gentiles, and Apocalyptic Hope: Another Look at Galatians 1 and 2." *Journal of Theological Studies,* n.s. 42 (1991): 532–564.

Frege, Gottlob. "Über Sinn und Bedeutung." *Zeitschrift für Philosophie und philosophische Kritik* 100 (1892): 25–50.

Frei, Hans W. *The Eclipse of Biblical Narrative: A Study in Eighteenth and Nineteenth Century Hermeneutics.* New Haven: Yale University Press, 1980.

Furnish, Victor Paul. *II Corinthians.* Anchor Bible 32A. Garden City, N.Y.: Doubleday, 1984.

Gager, John G. "Messiahs and Their Followers." Pp. 37–46 in *Toward the Millennium: Messianic Expectations from the Bible to Waco.* Edited by Peter Schäfer and Mark R. Cohen. Studies in the History of Religions 77. Leiden: Brill, 1998.

———. *The Origins of Anti-Semitism: Attitudes toward Judaism in Pagan and Christian Antiquity.* Oxford: Oxford University Press, 1979.

———. *Reinventing Paul.* Oxford: Oxford University Press, 2000.

Galsterer, H. "A Man, a Book, and a Method: Sir Ronald Syme's *Roman Revolution* after Fifty Years." Pp. 1–20 in *Between Republic and Empire: Interpretations of Augustus and His Principate.* Edited by Kurt A. Raaflaub and Mark Toher. Berkeley: University of California Press, 1993.

Gaston, Lloyd. "Paul and the Torah." Pp. 15–34 in *Paul and the Torah.* Vancouver: University of British Columbia Press, 1987. Reprint of "Paul and the Torah." Pp. 48–71 in *Antisemitism and the Foundations of Christianity.* Edited by Alan T. Davies. New York: Paulist, 1979.

Gaventa, Beverly Roberts. "On the Calling-into-Being of Israel: Romans 9:6–29." Pp. 255–269 in *Between Gospel and Election: Explorations in the Interpretation of Romans 9–11.* Edited by Florian Wilk and J. Ross Wagner with the assistance of Frank Schleritt. Wissenschaftliche Untersuchungen zum Neuen Testament 257. Tübingen: Mohr Siebeck, 2010.

Gerdmar, Anders. *Roots of Theological Anti-Semitism: German Biblical Interpretation and the Jews, from Herder and Semler to Kittel and Bultmann.* Studies in Jewish History and Culture 20. Leiden: Brill, 2009.

Goldstein, Jonathan A. "How the Authors of 1 and 2 Maccabees Treated the 'Messianic' Promises." Pp. 69–96 in *Judaisms and Their Messiahs at the Turn of the Christian Era*. Edited by Jacob Neusner, William Scott Green, and Ernest Frerichs. Cambridge: Cambridge University Press, 1987.

Goodwin, W. W. *Greek Grammar*. Revised by C. B. Gulick. Boston: Ginn, 1930.

Green, William Scott. "Introduction: Messiah in Judaism: Rethinking the Question." Pp. 1–13 in *Judaisms and Their Messiahs at the Turn of the Christian Era*. Edited by Jacob Neusner, William Scott Green, and Ernest Frerichs. Cambridge: Cambridge University Press, 1987.

Greenstone, Julius H. *The Messiah Idea in Jewish History*. Philadelphia: Jewish Publication Society, 1906.

Gressmann, Hugo. *Der Messias*. Göttingen: Vandenhoeck & Ruprecht, 1929.

Hahn, Ferdinand. *The Titles of Jesus in Christology*. Translated by Harold Knight and George Ogg. London: Lutterworth, 1969.

Hare, Douglas R. A. "When Did 'Messiah' Become a Proper Name?" *Expository Times* 121 (2009): 70–73.

Harland, Philip A. "Familial Dimensions of Group Identity: 'Brothers' (ΑΔΕΛΦΟΙ) in Associations of the Greek East." *Journal of Biblical Literature* 124 (2005): 491–513.

Harrer, G. A. "Saul Who Is Also Called Paul." *Harvard Theological Review* 33 (1940): 19–34.

Harrisville, Roy A. "Paul and the Psalms: A Formal Study." *Word and World* 5 (1985): 168–179.

Harvey, A. E. *Jesus and the Constraints of History*. Philadelphia: Westminster, 1982.

Hatch, E., and H. A. Redpath. *Concordance to the Septuagint and Other Greek Versions of the Old Testament*. 2 vols. Oxford: Clarendon, 1897. Suppl., 1906. Repr., Grand Rapids, Mich.: Baker, 1998.

Hay, David M. *Glory at the Right Hand: Psalm 110 in Early Christianity*. Society of Biblical Literature Monograph Series 18. Nashville: Abingdon, 1973.

Hays, Richard B. "Christ Prays the Psalms: Israel's Psalter as Matrix of Early Christology." Pp. 101–118 in *The Conversion of the Imagination: Paul as Interpreter of Israel's Scripture*. Grand Rapids, Mich.: Eerdmans, 2005.

———. *The Conversion of the Imagination: Paul as Interpreter of Israel's Scripture*. Grand Rapids, Mich.: Eerdmans, 2005.

———. *Echoes of Scripture in the Letters of Paul*. New Haven: Yale University Press, 1989.

———. *The Faith of Jesus Christ: The Narrative Substructure of Galatians 3:1–4:11*. 2d ed. Biblical Resource Series. Grand Rapids, Mich.: Eerdmans, 2002.

———. "'Have We Found Abraham to Be Our Forefather according to the Flesh?' A Reconsideration of Rom 4:1." *Novum Testamentum* 27 (1985): 76–98.

———. "Πίστις and Pauline Christology: What Is at Stake?" Pp. 35–60 in *Pauline Theology*. Vol. 4, *Looking Back, Pressing On*. Edited by David M. Hay and E. Elizabeth Johnson. Atlanta: Scholars Press, 1997.

Heitmüller, Wilhelm. "Zum Problem Jesus und Paulus." *Zeitschrift für die neutestamentliche Wissenschaft und die Kunde der älteren Kirche* 13 (1912): 320–337.

Heliso, Desta. Pistis *and the Righteous One: A Study of Romans 1:17 against the Background of Scripture and Second Temple Jewish Literature.* Wissenschaftliche Untersuchungen zum Neuen Testament. Second Series 235. Tübingen: Mohr Siebeck, 2007.

Hemer, Colin J. "The Name of Paul." *Tyndale Bulletin* 36 (1985): 179–183.

Hengel, Martin. "Christological Titles in Early Christianity." Pp. 359–390 in *Studies in Early Christology.* Edinburgh: Clark, 1995.

———. " 'Christos' in Paul." Pp. 65–77 in *Between Jesus and Paul: Studies in the Earliest History of Christianity.* Translated by John Bowden. Philadelphia: Fortress, 1983. Translation of "Erwägungen zum Sprachgebrauch von Χριστός bei Paulus und in der vorpaulinischen Überlieferung." Pp. 135–158 in *Paul and Paulinism: Essays in Honour of C. K. Barrett.* Edited by Morna D. Hooker and S. G. Wilson. London: SPCK, 1982.

———. *Crucifixion.* Translated by John Bowden. Philadelphia: Fortress, 1997.

———. "Jesus, the Messiah of Israel." Pp. 1–71 in *Studies in Early Christology.* Edinburgh: T. & T. Clark, 1995.

———. *Judaism and Hellenism: Studies in Their Encounter in Palestine during the Early Hellenistic Period.* Translated by John Bowden. Philadelphia: Fortress, 1974.

———. *Studies in Early Christology.* Edinburgh: T. & T. Clark, 1995.

Heschel, Susannah. *Abraham Geiger and the Jewish Jesus.* Chicago Studies in the History of Judaism. Chicago: University of Chicago Press, 1998.

———. *The Aryan Jesus: Christian Theologians and the Bible in Nazi Germany.* Princeton, N.J.: Princeton University Press, 2008.

Higgins, A. J. B. "Jewish Messianic Belief in Justin Martyr's *Dialogue with Trypho.*" *Novum Testamentum* 9 (1967): 298–305.

Hill, C. E. "Paul's Understanding of Christ's Kingdom in 1 Cor 15:20–28." *Novum Testamentum* 30 (1988): 297–320.

Himmelfarb, Martha. "Judaism and Hellenism in 2 Maccabees." *Poetics Today* 19 (1998): 19–40.

———. *Tours of Hell: An Apocalyptic Form in Jewish and Christian Literature.* Philadelphia: University of Pennsylvania Press, 1983.

Hoehner, Harold W. *Herod Antipas.* Society for New Testament Studies Monograph Series 17. Cambridge: Cambridge University Press, 1972.

Holtzmann, Heinrich Julius. *Lehrbuch der neutestamentlichen Theologie.* 2 vols. Freiburg: Mohr, 1897.

———. "Die Messiasidee zur Zeit Jesu." *Jahrbuch für deutsche Theologie* 12 (1867): 389–411.

Hooker, Morna D. "ΠΙΣΤΙΣ ΧΡΙΣΤΟΥ." *New Testament Studies* 35 (1989): 321–342.

———. *Paul: A Short Introduction.* Oxford: Oneworld, 2003.

Horbury, William. *Jewish Messianism and the Cult of Christ.* London: SCM, 1998.

———. *Messianism among Jews and Christians: Twelve Biblical and Historical Studies.* London: T. & T. Clark, 2003.

———. "Messianism in the Old Testament Apocrypha and Pseudepigrapha." Pp. 35–64 in *Messianism among Jews and Christians: Twelve Biblical and Historical Studies.* London: T. & T. Clark, 2003.

Horsley, Richard A., ed. *Paul and Empire: Religion and Power in Roman Imperial Society.* Harrisburg, Pa.: Trinity, 1997.

———, ed. *Paul and Politics: Ekklesia, Israel, Imperium, Interpretation: Essays in Honor of Krister Stendahl.* Harrisburg, Pa.: Trinity, 2000.

———, ed. *Paul and the Roman Imperial Order.* Harrisburg, Pa.: Trinity, 2004.

———, and John S. Hanson. *Bandits, Prophets, and Messiahs: Popular Movements at the Time of Jesus.* Minneapolis: Winston, 1985.

Hultgren, Arland J. "The *Pistis Christou* Formulation in Paul." *Novum Testamentum* 22 (1980): 248–263.

Hurtado, Larry. *Lord Jesus Christ: Devotion to Jesus in Earliest Christianity.* Grand Rapids, Mich.: Eerdmans, 2003.

———. "Paul's Christology." Pp. 185–198 in *The Cambridge Companion to St. Paul.* Edited by James D. G. Dunn. Cambridge: Cambridge University Press, 2003.

Idel, Moshe. *Messianic Mystics.* New Haven: Yale University Press, 1998.

Jastrow, Marcus. *Dictionary of the Targumim, the Talmud Babli and Yerushalmi, and the Midrashic Literature.* 2 vols. New York: Putnam, 1903.

Jespersen, Otto. *The Philosophy of Grammar.* London: Allen & Unwin, 1924.

Jewett, Robert. "The Redaction and Use of an Early Christian Confession in Romans 1:3–4." Pp. 99–122 in *The Living Text: Essays in Honor of Ernest W. Saunders.* Edited by Dennis E. Groh and Robert Jewett. Lanham, Md.: University Press of America, 1985.

Johnson, Luke Timothy. "Rom 3:21–26 and the Faith of Jesus." *Catholic Biblical Quarterly* 44 (1982): 77–90.

Jonge, Marinus de. "The Earliest Christian Use of *Christos*: Some Suggestions." *New Testament Studies* 32 (1986): 321–343.

———. "The Use of the Word 'Anointed' in the Time of Jesus." *Novum Testamentum* 8 (1966): 132–148.

Judge, E. A. "The Early Christians as a Scholastic Community." *Journal of Religious History* 1 (1960): 4–15, 125–137.

Juel, Donald. *Messianic Exegesis: Christological Interpretation of the Old Testament in Early Christianity.* Philadelphia: Fortress, 1988.

Kajanto, Iiro. *Supernomina: A Study in Latin Epigraphy.* Helsinki: Societas Scientarum Fennica, 1966.

Karrer, Martin. *Der Gesalbte: Die Grundlagen des Christustitels.* Forschungen zur Religion und Literatur des Alten und Neuen Testaments 151. Göttingen: Vandenhoeck & Ruprecht, 1991.

————. *Jesus Christus im Neuen Testament.* Grundrisse zum Neuen Testament 11. Göttingen: Vandenhoeck & Ruprecht, 1998.

Käsemann, Ernst. *Commentary on Romans.* Translated and edited by Geoffrey W. Bromiley. Grand Rapids, Mich.: Eerdmans, 1980.

Keck, Leander E. "Christology, Soteriology, and the Praise of God (Romans 15:7–13)." Pp. 85–97 in *The Conversation Continues: Studies in Paul and John in Honor of J. Louis Martyn.* Edited by Robert T. Fortna and Beverly Roberts Gaventa. Nashville: Abingdon, 1990.

————. " 'Jesus' in Romans." *Journal of Biblical Literature* 108 (1989): 443–460.

Keesmaat, Sylvia C. "The Psalms in Romans and Galatians." Pp. 139–162 in *The Psalms in the New Testament.* Edited by Steve Moyise and M. J. J. Menken. London: T. & T. Clark, 2004.

Kennedy, H. A. A. *St. Paul and the Mystery Religions.* London: Hodder & Stoughton, 1913.

Keynes, John Neville. *Studies and Exercises in Formal Logic.* New York: Macmillan, 1884.

King, Karen L. *What Is Gnosticism?* Cambridge, Mass.: Harvard University Press, 2005.

Kirk, J. R. Daniel. *Unlocking Romans: Resurrection and the Justification of God.* Grand Rapids, Mich.: Eerdmans, 2008.

Kittel, Gerhard, and Gerhard Friedrich, eds. *Theological Dictionary of the New Testament.* Translated by Geoffrey W. Bromiley. 10 vols. Grand Rapids: Eerdmans, 1964–1976.

Klausner, Joseph. *The Messianic Idea in Israel: From Its Beginning to the Completion of the Mishnah.* Translated by W. F. Stinespring. New York: Macmillan: 1955.

Kneissl, Peter. *Die Siegestitulatur der römischen Kaiser: Untersuchungen zu d. Siegerbeinamen d. 1. u. 2. Jahrhunderts.* Hypomnemata 23. Göttingen: Vandenhoeck & Ruprecht, 1969.

Knoppers, Gary N. Review of Antii Laato, *A Star Is Rising: The Historical Development of the Old Testament Royal Ideology and the Rise of the Jewish Messianic Expectations. Journal of Biblical Literature* 117 (1998): 732–735.

Koch, Dietrich-Alex. *Die Schrift als Zeuge des Evangeliums: Untersuchungen zur Verwendung und zum Verständnis der Schrift bei Paulus.* Tübingen: Mohr Siebeck, 1986.

Koch, Klaus. "Messias und Menschensohn." Pp. 235–266 in *Vor der Wende der Zeiten: Beiträge zur apokalyptischen Literatur.* Neukirchen-Vluyn: Neukirchener Verlag, 1996.

————. "Stages in the Canonization of the Book of Daniel." Pp. 421–446 in *The Book of Daniel: Composition and Reception.* Edited by John J. Collins and Peter W. Flint. Supplements to Vetus Testamentum 83. Leiden: Brill, 2001.

Kramer, Werner. *Christ, Lord, Son of God.* Translated by Brian Hardy. Studies in Biblical Theology 50. London: SCM, 1966. Translation of *Christos Kyrios Gottessohn: Untersuchungen zu Gebrauch und Bedeutung der christologischen Bezeichnungen bei Paulus und den vorpaulinischen Gemeinden.* Abhandlungen zur Theologie des Alten und Neuen Testaments 44. Zurich: Zwingli, 1963.

Kraus, Hans-Joachim. *Theology of the Psalms*. Translated by Keith Crim. Minneapolis: Fortress, 1992.

Kripke, Saul. *Naming and Necessity*. Cambridge, Mass.: Harvard University Press, 1980.

Kronenfeld, David, and Gabriella Rundblad. "The Semantic Structure of Lexical Fields: Variation and Change." Pp. 67–114 in *Words in Time: Diachronic Semantics from Different Points of View*. Edited by Regine Eckardt, Klaus von Heusinger, and Christoph Schwarze. Berlin: de Gruyter, 2003.

Kugel, James L. *The Bible as It Was*. Cambridge, Mass.: Harvard University Press, 1999.

———, and Rowan A. Greer. *Early Biblical Interpretation*. Philadelphia: Westminster, 1986.

Kümmel, Werner Georg. *The New Testament: A History of the Investigation of Its Problems*. Translated by S. McLean Gilmour and Howard Clark Kee. Nashville: Abingdon, 1972.

———. "Rudolf Bultmann als Paulusforscher." Pp. 174–193 in *Rudolf Bultmanns Werk und Wirkung*. Edited by B. Jaspert. Darmstadt: Wissenschaftlichebuchgesellschaft, 1984.

———. *The Theology of the New Testament according to Its Major Witnesses: Jesus-Paul-John*. Translated by John E. Steely. Nashville: Abingdon, 1973.

Laato, Antii. *A Star Is Rising: The Historical Development of the Old Testament Royal Ideology and the Rise of the Jewish Messianic Expectations*. Atlanta: Scholars Press, 1997.

Lagrange, M.-J. *Saint Paul Épitre aux Romains*. Études bibliques. Paris: Lecoffre, 1916.

Lake, Kirsopp. "Simon, Cephas, Peter." *Harvard Theological Review* 14 (1921): 95–97.

Lambertz, M. "Zur Ausbreitung des Supernomen oder Signum im römischen Reiche." *Glotta* 4 (1913): 78–143; 5 (1914): 99–169.

Lambrecht, Jan. "Paul's Christological Use of Scripture in 1 Cor 15:20–28." *New Testament Studies* 28 (1982): 502–527.

La Piana, George. "Cephas and Peter in the Epistle to the Galatians." *Harvard Theological Review* 14 (1921): 187–193.

Leary, T. J. "Paul's Improper Name." *New Testament Studies* 38 (1992): 467–469.

Letronne, J.-A. "Observations philologiques et archéologiques sur l'étude des noms propres grecs." *Annales de l'Institut Archéologique* 17 (1845): 251–346.

Levenson, Jon D. *The Death and Resurrection of the Beloved Son: The Transformation of Child Sacrifice in Judaism and Christianity*. New Haven: Yale University Press, 1993.

Levey, Samson H. *The Messiah: An Aramaic Interpretation: The Messianic Exegesis of the Targum*. Monographs of the Hebrew Union College 2. Cincinnati: Hebrew Union College Press, 1974.

Liddell, H. G., R. Scott, and H. S. Jones. *A Greek-English Lexicon*. 9th ed. Oxford: Oxford University Press, 1996.

Lietzmann, Hans. *Einführung in die Textgeschichte der Paulusbriefe: An die Römer*. Handbuch zum Neuen Testament 8. Tübingen: Mohr Siebeck, 1928.

Lightfoot, Joseph Barber. *The Epistle of St. Paul to the Galatians.* Grand Rapids, Mich.: Zondervan, 1971.

Linnemann, Eta. "Tradition und Interpretation in Röm 1,3f." *Evangelische Theologie* 31 (1971): 264–275.

Louw, Johannes P., and Eugene A. Nida. *Greek-English Lexicon of the New Testament Based on Semantic Domains.* New York: United Bible Societies, 1988.

Lust, Johan. *Messianism and the Septuagint: Collected Essays.* Edited by K. Hauspie. Bibliotheca ephemeridum theologicarum lovaniensium 178. Leuven: Peeters, 2004.

Lyons, John. *Language and Linguistics: An Introduction.* Cambridge: Cambridge University Press, 1981.

Mack, Burton L. *A Myth of Innocence: Mark and Christian Origins.* Philadelphia: Fortress, 1988.

MacRae, George, S. J. "Messiah and Gospel." Pp. 169–186 in *Judaisms and Their Messiahs at the Turn of the Christian Era.* Edited by Jacob Neusner, William Scott Green, and Ernest Frerichs. Cambridge: Cambridge University Press, 1987.

Marcus, Joel. "Mark 14:61: 'Are You the Messiah-Son-of-God?' " *Novum Testamentum* 31 (1989): 125–141.

Marshall, Bruce A. "Crassus and the Cognomen Dives." *Historia* 22 (1973): 459–467.

Martin, Dale B. *The Corinthian Body.* New Haven: Yale University Press, 1999.

———. "Paul and the Judaism/Hellenism Dichotomy: Toward a Social History of the Question." Pp. 29–61 in *Paul beyond the Judaism/Hellenism Divide.* Edited by Troels Engberg-Pedersen. Louisville, Ky.: Westminster John Knox, 2001.

Martyn, J. Louis. "Epistemology at the Turn of the Ages." Pp. 89–110 in *Theological Issues in the Letters of Paul.* Edinburgh: T. & T. Clark, 1997.

———. *Galatians: A New Translation with Introduction and Commentary.* Anchor Bible 33A. New York: Doubleday, 1997.

———. *Theological Issues in the Letters of Paul.* Edinburgh: T. & T. Clark, 1997.

Mason, Steve. "Jews, Judaeans, Judaizing, Judaism: Problems of Categorization in Ancient History." *Journal for the Study of Judaism* 38 (2007): 457–512.

———. *Life of Josephus.* Vol. 9 of *Flavius Josephus: Translation and Commentary.* Edited by Steve Mason. Leiden: Brill, 2001.

Matthews, Elaine. "Names, Personal, Greek." Pp. 1022–1024 in *The Oxford Classical Dictionary.* Edited by S. Hornblower and A. Spawforth. 3d ed. Oxford: Oxford University Press, 2003.

Mays, James L. "The David of the Psalms." *Interpretation* 40 (1986): 143–155.

McCartney, E. S. "Puns and Plays on Proper Names." *Classical Journal* 14 (1919): 343–358.

McCasland, S. Vernon. "Christ Jesus." *Journal of Biblical Literature* 65 (1946): 377–383.

McDowell, John. "On the Sense and Reference of a Proper Name." *Mind* 86 (1977): 159–185.

McFayden, Donald. *The History of the Title Imperator under the Roman Empire.* Chicago: University of Chicago Press, 1920.

McLean, B. H. *An Introduction to Greek Epigraphy of the Hellenistic Periods.* Ann Arbor: University of Michigan Press, 2002.

McWhorter, Ashton Waugh. "A Study of the So-Called Deliberative Type of Question." *Transactions and Proceedings of the American Philological Association* 41 (1910): 157–168.

Meeks, Wayne A. *The First Urban Christians: The Social World of the Apostle Paul.* 2d ed. New Haven: Yale University Press, 2003.

Metzger, Bruce M. "The Punctuation of Rom 9:5." Pp. 95–122 in *Christ and the Spirit in the New Testament.* Edited by Barnabas Lindars and Stephen S. Smalley. Cambridge: Cambridge University Press, 1973.

Meulen, Alice ter. "Logic and Natural Language." Pp. 461–483 in *The Blackwell Guide to Philosophical Logic.* Edited by Lou Goble. Oxford: Blackwell, 2001.

Meyer, Ben F. Review of A. E. Harvey, *Jesus and the Constraints of History. Journal of Biblical Literature* 103 (1984): 652–654.

Michaels, J. Ramsey. "Catholic Christologies in the Catholic Epistles." Pp. 268–291 in *Contours of Christology in the New Testament.* Edited by Richard N. Longenecker. Grand Rapids, Mich.: Eerdmans, 2005.

Michel, Otto. *Der Brief an die Römer übersetzt und erklärt.* Kritisch-exegetischer Kommentar über das Neue Testament. Göttingen : Vandenhoeck & Ruprecht, 1955.

Mildenberg, Leo. *The Coinage of the Bar Kokhba War.* Zurich: Schweizerische Numismatische Gesellschaft, 1984.

Mill, John Stuart. *A System of Logic, Ratiocinative and Inductive.* London: Parker, 1843.

Miller, Merrill P. "The Anointed Jesus." Pp. 375–416 in *Redescribing Christian Origins.* Edited by Ron Cameron and Merrill P. Miller. Society of Biblical Literature Symposium Series 28. Atlanta: Society of Biblical Literature, 2004.

———. "The Problem of the Origins of a Messianic Conception of Jesus." Pp. 301–336 in *Redescribing Christian Origins.* Edited by Ron Cameron and Merrill P. Miller. Society of Biblical Literature Symposium Series 28. Atlanta: Society of Biblical Literature, 2004.

Minear, Paul S. *The Obedience of Faith: The Purposes of Paul in the Epistle to the Romans.* Studies in Biblical Theology. Second Series 19. London: SCM, 1971.

Missiou, Anna. "The Hellenistic Period." Pp. 325–341 in *A History of Ancient Greek: From the Beginnings to Late Antiquity.* Edited by A.-F. Christidis. Cambridge: Cambridge University Press, 2007.

Mitchell, Margaret M. *Paul and the Rhetoric of Reconciliation: An Exegetical Investigation of the Language and Composition of 1 Corinthians.* Louisville, Ky.: Westminster John Knox Press, 1993.

Moule, C. F. D. *An Idiom Book of New Testament Greek.* Cambridge: Cambridge University Press, 1963.

Moulton, J. H., and G. Milligan. *The Vocabulary of the Greek Testament Illustrated from the Papyri and Other Non-Literary Sources.* London: Hodder & Stoughton, 1949.

Momigliano, Arnaldo. "The Second Book of Maccabees." *Classical Philology* 70 (1975): 81–88.

Mommsen, Theodor. "Die römischen Eigennamen." Pp. 3–68 in vol. 1 of *Römische Forschungen.* 2 vols. Berlin: Weidmann, 1864.

Moo, Douglas J. "The Christology of the Early Pauline Letters." Pp. 169–192 in *Contours of Christology in the New Testament.* Edited by Richard N. Longenecker. Grand Rapids, Mich.: Eerdmans, 2005.

Morgan, Robert. *The Nature of New Testament Theology: The Contribution of William Wrede and Adolf Schlatter.* Edited and translated and with an introduction by Robert Morgan. Studies in Biblical Theology. Second Series 25. London: SCM, 1973.

Morgenstern, Arie. *Hastening Redemption: Messianism and the Resettlement of the Land of Israel.* Translated by Joel A. Linsider. Oxford: Oxford University Press, 2006.

Mowinckel, Sigmund. *He That Cometh: The Messiah Concept in the Old Testament and Later Judaism.* Translated by G. W. Anderson. Grand Rapids, Mich.: Eerdmans, 2005.

———. *The Psalms in Israel's Worship.* Translated by D. R. Ap-Thomas. 2 vols. Grand Rapids, Mich.: Eerdmans, 2004.

"Mr. Trollope's Novels." *National Review* (October 1858): 416–435. Repr., pp. 80–89 in *Anthony Trollope: The Critical Heritage.* Edited by Donald Smalley. London: Routledge, 1996.

Muraoka, T. *Hebrew/Aramaic Index to the Septuagint.* Grand Rapids, Mich.: Baker, 1998.

Murphy-O'Connor, Jerome. *Keys to First Corinthians: Revisiting the Major Issues.* Oxford: Oxford University Press, 2009.

Najman, Hindy. "Torah of Moses: Pseudonymous Attribution in Second Temple Writings." Pp. 202–216 in *The Interpretation of Scripture in Early Judaism and Christianity: Studies in Language and Tradition.* Edited by Craig A. Evans. Sheffield: Sheffield Academic, 2000.

Neill, Stephen. *The Interpretation of the New Testament: 1861–1961.* Oxford: Oxford University Press, 1964.

Neugebauer, Fritz. *In Christus: Eine Untersuchung zum paulinischen Glaubensverständnis.* Göttingen: Vandenhoeck & Ruprecht, 1961.

Neusner, Jacob. "Mishnah and Messiah." Pp. 265–282 in *Judaisms and Their Messiahs at the Turn of the Christian Era.* Edited by Jacob Neusner, William Scott Green, and Ernest Frerichs. Cambridge: Cambridge University Press, 1987.

———. "Preface." Pp. ix–xiv in *Judaisms and Their Messiahs at the Turn of the Christian Era.* Edited by Jacob Neusner, William Scott Green, and Ernest Frerichs. Cambridge: Cambridge University Press, 1987.

———, William Scott Green, and Ernest Frerichs, eds. *Judaisms and Their Messiahs at the Turn of the Christian Era.* Cambridge: Cambridge University Press, 1987.

Nickelsburg, George W. E. "Salvation without and with a Messiah: Developing Beliefs in Writings Ascribed to Enoch." Pp. 49–68 in *Judaisms and Their Messiahs at the Turn of the Christian Era*. Edited by Jacob Neusner, William Scott Green, and Ernest Frerichs. Cambridge: Cambridge University Press, 1987.

Niebuhr, Karl-Wilhelm. "Jesus Christus und die vielfältigen messianischen Erwartungen Israels: Ein Forschungsbericht." Pp. 337–345 in *Der Messias*. Edited by Ingo Baldermann, Ernst Dassmann, and Ottmar Fuchs. Jahrbuch für Biblische Theologie 8. Neukirchen-Vluyn: Neukirchener Verlag, 1993.

Nöldeke, Theodor. *Compendious Syriac Grammar*. Translated by James A. Crichton. Winona Lake, Ind.: Eisenbrauns, 2001.

Norden, Eduard. "Josephus und Tacitus über Jesus Christus und eine messianische Prophetie." *Neue Jahrbücher für klassische Altertum* 31 (1913): 636–666.

Novenson, Matthew V. "The Jewish Messiahs, the Pauline Christ, and the Gentile Question." *Journal of Biblical Literature* 128 (2009): 373–389.

Oegema, Gerbern S. *The Anointed and His People: Messianic Expectations from the Maccabees to Bar Kokhba*. Journal for the Study of the Pseudepigrapha Supplement Series 27. Sheffield: Sheffield Academic, 1998.

Oesterley, W. O. E. *The Evolution of the Messianic Idea: A Study in Comparative Religion*. New York: Dutton, 1908.

Parker, Robert. "Theophoric Names and the History of Greek Religion." Pp. 53–80 in *Greek Personal Names: Their Value as Evidence*. Edited by Simon Hornblower and Elaine Matthews. Proceedings of the British Academy 104. Oxford: Oxford University Press, 2000.

Pascuzzi, Maria A. "Baptism-Based Allegiance and the Divisions in Corinth: A Reexamination of 1 Corinthians 1:13–17." *Catholic Biblical Quarterly* 71 (2009): 813–829.

Pelham, H. F. *Outlines of Roman History*. 4th ed. London: Rivingtons, 1905.

Pietersma, Albert. "Messianism and the Greek Psalter: In Search of the Messiah." Pp. 49–75 in *The Septuagint and Messianism*. Edited by Michael A. Knibb. Bibliotheca ephemeridum theologicarum lovaniensium 195. Leuven: Peeters, 2006.

———. "Septuagintal Exegesis and the Superscriptions of the Greek Psalter." Pp. 443–475 in *The Book of Psalms: Composition and Reception*. Edited by Peter W. Flint and Patrick D. Miller. Supplements to Vetus Testamentum 99. Leiden: Brill, 2005.

Pomykala, Kenneth E. *The Davidic Dynasty Tradition in Early Judaism: Its History and Significance for Messianism*. Early Judaism and Its Literature 7. Atlanta: Scholars Press, 1995.

———. Review of William Horbury, *Jewish Messianism and the Cult of Christ*. *Journal of Biblical Literature* 119 (2000): 351–353.

Popkes, Wiard. "1 Kor 2,2 und die Anfänge der Christologie." *Zeitschrift für die neutestamentliche Wissenschaft und die Kunde der älteren Kirche* 95 (2004): 64–83.

Porter, J. R. "The Legal Aspects of the Concept of 'Corporate Personality' in the Old Testament." *Vetus Testamentum* 15 (1965): 361–380.

Porter, Stanley E. *The Messiah in the Old and New Testaments*. Grand Rapids, Mich.: Eerdmans, 2007.

Poythress, Vern S. "Is Romans 1:3–4 a Pauline Confession after All?" *Expository Times* 87 (1976): 180–183.

Räisänen, Heikki. *Paul and the Law*. Tübingen: Mohr, 1987.

Rajak, Tessa. *Translation and Survival: The Greek Bible of the Ancient Jewish Diaspora*. Oxford: Oxford University Press, 2009.

Ramsay, W. M. *St. Paul the Traveller and the Roman Citizen*. London: Hodder & Stoughton, 1895.

Ravin, Yael, and Claudia Leacock. "Polysemy: An Overview." Pp. 1–29 in *Polysemy: Theoretical and Computational Approaches*. Edited by Yael Ravin and Claudia Leacock. Oxford: Oxford University Press, 2000.

Rawlinson, A. E. J. *The New Testament Doctrine of the Christ*. London: Longmans, 1926.

Reider, Joseph. *An Index to Aquila*. Completed and revised by Nigel Turner. Supplements to Vetus Testamentum 12. Leiden: Brill, 1966.

Richard, Earl. *Jesus, One and Many: The Christological Concept of New Testament Authors*. Wilmington, Del.: Glazier, 1988.

Roberts, J. J. M. "The Old Testament's Contributions to Messianic Expectations." Pp. 39–51 in *The Messiah: Developments in Earliest Judaism and Christianity*. Edited by James H. Charlesworth. Minneapolis: Fortress, 1992.

Rogerson, J. W. "The Hebrew Conception of Corporate Personality: A Re-Examination." *Journal of Theological Studies* 21 (1970): 1–16.

Rösel, Martin. "Die Psalmüberschriften des Septuaginta-Psalter." Pp. 125–148 in *Der Septuaginta-Psalter: Sprachliche und theologische Aspekte*. Edited by Erich Zenger. Herders biblische Studien 32. Freiburg: Herder, 2001.

Rosenthal, Keith. "Rethinking the Messianological Vacuum: The Prevalence of Jewish Messianism during the Second Temple Period." Ph.D. diss., Graduate Theological Union, 2006.

Ruether, Rosemary Radford. *Faith and Fratricide: The Theological Roots of Anti-Semitism*. New York: Seabury, 1974.

———. *To Change the World: Christology and Cultural Criticism*. New York: Crossroad, 1981.

Russell, Bertrand. "On Denoting." *Mind* 14 (1905): 479–493.

Sacy, A. I. Silvestre de. *Principles of General Grammar*. Translated by David Fosdick. New York: Leavitt, 1834.

Sæbø, Magne. "On the Relationship between 'Messianism' and 'Eschatology' in the Old Testament: An Attempt at a Terminological and Factual Clarification." Pp. 197–231 in *On the Way to Canon: Creative Tradition History in the Old Testament*. Journal for the Study of the Old Testament Supplement Series 191. Sheffield: Sheffield Academic, 1998.

Sanday, William, and Arthur C. Headlam. *A Critical and Exegetical Commentary on the Epistle to the Romans*. International Critical Commentary. Edinburgh: T. & T. Clark, 1977.

Sanders, Carol. "Introduction: Saussure Today." Pp. 1–8 in *The Cambridge Companion to Saussure*. Edited by Carol Sanders. Cambridge: Cambridge University Press, 2004.

Sanders, E. P. *Judaism: Practice and Belief, 63 BCE–66 CE*. 4th ed. London: SCM, 2005.

———. *Paul and Palestinian Judaism: A Comparison of Patterns of Religion*. Philadelphia: Fortress, 1977.

Sandmel, Samuel. *The Genius of Paul: A Study in History*. New York: Schocken, 1958.

———. "The Haggadah within Scripture." *Journal of Biblical Literature* 80 (1961): 105–122.

———. "Parallelomania." *Journal of Biblical Literature* 81 (1962): 1–13.

Saussure, Ferdinand de. *Course in General Linguistics*. Edited by Charles Bally, Roy Harris, Albert Sechehaye, and Albert Riedlinger. Translated Roy Harris. 3d ed. Chicago: Open Court, 1986.

———. *Writings in General Linguistics*. Edited by Simon Bouquet and Rudolf Engler. Translated by Carol Sanders, Matthew Pires, and Peter Figueroa. Oxford: Oxford University Press, 2006.

Schäfer, Peter. *Der Bar Kokhba-Aufstand: Studien zum zweiten jüdischen Krieg gegen Rom*. Texte und Studien zum antiken Judentum 1. Tübingen: Mohr Siebeck, 1981.

———. "Diversity and Interaction: Messiahs in Early Judaism." Pp. 15–35 in *Toward the Millennium: Messianic Expectations from the Bible to Waco*. Edited by Peter Schäfer and Mark R. Cohen. Studies in the History of Religions 77. Leiden: Brill, 1998.

Schaper, Joachim. *Eschatology in the Greek Psalter*. Wissenschaftliche Untersuchungen zum Neuen Testament. Second Series 76. Tübingen: Mohr Siebeck, 1995.

Schiffman, Lawrence H. "Messianic Figures and Ideas in the Qumran Scrolls." Pp. 116–129 in *The Messiah: Developments in Earliest Judaism and Christianity*. Edited by James H. Charlesworth. Minneapolis: Fortress, 1992.

Schlier, Heinrich. "Eine christologische Credoformel der römischen Gemeinde: Zu Röm 1,3f." Pp. 56–69 in *Der Geist und Die Kirche*. Vol. 4 of *Exegetische Aufsätze und Vorträge*. 4 vols. Freiburg: Herder, 1980.

Schmithals, Walter. *Gnosticism in Corinth*. Translated by John E. Steely. Nashville: Abingdon, 1971.

Schnelle, Udo. *Apostle Paul: His Life and Theology*. Translated by M. Eugene Boring. Grand Rapids, Mich.: Baker Academic, 2005.

———. *Gerechtigkeit und Christusgegenwart: Vorpaulinische und paulinische Tauftheologie*. Göttingen: Vandenhoeck & Ruprecht, 1983.

Schoeps, Hans-Joachim. *Paul: The Thought of the Apostle in the Light of Jewish Religious History*. Translated by Harold Knight. London: Lutterworth, 1961.

Scholem, Gershom. *Major Trends in Jewish Mysticism*. Jerusalem: Schocken, 1941.

———. *The Messianic Idea in Judaism and Other Essays on Jewish Spirituality*. New York: Schocken, 1971.

———. *Sabbatai Sevi: The Mystical Messiah, 1626–1676.* Translated by R. J. Zwi Werblowsky. Princeton, N.J.: Princeton University Press, 1973.

———. "Toward an Understanding of the Messianic Idea in Judaism." Pp. 1–36 in *The Messianic Idea in Judaism and Other Essays on Jewish Spirituality.* New York: Schocken, 1971.

Schorsch, Ismar. *From Text to Context: The Turn to History in Modern Judaism.* Waltham, Mass.: Brandeis University Press, 1994.

Schreiber, Stefan. *Gesalbter und König: Titel und Konzeptionen der königlichen Gesalbtenerwartung in frühjüdischen und urchristlichen Schriften.* Berlin: de Gruyter, 2000.

Schürer, Emil. *The History of the Jewish People in the Age of Jesus Christ.* 3 vols. Revised and edited by Geza Vermes and Fergus Millar. Edinburgh: T. & T. Clark, 1973–1987.

———. *A History of the Jewish People in the Time of Jesus Christ.* 2d ed., 5 vols. Translated by John Macpherson, Sophia Taylor, and Peter Christie. Edinburgh: T. &. T. Clark, 1901.

Schütz, John Howard. *Paul and the Anatomy of Apostolic Authority.* Society for New Testament Studies Monograph Series 26. Cambridge: Cambridge University Press, 1975.

Schwartz, Daniel R. "'Judaean' or 'Jew'? How Should We Translate IOUDAIOS in Josephus?" Pp. 3–27 in *Jewish Identity in the Greco-Roman World.* Edited by Jörg Frey, Daniel R. Schwartz, and Stephanie Gripentrog. Arbeiten zur Geschichte des antiken Judentums und des Urchristentums 71. Leiden: Brill, 2007.

Schwartz, Dov. "The Neutralization of the Messianic Idea in Medieval Jewish Rationalism." *Hebrew Union College Annual* 64 (1993): 37–58 (Hebrew).

Schweitzer, Albert. *The Mysticism of Paul the Apostle.* Translated by W. Montgomery. New York: Holt, 1931.

———. *Paul and His Interpreters.* Translated by W. Montgomery. London: Black, 1912.

———. *The Quest of the Historical Jesus.* Translated by W. Montgomery. New York: Macmillan, 1968.

Schweizer, Eduard. "Römer 1,3f. und der Gegensatz von Fleisch und Geist vor und bei Paulus." *Evangelische Theologie* 15 (1955): 563–571.

Scott, Ernest F. "What Did the Idea of Messiah Mean to the Early Christians?" *Journal of Religion* 1 (1921): 418–420.

Scott, James. "Historical Development of the Messianic Idea." *Old Testament Student* 7 (1888): 176–180.

Searle, John R. "Proper Names." *Mind* 67 (1958): 166–173.

Segal, Alan F. "Paul's Jewish Presuppositions." Pp. 159–172 in *The Cambridge Companion to St. Paul.* Edited by James D. G. Dunn. Cambridge: Cambridge University Press, 2003.

———. *Paul the Convert: The Apostolate and Apostasy of Saul the Pharisee.* New Haven: Yale University Press, 1990.

————. *Two Powers in Heaven: Early Rabbinic Reports about Christianity and Gnosticism.* Studies in Judaism in Late Antiquity 25. Leiden: Brill, 1977.

Sevenster, Gerhard. *De Christologie van het Nieuwe Testament.* Amsterdam: Uitgeversmaatschappij, 1946.

Shanker, Stuart, ed. *Ludwig Wittgenstein: Critical Assessments.* 2 vols. London: Routledge, 1996.

Sherwin-White, A. N. *Roman Society and Roman Law in the New Testament.* Oxford: Clarendon, 1963.

Silva, Moisés. *Biblical Words and Their Meaning: An Introduction to Lexical Semantics.* 2d ed. Grand Rapids, Mich.: Zondervan, 1994.

Silver, Abba Hillel. *A History of Messianic Speculation in Israel from the First through the Seventeenth Centuries.* New York: Macmillan, 1927.

Smith, Elsdon C. *The Story of Our Names.* New York: Harper, 1950.

Smith, Jonathan Z. *Drudgery Divine: On the Comparison of Early Christianities and the Religions of Late Antiquity.* Chicago: University of Chicago Press, 1990.

Smith, Morton. "The Reason for the Persecution of Paul and the Obscurity of Acts." Pp. 261–268 in *Studies in Mysticism and Religion Presented to Gershom G. Scholem on His Seventieth Birthday.* Edited by E. E. Urbach, R. J. Zwi Werblowsky, and C. Wirszubski. Jerusalem: Magnes, 1967.

————. "What Is Implied by the Variety of Messianic Figures?" *Journal of Biblical Literature* 78 (1959): 66–72.

Smith-Bannister, S. *Names and Naming Patterns in England 1538–1700.* Oxford: Oxford University Press, 1997.

Smyth, Herbert Weir. *Greek Grammar.* Cambridge, Mass.: Harvard University Press, 1920.

Soames, Scott. *Reference and Description.* Princeton, N.J.: Princeton University Press, 2005.

Sokoloff, Michael. *A Dictionary of Jewish Babylonian Aramaic of the Talmudic and Geonic Periods.* Baltimore: Johns Hopkins University Press, 2002.

Solin, Heikki. *Namenpaare: Eine Studie zur römischen Namengebung.* Helsinki: Societas Scientiarum Fennica, 1990.

————. "Names, Personal, Roman." Pp. 1024–1026 in *The Oxford Classical Dictionary.* Edited by S. Hornblower and A. Spawforth. 3d ed. Oxford: Oxford University Press, 2003.

Stanley, Christopher D. *Paul and the Language of Scripture: Citation Technique in the Pauline Epistles and Contemporary Literature.* Society for New Testament Studies Monograph Series 74. Cambridge: Cambridge University Press, 1992.

Stendahl, Krister. *Paul among Jews and Gentiles.* Philadelphia: Fortress, 1976.

Stone, Michael E. "The Concept of the Messiah in IV Ezra." Pp. 295–312 in *Religions in Antiquity: Essays in Memory of Erwin Ramsdell Goodenough.* Edited by Jacob Neusner. Leiden: Brill, 1968.

————. "The Question of the Messiah in 4 Ezra." Pp. 209–224 in *Judaisms and Their Messiahs at the Turn of the Christian Era*. Edited by Jacob Neusner, William Scott Green, and Ernest Frerichs. Cambridge: Cambridge University Press, 1987.

Stowers, Stanley K. *Letter Writing in Greco-Roman Antiquity*. Philadelphia: Westminster, 1986.

————. *A Rereading of Romans: Justice, Jews, and Gentiles*. New Haven: Yale University Press, 1994.

Strack, H. L., and Günter Stemberger. *Introduction to the Talmud and Midrash*. Translated by Markus Bockmuehl. Edinburgh: T. & T. Clark, 1991.

Strauss, David Friedrich. *The Life of Jesus Critically Examined*. Translated by George Eliot. Philadelphia: Fortress, 1972. Translation of *Das Leben Jesu, kritisch bearbeitet*. 2 vols. Tübingen: Osiander, 1835.

Strauss, Mark L. *The Davidic Messiah in Luke-Acts: The Promise and Its Fulfillment in Lukan Christology*. Journal for the Study of the New Testament Supplement Series 110. Sheffield: Sheffield Academic, 1995.

Stuckenbruck, Loren T. *Angel Veneration and Christology: A Study in Early Judaism and in the Christology of the Apocalypse of John*. Wissenschaftliche Untersuchungen zum Neuen Testament. Second Series 70. Tübingen: Mohr Siebeck, 1995.

————. "Messianic Ideas in the Apocalyptic and Related Literature of Early Judaism." Pp. 90–113 in *The Messiah in the Old and New Testaments*. Edited by Stanley E. Porter. Grand Rapids, Mich.: Eerdmans, 2007.

Stuhlmacher, Peter. "Der messianische Gottesknecht." Pp. 131–154 in *Der Messias*. Edited by Ingo Baldermann, Ernst Dassmann, and Ottmar Fuchs. Jahrbuch für Biblische Theologie 8. Neukirchen-Vluyn: Neukirchener Verlag, 1993.

Syme, Ronald. "Imperator Caesar: A Study in Nomenclature." *Historia* 7 (1958): 172–188.

Taubes, Jacob. *The Political Theology of Paul*. Edited by Aleida Assmann and Jan Assmann. Translated by Dana Hollander. Cultural Memory in the Present. Stanford: Stanford University Press, 2004.

Thackeray, H. St. J. *The Relation of St. Paul to Contemporary Jewish Thought*. London: Macmillan, 1900.

Theissen, Gerd. "Soziale Schichtung in der korinthischen Gemeinde." *Zeitschrift für die neutestamentliche Wissenschaft und die Kunde der älteren Kirche* 65 (1974): 232–272.

Thompson, Anne. "Ancient Greek Personal Names." Pp. 677–692 in *A History of Ancient Greek: From the Beginnings to Late Antiquity*. Edited by A.-F. Christidis. Cambridge: Cambridge University Press, 2007.

Tishby, Isaiah. "The Messianic Idea and Messianic Trends at the Beginning of Hasidism." *Zion* 32 (1967): 1–45 (Hebrew).

Trollope, Anthony. *The Chronicles of Barsetshire*. 8 vols. London: Chapman & Hall, 1878–1879.

Turner, Max. "Modern Linguistics and the New Testament." Pp. 146–174 in *Hearing the New Testament: Strategies for Interpretation*. Edited by Joel B. Green. 2d ed. Grand Rapids, Mich.: Eerdmans, 2010.

Turner, Nigel. *A Grammar of New Testament Greek III: Syntax*. Edinburgh: T. & T. Clark, 1963.

Ulrichs, Karl Friedrich. *Christusglaube: Studien zum Syntagma pistis Christou und zum paulinischen Verständnis von Glaube und Rechtfertigung*. Wissenschaftliche Untersuchungen zum Neuen Testament. Second Series 227. Tübingen: Mohr Siebeck, 2007.

Urdahl, Lloyd B. Review of Iiro Kajanto, *Supernomina: A Study in Latin Epigraphy*. *Classical Journal* 63 (1967): 140–141.

Van der Woude, A. S. *Die messianischen Vorstellungen der Gemeinde von Qumrân*. Studia semitica neerlandica 3. Assen: Van Gorcum, 1957.

VanderKam, James C. *The Dead Sea Scrolls Today*. Grand Rapids, Mich.: Eerdmans, 1994.

Vermes, Geza. "Jewish Literature and New Testament Exegesis: Reflections on Method." Pp. 74–88 in *Jesus and the World of Judaism*. London: SCM, 1983.

———. "Jewish Studies and New Testament Interpretation." Pp. 58–73 in *Jesus and the World of Judaism*. London: SCM, 1983.

———. "Methodology in the Study of Jewish Literature in the Greco-Roman Period." *Journal of Jewish Studies* 36 (1985): 143–158.

———. *Post-Biblical Jewish Studies*. Leiden: Brill, 1975.

———. *Scripture and Tradition in Judaism: Haggadic Studies*. 2d ed. Leiden: Brill, 1973.

Waddell, James A. *The Messiah: A Comparative Study of the Enochic Son of Man and the Pauline Kyrios*. London: T. & T. Clark, 2011.

Wagner, J. Ross. *Heralds of the Good News: Isaiah and Paul "in Concert" in the Letter to the Romans*. Supplements to Novum Testamentum 101. Leiden: Brill, 2002.

Walbank, F. W. "Monarchies and Monarchic Ideas." Pp. 62–100 in vol. 7.1 of *The Cambridge Ancient History*. 14 vols. 2d ed. Cambridge: Cambridge University Press, 1970–2005.

Walker, Donald Dale. *Paul's Offer of Leniency (2 Cor 10:1): Populist Ideology and Rhetoric in a Pauline Letter Fragment*. Wissenschaftliche Untersuchungen zum Neuen Testament. Second Series 152. Tübingen: Mohr Siebeck, 2002.

Watson, Francis. *Paul and the Hermeneutics of Faith*. London: T. & T. Clark, 2004.

Wedderburn, A. J. M. "The Body of Christ and Related Concepts in 1 Corinthians." *Scottish Journal of Theology* 2 (1971): 74–96.

———. "Some Observations on Paul's Use of the Phrases 'In Christ' and 'With Christ.'" *Journal for the Study of the New Testament* 25 (1985): 83–97.

Weiss, Bernhard. "Der Gebrauch des Artikels bei den Eigennamen." *Theologische Studien und Kritiken* 86 (1913): 349–389.

Whitsett, Christopher G. "Son of God, Seed of David: Paul's Messianic Exegesis in Rom 1:3–4." *Journal of Biblical Literature* 119 (2000): 661–681.

Wilcox, Max. "The Promise of the 'Seed' in the New Testament and the Targumim." *Journal for the Study of the New Testament* 5 (1979): 2–20.

Williams, H. H. Drake, III. "The Psalms in 1 and 2 Corinthians." Pp. 163–180 in *The Psalms in the New Testament*. Edited by Steve Moyise and M. J. J. Menken. London: T. & T. Clark, 2004.

Williams, Margaret H. "Exarchon: An Unsuspected Jewish Liturgical Title from Ancient Rome." *Journal of Jewish Studies* 51 (2000): 77–87.

———. "Jewish Festal Names in Antiquity: A Neglected Area of Onomastic Research." *Journal for the Study of Judaism* 36 (2005): 21–40.

———. "The Jews of Corycus: A Neglected Diasporan Community from Roman Times." *Journal for the Study of Judaism* 25 (1994): 274–286.

———. "Semitic Name-Use by Jews in Roman Asia Minor and the Dating of the Aphrodisias Stele Inscriptions." Pp. 173–197 in *Old and New Worlds in Greek Onomastics*. Edited by Elaine Matthews. Proceedings of the British Academy 148. Oxford: Oxford University Press, 2007.

———. "The Use of Alternative Names by Diaspora Jews in Late Antiquity." *Journal for the Study of Judaism* 38 (2007): 307–327.

Williams, Sam K. "Again *Pistis Christou.*" *Catholic Biblical Quarterly* 49 (1987): 431–447.

Wilson, Robert Dick. "Royal Titles in Antiquity: An Essay in Criticism, Article Four: The Titles of the Greek Kings." *Princeton Theological Review* 3 (1905): 238–267.

Wittgenstein, Ludwig. *Philosophical Investigations*. Translated by G. E. M. Anscombe. Oxford: Blackwell, 1953.

Wrede, William. *Paul*. Translated by Edward Lummis. London: Green, 1907. Translation of *Paulus*. Halle: Gebauer-Schwetschke, 1904.

Wright, N. T. "Adam, Israel and the Messiah." Pp 18–40 in *The Climax of the Covenant: Christ and the Law in the Pauline Theology*. Edinburgh: T. & T. Clark, 1991.

———. "ΧΡΙΣΤΟΣ as 'Messiah' in Paul: Philemon 6." Pp. 41–55 in *The Climax of the Covenant: Christ and the Law in the Pauline Theology*. Edinburgh: T. & T. Clark, 1991.

———. *The Climax of the Covenant: Christ and the Law in the Pauline Theology*. Edinburgh: T. & T. Clark, 1991.

———. *Jesus and the Victory of God*. London: SPCK, 1996.

———. "The Messiah and the People of God: A Study in Pauline Theology with Particular Reference to the Argument of the Epistle to the Romans." Ph.D. diss., University of Oxford, 1980.

———. *The New Testament and the People of God*. London: SPCK, 1992.

———. *Paul: In Fresh Perspective*. Minneapolis: Fortress, 2005.

———. *The Resurrection of the Son of God*. Minneapolis: Fortress, 2003.

———. *What Saint Paul Really Said: Was Paul of Tarsus the Real Founder of Christianity?*
Grand Rapids, Mich.: Eerdmans, 1997.

Zeller, Dieter. "Zur Transformation des Χριστός bei Paulus." Pp. 155–167 in *Der Messias*.
Edited by Ingo Baldermann, Ernst Dassmann, and Ottmar Fuchs. Jahrbuch für
Biblische Theologie 8. Neukirchen-Vluyn: Neukirchener Verlag, 1993.

Zetterholm, Magnus, ed. *The Messiah in Early Judaism and Christianity*. Minneapolis:
Fortress, 2007.

———. "Paul and the Missing Messiah." Pp. 33–55 in *The Messiah in Early Judaism and
Christianity*. Edited by Magnus Zetterholm. Minneapolis: Fortress, 2007.

Ziegler, Joseph. *Untersuchungen zur Septuaginta des Buches Isaias*. Alttestamentliche
Abhandlungen 12.3. Münster: Aschendorff, 1934.

Index of Subjects

Index of Ancient Sources

Index of Modern Authors